D1329498

The United States and Coercive Diplomacy

The United States
and Coercive Diplomacy

edited by Robert J. Art
and Patrick M. Cronin

UNITED STATES INSTITUTE OF PEACE PRESS
Washington, D.C.

The views expressed in this book are those of the authors alone. They do not necessarily reflect views of the United States Institute of Peace.

UNITED STATES INSTITUTE OF PEACE
1200 17th Street NW, Suite 200
Washington, DC 20036-3011

First published 2003

Printed in the United States of America

The paper used in this publication meets the minimum requirements of American National Standards for Information Science—Permanence of Paper for Printed Library Materials, ANSI Z39.48-1984.

Library of Congress Cataloging-in-Publication Data
The United States and coercive diplomacy / edited by Robert J. Art and Patrick M. Cronin
     p. cm.
   Includes bibliographical references and index.
   ISBN 1-929223-45-5 (cloth : alk. paper) — ISBN 1-929223-44-7 (paper : alk. paper)
      1. United States—Foreign relations—1993-2001. 2. Diplomacy. 3. Aggression (International law) I. Art, Robert J. II. Cronin, Patrick M., 1958-

JZ1480.U553 2003
327.73'009'049–dc21

                                                              2003041666

Contents

Foreword

Alexander L. George

Coercive diplomacy (or *compellence*, as some prefer to call it) employs threats of force to persuade an opponent to call off or undo its encroachment—for example, to halt an invasion or give up territory that has been occupied. Coercive diplomacy differs, therefore, from the strategy of deterrence, which involves attempts to dissuade an adversary from undertaking an action that has not yet been initiated.

Coercive diplomacy is also different from use of military force to reverse an encroachment. Coercive diplomacy seeks to persuade the adversary to cease its aggression rather than bludgeon him with military force into stopping. In coercive diplomacy, one gives the opponent an opportunity to stop or back off before employing force against it. Threats or quite limited use of force are closely coordinated with appropriate diplomatic communications to the opponent. Important signaling, bargaining, and negotiating components are built into the strategy of coercive diplomacy.

Coercive diplomacy is an attractive strategy insofar as it offers the possibility of achieving one's objectives economically, with little if any bloodshed, and with fewer political and psychological costs than warfare exacts and with less risk of conflict escalation. There is all the more reason, therefore, to take sober account of the difficulties this strategy encounters.

The concept of coercive diplomacy is converted into a specific strategy tailored to a particular situation only when the policymaker decides four important questions: (1) what to demand of the adversary; (2) whether—and how—to create in the opponent's minds a sense of urgency to comply with the demand; (3) how to create and convey a threat of punishment for noncompliance with the demand that is sufficiently credible and potent enough in the adversary's mind to persuade the adversary that compliance is more in its interest than facing the consequences of noncompliance; and (4) whether to couple the threatened punishment with positive inducements—a "carrot"—to make it easier for the adversary to comply.

It should be obvious that the more far-reaching the demand on the opponent, the stronger will be its motivation to resist—and the more difficult the task of coercive diplomacy. Depending on the answers the policymaker gives to the second and third questions, there will be significantly different variants of the strategy. The three major variants are (1) the *ultimatum*, explicit or tacit, in which a deadline is given for compliance backed by a credible threat of strong punishment; (2) the weaker *gradual turning of the screw*, in which a sense of urgency for compliance is diluted and backed only with the threat of incrementally severe punishment over time; and (3) the even weaker *try-and-see* variant of the strategy that lacks both urgency for compliance and a clear threat of strong punishment for noncompliance.

On many occasions during the Cold War and since, U.S. policymakers have attempted coercive diplomacy against different adversaries. The present study analyzes and compares eight important post–Cold War cases. The editors, Patrick Cronin and Robert Art, have produced an exemplary study that adds significantly to our understanding of the uses and limitations of this strategy. They recruited exceptionally talented scholars to undertake each case study and these individuals responded by producing incisive, sophisticated analyses.

In the opening and closing chapters, Robert Art produces a major elaboration and refinement of the theory and practice of coercive diplomacy. He finds that the eight new case studies generally support the major findings of earlier research on the Cold War cases. In addition, many important new insights are offered that greatly enrich understanding of the complex challenges and limitations as well as the uses of this strategy under different circumstances.

Among the many important contributions of this new study sponsored by the United States Institute of Peace, only a few will be mentioned here. Art provides an incisive, multisided analysis of the difficulties that may undermine the target's willingness to comply with demands made by the coercing state. Thus, the case studies show that the target may be quite concerned about the effect of allowing itself to be coerced on its credibility and its power stakes. If it gives in to the coercer's demand, the target may worry whether this will be the last demand or only the first in a series of demands. Moreover, accepting the coercing power's demands is seldom cost-free in terms of its implications for the target's remaining power. For example, when the United States attempted to set up representative councils in Somalia in March 1993, Mohammed Farah Aideed, the most powerful of the local warlords, realized that to agree would mean a loss of territory under his control and hence a reduction in his power. Similarly, Iraq and North Korea both faced a considerable weakening of their power position if they complied with U.S. demands to stop programs for acquiring weapons of mass destruction.

This volume emphasizes that it becomes more difficult to achieve coercive diplomacy when there is more than a single state employing that strategy and more than a single target. In five of the cases examined (Bosnia, Kosovo, Iraq, Somalia, and North Korea), the coalition engaging in coercive diplomacy may have been united in its goal but often divided on the means to achieve it. In such cases, as Steven Burg notes in his case study of Kosovo and Bosnia, the actions to hold a coalition together can degrade the effectiveness of its effort. In Somalia, the faction led by Ali Mahdi Mohammed cooperated more with the United Nations than did the stronger faction led by Aideed, who viewed the United Nations' actions as hurting his interests and benefiting Mahdi's. This set the stage for the armed confrontation between the UN forces and Aideed's supporters that led to the collapse of the UN mission in Somalia.

The United States and Coercive Diplomacy highlights the fact that the targets of coercion often develop "countercoercion" techniques that constrain the coercing power's ability to pursue a strong course of action. One device that Serbian president Slobodan Milosevic hit upon was to hold back use of his surface-to-air missiles (SAMs). This tactic forced NATO pilots to fly at higher altitudes to avoid possible attack by those SAMs held in abeyance, thereby reducing their ability to take out Serb armored tanks.

Four of the cases—Haiti, Bosnia, Somalia, and Kosovo—illustrate how difficult it is to use coercive diplomacy on behalf of humanitarian goals.

Earlier research on coercive diplomacy had already focused on the importance of adding meaningful positive incentives in a combined "carrot-and-stick" variant of the strategy. The present study adds to this by noting that, in general, positive inducements should not be offered before undertaking coercive threats or limited military action. This echoes an earlier finding that during an early stage of the Cuban missile crisis, President Kennedy rejected advice to offer Premier Khrushchev concessions, saying that option should be put off until the United States had succeeded in impressing the Soviet leaders with actions and statements that unmistakably conveyed U.S. resolve to get the missiles out of Cuba.

Robert Art also provides an excellent, badly needed discussion of the difficulty of deciding whether coercive diplomacy was successful in many cases. Some of the eight cases, he finds, are difficult to code as either successes or failures. Two (Kosovo and North Korea) are clear cases of failed coercive diplomacy—although, as Art notes, "failure in the Korean case did not become apparent until eight years after a seemingly successful outcome." Bosnia and Haiti can be regarded as successful but might well be regarded as at the border between coercive diplomacy and full-scale military coercion. Somalia, Iraq, and the response to terrorism are complex cases of coercive diplomacy. There were two separate instances of the strategy in Somalia between 1992 and 1994, six in Iraq between 1990 and 1998, and three in response to terrorism between 1993 and 2001. Although there were both successes and failures within each case, Art concludes overall that all three have to be judged as failures. Art finds the China case the hardest to code as either success or failure because U.S. actions were a response to China's own coercive diplomacy directed at Taiwan and the United States whereas Washington's response was as much an exercise in deterrence as coercive in nature. (As William Drennan points out in the subtitle of his chapter, the question "Who's Coercing Whom?" arises also in the case of North Korea.)

The task of assessing the success or failure of coercive diplomacy is further complicted when it is chosen as a "default" option by policymakers because the alternatives of doing nothing or using force are rejected, at least for the time being. On several occasions the United States has resorted initially to coercive diplomacy even though it did not expect it to be effective. In some instances, coercive diplomacy was undertaken because policymakers thought it politically necessary to do so prior to undertaking necessary military action. This was the case in the events leading to the Gulf War in 1991 because U.S. leaders believed that alliance partners, including the United Nations, as well as domestic U.S. opinion would not support an immediate military response to Iraq's aggression unless diplomatic efforts, including sanctions and coercive diplomacy, were tried first and shown to be ineffective. By doing so, the legitimacy required for the military response could be better achieved. Again in the crisis that began in the latter part of 2002 over Iraq's noncompliance with UN resolutions and its pursuit of weapons of mass destruction, those in the Bush administration dubious of the worth and relevance of inspections in Iraq appear to have reluctantly accepted an effort at coercive diplomacy in order to build support eventually for military action.

Art concludes the study with a set of important general guidelines for policy. One of them may be noted here: "Do not resort to coercive diplomacy unless, should it fail, you are prepared to go down the path of war or you have prepared a suitable escape hatch." This sage advice has been heeded on some occasions—witness, for example, the readiness to respond with an air war to coercive diplomacy's failure in Kosovo in 1999—but not on others—as in Somalia in 1994, when the failure to prepare a political escape hatch resulted in the humiliating withdrawal of U.S. forces.

There are other dangers, too, in pursuing coercive diplomacy if the target opts not to comply with the coercer's demands. In the first place, the target may reject the ultimatum as a bluff, presenting the coercer with Art's stark options of entering war or exiting either through a modestly dignified escape hatch or through a comprehensively humiliating climb-down. In the second place, the target may take the ultimatum very seriously indeed and decide to act preemptively—as the Japanese did at Pearl Harbor—inflicting heavy losses on the coercer or its allies. In the third place, the target may regard the ultimatum as credible and likely to be enforced with military action but refuse to back down for reasons such as honor and prestige and/or because it feels that it can tolerate the damage from the impending war. Finally, the target may indicate conditional or equivocal acceptance of the ultimatum in a way that would erode the willingness or ability of the coercer or the coercer's allies to pursue their declared course and enforce the ultimatum. This fourth danger was much on the minds of U.S. policymakers in the first Gulf crisis of 1990–91, once the United States had issued a specific ultimatum with January 15 as the deadline for Saddam Hussein's compliance. As the deadline approached, however, policymakers became increasingly concerned that Saddam might announce a partial or conditional withdrawal from Kuwait, thereby defusing the impact of the ultimatum and the threat of a war. This possibility was referred to by well-informed journalists as Washington's "nightmare scenario," and very detailed contingency plans were made to deal with such a contingency and were discussed with coalition partners. In the event, and much to the relief of administration officials, Saddam failed to do so, making it easier for the allied coalition to initiate war immediately after January 15.

In short, coercive diplomacy may sometimes promise substantial rewards at relatively modest cost but it is always fraught with difficulties and potential dangers. As this volume confirms, it often fails, and when it fails it presents U.S. policymakers with hard choices between war and political retreat. In those comparatively rare cases when coercive diplomacy is employed chiefly to legitimize subsequent U.S. military action, its failure may not be entirely unwelcome in Washington. But in most instances, failure exacts a heavy price. Hence the importance of policymakers being well schooled not only in the capabilities but also in the complications and limitations of coercive diplomacy. Hence, too, the value of this volume, which offers policymakers as well as scholars a remarkably broad-ranging and unusually insightful assessment of the recent history and the enduring advantages and drawbacks of coercive diplomacy.

Acknowledgments

The idea for this book originated with Richard H. Solomon, president of the United States Institute of Peace. Patrick M. Cronin, during his tenure at the Institute as director of Research and Studies, and Robert J. Art, Herter Professor of International Relations at Brandeis University, served as the project's codirectors. Two conferences were held at the Institute during the course of a year to refine the project and to provide feedback on the chapters produced by the contributors.

Art and Cronin would like to thank the following individuals for their assistance with this project: our contributors, for putting up with our demands for numerous revisions; Alexander George, for helping us define the project, carefully critiquing the entire manuscript, and writing the foreword; Bruce Jentleson, for his guidance on how to preserve coherence in the project; Paul Stares, director of research and studies at the Institute, for his support in helping us finish the project; two anonymous reviewers, for their helpful suggestions on how to improve the manuscript; Barry Posen, Richard Ullman, Morton Halperin, Ivo Daalder, Robert Gallucci, Dan Byman, Kenneth Menkhaus, Bruce Hoffman, John Fox, and Michael Desch, for their perceptive commentaries on the draft chapters; the other participants at the conferences, too numerous to mention here, for their valuable interventions; Dan Snodderly and Nigel Quinney, for their excellent editorial assistance and general guidance; Donna Ramsey Marshall and Christina Zechman Brown, for their yeoman work with logistics and travel schedules and for their unremitting cheerfulness; and David Sweet, for his careful copyediting.

R.J.A.
P.M.C.

Contributors

Jon B. Alterman is director of the Middle East Program at the Center for Strategic and International Studies.

Robert J. Art is Christian A. Herter Professor of International Relations at Brandeis University and director of MIT's Seminar XXI Program.

Nora Bensahel is an analyst at the RAND Corporation in Washington, D.C.

Steven L. Burg is Adlai Stevenson Professor of International Politics and chair, Department of Politics, Brandeis University.

Martha Crenshaw is the Colin and Nancy Campbell Professor of Global Issues and Democratic Thought in the Department of Government, Wesleyan University.

Patrick M. Cronin is assistant administrator for budget and policy, the Agency for International Development, United States Department of State.

William M. Drennan is deputy director of the Research and Studies Program at the United States Institute of Peace.

Robert A. Pastor is vice president of international affairs, professor of international relations, and director of the Center for Democracy and Election Management at American University.

Robert S. Ross is professor of political science at Boston College and a research associate at the East Asian Institute, Harvard University.

The United States and Coercive Diplomacy

1

Introduction

ROBERT J. ART

THE DECADE AFTER THE COLD WAR'S DEMISE is often viewed as the era when economics reigned supreme. With the end of the Soviet-U.S. conflict and the subsequent collapse of the Soviet Union, it looked to many as if the overweening role that military power had played in international politics in general and in U.S. foreign policy in particular would come to an end. The United States and large parts of the world began to experience unparalleled prosperity, democratic market capitalism appeared to be the wave of the future, and globalization seemed to be an unstoppable force. Subsequent events, however, belied the prognostications about the devaluation of force, at least in U.S. foreign policy.

Indeed, during the dozen years between 1990 and 2001, the United States continued to rely heavily on its military instrument to achieve its foreign policy goals. During these years the United States maintained more than a quarter of a million troops abroad. In Europe the United States did not disband the NATO alliance but in fact enlarged it, thereby expanding its commitments to defend more nations against attack. Through military training and military education programs under NATO's Partnership for Peace Program, the United States established military ties with most of the other nations of Europe (and several in Central Asia) that were not yet permitted to join NATO. With a short but effective bombing campaign against the Bosnian Serbs in September 1995, the United States helped bring the Bosnian War to

3

an end, and in 1999, in a more sustained and intense bombing campaign against Serbia, it effectively ended Serbian control over Kosovo. In East Asia the United States reinvigorated the alliance with Japan in the middle of the decade and sought to make it less a unilateral U.S. guarantee and more a two-way street. Later in the decade the United States began to bolster its alliance ties with Australia and the Philippines. In 1994 the United States found itself in a severe crisis with North Korea over the latter's nuclear weapons program and came, according to those intimately involved in the crisis, very close to war. In the 1996 Taiwan Strait crisis, the United States demonstrated its naval muscle to China and reaffirmed its quasi-alliance commitments to Taiwan, in part to reaffirm its other bilateral commitments in East Asia. In the Middle East in 1990–91, the United States planned for and then waged war against Iraq, evicted it from Kuwait, and then continued throughout the decade, in conjunction with the British, to coerce, punish, and generally harass Saddam Hussein's regime. In the Caribbean in 1994, the United States invaded Haiti to evict a thuggish military government and install the rightfully elected one. In Africa in 1992, it sent its soldiers into Somalia to feed starving civilians. In 1998 the United States launched cruise missile strikes against Sudan and Afghanistan in a bid to punish al Qaeda, the terrorist organization led by Osama bin Laden, for its bombing of U.S. embassies in Kenya and Tanzania, and in 2001 it waged war against the Taliban regime and al Qaeda in Afghanistan in response to the latter's September 11 attack on New York and Washington. Finally, throughout the decade U.S. military forces were engaged in numerous diplomatic, training, and other exercises with well over one hundred militaries in the world. In short, during the twelve years after the Cold War, the U.S. military was busy.

Several factors account for Washington's heavy reliance on its military forces during these years. First, there was no other superpower to constrain it. As a consequence, the United States did not need to worry that its actions would be countered by another power with global reach, nor did it have to fear the escalatory dangers that a confrontation with such a power could bring. Second, the troubles of the world did not magically go away with the end of the Cold War. Indeed, many regional disputes that had been suppressed by the U.S.-Soviet competition forced their way into the international limelight. Third, as a status quo power, the United States believed it could not ignore many of these disputes because they were felt to affect its global interests adversely. Fourth, many of the disputes that ultimately came to require the use of U.S. and allied military power were not solved through the prior exercise of political and economic means. Fifth, the United States found itself in the enviable position of having the only military force that could operate globally, but also, as a consequence, in the unenviable position of being frequently asked to use that force to help solve world problems. Sixth, finally, threats arose that challenged core and long-standing U.S. interests or those of its allies and that required the use of military force. For whatever reasons, after the Cold War's end the United States resorted to its military instrument on numerous occasions and in many ways to advance its political goals.

This volume examines one particular way that the United States employed its military forces after the Cold War's demise: its resort to "coercive diplomacy." As we shall see, coercive diplomacy is not meant to entail war, but instead employs military power short of war to bring about a change in a target's policies or in its political makeup. The chapters in this volume analyze eight instances—a few of which feature multiple episodes—between 1990 and 2001 when the United States employed coercive diplomacy to achieve its goals: Somalia (1992–94), Haiti (1994), North Korea (1994), Bosnia (1995), China (1996), Iraq (1990–98), Kosovo (1999), and combating terrorism (1993, 1998, and 2001).

These cases are important to examine because the conditions that gave rise to them will not soon disappear. This means that there will be more U.S. attempts to employ coercive diplomacy in the future. For starters, the United States will remain a global military power and will likely continue with its overseas military presence for the next several decades, while other states will continue to call upon it to use its military power on their behalf. Civil wars will continue to happen, especially in Africa, and the demands for military intervention to stop them will continue. The Persian Gulf and its oil supplies will remain important to the United States and the world and so, consequently, will the need to protect them from aggression. The United States and its allies will be in the Balkans for a generation, and their position is likely to be challenged by groups within the region. China's power will continue to grow—and along with it the threat to Taiwan—giving rise to future crises between China and the United States. North Korea may implode, but other states that the United States opposes will attempt to acquire or may even obtain nuclear weapons and may then threaten to sell them or the raw materials to produce the weapons to other actors, including terrorists, requiring U.S. attempts to prevent their acquisition or sale. Down the road, still other states that the United States opposes will likely acquire nuclear weapons and then use them as a deterrent shield behind which to challenge U.S. interests in their region, calling forth U.S. attempts to check or reverse these challenges. Other terrorist groups may well attempt additional grand terror attacks with conventional means against the U.S. homeland, as al Qaeda did in September 2001. Al Qaeda or other terrorist groups may well acquire chemical and biological weapons, and perhaps even nuclear ones, too, and may threaten to use them against the United States unless it bends to their will. Finally, in spite of the lesson that the United States taught with its overthrow of the Taliban regime in Afghanistan, some states may sponsor grand terror attacks against the United States or its forces abroad.

In short, the need to back U.S. diplomacy with force will not go away; consequently, political-military coercion short of all-out war will remain a highly attractive option to U.S. leaders. Therefore, these leaders need to understand what coercive diplomacy can and cannot accomplish. That is the purpose of this volume: to assess coercive diplomacy's efficacy for U.S. statecraft.

WHAT IS COERCIVE DIPLOMACY?

Coercive diplomacy is, in Alexander George's words, "forceful persuasion": the attempt to get a target—a state, a group (or groups) within a state, or a nonstate actor—to change its objectionable behavior through either the threat to use force or the actual use of limited force. It is a strategy that "seeks to *persuade* an opponent to cease his aggression rather than bludgeon him into stopping."[1]

Coercive diplomacy can include, but need not include, positive inducements, and these inducements can involve either a transfer of resources
to the target or the offer of things that do not involve resource transfer
but that are nonetheless of tangible benefit to the target. Coercive diplomacy is intended to be an alternative to war, even though it involves
some employment of military power to achieve a state's desired objective. It is a technique for achieving objectives "on the cheap" and has
allure because it promises big results with small costs (to the coercer).
Next to outright war, however, coercive diplomacy represents the most
dangerous way to use a state's military power because, if coercive diplomacy fails, the state that tries it then faces two stark choices: back down
or wage war. The first risks loss of face and future bargaining power; the
second, loss of life and military defeat. Because both outcomes
are possible, a state should never undertake coercive diplomacy lightly.

In this volume we distinguish between coercive diplomacy and coercive attempts. The feature that distinguishes the two is the presence or
absence of the employment of force. Coercive diplomacy has as one of
its essential features, and often its only feature, the threat or the limited
use of force. Coercive attempts utilize levers over a target, but these
levers do not involve the threat or use of force. Therefore, we have
excluded from our cases of coercive diplomacy those coercive attempts
that involve only the use of economic sanctions, only the withholding
of benefits to a target, only the cessation of benefits that a target currently enjoys, or more generally any coercive attempt that does not
entail some employment of military power. Clearly, all these actions are
coercive in nature, but they do not constitute coercive diplomacy as we
have defined it. In distinguishing between coercive attempts and coercive diplomacy, we follow the convention set by George: coercive diplomacy must involve the threat or limited use of force, even though it can
also include some of these other types of coercive actions.

Because it entails coercion, coercive diplomacy is a form of
compellence—a term first coined by Thomas Schelling in order to distinguish it from deterrence. For Schelling, the distinction between compellence and deterrence is the difference between an action "intended
to make an adversary do something"—compellence—and an action
"intended to keep him from starting something"—deterrence.[2] The

change in behavior sought by compellence can be manifested in one of two ways: either the adversary starts doing something it is not now doing, or the adversary stops doing something it is now doing. Either way, the adversary changes its behavior. Deterrence, in contrast, is a strategy designed to prevent an adversary from changing its behavior by dissuading it from initiating an action. Deterrence seeks to get the adversary not to change its behavior—that is, to continue "not doing what it is not doing." Thus, compellence aims to alter an adversary's behavior; deterrence, to keep it the same. Deterrence generally involves only threats to use force, whereas compellence can involve both the threat to use force and the actual use of force. In a deterrent situation, if the threat has to be carried out, then, by definition, the adversary has changed its behavior and deterrence has failed. In contrast, because compellence can entail both threats and actual use of force, compellence has not necessarily failed if the threats are carried out.

Although deterrence and compellence are analytically distinct strategies, they usually become conflated when disputing parties contest the legitimacy of the status quo, which they generally do. The deterrer defends the status quo because of the benefits it confers; the target tries to overthrow the status quo because of the injury it inflicts. The target views the deterrer's attempt to maintain the status quo as compellence: "You are coercing me (the target) to accept a situation that benefits you but not me." If the target attempts to alter the status quo, however, then the deterrer will view that attempt as compellence: "You are attempting to coerce me (the deterrer) to stop defending the status quo and accept a revision in it that is less beneficial to me." In such a situation, deterrence and compellence become intermingled. Similarly, deterrent threats can become transformed into compellent actions in situations where deterrence has failed, for in that case the would-be deterrer must decide whether to carry out its threat. If it does so, not for purposes of revenge but to get the adversary to stop its objectionable behavior, then, by definition, execution of the deterrent threat becomes a compellent action. Finally, the deterrer may calculate that deterrence is weakening, even though it has not totally failed, and may decide to bolster deterrence by engaging in actions that are compellent in nature. In that case, compellence is exercised to deter.[3]

Compellence can come in three doses or forms: (1) diplomatic use—the issuance of threats to use force against an adversary if it does not change its behavior, (2) demonstrative use—the exemplary and limited uses of force, and (3) full-scale use, or war—the use of whatever amount of force it takes to get the adversary to change its behavior. The first form of compellence does not use force physically against the target state but only threatens use. The second form uses "just enough force of an appropriate kind to demonstrate resolution to protect one's interests and to establish the credibility of one's determination to use more force if necessary."[4] The third form is to be understood as war—the large-scale use of military power to make the adversary change its behavior. In this volume we follow Alexander George and define coercive diplomacy to encompass only the first two forms of compellence—the diplomatic and demonstrative uses of force. The third form—war—is coercion but not coercive diplomacy, even though diplomacy is never totally absent from war.[5]

The meanings of threat and war are clear. Threat can involve mobilizing and moving large amounts of military force to make the coercer's seriousness of purpose as credible as possible to the target state, or it can simply mean the issuance of verbal warnings. The one thing threat does not mean is the actual physical use of force against the target. War involves sustained, large-scale combat operations against the target, with the goal of either militarily defeating it or bringing about its surrender short of achieving a complete victory over it. Either way, war involves the use of force that is massive, at least to the target.

The meaning of demonstrative use is more difficult to pin down. Although George argues that demonstrative should mean only the "quite limited" use of force, we have used a somewhat broader meaning of demonstrative use. How much is "just enough force" to demonstrate resolution and establish credibility can vary enormously from one situation to another and depends on the nature of the coercer's goals, on the one hand, and on the military capabilities and intensity of interests of the target, on the other.[6] We have therefore defined demonstrative use to include both exemplary and limited use. Exemplary use serves as both a model and a warning of what can or will come: "You did not believe my threat; here is an example for you to chew on of what I can do to you if you do not change your ways." Exemplary use can encompass a one-time employment of force, or a few instances of use, but the major constraint is that it is at the low end of force employment, close to the boundary between threat and use. Exemplary use means moving just beyond the border of threat to make clear by the actions taken that the coercer is deadly serious about escalating the use of force if the target does not comply. In this volume limited use can mean anything from one to several steps beyond exemplary use. The meaning of limited use is this: "You failed to take both my threat and my exemplary use seriously; you obviously need more persuading; let me now give you a better idea of the consequences that your continued noncompliance will bring." More force is used, but not so much such that the boundary to war has been crossed.

A central point follows when coercive diplomacy is conceived to encompass only threat and demonstrative use, but not full-scale use: coercive diplomacy has failed when full-scale use occurs. Wherever one draws the line between limited and full-scale use, if the coercer has to cross that line to achieve its objectives, then, by definition, coercive diplomacy has failed. In this case, war, not coercive diplomacy, produced the change. Any employment of force beyond threat, exemplary use, or limited use signals the failure of coercive diplomacy, even though the subsequent full-scale use of force may succeed in accomplishing the original objectives. As a consequence, exactly where the boundary between limited and full-scale use is drawn becomes crucial for coding cases in which limited use involves escalatory steps that skirt the boundary. Such cases can be coded as either successes or failures of coercive diplomacy, depending on which side of the boundary it is placed. Categorizing such cases becomes an exercise in qualitative judgment.

Washington's Coercive Diplomatic Gambits, 1990–2001

In seeking to evaluate the efficacy of coercive diplomacy, we build upon the path-breaking work of Alexander George, who was the first to define and systematically assess this diplomatic technique.[7] George and his colleagues studied seven cases in which the United States resorted to coercive diplomacy: U.S. opposition to Japanese expansion in the late 1930s, the Laos crisis of 1961–62, the Cuban missile crisis of 1962, U.S. coercive pressure on North Vietnam in 1965, U.S. coercive pressure against Nicaragua in the early 1980s, U.S. coercive pressure against Libya in the 1980s, and U.S. coercive diplomacy in the Persian Gulf crisis of 1990–91.[8] Our volume adds eight cases to the seven previously studied. The eight cases examined here, together with the United States' prime goals in each, are listed in table 1. These fifteen cases (George's seven and our eight) span a sixty-year period and provide a good base from which to draw some suggestive conclusions about the utility of coercive diplomacy, as will be made clear in chapter 9.

Three of our cases—Iraq, China, and North Korea—involved states that had nuclear, biological, and/or chemical weapons. Two of the cases—Somalia and Bosnia—involved states in which civil wars ensued after the state's authority had disintegrated. Two cases—Haiti and Kosovo—involved states whose governments were engaged in savage repression of their peoples. And one—the campaign against terrorists—involved either state-sponsored terrorism or nonstate groups that were aided and abetted in one form or another by state sponsors. Two cases—Haiti and Bosnia—fall right on the boundary between coercive diplomacy and war. (The 1994 Haitian case involved the landing of an invasion force as the Cedras government finally complied with U.S. demands. The 1995 Bosnian case involved the coercive use not only of NATO airpower but also of an increasingly successful Croatian-Muslim ground war offensive against the Bosnian Serbs.) Two cases—North Korea and China—involved a situation in which the United States and its adversary were each engaged in exerting coercive diplomacy against the other. One case—China—involved a U.S. attempt to use coercive diplomacy to shore up deterrence. In half of our cases, the United States offered some type of positive inducement to help persuade the adversary to bend to Washington's will, in addition to issuing threats to resort to force, with some degree of success.

Table 1. U.S. Coercive Diplomacy Cases, 1990–2001

Case	Specific U.S. Goals
Somalia 1992–94	End starvation and reconstruct the government
Haiti 1994	Install a new government
North Korea 1994	Freeze the nuclear weapons program
Bosnia 1995	Reduce Serbian conquest and end the Bosnian war
China 1996	Demonstrate U.S. resolve and stop China from coercing Taiwan
Iraq 1990–98	Free Kuwait and destroy Iraq's weapons of mass destruction
Kosovo 1999	End Serb repression of Albanian Kosovars
Terrorism 1993, 1998, and 2001	Retaliate against terrorists and force state actors to yield them up

In three cases coercive diplomacy did not work at all and the United States therefore went beyond the demonstrative use of force to full-scale war: Iraq in 1991, Afghanistan in 2001, and Kosovo in 1999. In two cases coercive diplomacy was a borderline success because the United States resorted to measures that arguably crossed the boundary of limited use: Haiti in 1994 and Bosnia in 1995. In two cases—Somalia in 1992–93 and North Korea in 1994—coercive diplomacy ultimately failed, although it did enjoy some success initially. In one case the results of coercive diplomacy were ambiguous: China in 1996. The results of coercive diplomacy in dealing with terrorism are also problematic but are mostly failures. Based on these results, coercive diplomacy appears to be an instrument that fails more often than it succeeds. More refined results are presented in chapter 9, after the eight cases are broken down into their multiple episodes and then reanalyzed, but the overall result—that failures exceed successes—does not change.

Any final judgments about the overall record of these cases, however, must be held in reserve because four them—North Korea, Iraq, China, and terrorism—are ongoing sagas. The ultimate fate of North Korea's nuclear weapons program is still to be determined. As of this writing (March 2003), the results of the U.S. war to overthrow Saddam Hussein's government and rid Iraq of weapons of mass destruction are not yet clear. The Chinese-Taiwanese relationship is quiescent for now, but the underlying issue is not resolved; therefore, the ultimate meaning of the 1996 crisis for U.S.-China relations cannot be fully determined. Finally, the battle against al Qaeda is by no means won, and the efficacy of the coercive principle set by the 2001 war against Afghanistan— that states that harbor terrorist organizations aiming to attack the United States will be held to account—has yet to be fully tested. Nonetheless, even though these four cases are ongoing, they can still be treated as discrete incidents in their own right, and all eight cases can be viewed as a snapshot of a given time period. Moreover, because the results from our period accord reasonably well with those from the larger time span covered by Alexander George and his colleagues, we should have a high degree of confidence about the overall conclusions reached in this volume regarding the efficacy of coercive diplomacy.

Finally, every one of our cases, taken as a whole or as a set of multiple episodes, represents a legitimate example of coercive diplomacy because each one satisfies the two conditions laid down by Alexander George. First, in each case the United States was trying to compel the target (or targets) to change its behavior. Second, in each case the United States either found that diplomacy alone could not produce this change in behavior or else believed that diplomacy by itself could not do so and, as a consequence, bolstered its diplomacy by issuing threats to resort to force, by engaging in the demonstrative use of force, or by doing both. The employment of force short of war to produce a change in the target's behavior is the hallmark of these cases.

Somalia

In the Somalian case, as Nora Bensahel shows, the United States had two objectives: to relieve the widespread starvation of civilians and then to support the United Nations and its efforts at civil and governmental reconstruction. The United States acted to coerce the warlords to stop using starvation of noncombatants as one of their means to wage war against one another. Robert Oakley, Washington's representative in Somalia, made crystal clear to these warlords that if they interfered with the delivery of food or attacked U.S. troops, they would be met with overwhelming force. This phase of the operation proved successful. In the next phase, after the United States had engaged in half-hearted attempts to disarm the warlords and had twenty-four of its peacekeepers killed in the process, the United Nations tried to hunt down the killers, ended up in a firefight with the troops of the most powerful warlord (Mohammed Farah Aideed), and subsequently evacuated its forces from Somalia. This phase of governmental reconstruction was an abject failure.

Bosnia and Kosovo

Steven Burg treats the Bosnian and Kosovo cases together in one chapter. In Bosnia the United States, together with its NATO allies, acted to bring an end to the Bosnian War by coercing the Serbs and the Muslims to stop the fighting and ultimately to reach a peace accord. It used air strikes, as well as heavy artillery pounding by British, French, and Dutch forces, to coerce the Serbs to the bargaining table and then employed the threat to stop the air strikes to achieve the same objective with the Muslims. This case is a borderline success for coercive diplomacy because Serb compliance also depended upon the rapid advances made by the Croats in their full-scale ground offensive war against the Serbs in western Bosnia. In Kosovo the United States, once again in concert with its NATO allies, acted to stop Slobodan Milosevic's oppressive and repressive counterguerrilla policies against the Albanian Kosovars. It threatened to bomb Serbian forces in Kosovo and Serbia proper unless Milosevic stopped his counterinsurgency campaign against the Albanians. Coercive diplomacy ultimately failed and only a full-scale air war brought Serb compliance with NATO's demands.

Haiti

The goal in the Haitian case was to get rid of a repressive military government and reinstate the freely elected government of Jean-Bertrand Aristide. To achieve this objective, the United States threatened to invade unless Raoul Cedras and his military cohorts who ran the government gave up power. They did so, but only after the United States invaded the country. (As Robert Pastor points out in his chapter, military leaders reached an agreement not to oppose the U.S. invasion as the troops were landing, but they signed an agreement for the change of government only the day after the invasion.) This case falls on the borderline between coercive diplomacy and war because invasion of a country, especially one that takes place without loss of life on either side, is difficult to code and can be viewed as either a success or failure of coercive diplomacy. I have coded it as a borderline success, for reasons I make clear in chapter 9, although Robert Pastor's judgment is that it was a failure of coercive diplomacy, as he makes clear in his chapter. The difference in coding illustrates the difficulty of drawing judgments about cases that fall squarely on the borderline.

North Korea

The North Korean case centered on Washington's attempt to convince the Kim Il Sung government to halt its program to acquire nuclear weapons. To achieve this objective, as William Drennan explains, the United States threatened to impose economic sanctions on North Korea, which the North Koreans said would be a cause for war, and then it made threats to use force unless the North Koreans stopped proceeding with their weapons program. The United States ultimately succeeded in stopping the North from reprocessing its plutonium, but after the North Koreans had agreed to freeze that program, they began, covertly in 1997 or 1998, to open another route—uranium enrichment—to acquire nuclear weapons, as the U.S. government discovered in the fall of 2002. Even the partial success of coercive diplomacy—the freeze on plutonium reprocessing—worked only because former president Jimmy Carter made a trip to Pyongyang in June 1994 and through his unauthorized actions, especially his public declaration that sanctions were dead, helped avert what appeared to most in the U.S. government in the early summer of 1994 to be a collision course to war. Overall, this case represents a failure of coercive diplomacy because even though it adhered to the freeze on its reprocessing program, North Korea contravened both the terms and the spirit of the October 1994 Agreed Framework by beginning the uranium enrichment program.

China

As Robert Ross shows, in the 1996 crisis, the United States acted to demonstrate to China the seriousness of its commitment to ensure the peaceful resolution of Taiwan's status and, in the process, to shore up its alliances in East Asia. In 1996 China resorted to displays of force by firing missiles around Taiwan's waters in order to halt what it viewed as Taiwan's creeping moves toward independence. The United States responded with its own coercive actions: it sent two aircraft carrier battle groups into the Taiwan Strait to send a message to China that the United States was serious about its commitment to the peaceful resolution of Taiwan's status. Clearly, Washington's actions were designed to shore up the credibility of the U.S. commitment to come to Taiwan's aid with military force should China attack it or otherwise try to coerce it, and in this sense the United States was shoring up its deterrent posture. Looked at another way, however, the United States was also engaged in coercive diplomacy: it was making a display of force and an implicit threat to use its air and naval power to stop China from its future attempts to use coercive diplomacy against Taiwan. The China case falls into that category of coercive diplomacy discussed earlier, when threats or limited use are employed to strengthen deterrence because the deterrer believes that its deterrence posture is weakening.

Iraq

Jon Alterman demonstrates that the Iraqi case involved a series of six discrete coercive diplomatic incidents, beginning in the fall of 1990 with the attempt to reverse Saddam Hussein's invasion of Kuwait and ending in December 1998 with the attempt to force Saddam to allow UN inspectors back into Iraq. As he points out, before August 1990 Washington's goal was to engage Iraq, not coerce it; after December 1998 the goal was to change the regime, not coerce it, and regime change in the case of Iraq would likely mean death for its key members. In the Iraqi case the United States threatened war in 1990 unless Saddam Hussein evacuated Kuwait, and then, after the war was won, it used the threat of air strikes and actual air strikes to coerce Saddam into stopping his interference with the weapons inspectors.

The Iraqi case also involved four other goals. The first goal was the destruction of a significant portion of Iraq's conventional military power, which only war could accomplish. The second was the containment of Iraq within its borders once the war was won, which was accomplished mainly through deterrence. The third was to keep Iraq's conventional forces in a weak state, which was accomplished by a combination of economic sanctions and military blockade. The fourth was to destroy Iraq's nuclear, biological, and chemical (NBC) weapons programs, which was only partially successful. In the Iraqi case, therefore, war waging, deterrence, economic and military containment, NBC disarmament, and coercive diplomacy were all present. Alterman confines his analysis to the discrete coercive diplomatic attempts that took place within the general deterrence and containment rubric, and while deterrence and containment worked, Alterman concludes that Washington's coercive diplomatic attempts over this nine-year period brought mixed results. For reasons spelled out in chapter 9, I judge these multiple coercive diplomatic attempts overall to be a failure.

Terrorism

Finally, the responses to terrorism involved attempts to find ways to stop contemplated and actual attacks against Americans overseas and at home, and employed threats or limited uses of force to achieve these objectives. The threat in September 2001 to subject the Taliban government to the same fate as al Qaeda unless it turned over the al Qaeda leadership clearly fits the profile of a coercive diplomacy gambit, but so, too, do the other cases. Retaliation against Saddam's intelligence headquarters complex in 1993 in response to his attempts to kill former president Bush may be classified as retaliation but also as coercion: the use of force to change Saddam's behavior. Similarly, the 1999 attacks against al Qaeda camps in Afghanistan can be seen as

retaliation for the bombings of the U.S. embassies in Kenya and
Tanzania, and also as an outright attempt to kill Bin Laden. Retaliation and decapitation of a terrorist organization's leadership is a
form of coercive diplomacy; after all, both are designed to get the terrorist organization to stop its terrorist attacks. Judging the efficacy
of coercive diplomacy against terrorists is exceedingly difficult, as
Martha Crenshaw explains, but she concludes that overall this technique has not worked well.

Chapters 2 through 8 flesh out the brief descriptions of the eight cases
presented here. In each case the author lays out the essential details of
the story and then addresses three fundamental questions: what goals
did the United States seek, how did it employ threats of force to
achieve them, and what results did coercive diplomacy produce?
Chapter 9 puts the case studies into an analytic summary and derives
conclusions and policy prescriptions by answering these five questions:

- Why is coercive diplomacy difficult?
- What are the prerequisites for the successful exercise of coercive
  diplomacy?
- What is the United States' experience with coercive diplomacy?
- When does coercive diplomacy work?
- What guidelines can be offered to U.S policymakers who may con-
  template resort to coercive diplomacy?

NOTES

1. Alexander L. George, *Forceful Persuasion: Coercive Diplomacy as an
Alternative to War* (Washington, D.C.: United States Institute of Peace Press,
1991), 5 (emphasis in original).

2. Thomas C. Schelling, *Arms and Influence* (New Haven, Conn.: Yale
University Press, 1966), 69.

3. The 1996 Taiwan Strait crisis is a good example of the bolstering of
deterrence by compellent actions and is discussed later. For further discus-

sion on the conflation of compellence and deterrence, see Daniel L. Byman, Matthew C. Waxman, and Eric Larson, *Airpower as a Coercive Instrument* (Santa Monica, Calif.: RAND, 1999), 10–15.

4. George, *Forceful Persuasion*, 5.

5. By treating coercive diplomacy as a form of compellence, however, we depart somewhat from George's usage. He does not put coercive diplomacy under the general rubric of compellence for two reasons. First, he believes that compellence implies "exclusive or heavy reliance on coercive threats to influence an adversary," whereas he wishes "to emphasize the possibility of a more flexible diplomacy that can employ noncoercive persuasion and accommodation as well as coercive threats." Second, he believes that coercive diplomacy implies a defensive use of coercion, not an offensive use, or what he calls blackmail. Defensive use constitutes an effort "to persuade an opponent to stop and/or undo an action he is already embarked upon," whereas offensive use constitutes an aggressive effort "to persuade a victim to give up something of value without putting up resistance." As a consequence, George treats coercive diplomacy as something distinct from compellence, even though he argues that "coercive diplomacy is a response to an encroachment already undertaken." (Quotes are from George, *Forceful Persuasion*, 5.) We find neither point compelling. First, what is defensive lies in the eyes of the beholder. The coercer views its attempt to change the target's behavior as defensive because it wants to stop the target's objectionable behavior. The target, however, does not view its behavior as objectionable because it is trying to alter a situation that it considers unjust or unacceptable; consequently, from its standpoint the actions it is taking are also defensive. Moreover, the target's objectionable behavior may have been unprovoked, though the target more likely views its behavior as a response to prior actions of the coercer or others. Second, nothing that Schelling wrote about compellence implied that it had to be mostly coercive. Indeed, a strong emphasis on communication and bargaining is found throughout his work. For both reasons, then, we treat coercive diplomacy as a form of compellence and make no distinction between defensive coercive diplomacy and offensive coercive diplomacy.

6. George, *Forceful Persuasion*, 5.

7. See Alexander L. George, David K. Hall, and William E. Simons, *The Limits of Coercive Diplomacy—Laos, Cuba, Vietnam* (Boston: Little, Brown, 1971); and Alexander L. George and William E. Simons, *The Limits of Coercive Diplomacy*, 2d ed. (Boulder, Colo.: Westview Press, 1994). Other useful works on coercive diplomacy are Lawrence Freedman, ed., *Strategic Coercion: Concepts and Cases* (Oxford: Oxford University Press, 1998); Peter

Jakobsen, *Western Use of Coercive Diplomacy after the Cold War: A Challenge for Theory and Practice* (New York: St. Martin's Press, 1998); Donald C. F. Daniel and Bradd C. Hayes, with Chantal de Jonge Oudraat, *Coercive Inducement and the Containment of International Crises* (Washington, D.C.: United States Institute of Peace Press, 1999); Byman et al., *Airpower as a Coercive Instrument*; Daniel L. Byman and Matthew C. Waxman, *The Dynamics of Coercion: American Foreign Policy* (Cambridge: Cambridge University Press, 2002); and David E. Johnson, Karl P. Mueller, and William H. Taft, *Conventional Coercion across the Spectrum of Operations: The Utility of U.S. Military Forces in the Emerging Security Environment* (Santa Monica, Calif.: RAND, 2002).

8. These cases were examined in the first and second editions of *The Limits of Coercive Diplomacy*. The second edition revised three cases—Laos, Cuba, and Vietnam—that appeared in the first edition.

2

Humanitarian Relief and Nation Building in Somalia

NORA BENSAHEL

URING 1991 AND 1992 SOMALIA SUFFERED from a widespread famine. Almost 20 percent of Somalia's eight million residents were in immediate danger of starvation, and more than half the population required some form of external assistance. The United Nations spent almost two years trying to achieve a diplomatic settlement to the factional fighting that was causing the famine, without much success. As the famine continued to spread, the United States proposed a two-phased military intervention in Somalia. According to the concept of operations announced by President George Bush, the United States would lead a multinational coalition into Somalia in order to stabilize the security situation and ensure the safe delivery of relief supplies. Once this objective had been achieved, the United States would transfer responsibility for the intervention to the United Nations, which would continue humanitarian relief efforts while embarking on a program of civil reconstruction. UN secretary-general Boutros Boutros-Ghali tacitly accepted this proposal, and the international intervention in Somalia commenced in December 1992.

This chapter argues that the United States successfully pursued a strategy of coercive diplomacy during the first phase of this intervention.

21

Its overwhelming military power made its threats credible, and its objective of humanitarian relief did not challenge the core interests of the faction leaders. The United Nations, by contrast, possessed neither of these favorable conditions. Its weak military capabilities reduced the credibility of its threats to use force, and its objectives of forcible disarmament and national reconstruction fundamentally challenged the interests of Mohammed Farah Aideed, one of the main faction leaders. The United Nations therefore encountered much more resistance than it had anticipated, including numerous attacks on UN peacekeepers during the summer of 1993. With support from the United States, the United Nations responded by emphasizing the coercive elements of its strategy and seeking accountability for those involved in the attacks. This decision resulted in more than four months of armed conflict, drawing U.S. forces directly into combat with Aideed's faction. This conflict culminated in the October 3 firefight, an incident that caused the United States to withdraw its forces from Somalia and that inevitably led to the withdrawal of the United Nations.

This chapter is divided into four sections. The first section describes the early, and ultimately unsuccessful, diplomatic efforts to resolve the conflict and end the famine. The second section addresses the initial phase of the military intervention in Somalia, when the United States pursued a strategy of coercive diplomacy that blended the credible threat of force with diplomatic outreach efforts to the faction leaders. The third section details the changes that occurred after the United Nations took responsibility for the military intervention in May 1993 and explains why the United Nations soon found itself pursuing a military policy based on coercion. The fourth section concludes with some reflections on the international intervention in Somalia and the lessons that it provides for the study of coercive diplomacy.

DIPLOMACY: JANUARY 1991 TO NOVEMBER 1992

Somalia's government collapsed in January 1991. President Mohammed Siad Barre fled the capital, Mogadishu, after decades of factional challenges to his military dictatorship and more than two years of civil war. His departure left Somalia without a functioning government, and armed factions quickly started fighting for control of the war-torn country. Among the dozens of factions seeking power, two of the most important were led by Ali Mahdi Mohammed and Mohammed Farah Aideed. The two men had been aligned with the same faction, the United Somali Congress (USC), during the civil war, united in their desire to drive Siad Barre out of power. Once they had achieved this goal, they quickly turned against each other in a battle for political control of the country. Both men believed that they would gain control of Somalia as a whole if they gained control of Mogadishu, but each one maintained his power base in a different part of the city. Ali Mahdi's background as a civilian and a businessman appealed to urban residents in northern Mogadishu, while Aideed, a former general with extensive military experience, drew strong support in the southern parts of the city. Mogadishu, a city of more than a million people, remained extremely tense throughout the spring of 1991, and the two factions clashed on several occasions in May. In an effort to quell the violence, the USC elected Aideed as its party chairman in June. The USC hoped that this would resolve the power struggle, but the following month, Ali Mahdi declared himself interim president of Somalia. Fighting broke out once again in September, and the streets of Mogadishu had turned into a full battle zone by November.[1]

Civil war also spread throughout the rest of the country during 1991, as various clans took advantage of the security vacuum created by Siad Barre's departure. Somalia had always been a poor country, but this civil war destroyed much of the country's infrastructure. More than a million Somalis left their homes, which caused massive disruptions in food production and distribution. Combatants pursued a scorched-earth policy, deliberately destroying productive agricultural lands, grain and seed stocks, and irrigation systems in order to deprive their opponents of food and water.[2] As the fighting continued, famine began to spread on an unprecedented scale. Within the year an estimated 4.5 million people—more than half of Somalia's population—required urgent assistance. More than 1.5 million people faced an immediate risk of starvation, including more than 1 million children.[3]

Relief organizations from around the world poured into Somalia to try to help the people in need.[4] Yet the armed conflicts continued to get worse throughout 1991, making it increasingly difficult for the relief agencies to do their work. In late December the outgoing UN secretary-general, Javier Pérez de Cuéllar, asked the Security Council to consider the situation in Somalia and announced that Under Secretary-General James Jonah would soon travel to Somalia.[5]

Jonah conducted a fact-finding mission in Mogadishu in January 1992 to see whether Ali Mahdi and Aideed would accept a UN mediation effort.[6] Jonah met with both faction leaders during his trip and concluded that Aideed would probably not welcome a UN role. Despite this recommendation, and despite some opposition from the permanent members of the Security Council, the new secretary-general, Boutros Boutros-Ghali, supported proactive measures to resolve this conflict.[7] Ali Mahdi welcomed these efforts, but Aideed opposed UN involvement for two reasons. First, Aideed believed that Jonah's diplomatic efforts favored Ali Mahdi, and he feared that the United Nations would legitimize Ali Mahdi's claim to the presidency simply by bringing him to the negotiation table.[8] Second, and perhaps more important, Aideed was militarily stronger than Ali Mahdi. His forces were much more experienced and possessed many heavy weapons that had been taken from Siad Barre's warehouses. Aideed believed that he could defeat Ali Mahdi's forces within several weeks, so he had little incentive to cooperate with UN mediation efforts. It is therefore not surprising that Ali Mahdi, as the weaker party, welcomed the UN role, while Aideed, as the stronger party, opposed it.[9]

Skirmishes between the two factions intensified in January, but the United Nations continued to pursue a diplomatic settlement. Both factions accepted an invitation from Boutros-Ghali to meet in New York to discuss a cease-fire, and the two delegations reached a tentative agreement on February 14. Jonah went back to Mogadishu to work out the specifics, and after four days of intense negotiations, Ali Mahdi and Aideed signed an official cease-fire. However, this official agreement did not stop the fighting on the ground. The UN special coordinator for the delivery of humanitarian aid, David Bassiouni, intensified his efforts to secure the delivery of relief supplies after the factions signed the cease-fire, but the anarchic security situation still interfered with his work. Ali Mahdi and Aideed often broke their agreements to provide air and port access, and Mogadishu continued to be plagued by looting and extortion.[10]

As the famine continued to spread, the United Nations decided to take stronger action. On April 24, 1992, the Security Council approved Resolution 751, which established the United Nations Operation in Somalia (UNOSOM).[11] The resolution authorized UNOSOM to immediately deploy fifty unarmed observers to monitor the cease-fire and allowed for the possibility of deploying up to five hundred peacekeepers in the future. Aideed was furious at this new development, because, in the words of one analyst, he viewed the resolution as "potentially lethal."[12] It seemed to confirm his suspicions that the United Nations was biased in favor of Ali Mahdi, since he believed that any external security force that restored law and order would also legitimize Ali Mahdi's claim to the presidency. Over the next two months Mohamed Sahnoun, the special representative of the secretary-general (SRSG), worked hard to convince Aideed to support the UN resolution and the deployment of the fifty military observers. Aideed finally gave his consent, only to withdraw it again after discovering that a UN-chartered aircraft had also been chartered by Ali Mahdi to deliver military equipment and to distribute his new currency.[13] Sahnoun made several public statements defending Aideed's position, which annoyed the United Nations but placated Aideed. After numerous conversations with Sahnoun, Aideed restored his consent to the deployment of the fifty military observers.[14]

Once again this UN action did little to stem the growing humanitarian disaster. Relief agencies still could not establish food distribution networks, and most of the relief supplies sent to Somalia never made it out of the ports or airports because of violence and looting. In a July report to the Security Council, Boutros-Ghali wrote, "Many of the most destitute are located in the interior of the country, not easily accessible from the major ports. The mounting of an urgent airlift operation may be the only way to reach those areas and should be undertaken as soon as possible."[15] The Security Council responded by passing Resolution

767, authorizing an airlift of food and relief supplies into the most urgently affected areas of Somalia.[16] Although the report and the resolution did not mention any specific countries by name, only the United States possessed the military capability to conduct such an airlift. After several weeks of internal debate among senior administration officials, President Bush approved the use of U.S. assets and troops for the airlift.[17] The operation, which soon became known as Provide Relief, conducted almost twenty-five hundred flights between August and November 1992 and delivered more than twenty-five thousand metric tons of food—enough for 112 million meals.[18]

The airlift did relieve some of the most urgent suffering, but it could not address the deteriorating security situation throughout the country. Special Representative Sahnoun intensified his efforts to secure approval for the deployment of the five hundred peacekeepers that had been authorized by Resolution 751. In mid-August Ali Mahdi and Aideed finally gave their consent to this peacekeeping force, which would be staffed by a Pakistani battalion.[19] The Pakistani forces faced initial transportation problems that delayed their deployment, but those problems were solved when the United States volunteered to transport the battalion to Somalia.[20] As these peacekeepers started deploying, the Security Council took an action that almost jeopardized the entire operation. Acting on a recommendation from Boutros-Ghali, the Security Council adopted Resolution 775, which authorized UNOSOM to include up to three thousand additional peacekeepers.[21] However, this decision was taken without consulting the faction leaders or UN personnel in the field. Sahnoun had no idea that the resolution was even being considered and first heard about the decision while listening to a BBC radio broadcast.[22] Aideed reacted furiously: he believed that the United Nations had deliberately deceived him, since he had just given his consent for the five hundred peacekeepers. He responded by placing significant restrictions on the deploying Pakistani forces, which effectively trapped the UNOSOM peacekeepers at the airport. They remained ensconced at the airport throughout the fall, unable to even attempt to fulfill their mission of protecting food and other relief supplies.[23]

Aideed had never liked the idea of an international intervention in

Somalia, but this incident seems to have convinced him once and for all that the United Nations was biased against him. Sahnoun continued his intense diplomatic efforts through the fall of 1992 in an effort to ease the restrictions facing the United Nations and to respond to the concerns of local clan leaders throughout the country. Yet his activities increasingly incurred the wrath of UN Headquarters in New York, as he seemed to ignore Aideed's many anti-UN statements and sometimes criticized his UN superiors as well. Sahnoun was essentially forced to resign from his position in October, which complicated UN relations with the faction leaders even more. Boutros-Ghali named Ismat Kittani to replace Sahnoun, and the styles of the two men could not have been more different. Whereas Sahnoun had actively sought meetings and cultivated personal relations with faction leaders throughout the country, Kittani was more formal and reserved. He asked the faction leaders to come to him for meetings instead of the other way around and often had his staff members meet with the faction leaders instead of meeting with them himself. Aideed was particularly offended by the new representative's style, believing that Kittani epitomized the United Nations' desire to undermine his power and authority.[24]

By November 1992 Aideed and Ali Mahdi had essentially suspended their negotiations with the United Nations. Diplomatic efforts to end the humanitarian disaster had clearly failed, as the scale of the suffering continued to increase. Operation Provide Relief did save some lives, but the vast majority of Somalis were still not receiving any form of aid.[25] The famine had claimed more than half a million victims by this point, including more than 25 percent of children under age five in southern Somalia. The statistics were even more horrific in cities such as Baidoa, which had already lost 40 percent of its population and 70 percent of children under age five.[26] UNOSOM did include a small military component, but the Pakistani peacekeepers were completely hamstrung by the need to secure approval from the warring factions before taking any action that involved leaving the airport. At this point, it became clear that the human suffering in Somalia could not be relieved through diplomatic efforts alone. A more forceful approach would be needed.

COERCIVE DIPLOMACY: NOVEMBER 1992 TO MAY 1993

As the crisis worsened during the summer and fall of 1992, Bush administration officials began to realize that U.S. interests in Somalia went beyond simply feeding the hungry. According to Ken Menkhaus, a consensus emerged that "while isolated crises like Somalia were not in themselves vital to U.S. national interests, collectively the growing instances of state collapse, ethnic wars and anarchy did pose a threat to U.S. interests in the post–Cold War era."[27] Bush administration officials believed that the United Nations possessed the legitimacy necessary to address these types of conflicts but lacked the institutional capacity to conduct effective military operations—a lesson seemingly confirmed by the concurrent UN peacekeeping operation in Bosnia.[28] They concluded that the United States would have to lead any military intervention into Somalia, since it was the only country capable of making such an intervention work.[29] As Admiral Jonathan Howe later wrote, "Alone among the nations of the world, the United States had the lift and logistical infrastructure to establish a large force rapidly in a remote area in which civil institutions and services were nonexistent and where violent opposition to even a humanitarian mission could be encountered."[30]

On November 25 President Bush approved the plans for a two-phased military intervention.[31] Phase I involved a multinational coalition, known as the Unified Task Force (UNITAF), whose mission would be to provide a secure environment for the delivery of relief aid in southern Somalia.[32] The United States would contribute two divisions to UNITAF, totaling approximately thirty thousand troops, and would retain exclusive command authority over the entire operation. Once the south had been secured, Phase II would begin: UNITAF would transfer control of the operation to a new UN force, called the United Nations Operation in Somalia II (UNOSOM II). The United States would gradually draw down its forces after the transfer of authority, leaving the United Nations to consolidate the zone of stability in the south and to expand that zone to the north. In other words, the United States would use its unique military capabilities to launch the operation and provide short-term humanitarian relief.

Once the operation was up and running, the United Nations would take over the longer-term task of reconstructing and rebuilding Somalia.[33]

Boutros-Ghali, along with other UN officials, did not like the idea of taking responsibility for the mission so quickly. He knew that the United Nations lacked the capacity to disarm the factions, which he believed to be the only way to permanently stabilize the security situation. He wanted the United States to pursue active disarmament, since that would be the only way for the United Nations to maintain order once it took over the mission.[34] On November 29 he presented several intervention options to the Security Council, ranging from no additional action to comprehensive intervention.[35] On December 3 the Security Council adopted Resolution 794, which authorized member states to carry out a peace enforcement operation under Chapter VII of the UN Charter.[36] For all intents and purposes, this resolution meant that the United Nations accepted the U.S. operational plan. UN officials did remain wary that UNITAF would want to depart too quickly, forcing the United Nations to take over a situation that it could not control. But at this point, both the Security Council and the secretary-general believed that the Somalia intervention would alleviate some of the suffering, that it would set a good precedent for the United Nations' role in the post–Cold War world, and that they could not afford to wait.[37] They agreed to move forward with the U.S.-led intervention, despite the UN reservations.

UNITAF epitomized the concept of coercive diplomacy: the United States endeavored to create a stable security environment through diplomatic initiatives backed by the threat of force. President Bush named Ambassador Robert Oakley as his special envoy for Somalia and charged him with coordinating the civilian effort and leading the diplomatic outreach to the faction leaders. As Oakley later described, "As far as possible, our work would be achieved by dialogue and co-option, using implicit threats of coercion to buttress requests for cooperation among the factions and with UNITAF."[38] However, UNITAF made it clear that it would achieve its objectives, with or without the agreement of the faction leaders. UNITAF possessed a significant amount of military force, spearheaded by the two U.S. divisions, and its troops operated under robust rules of engagement. In addition to the standard self-defense clause, UNITAF was authorized to enforce what it called the "four no's": no banditry, no roadblocks, no visible weapons, and no technicals.[39] Its goals were to secure the Mogadishu port and airfield, secure regional airfields in southern Somalia, open the roads for truck transport, and provide security for the safe conduct of humanitarian operations.[40] Oakley would do his best to secure the consent of the faction leaders for these activities, but if diplomatic efforts failed, UNITAF would achieve these objectives through the use of force.

Oakley started reaching out to the faction leaders before the first UNITAF forces arrived in Somalia. He met with Aideed and Ali Mahdi on December 7 and 8, 1992, in order to secure an uncontested landing for the United States Marine Corps. Both faction leaders promised to use their radio transmissions and clan connections to urge their followers to stay away from the Mogadishu port and airport, and the marines landed without incident on the night of December 8.[41] Ali Mahdi seemed to genuinely welcome the UNITAF deployment, but Aideed remained much more reserved. As John Hirsch and Robert Oakley later wrote, "It was perceptible, beneath the apparently warm welcome, that [Aideed] still harbored deep reservations about the effect of foreign forces on his interests, but it was even clearer that he was not in a mood to challenge them at the outset."[42] Oakley had convinced Aideed that UNITAF had a substantial amount of firepower at its disposal and that it would not hesitate to use force against those who challenged it. On December 11 Oakley invited both faction leaders to a meeting with Special Representative Kittani and Lieutenant General Robert Johnston, the UNITAF commander, to remind them of the "potentially disastrous" results of a confrontation with UNITAF forces. Oakley recalled that in persuading them to attend, "I reminded them of the massive firepower that had been used so effectively during Desert Storm. I remarked that it would be better if they discussed security problems with General Johnston."[43]

During this meeting Ali Mahdi and Aideed agreed to establish a joint security committee. Although the committee was created to provide a neutral forum for the factions to continue their peace discussions, it also became the primary mechanism for communication between UNITAF and the faction leaders. This committee met every day during the UNITAF deployment. The committee met at Oakley's compound, since it was a safe, neutral site, and its meetings often included U.S. military and civilian officials. These meetings gave UNITAF personnel a chance to explain the reasons for their actions and to communicate actions that they intended to take in the upcoming days. These meetings continued regularly, even when relations with the faction leaders became tense.[44] While these meetings occurred in Mogadishu, Oakley's diplomatic efforts also reached out to other areas of the country. He went to Baidoa on December 15 to secure another uncontested entry of U.S. Marine forces and to start a dialogue on ways to restore local political institutions. During his meetings with a wide range of community leaders, he stressed that UNITAF would not seek to impose any particular settlement and that the people would be able to select their leaders in accordance with their local traditions. Baidoa became a model for the other humanitarian relief sectors.[45] Before UNITAF forces arrived in any sector, Oakley and other diplomatic personnel met with local leaders, established civil-military coordination centers, and encouraged local leaders to promote political reconstruction.[46]

The factions did occasionally challenge UNITAF's authority, but these skirmishes were usually settled through the quick and impartial use of force. Aideed's faction, now known as the Somali National Alliance (SNA),[47] engaged in what Walter Clarke described as "petty harassment" of UNITAF forces.[48] The first incident occurred three days after UNITAF arrived, when two technicals opened fire at night on UNITAF helicopters and were immediately destroyed by rocket fire. Oakley responded with diplomacy, not the further use of force. He called both Ali Mahdi and Aideed and said that he did not know who was responsible for the attacks, but he urged both men to go on the radio and tell their followers that the incident had been a mistake and that they should refrain from such confrontations in the future. They did so, and the situation was defused.[49] A few more incidents did occur during the following weeks, and UNITAF responded to these with the exemplary use of force. After Christmas one of the smaller factions started a series of artillery attacks in Mogadishu's northeastern suburbs—and marine helicopters quickly found and destroyed their weapons.[50] However, the exemplary use of force was always combined with a diplomatic initiative. After each incident Oakley would travel with a military representative to the area of confrontation. They would discuss the incident with the commander in charge and find ways to avoid escalating the incident into a major confrontation. As Oakley later explained, "We just kept up the dialogue. We didn't allow an adversarial relationship to develop."[51]

The only major challenge occurred in February 1993, after a series of factional conflicts in the city of Kismayo. Two local leaders, Colonel Jess and General Morgan, had been fighting to gain control of the city for several weeks, and UNITAF stepped in after a series of attacks and looting on February 23.[52] Several reports indicated that Morgan had defeated Jess and taken control of the city. Since Jess was one of his allies, Aideed was enraged and believed that UNITAF had let this happen. Aideed's supporters mounted a series of demonstrations outside the U.S. embassy compound and UN headquarters and planned a deliberate attack on a group of Nigerian UNITAF forces. Oakley and Johnston conferred with several other U.S. officials and determined that the fighting was confined to a small area of Mogadishu controlled by Aideed and the SNA. They concluded that the best response was no response: they would wait for the demonstration to "burn itself out," according to Hirsch and Oakley. Mogadishu returned to normal within two days. Oakley told the press that this incident demonstrated UNITAF's strength and its commitment to the reconciliation process, but he privately conveyed a stern warning to Aideed.[53] Oakley recalled that he and a marine general "had a very private, very pointed talk with Aideed about what would happen to him if there were to be a repeat," telling him that he would be held personally responsible for any further attacks on UNITAF forces.[54] Aideed got the message, and the SNA did not challenge UNITAF forces in Mogadishu again.[55]

These incidents notwithstanding, Aideed and Ali Mahdi generally respected UNITAF's authority. At least three factors contributed to the success of this first phase of the Somalia intervention. First, UNITAF was an extremely capable military force: it had a lot of firepower at its disposal and benefited from the U.S. military's organizational and logistical strengths.[56] These capabilities, combined with tough rules of engagement, allowed UNITAF to respond quickly and effectively to factional challenges. To use the language of deterrence theory, UNITAF clearly communicated a credible threat of retaliation that would impose high costs on those who challenged its authority. Even though Aideed did not like the entire concept of an intervention force, he seems to have calculated that the costs of confronting UNITAF would outweigh the benefits. Second, UNITAF maintained a position of impartiality and came to be seen as an honest broker by most of the faction leaders. Oakley believed that the U.S. experience in Lebanon clearly demonstrated the importance of impartial intervention forces and the dangers of deviating from impartiality.[57] UNITAF forces thus took great pains to balance their weapons raids so that they affected all areas and all factions within Mogadishu.[58] Oakley worked hard to lead with diplomacy and used coercive methods only as a last resort.

Third, and perhaps most important, the operational objectives were limited in scope. UNITAF's mandate deliberately excluded forcible disarmament of the factions—a policy decision that UNOSOM II later reversed, as will be described later.[59] For UNITAF, out of sight was really out of mind: weapons were confiscated only when they were blatantly displayed or used against UNITAF personnel. U.S. military and civilian officials agreed that UNITAF did not possess enough power to conduct a forcible disarmament campaign, which would undoubtedly entangle UNITAF in a series of violent confrontations with the well-armed factions.[60] Aideed understood that UNITAF would confiscate any weapons that it came across, but that it would not actively seek to locate and destroy those weapons. So in order to retain control of his considerable arsenal, he moved most of his heavy weapons out of Mogadishu. UNITAF allowed him to do so, for as Oakley explains, "there was no perceived need to confront Aideed over the disappearance of the weapons as long as they posed no threat to UNITAF forces or humanitarian operations."[61]

UNITAF successfully achieved its primary goal of securing the safe delivery of relief supplies. UNITAF also seems to be an excellent example of coercive diplomacy: it achieved its objectives by blending serious diplomatic initiatives with the credible threats and the exemplary use of force. However, at least two mitigating factors must be considered before holding UNITAF up as a model of successful coercive diplomacy. The first is the same as one of the factors that contributed to its operational success: UNITAF possessed limited objectives. This made its operational tasks much easier, but it also meant that UNITAF never fundamentally challenged the interests or the power of the strongest faction leaders. A forcible disarmament campaign would have antagonized Aideed by removing his greatest source of strength in the struggle for control of Somalia. By rejecting this option and by overlooking Aideed's weapons movements, UNITAF secured at least the grudging consent of all faction leaders. Given this narrow set of objectives and an overwhelming military capability, it would have been surprising had UNITAF *not* been a major success.[62]

The second mitigating factor is that UNITAF's clearly stated withdrawal timetable created strong incentives for the faction leaders to simply wait out the operation. From the earliest days of the operation, the United States emphasized that UNITAF would only last several months and that it would transfer authority to the United Nations as soon as the security situation had been stabilized. These statements were designed to bolster the reputation of the United Nations, but they also signaled the limits to U.S. involvement in Somalia. The faction leaders knew that the UN-led operation would be much weaker than the U.S.-led operation, so they calculated that they would be better off if they played along with UNITAF, waited until the U.S. forces went home, and then challenged the weaker UN operation. As Walter Clarke and Jeffrey Herbst later wrote, "one of the fundamental mistakes in attributing success to the United States and failure to the UN is that the American forces made it so clear that they would not challenge the warlords and that they would be in Somalia for such a short period of time that it was in the interests of the warlords not to hinder the Americans and to speed their departure."[63]

As the United States prepared to transfer authority from UNITAF to UNOSOM II, the United Nations grew increasingly concerned that it would not be ready to take over the operation. Secretary-General Boutros-Ghali believed that UNOSOM II would not be able to main-

tain a stable situation in Somalia unless UNITAF had forcibly dis-
armed the factions—even though UNITAF clearly stated that it would
not pursue a disarmament policy.[64] This disagreement had delayed
joint planning for the transition to UNOSOM II, which did not really
start until mid-March.[65] The United States remained eager to transfer
authority to the United Nations and turned down a UN request to
delay the transfer by a month so that UNOSOM II would have more
time to prepare for its military deployment and to build up its civilian
staff.[66] The turnover proceeded as scheduled on May 4, as UNITAF
was officially disbanded and UNOSOM II took responsibility for the
international intervention in Somalia.

Between November 1992 and May 1993, the United States successfully used a strategy of coercive diplomacy to achieve its objectives in Somalia. It blended ongoing diplomatic initiatives with the
exemplary use of force in order to convince the main warlords to
cease their fighting and allow humanitarian relief efforts to reach
starving populations. However, part of the reason why this strategy of
coercive diplomacy worked was that it was explicitly temporary: the
warlords knew that the United States would be pulling out its highly
capable military forces in a few months and they would be replaced
by less capable forces under United Nations command. They therefore faced strong incentives to comply with U.S. demands and halt
their fighting for a few months, calculating that they could resume
their struggle for power once UNITAF withdrew from Somalia.

COERCION: JUNE 1993 TO OCTOBER 1993

Whereas UNITAF started its deployment from a position of strength,
UNOSOM II started its deployment from a position of weakness. Relief
workers and Somalis alike feared that the transfer of authority would
lead to a resumption of factional fighting, and UN officials expected that
Aideed would challenge UNOSOM II soon after the handover.[67] At least
four factors contributed to this pessimistic assessment.

First, UNOSOM II was militarily weaker than UNITAF had been.
Its area of responsibility expanded to include all of Somalia, not just
the southern part of the country, but its authorized force strength was

reduced by 20 percent, to include a maximum of twenty-eight thousand troops.[68] Some of UNITAF's most capable units were withdrawing, including contingents from Australia, Canada, and the U.S. Marine Corps, and UN officials worried that the number of troops on the ground for UNOSOM II could dip as low as sixteen thousand. This would require the UN command to move forces out of Mogadishu to cover gaps in other areas, which could seriously destabilize the capital. Furthermore, the United Nations had to create an integrated operation using force contributions from more than twenty different countries, which were often small units that had not worked with each other before. UNOSOM II therefore faced significant problems that resulted from interoperability challenges, insufficient weaponry, and varied states of training and readiness.[69]

The United States did make a fairly significant force contribution to UNOSOM II, including more than three thousand U.S. logistics troops that reported through the UN chain of command. If the UNOSOM II commander ran into trouble, he could request additional support from a 1,300-person U.S. Quick Reaction Force (QRF) and from the First Marine Expeditionary Force (I MEF), which remained under a U.S. chain of command.[70] However, these forces paled in comparison to the sheer number of U.S. forces that had been deployed during UNITAF, which fueled the perception that UNOSOM II was a much weaker operation. As Hirsch and Oakley explain, "The departure of the heavily armed, aggressively patrolling Marines from south Mogadishu obviously had a greater psychological effect on the Somalis, especially the SNA, than the continued presence of a QRF from the Tenth Mountain Division."[71] These impressions were only intensified when UNOSOM II manifested some obvious command-and-control problems and when a lack of personnel and equipment caused the Pakistani contingent in Mogadishu to reduce the number of street patrols.[72]

Second, the United Nations was not seen as an impartial organization. Even though Aideed probably would have believed that any external intervention force was biased against him, he particularly distrusted the United Nations. He remained angry with the Security Council for having approved an additional three thousand peacekeepers without consulting him first, and he deeply disliked Secretary-

General Boutros-Ghali. Aideed held Boutros-Ghali personally responsible for Egypt's strong support of the Siad Barre regime when the secretary-general was the Egyptian minister of state for foreign affairs.[73] As Gérard Prunier recounts, Boutros-Ghali "was never seen by the Somalis as a neutral player but rather as somebody who still had the same political agenda, using the UN's rather than Cairo's resources."[74] When Boutros-Ghali arrived in Mogadishu on January 3, 1993, during a stopover on his way to a peace conference in Addis Ababa, Aideed organized a large demonstration against the United Nations. The protests prevented Boutros-Ghali from visiting the UNOSOM II headquarters and fueled the mutual distrust between the two men.[75]

Third, UNOSOM II pursued a policy of disarmament that threatened the interests of some of the faction leaders. Security Council Resolution 814 gave UNOSOM II a substantially expanded mandate, emphasizing the importance of disarmament and nation building throughout Somalia.[76] UNOSOM II initially inherited UNITAF's rules of engagement, which allowed force to be used only after a direct confrontation. In late May, however, UNOSOM II commander Cevic Bir issued Fragmentary Order 39, which stated that "[o]rganized, armed militias, technicals, and other crew-served weapons can be *engaged without provocation*" (emphasis added).[77] This order allowed UNOSOM II to actively pursue disarmament by forcibly removing these types of weapons from their Somali owners. Although in principle this order applied to all the armed factions, in reality it set the stage for a confrontation with the SNA. Ali Mahdi had voluntarily turned over all his weapons to UNITAF back in February, but Aideed had moved his outside Mogadishu. When UNITAF transferred power to UNOSOM II, Aideed simply moved those weapons back into the city. Since Aideed was the only faction leader who still possessed these types of weapons, Fragmentary Order 39 set UNOSOM II on a collision course with the SNA.

Fourth, Aideed did not like UN efforts toward political reconstruction. In March 1993 Aideed and the fourteen other recognized faction leaders attended the UN-sponsored Conference on National Reconciliation, held in Addis Ababa. At the end of the conference, the faction leaders signed an accord that committed them to establish representative councils at the local and district levels. Aideed and the other leaders quickly demonstrated that they had no intention of abiding by their commitments, but the United Nations continued to push for the creation of these representative councils.[78] Led by Admiral Jonathan Howe (ret.), the new special representative of the secretary-general, UNOSOM II's civilian authorities believed that these councils were a crucial first step toward national reconstruction. However, these representative councils were not at all in Aideed's interests. Aideed simply did not have the popular support necessary to guarantee a majority in these councils. As Howe later recalled, "if the UN mandate was carried out, Aideed was not going to be the leader of the country. In fact, he was going to lose a lot of territory and power, simply through the process of some sort of representative government emerging."[79] Thus, Aideed had every incentive to challenge the authority of the United Nations, since its objectives of disarmament and political reconstruction were completely antithetical to his core interests.

It did not take long for the expected confrontation to occur. Immediately after the transfer of authority, forces aligned with Aideed attacked Belgian peacekeepers in Kismayo. The Belgians successfully repelled the attack, and UN personnel suspected that this might have been the challenge that they had been led to expect. A few days later, however, the United States received information that Aideed's people had threatened to kill an American. U.S. officials made this information public by putting it in the *Washington Post* and broadcasting it over the Voice of America and the BBC, in an effort to warn people and to deter the attack. UN personnel were urged to be careful, since people of any nationality can be mistaken for Americans.[80] Tension continued to brew during May. SNA heavy weapons grew increasingly noticeable throughout Mogadishu, and Aideed used his radio station to broadcast a series of blistering attacks against the United Nations.

On June 4 UNOSOM II officials told one of Aideed's midlevel officials that they would inspect one of his weapons storage areas the following day.[81] UNITAF had authorized this storage area during its phase of the deployment and had inventoried and inspected the weapons contained inside. After UNITAF withdrew from Somalia, UNOSOM II continued its policy of routinely inspecting these weapons sites to verify the status of the stockpiles. UNOSOM II generally prenotified local parties about upcoming inspections, so this message to Aideed's representatives on June 4 was nothing out of the ordinary. However, Aideed reacted to this message far more strongly than he ever had before. Aideed's representative apparently told Major General Thomas Montgomery, the UNOSOM II deputy commander, that inspecting this arsenal without Aideed's personal agreement "would lead to war," but Montgomery did not share this information with the Pakistani forces that were scheduled to accompany the weapons inspectors.[82] The inspection began as scheduled on the morning of June 5, and the Pakistani forces went in unarmed vehicles since they remained unaware of the potential for hostility.[83] Most of the inspections were conducted without serious incident, despite protests and verbal harassment at some of the sites. By 10:00 A.M., however, demonstrations had erupted throughout the city, and within a couple of hours Pakistani forces were attacked in several different locations. These attacks appear to have been triggered by a rumor that UNOSOM II had closed down Aideed's radio station, which was situated in one of the weapons storage sites.[84] One set of Pakistani forces was attacked at a food distribution station, while another group of Pakistani units encountered an ambush on 21 October Road, one of the main transit routes through the city. By early afternoon armed Italian forces and elements of the QRF had been called in to help the Pakistani forces out of the ambush, but it took them a long time to arrive on the scene.[85] By the end of the day, twenty-four Pakistani soldiers were dead, ten were missing, and fifty-four were wounded.[86]

It was not immediately clear whether Aideed's forces preplanned these attacks, but the United Nations needed to formulate a response as quickly as possible.[87] Both UN and U.S. decision makers immediately agreed that the people responsible for the attacks had to be held accountable for their actions. Otherwise, the United Nations would be sending the message that peacekeepers could be killed with impunity—which would set a terrible precedent, not only in Somalia, but also throughout the world. On June 6 the Security Council adopted Resolution 837, which condemned the attacks and authorized UNOSOM II "to take all measures necessary against all those responsible for the armed attacks" the previous day.[88] It held Aideed responsible by specifically naming the SNA in the text of the resolution.[89]

Resolution 837 became the turning point in the entire operation, since, as one analyst explains, it was "tantamount to a declaration of war against Aideed's militia."[90] UNOSOM II's civilian staff repeatedly attempted to engage Aideed diplomatically after the resolution was passed, but Aideed showed no interest in these negotiations. As Howe later explained, "There was nothing there that we could see that offered us hope, that if we just worked for a peaceful accommodation, that something satisfactory might work out."[91] UNOSOM II forces clashed with the SNA repeatedly during the next couple of weeks, as large crowds protested the United Nations' efforts to confiscate heavy weapons. On May 13 Aideed's supporters organized a demonstration near the press hotel in south Mogadishu. During the demonstration several Somali gunmen on nearby roofs started shooting at the Pakistani UNOSOM II contingent in the area. When the Pakistanis returned fire, other Somali gunmen in the back of the crowd started firing on their own people. Their intent was to embarrass the United Nations by making it seem as though the Pakistani peacekeepers had started shooting into the crowd. Since the demonstration occurred right in front of the press hotel, images of the Somali dead and wounded were quickly transmitted around the world, creating the impression that the United Nations had caused the incident.[92]

On June 17 the United Nations announced for the first time that UNOSOM II intended to arrest Aideed. Resolution 837 had named the SNA in general, not Aideed, and UN officials had spent almost two weeks debating the wisdom of making this announcement. The UN military command planned to raid Aideed's compound on the seventeenth because it contained command-and-control facilities and weapons and ammunition stores. The military commanders argued that it would be illogical for them to go through Aideed's headquarters without the authority to arrest him. UN civilian officials agreed, hoping that once Aideed had been held accountable, the SNA could be brought into the peace process again and the process of national reconstruction could continue. This particular raid was unsuccessful, but the arrest order remained in place. After unsuccessfully searching for a couple of weeks, UN military intelligence personnel told Howe that their threat to arrest Aideed had no credibility with the people of Mogadishu, since they believed that the United Nations would offer a reward for Aideed's capture if it was really serious about finding him. Once he received funding authorization from the United Nations, Howe approved a $25,000 reward for information leading to the arrest of Aideed.[93]

By the end of June the intervention in Somalia had shifted irrevocably from coercive diplomacy to all-out coercion. UNOSOM II's civilian side continued to pursue efforts at peaceful reconciliation, but its military policies had essentially declared war on Aideed. Several of the troop-contributing countries objected to this military policy, and Italy in particular argued that peace could be achieved only by negotiating and compromising with the faction leaders.[94] The United Nations ignored this argument, but it probably would have been too late to reverse course anyway. The damage had already been done: once Resolution 837 branded Aideed a criminal, it removed any incentive for him to negotiate peacefully with the United Nations. From Aideed's perspective, it proved once and for all that the United Nations was determined to prevent him from gaining control of Somalia. The United Nations continued to pursue diplomatic initiatives with all the factions throughout the summer of 1993. Many faction leaders did cooperate with the United Nations, but Aideed showed no interest in these initiatives. He fit the classic definition of a spoiler, taking actions that undermined the implementation of the Addis Ababa accords.[95] There could be little hope for a diplomatic settlement while the United Nations remained determined to capture Aideed, and Aideed remained determined to get the United Nations out of Somalia.

During the summer of 1993 the conflict between UNOSOM II and the SNA escalated dramatically. Hirsch and Oakley describe this confrontation as "almost an obsession," as SNA actions became increasingly militant. Some Somalis started to rally around Aideed, giving him both political and military support as he fought back against the United Nations' aggressive actions.[96] UNOSOM II found itself unprepared for these reprisals and started requesting support from the QRF more frequently. Since the other national contingents within UNOSOM did not possess the capability to stage an intensive hunt for Aideed, the

QRF became increasingly drawn into routine patrol and search operations in Mogadishu. However, even these well-armed U.S. units found
it difficult to track down the ever-elusive Aideed. In early July the UN
command requested that the United States send in a team of special
forces in order to capture Aideed.[97] Howe had been lobbying the United
States to deploy these forces ever since the June 5 attacks, believing that
only a specially trained force could snatch Aideed without causing significant collateral damage.[98] Generals Joseph Hoar and Colin
Powell continually opposed this request until August 22, when six
U.S. soldiers were wounded in a land mine explosion. This incident
caused them to rethink their positions, and they reluctantly decided to
send in a special task force to stop further attacks on U.S. forces.[99] On
their recommendation, President Clinton approved deploying Task
Force Ranger to Somalia, which included U.S. Army Rangers and
Delta Force commandos. Their orders were to catch Aideed whenever
and however they could.[100] Task Force Ranger initially thought that
capturing Aideed would be a relatively straightforward task, but Aideed
eluded them through late August and September. Violence escalated
throughout Mogadishu as these special forces aggressively pursued
Aideed, and relief efforts decreased dramatically through this period.[101]

By the end of the summer, the United States had started reevalu-
ating the utility of this policy. An August 1993 interagency trip to
Somalia reported that the civil war had ended, that banditry was
decreasing, and that emergency food programs could soon end.[102] Yet
the number of attacks on both U.S. and UN peacekeepers continued
to rise, and U.S. defense officials estimated that the chances of finding Aideed were now as low as one in four.[103] In late September the
United States told Boutros-Ghali that UNOSOM II should emphasize
political reconciliation and de-emphasize the military pursuit of
Aideed.[104] The secretary-general rejected the new U.S. position, arguing that a lasting peace could not be achieved until Aideed was held
responsible for the attacks on UN peacekeepers.[105] Undeterred by this
UN opposition, Clinton administration officials decided by the last
week of September to pursue a diplomatic solution in Somalia.[106] The
administration announced this policy shift on September 27, stating
that the United States had moved away from the goal of capturing

Aideed and instead would focus on ways to isolate him diplomatically. Yet despite this stated policy change, the United States did not revoke its military orders to hunt down and capture Aideed. U.S. policy thus contained an inherent contradiction: the stated political objective now emphasized diplomacy, but U.S. leaders had not yet given up the military objective of capturing Aideed.[107]

Unfortunately, U.S. servicemen literally got caught in the crossfire between these two incompatible objectives. Since their orders had not changed, U.S. forces continued their aggressive efforts to find and capture Aideed.[108] On October 3 Task Force Ranger received an intelligence report that Aideed and his advisers were meeting in the Olympic Hotel. The Rangers responded within two hours, and although they did not find Aideed, they took several Somalis prisoner. This part of the operation passed without incident, but as they were leading the prisoners out of the hotel, they learned that a Blackhawk helicopter had been shot down. The crash site was about five blocks away from the hotel, so the closest Rangers went in to rescue the Blackhawk crew. One group of SNA forces trapped about ninety Rangers at the crash site, resulting in a massive firefight. Another group of SNA forces barricaded the streets and prevented U.S. reinforcements from reaching the Rangers.

During the next fifteen hours, U.S. and UNOSOM II forces struggled to deploy to the crash scene. An operation that was initially scheduled to last no more than ninety minutes ended up lasting all night long, and eighteen U.S. soldiers died in the firefight.[109] Aideed's forces claimed the body of one of the U.S. casualties and dragged it through the streets of Mogadishu, creating the most enduring image of the entire operation. This incident led to a firestorm of congressional criticism and an immediate policy review in Washington. Clinton administration officials were aware that much more than Somalia was at stake here: this incident would affect the future role of the United Nations in the post–Cold War world.[110] They did not want to continue the military effort against Aideed, but they feared that ordering an immediate withdrawal of U.S. forces would set a terrible precedent. They decided on a middle course: they would propose a diplomatic settlement with a phased U.S. withdrawal, so that the withdrawal would not be seen as a direct consequence of the firefight.[111] During a speech to the nation on October 7, President Clinton admitted that personalizing the conflict against Aideed had been a mistake and announced that all U.S. forces would withdraw from Somalia by March 31, 1994.[112]

Ironically, the United States reverted to a policy based on diplomacy in the wake of this incident. Clinton ordered the Joint Chiefs of Staff (JCS) and United States Central Command (CENTCOM) to cease any military actions against Aideed or the SNA that were not in self-defense. He also reappointed Oakley as his special envoy and charged him with reopening a political dialogue with the faction leaders. Oakley's efforts included attempts to strengthen the political reconciliation process, to accelerate humanitarian relief programs, and to support the development of a Somali police force.[113] Some of these efforts were successful, such as convincing Aideed to attend informal peace talks in Addis Ababa in December.[114] However, Aideed cooperated with this new international approach only when he believed that doing so would not undermine his power base. The United States and the United Nations were simply too weak to convince Aideed to take any actions that went against his interests. The United States had little bargaining power at this point, since its withdrawal date was set, and the United Nations was struggling to reconstitute UNOSOM II.[115] The U.S. withdrawal announcement had set off a "stampede for the door," according to Howe, as many troop contributors decided to withdraw their forces as well.[116] Boutros-Ghali wrote letters to forty-two UN member states, requesting new contributions for UNOSOM II, but he did not receive a single positive response.[117]

Small detachments of U.S. forces started leaving Somalia in February 1994, and the United States completed its withdrawal on March 25, 1994.[118] The United States left behind a gutted UNOSOM II: all the experienced units had already gone home, leaving behind units that lacked advanced equipment and operational experience.[119] The remaining units turned ever more inward, as few military or civilian personnel left their compounds. One analyst described UNOSOM II as doing little more than protecting itself, as its forces were "[e]ncamped in heavily fortified compounds, and operating under self-imposed risk-adverse rules of engagement."[120] Not surprisingly, the security situation quickly began to deteriorate, and soon there were as many technicals on the streets of Mogadishu as there had been before the UNITAF intervention in December 1992.[121] By the end of 1994 Boutros-Ghali concluded that UNOSOM II no longer possessed the capability to carry out its mission in such a difficult situation.[122] UNOSOM II's final withdrawal date was set for March 31, 1995, and various contingents left Somalia during the fall and winter months. Interestingly, U.S. forces deployed to Somalia one last time, to participate in a withdrawal operation known as United Shield.[123] This operation commenced on February 28, 1995, and the last UNOSOM II forces left Somalia safely on March 3.[124]

By the end of 1993 the international community had used strategies of diplomacy, coercive diplomacy, and finally straight coercion in order to convince the warlords to lay down their weapons long enough for humanitarian relief and political reconstruction efforts to take hold. None of the strategies ended in success. Somalia remains a failed state today, with continued factional fighting, no effective central government, and an ongoing humanitarian crisis.[125]

CONCLUSION: COERCIVE DIPLOMACY AND SOMALIA

The international intervention in Somalia provides a unique opportunity to draw lessons about coercive diplomacy since it encompasses two distinct military operations. UNITAF must be considered an operational success since it compelled the faction leaders to stop interfering with the delivery of relief supplies and humanitarian assistance. UNOSOM II, on the other hand, was an operational failure. It did achieve some humanitarian goals, but the June 5 attack drew the United Nations into a personalized conflict with Aideed. Political reconstruction efforts continued throughout the summer, but the military confrontation with Aideed continued as well. Somalia became a synonym for failure after the October 3 firefight, and the legacy of that experience still haunts U.S. foreign policy today.

Why did UNOSOM II fail when UNITAF had succeeded? Simply put, UNITAF used the credible threat of military force to achieve a narrow set of objectives, while UNOSOM II relied on a far weaker military force to achieve a much broader set of objectives. UNITAF had a massive amount of firepower at its disposal and demonstrated a willingness to use that force against those who challenged its authority. UNOSOM II consisted of far less capable units, which reduced the credibility of its threats to use force. Even more important, UNITAF's objective of humanitarian relief did not fundamentally threaten the interests of the faction leaders. Aideed may not have liked the UNITAF intervention, but he understood that it would not interfere directly with his quest for political control over Somalia as long as he did not use military force. Since the United States had announced its intention to withdraw from Somalia within a matter of months, Aideed's best strategy was simply to wait out the United States and then reassert his drive for national political power. UNOSOM II, by contrast, posed a fundamental threat to Aideed's core interests. Aideed relied on his substantial arsenal to give him an advantage over Ali Mahdi in the fight for political control. He saw the United Nations' disarmament campaign as a zero-sum game: each weapon that he gave up would reduce his own power and therefore increase the chances that Ali Mahdi would gain control over Somalia. Furthermore, the United Nations' effort to implement the Addis Ababa accords directly threatened his claim to power since he did not have enough supporters to guarantee victory in open elections. It is therefore not surprising that Aideed chose to challenge a relatively weak intervention force that posed such a serious threat to his core interests.

Somalia demonstrates that coercive diplomacy is a remarkably challenging strategy since it requires the credible threat of military force to be carefully balanced with intensive diplomatic bargaining efforts. Coercive diplomacy is an appropriate strategy only when the target has some sort of incentive to cooperate with the coercer in finding a diplomatic solution. UNITAF managed to strike the right balance between threats and diplomacy, but its success was tempered by the fact that its narrowly defined objectives and its publicly announced withdrawal schedule gave Aideed a strong incentive to wait out the United States. Coercive diplomacy failed during UNOSOM II because it was an inappropriate strategy for the circumstances. Its weakened military forces did not pose a credible threat to the faction leaders, and its objectives of forcible disarmament and national reconciliation threatened one of Aideed's core interests. Under such circumstances, it is not surprising that Aideed chose a counterstrategy based on confrontation rather than cooperation and that the United Nations did not possess the requisite amount of force to pose a credible threat of escalation.

NOTES

The author wishes to thank Robert Art, Michele Flournoy, Admiral Jonathan Howe (ret.), Kenneth Menkhaus, and Ambassador Robert Oakley for their comments and their assistance with this project.

1. John L. Hirsch and Robert B. Oakley, *Somalia and Operation Restore Hope* (Washington, D.C.: United States Institute of Peace Press, 1995), 12–16. For more on the collapse of Somalia and the outbreak of civil war, see Kenneth Menkhaus and Louis Ortmayer, "Somalia: Misread Crises and Missed Opportunities," in *Opportunities Missed, Opportunities Seized: Preventive Diplomacy in the Post–Cold War World*, ed. Bruce W. Jentleson (Lanham, Md.: Rowman and Littlefield, 2000), 211–237.

2. Terence Lyons and Ahmed I. Samatar, *Somalia: State Collapse, Multilateral Intervention, and Strategies for Political Reconstruction* (Washington, D.C.: Brookings Institution, 1995), 22–23; and United Nations, *The United Nations and Somalia, 1992–1996* (New York: United Nations Department of Public Information, 1996), 14.

3. John G. Sommer, *Hope Restored? Humanitarian Aid in Somalia, 1990–1994* (Washington, D.C.: Refugee Policy Group, Center for Policy Analysis and Research on Refugee Issues, 1994), 11; and United Nations, *The United Nations and Somalia*, 3–15.

4. At the peak of the crisis, there were at least forty-nine different relief organizations operating in Somalia. Kenneth Allard, *Somalia Operations: Lessons Learned* (Washington, D.C.: National Defense University Press, 1995), 66.

5. United Nations, *The United Nations and Somalia*, 113–114.

6. For Jonah's comments upon his return, see Keith Richburg, "Envoy Finds Somalia in Dissolution," *Washington Post*, January 7, 1992.

7. James L. Woods, "U.S. Government Decisionmaking Processes during Humanitarian Operations in Somalia," in *Learning from Somalia: The Lessons of Armed Humanitarian Intervention*, ed. Walter Clarke and Jeffrey Herbst (Boulder, Colo.: Westview Press, 1997), 152.

8. Walter Clarke, "Failed Visions and Uncertain Mandates in Somalia," and John Drysdale, "Foreign Military Intervention in Somalia: The Root Cause of the Shift from UN Peacekeeping to Peacemaking and Its Consequences," in *Learning from Somalia*, 5, 120, respectively.

9. Hirsch and Oakley, *Somalia and Operation Restore Hope*, 14, 19; and Donald C. F. Daniel and Bradd C. Hayes with Chantal de Jonge Oudraat, *Coercive Inducement and the Containment of International Crises* (Washington, D.C.: United States Institute of Peace Press, 1999), 85.

10. Hirsch and Oakley, *Somalia and Operation Restore Hope*, 20–21.

11. S/RES/751 (1992), April 24, 1992, in United Nations, *The United Nations and Somalia*, 166–167.

12. Drysdale, "Foreign Military Intervention in Somalia," 121.

13. Jonathan Stevenson, "Hope Restored in Somalia?" *Foreign Policy* 91 (summer 1993): 145; Hirsch and Oakley, *Somalia and Operation Restore Hope*, 22–23; and Drysdale, "Foreign Military Intervention in Somalia," 123.

14. Hirsch and Oakley, *Somalia and Operation Restore Hope*, 22–23.

15. S/24343, July 22, 1992, in United Nations, *The United Nations and Somalia*, 178.

16. S/RES/767 (1992), July 27, 1992, in ibid., 179–180.

17. For more details on the U.S. decision-making process, see Ken Menkhaus, *Key Decisions in the Somalia Intervention*, Pew Case Studies in International Affairs, Case 464 (Washington, D.C.: Institute for the Study of Diplomacy, School of Foreign Service, Georgetown University, 1995); and Nora Bensahel, "The Coalition Paradox: The Politics of Military Cooperation" (Ph.D. diss., Department of Political Science, Stanford University, 1999).

18. Sommer, *Hope Restored?* 24.

19. There seems to be some controversy over the exact date that this agreement was reached: Hirsch and Oakley state that it occurred on August 10, while the official UN account of the operation puts the date at August 12. See Hirsch and Oakley, *Somalia and Operation Restore Hope*, 26; and United Nations, *The United Nations and Somalia*, 26.

20. United Nations, *The United Nations and Somalia*, 26.

21. For Boutros-Ghali's report, see S/24452, August 14, 1992, in United Nations, *The United Nations and Somalia*, 183–189. For the text of the resolution, see S/RES/775 (1992), August 28, 1992, in ibid., 189–190.

22. Mohamed Sahnoun, *Somalia: The Missed Opportunities* (Washington, D.C.: United States Institute of Peace Press, 1994), 39; Hirsch and Oakley, *Somalia and Operation Restore Hope*, 26; and William J. Durch, "Introduction to Anarchy: Humanitarian Intervention and 'State-Building' in Somalia," in *UN Peacekeeping, American Policy, and the Uncivil Wars of the 1990s*, ed. William J. Durch (New York: St. Martin's Press, 1996), 316.

23. Hirsch and Oakley, *Somalia and Operation Restore Hope*, 27; Jonathan Stevenson, *Losing Mogadishu* (Annapolis, Md.: Naval Institute Press, 1995), 44, 146; Susan Rosegrant and Michael D. Watkins, *A "Seamless" Transition: United States and United Nations Operations in Somalia–1992–1993 (A) and (B)*. Case Program C-09-96-1324.0 and C-09-96-1325.0 (Cambridge, Mass.: John F. Kennedy School of Government, Harvard University, 1996), A8; Clarke, "Failed Visions and Uncertain Mandates in Somalia," 8; and Woods, "U.S. Government Decisionmaking Processes during Humanitarian Operations in Somalia," 156.

24. Hirsch and Oakley, *Somalia and Operation Restore Hope*, 30–32.

25. Ironically, the amount of food reaching the needy actually dropped after the airlift started, as the new influx of food led to increased looting. Sahnoun, *Somalia*, 32–33; Sommer, *Hope Restored?* 27; and Herman J. Cohen, "Intervention in Somalia," in *The Diplomatic Record, 1992–1993*, ed. Allan E. Goodman (Boulder, Colo.: Westview Press, 1995), 62.

26. Hirsch and Oakley, *Somalia and Operation Restore Hope*, 31.

27. Menkhaus, *Key Decisions in the Somalia Intervention*, 8.

28. Somalia was seen, in stark and explicit contrast to Bosnia, as a relatively easy problem to solve. Acting Secretary of State Lawrence Eagleburger described the problem in Somalia as "one that we could do something about," and an unnamed Clinton administration official said that the United States was contemplating action in Somalia and not in Bosnia because "the risks are lower." Ibid., 8.

29. UN officials generally shared this assessment. Rosegrant and Watkins, *A "Seamless" Transition*," A13.

30. Jonathan Howe, "The United States and United Nations in Somalia: The Limits of Involvement," *Washington Quarterly* 18, no. 3 (summer 1995): 51.

31. For more on the U.S. decision-making process that led to this decision, see Robert B. Oakley, "An Envoy's Perspective," *Joint Force Quarterly* 2 (fall 1993): 45; and Rosegrant and Watkins, *A "Seamless" Transition*, A9–A13.

32. The exact mission statement called for the United States Central Command (CENTCOM) to "conduct joint and combined military operations in Somalia, to secure the major air and sea ports, key installations and food distribution points, to provide open and free passage of relief supplies, to provide security for convoys and relief organization operations and assist UN/NGOs in providing humanitarian relief under UN auspices." Waldo D. Freeman, Robert B. Lambert, and Jason D. Mims, "Operation Restore Hope: A US CENTCOM Perspective," *Military Review* 73, no. 9 (September 1993): 64.

33. General Colin Powell, then chairman of the Joint Chiefs of Staff (JCS), offered this conceptualization of the U.S. role in Somalia: "It's sort of like the cavalry coming to the rescue, straightening things out for a while and then letting the marshals come back to keep things under control." Sidney Blumenthal, "Why Are We in Somalia?" *New Yorker*, October 25, 1993, 57–58.

34. Durch, "Introduction to Anarchy," 319–321.

35. S/24868, November 30, 1992, in United Nations, *The United Nations and Somalia*, 209–212.

36. S/RES/794 (1992), in ibid., 214–216.

37. Ibid., 216.

38. Oakley, "An Envoy's Perspective," 47. See also Hirsch and Oakley, *Somalia and Operation Restore Hope*, 56.

39. Technicals are vehicles on which guns are mounted. F. M. Lorenz, "Law and Anarchy in Somalia," *Parameters* 23, no. 4 (winter 1993/94): 27–41; and Daniel and Hayes with de Jonge Oudraat, *Coercive Inducement and the Containment of International Crises*, 90.

40. Woods, "U.S. Government Decisionmaking Processes during Humanitarian Operations in Somalia," 159.

41. Oakley, "An Envoy's Perspective," 46.

42. Hirsch and Oakley, *Somalia and Operation Restore Hope*, 54.

43. Oakley, "An Envoy's Perspective," 46–47. See also comments by Andrew Natsios in Rosegrant and Watkins, *A "Seamless" Transition*, A18.

44. Hirsch and Oakley, *Somalia and Operation Restore Hope*, 58; Rosegrant and Watkins, *A "Seamless" Transition*, A20–A21, A24–A25; and Daniel and Hayes with de Jonge Oudraat, *Coercive Inducement and the Containment of International Crises*, 91–92.

45. UNITAF divided Somalia into nine humanitarian relief sectors: Mogadishu, Baidoa, Baledogle, Bardera, Belet Weyne, Jalalaqsi, Kismayo, Merca, and Oddur.

46. Joseph P. Hoar, "A CINC's Perspective," *Joint Force Quarterly* 2 (fall 1993): 59; and Oakley, "An Envoy's Perspective," 48–50.

47. In August 1992 Aideed consolidated his splinter group of the USC into the SNA. He also convinced several of the smaller factions to join the SNA. Durch, "Introduction to Anarchy," 316–317.

48. Clarke, "Failed Visions and Uncertain Mandates in Somalia," 12.

49. Ambassador Robert Oakley, interview with author, March 6, 2000.

50. Hirsch and Oakley, *Somalia and Operation Restore Hope*, 81.

51. Oakley, interview with author.

52. For a small-unit perspective on events in Kismayo, see Martin N. Stanton, "Task Force 2-87: Lessons from Restore Hope," *Military Review* 74, no. 9 (September 1994): 35–41.

53. Hirsch and Oakley, *Somalia and Operation Restore Hope*, 77–79.

54. Oakley, "An Envoy's Perspective," 53.

55. Oakley, interview with author. However, it should be noted that there were some incidents in Kismayo after this point.

56. Hirsch and Oakley, *Somalia and Operation Restore Hope*, 165.

57. Oakley, "An Envoy's Perspective," 52.

58. Hirsch and Oakley, *Somalia and Operation Restore Hope*, 60.

59. An early draft of UNITAF's mission statement included disarmament, but that provision was removed because CENTCOM and the JCS wanted to keep the mission as narrow and as streamlined as possible. Rosegrant and Watkins, *A "Seamless" Transition*, A16.

60. As General Joseph Hoar, then commander in chief of CENTCOM, explained, "Disarmament was excluded from the mission because it was neither realistically achievable nor a prerequisite for the core mission of providing a secure environment for relief operations." Hoar, "A CINC's Perspective," 58.

61. Oakley, "An Envoy's Perspective," 48.

62. I thank Ken Menkhaus for pointing this out.

63. Walter Clarke and Jeffrey Herbst, "Somalia and the Future of Humanitarian Intervention," in *Learning from Somalia*, 243. See also Walter S. Clarke, "Testing the World's Resolve in Somalia," *Parameters* 23, no. 4 (winter 1993/94): 53, 55; and Walter Clarke and Robert Gosende, "The Political Component: The Missing Vital Element in US Intervention Planning," *Parameters* 26, no. 3 (fall 1996): 42.

64. France and Italy also supported the secretary-general's position. Gérard Prunier, "The Experience of European Armies in Operation Restore Hope," in *Learning from Somalia*, 141–142.

65. Lorenz, "Law and Anarchy in Somalia," 37; Hirsch and Oakley, *Somalia and Operation Restore Hope*, 106–111; and David Bentley and Robert Oakley, *Peace Operations: A Comparison of Somalia and Haiti,* Strategic Forum 30 (Washington, D.C.: Institute for National Strategic Studies, National Defense University, 1995).

66. Admiral Jonathan Howe (ret.), interview with author, April 18, 2000. See also Howe, "The United States and United Nations in Somalia," 53.

67. Oakley, "An Envoy's Perspective," 50; Hirsch and Oakley, *Somalia and Operation Restore Hope*, 72, 115; Howe, "The United States and United Nations in Somalia," 53; and Woods, "U.S. Government Decisionmaking Processes during Humanitarian Operations in Somalia," 161. See also Keith B. Richburg, "Aideed Exploited U.N.'s Failure to Prepare," *Washington Post*, December 5, 1993.

68. UNITAF had been authorized to include as many as thirty-seven thousand troops. For the reasons why the United Nations thought that twenty-eight thousand troops would be sufficient, see S/25354, March 3, 1993, in United Nations, *The United Nations and Somalia*, 252, pars. 71–73.

69. Stevenson, "Hope Restored in Somalia?" 140–141; Howe, "The United States and United Nations," 53; and Rosegrant and Watkins, *A "Seamless" Transition*, A37, A40.

70. I MEF remained offshore, which meant that these forces were not always available in theater. Hirsch and Oakley, *Somalia and Operation Restore Hope*, 109; and Durch, "Introduction to Anarchy," 335.

71. Hirsch and Oakley, *Somalia and Operation Restore Hope*, 115.

72. Bentley and Oakley, *Peace Operations;* Hirsch and Oakley, *Somalia and Operation Restore Hope*, 114, 116; Cevic Bir, "Interoperability and Intervention Operations," *RUSI Journal* 142, no. 6 (December 1997): 22–26.

73. Hirsch and Oakley, *Somalia and Operation Restore Hope*, 19.

74. Prunier, "The Experience of European Armies in Operation Restore Hope," 146.

75. Hirsch and Oakley, *Somalia and Operation Restore Hope*, 101–102; and Rosegrant and Watkins, *A "Seamless" Transition*, A28.

76. Ironically, the United States drafted Resolution 814, even though it had refused to pursue such nation building tasks during the UNITAF deployment. For the text of the resolution, see S/RES/814 (1993), March 26, 1993, in United Nations, *The United Nations and Somalia*, 261–263.

77. Allard, *Somalia Operations*, 37; and F. M. Lorenz, "Rules of

Engagement in Somalia: Were They Effective?" *Naval Law Review* 42 (1995): 65–66.

78. Clarke, "Testing the World's Resolve in Somalia," 50–51; and Ken Menkhaus, "International Peacebuilding and the Dynamics of Local and National Reconciliation in Somalia," *Learning from Somalia*, 45–46. For the text of the Addis Ababa agreement, see United Nations, *The United Nations and Somalia*, 264–266.

79. Howe, interview with author.

80. Ibid.

81. The United States backed this action since Aideed had already been identified as the main obstacle to the implementation of Resolution 814. Hirsch and Oakley, *Somalia and Operation Restore Hope*, 117.

82. Stevenson, "Hope Restored in Somalia?" 119–120.

83. The Commission of Inquiry into armed attacks on UNOSOM II later concluded that the Pakistanis would have reorganized their forces and brought in stronger protective vehicles if they had been aware of Aideed's reaction to the inspection notification. The full text of the commission's report can be found in S/1994/653, June 1, 1994, in United Nations, *The United Nations and Somalia*, 368–416. The failure to notify the Pakistanis is discussed in paragraphs 215–219.

84. Robert Oakley describes the significance of the radio station: "What lay behind the confrontation at the armed weapons storage depot and elsewhere in the city between Aidid's forces and the Pakistanis was the belief by Aidid that the United Nations was going to close his radio station as an effort to put him out of business politically. So far as he was concerned, this was a 'causus belli.' He was going to react very strongly. The radio station happened to be in this particular weapon storage compound, so when the Pakistanis went to the weapon storage compound, the word went around to all of Aidid's people, the United Nations have seized the radio station. They responded violently in a number of different places." Oakley interview in "Ambush in Mogadishu," *Frontline*, which first aired on September 28, 1998. This and other interview transcripts can be found at www.pbs.org/wgbh/pages/frontline/shows/ambush/interviews.

85. The Pakistani brigade requested assistance from Italian tanks at 11:00 A.M. The Pakistanis thought that the tanks would be there within half an hour, but they did not arrive until 4:00 P.M. U.S. reconnaissance and Italian attack helicopters arrived at 1:20 P.M., but a friendly fire incident caused the Italian helicopters to withdraw. SNA forces continued to fire on the Pakistanis for the rest of the afternoon. See S/1994/653, in United Nations, *The United Nations and Somalia*, esp. 376.

86. This account of the attack relies heavily on S/26022, July 1, 1993, in United Nations, *The United Nations and Somalia*, 272–278.

87. For two contradictory reports on this question of premeditation, see S/26351, August 24, 1993, and S/1994/653, June 1, 1994, in United Nations, *The United Nations and Somalia*, 296–300, 368–416.

88. S/RES/837 (1993), June 6, 1993, in United Nations, *The United Nations and Somalia*, 267–268. Several reports indicate that pressure from the United States played a major role in reaching the decision to respond with force. Stevenson, "Hope Restored in Somalia?" 90; Sommer, *Hope Restored?* 78; Menkhaus, *Key Decisions in the Somalia Intervention*, 16, 24; and Colin Powell, *My American Journey* (New York: Ballantine Books, 1995), 568.

89. Pakistan wanted the resolution to mention Aideed by name, but the United States took that section out of the draft resolution. Hirsch and Oakley, *Somalia and Operation Restore Hope*, 118; and Rosegrant and Watkins, *A "Seamless" Transition*, B6.

90. Drysdale, "Foreign Military Intervention in Somalia," 132.

91. Howe, interview with author.

92. Ibid.

93. Ibid.

94. During the summer of 1993 Italy started ignoring orders from UNOSOM II and started negotiating with Aideed instead. For more on the conflict between Italy and the United Nations, see Bensahel, "The Coalition Paradox," 130–135.

95. According to Stephen Stedman, spoilers are "leaders and parties who believe that peace emerging from negotiations threatens their power, worldview, and interests, and use violence to undermine attempts to achieve it." Stephen John Stedman, "Spoiler Problems in Peace Processes," *International Security* 22, no. 2 (fall 1997): 5.

96. Hirsch and Oakley, *Somalia and Operation Restore Hope*, 121–124. For a discussion of problems that the United Nations faced during this summer, see Keith B. Richburg, "In War on Aideed, U.N. Battled Itself," *Washington Post*, December 6, 1993.

97. Michael R. Gordon, with John H. Cushman, Jr., "Missions in Somalia: After Hunting for Aidid, U.S. Is Blaming U.N. for Losses," *New York Times*, October 18, 1993; and Mark Bowden, *Black Hawk Down* (New York: Atlantic Monthly Press, 1999), 90–97.

98. Howe, interview with author.

99. Powell, *My American Journey*, 569.

100. Hirsch and Oakley describe Task Force Ranger as "a posse with standing authority to go after Aideed and his outlaw band." Hirsch and Oakley, *Somalia and Operation Restore Hope*, 125.

101. For a good description of how the conflict intensified, see Bowden, *Black Hawk Down*, 1–67.

102. Sommer, *Hope Restored?* 4.

103. Former secretary of defense William Perry, personal communication with author.

104. Hirsch and Oakley, *Somalia and Operation Restore Hope*, 126–127.

105. Menkhaus, *Key Decisions in the Somalia Intervention*, 19.

106. This policy review was sparked by a diplomatic cable, sent on September 17, entitled "The Making of a Deal." Keith B. Richburg, "U.S. Envoy to Somalia Urged Policy Shift before 18 GIs Died," *Washington Post*, November 11, 1993.

107. Gordon with Cushman, "Missions in Somalia."

108. Blumenthal, "Why Are We in Somalia?" 50; Menkhaus, *Key Decisions in the Somalia Intervention*, 19.

109. Bowden provides a comprehensive account of these events in *Black Hawk Down*.

110. Perry, personal communication with author.

111. Menkhaus, *Key Decisions in the Somalia Intervention*, 21–22; and Rosegrant and Watkins, *A "Seamless" Transition*, B15.

112. For the full text of Clinton's speech, see "Clinton's Words on Somalia: 'The Responsibilities of American Leadership,'" *New York Times*, October 8, 1993.

113. Hirsch and Oakley, *Somalia and Operation Restore Hope*, 128–132; Woods, "U.S. Government Decisionmaking Processes during Humanitarian Operations in Somalia," 165–166; and Daniel and Hayes with de Jonge Oudraat, *Coercive Inducement and the Containment of International Crises*, 105.

114. In order to convince Aideed to attend, Oakley decided to use a U.S. plane to transport Aideed to the conference. Oakley was later criticized for this decision, since it seemed to be a complete turnabout from the policy that had resulted in the death of the eighteen U.S. servicemen just two months earlier. Oakley knew that this action would be controversial. He believed that the talks would be doomed to failure if Aideed did not attend and that it was therefore worth withstanding this criticism. Hirsch and

Oakley, *Somalia and Operation Restore Hope*, 138–140; Oakley, interview with author; and Ken Menkhaus, "Getting Out vs. Getting Through: U.S. and U.N. Policies in Somalia," *Middle East Policy* 3, nos. 2–3 (March/April-May/June 1994): 138–140.

115. Durch, "Introduction to Anarchy," 347–348.

116. Howe, interview with author.

117. S/1994/12, January 6, 1994, in United Nations, *The United Nations and Somalia*, 352.

118. Fifty marines remained stationed in Mogadishu to guard the United States Liaison Office, the closest thing to a U.S. embassy. A marine amphibious force also remained offshore, in case violence required the evacuation of the one thousand U.S. citizens who remained in Somalia. Hirsch and Oakley, *Somalia and Operation Restore Hope*, 144; and Durch, "Introduction to Anarchy," 349.

119. Stevenson, "Hope Restored in Somalia?" xiv; and Sabine Cessou, "Tiers-mondisation des Casques bleus," *Jeune Afrique Économie* 177 (1994): 53. By July 1994 the only remaining force contributors were Australia, Bangladesh, Botswana, Egypt, India, Ireland, Malaysia, Nepal, Nigeria, Pakistan, Romania, and Zimbabwe. S/1994/839, July 18, 1994, in United Nations, *The United Nations and Somalia*, 421.

120. Menkhaus, "Getting Out vs. Getting Through," 147; and *Key Decisions in the Somalia Intervention*, 24.

121. Hirsch and Oakley, *Somalia and Operation Restore Hope*, 146.

122. One anecdote demonstrates the weakness of UNOSOM II at this time. In late July 1995 the SNA detained 150 UNOSOM II troops from Zimbabwe. These soldiers were held for a week, as UNOSOM II headquarters did not respond to repeated requests for help. The Zimbabwean soldiers finally surrendered, and the SNA forces stole their weapons as they were let go. Ibid., 147.

123. Ibid., 148; and F. M. Lorenz, "Forging Rules of Engagement: Lessons Learned in Operation United Shield," *Military Review* 75, no. 6 (November 1995): 17–25.

124. United Nations, *The United Nations and Somalia*, 76–77. See also Rick Atkinson, "Marines Launch Final Phase of Somalia Pullout," *Washington Post*, February 28, 1995.

125. A central government was officially established in recent years, but its powers are extremely limited. As of this writing, it effectively controls only a portion of Mogadishu, with warlords fighting for control of most of the rest of the country.

3

Coercive Diplomacy in the Balkans

The U.S. Use of Force in Bosnia and Kosovo

Steven L. Burg

THE USE OF COERCIVE DIPLOMACY in Bosnia by the United States, in cooperation with its NATO partners and local actors, succeeded in bringing the fighting in that country to an end and in persuading all sides to enter into a negotiated settlement of the war. The attempt by the United States to use coercive diplomacy to end the conflict in Kosovo, in contrast, failed. A prolonged effort during most of 1998 to use the threat of force to encourage the Serbs and Kosovar Albanians to negotiate an end to their conflict was transformed in late 1998 and early 1999 into what Alexander George calls a "blackmail strategy," or simple coercion, directed against Slobodan Milošević and the Serbs. The success of coercive diplomacy in Bosnia and its failure in Kosovo can be attributed to a number of factors. The most important may be the misreading by some senior U.S. policymakers of the lessons to be learned from the success in Bosnia. But the failure in Kosovo also raises the more fundamental question of whether the application of coercive diplomacy in this case was misconceived from the outset and made the resort to coercion inevitable.

This chapter reviews the characteristics of the coercive diplomacy practiced in Bosnia and the key factors that accounted for its success. I suggest that U.S. policymakers may have misread the Bosnian experience in precisely the manner anticipated by Alexander George, leading to the misapplication of coercive diplomacy in Kosovo. Furthermore, the chapter suggests that Western policymakers may have missed an opportunity to pursue an alternative, peaceful strategy for managing the conflict in Kosovo and identifies the factors that led them instead to rely on force and, ultimately, coercion.

COERCIVE DIPLOMACY IN BOSNIA

The war in Bosnia-Herzegovina was a multidimensional conflict, involving an internal struggle among three national groups (Bosnian Muslims, Bosnian Croats, and Bosnian Serbs), as well as conflicts between the Bosnian state and its neighbors, Croatia and Serbia. The Bosnian war took place in the context of the dissolution of the former Yugoslav federation, of which Bosnia-Herzegovina had been a constituent federal republic. The Bosnian Muslims, who constituted over 40 percent of the population in 1991, sought to follow the lead of Slovenia and Croatia and establish the Bosnian republic as an independent state. The Bosnian Croats and the Bosnian Serbs, however, each sought to separate those parts of Bosnia they claimed as "theirs" and either establish them as independent national states or attach them to their respective neighboring national states, Croatia and Serbia. The nationalist leaders of Croatia and Serbia, Franjo Tudjman and Slobodan Milošević supported the efforts of Bosnian Croat and Bosnian Serb nationalists to divide Bosnia. The war in Bosnia-Herzegovina thus involved competing and conflicting claims to national self-determination expressed as demands for independence on the part of the three major national groups in the republic, as well as the conflicting territorial ambitions and competing geostrategic interests of two neighboring states engaged in an ongoing war over the definition of their respective borders. For most of the war, the Bosnian Serbs—backed up by the Yugoslav (Serb) military—enjoyed substantial military superiority, which they employed to seize control of the territory to which they laid claim and ethnically "cleanse" it of Muslims and other non-Serbs. Although the Bosnian Muslims and the Bosnian Croats also engaged in ethnic cleansing in territories under their control, the scope and brutality of the ethnic cleansing carried out by the Serbs—and especially the massacre of thousands of defenseless Bosnian Muslim prisoners at Srebrenica in July 1995—gave rise to charges of war crimes, crimes against humanity, and genocide.

European and U.S. policymakers declined to intervene forcefully as the Bosnian tragedy unfolded. They chose instead to try to limit the humanitarian impact of the fighting by deploying a limited UN peacekeeping operation and a UN-led humanitarian relief operation to Bosnia while conducting negotiations to find a political solution to the conflict. The UN Protection Force in Bosnia (UNPROFOR) included troops from Britain, France, and other NATO and non-NATO states, but not the United States. (Some U.S. personnel participated in the headquarters and intelligence operations of UNPROFOR, but there was no significant U.S. troop presence on the ground.) The European states thus had a strong, concrete interest in ending the fighting in Bosnia and took the lead in diplomatic efforts to find a solution. Paul Shoup and I have documented the negotiation efforts in detail elsewhere.[1] Neotiations were carried out under the auspices of the International Conference on the Former Yugoslavia, which was cochaired by representatives of the UN secretary-general (at first, this was former U.S. secretary of state Cyrus Vance) and the European Union (at first, former British foreign secretary Lord David Owen). The Vance-Owen negotiations produced a proposed settlement in April 1993, but this plan failed for lack of enthusiasm on the part of the warring parties and for lack of support from either the Americans or the Europeans, neither of whom was prepared to supply the force that would be necessary to secure the plan's implementation. Vance was succeeded by former Norwegian prime minister Thorvald Stoltenberg in May 1993. The Owen-Stoltenberg peace plan proposed in August 1993 also failed to gain support. Several additional efforts to find a solution, based in large part on de facto partition plans, also failed. The last of these was attempted by the major powers—the United States, Russia, Britain, France, and Germany—acting in concert as the

Contact Group. The Contact Group plan for Bosnia was rejected by the Bosnian Serbs in July 1994. Although the Contact Group had characterized its proposal as an ultimatum that the Serbs had to accept, the group was unable to agree on any measures to back up its threat.

The United States had remained at the margins of diplomatic efforts to end the conflict in Bosnia for almost two years. Paul Shoup and I have demonstrated that the United States did not become seriously engaged in a strategy of coercive diplomacy in Bosnia until late 1994; that is, until after the failure of the Contact Group plan made it clear to U.S. policymakers that a credible threat of force was essential to any effort to negotiate an end to the fighting and after policymakers came to perceive the fighting as threatening U.S. national interests. From that point forward, the United States became increasingly determined to bring the fighting to an end.

Over the course of the war, the United States had participated in five attempts to use the threat of force to persuade or compel the Bosnian Serbs to cease certain actions. But these were limited in scope and intent. First, in response to the "strangulation" of Sarajevo by Serb forces that nearly surrounded the city in the summer of 1993, NATO issued a vague threat of future action against those who attacked UN forces or obstructed humanitarian aid. Despite signs of differences among the allies, the Bosnian Serbs ended their immediate threat to the city. Second, in February 1994 the United States and its NATO allies responded to a shelling of the Markala marketplace in Sarajevo attributed to the Bosnian Serbs by issuing an ultimatum to the Serbs to withdraw their heavy weapons from around the city or face an air attack by NATO. The NATO threat led the Bosnian Serbs to withdraw, and to the establishment of a heavy weapons exclusion zone around Sarajevo. Third, in April three limited air attacks—derisively characterized in the media as "pinpricks"—were carried out against Serb forces attacking the Muslim-held enclave of Goražde. These were followed by another ultimatum to the Serbs to withdraw and by at least some consideration of a more extensive use of force against them. But any effort to use such force was blocked by the special representative of the UN secretary-general, who exercised joint, or "dual key," control with NATO over the use of force by the West, which was operating in Bosnia under a UN mandate. An exclusion zone was established around Goražde, but the confrontation was allowed to wind down without a definitive conclusion. Fourth, in November 1994 NATO launched air attacks against a Serb airbase and three Serb SAM missile sites in the Bihać area in response to Serb attacks that threatened to overrun the Muslim-held enclave in western Bosnia. But the allies remained deeply divided over further action, and this crisis, too, ended inconclusively with little net change in the status quo. The fifth and final attempt to use force consisted of the use of airpower against a Bosnian Serb ammunition dump in May 1995, in order to back up an ultimatum to the Bosnian Serbs to withdraw weapons from the exclusion zone around Sarajevo. After the Serbs retaliated by shelling the city of Tuzla and killing seventy-one civilians, NATO launched a second air strike. This attack produced what Alexander George might characterize as an escalatory response on the part of the Bosnian Serbs: they seized UN personnel as hostages, using them as human shields against further attack and compelling NATO to cease its use of force—a response that NATO policymakers should have anticipated on the basis of similar Bosnian Serb reactions to the use of airpower against them at Bihać six months earlier. The May 1995 events contributed to both the collapse of the UN mission in Bosnia and the emergence of a comprehensive U.S. strategy of coercive diplomacy.

The U.S. and NATO threats to use force in connection with the 1993 crisis over the "strangulation" of Sarajevo and in response to the Markala marketplace massacre in February 1994 can be considered successful but limited acts of coercive diplomacy that displayed many of the characteristics identified by Alexander George.[2] George defines coercive diplomacy as an attempt to persuade an adversary to cease an aggression by backing up one's demands with a threat of punishment for noncompliance that the adversary considers credible and potent enough to induce compliance. A strategy of coercive diplomacy, George argues, allows for the possibility of flexible diplomacy, including the use of positive inducements credible and potent enough to achieve compliance. Force need not actually be used. But if it is, it is used in a limited fashion as a means to persuade the adversary to comply. In each of the Sarajevo cases, a threat of air attack was employed to compel the Bosnian Serbs to pull back from the city and reduce, at least temporarily, their attacks. Issuance of an ultimatum was accompanied by crisis negotiations with the party whose actions the coercer was trying to reverse. But in each case, special circumstances secured Serb compliance.

Shoup and I have pointed out that Bosnian Serb agreement was secured in no small part by the fact that in 1993 the Serbs were not required to withdraw so far as to prevent them from renewing artillery fire on the city and that they were able to secure UN occupation of strategic territory, thereby denying it to the Bosnian Muslims. Similarly, in 1994 negotiators agreed to prevent the Muslims from gaining control over territory relinquished by the Serbs by deploying Russian peacekeepers to the territory. In each case the demand advanced by the NATO allies was one to which the Serbs could agree, and agreement itself served Serb interests by keeping alive negotiations for a comprehensive cease-fire that would freeze existing Serb territorial gains. Thus, the Serbs did comply, making these exercises in coercive diplomacy successful, at least in the short run.

However, unlike in the situations reviewed by George, the crisis negotiations in both these instances were not carried out by the coercing party (NATO and the United States), but by a third party—the UN commander, who was not under the control of the coercing party and whose interests differed from those of the coercing party. The goals of coercive diplomacy were in each case limited in scope. Speaking of negotiations to end the overall conflict, Madeleine Albright, then U.S. ambassador to the United Nations, argued at the time of the 1994 threat that "[o]ur diplomacy must be backed by a willingness to use force when that is essential in the cause of peace. For it is only force plus diplomacy that can . . . break the stalemate in Geneva."[3] But the threat of force used to secure the pullback of the Serbs from around Sarajevo was not accompanied in either 1993 or 1994 by more comprehensive efforts—at least not on the part of the principal coercer, the United States—to settle the larger conflict.

In some respects, these attempts to use force made matters in

Bosnia worse. The apparent increase in U.S. and NATO involvement and the threat of force against the Serbs contributed in each case to a hardening of Bosnian Muslim positions in the negotiations over a political settlement taking place in Geneva under the auspices of the International Conference on the Former Yugoslavia (ICFY). This contradictory outcome suggests one of the difficulties of employing coercive diplomacy against only one party to a conflict involving multiple actors: a threat or inducement aimed at affecting the behavior of one target actor also affects the behaviors of others. Because the interests of the Bosnian actors were most often in opposition, threats or coercion applied against one actor in order to encourage that party to negotiate or comply would make one or more of the others less willing to negotiate or comply. The fact that the threat of force was not actually carried out in connection with either the "strangulation" crisis or the Markala marketplace massacre, and that the Serbs were able to keep their immediate concessions modest and reverse them later, weakened the credibility of subsequent U.S. and NATO threats in the eyes of both the Serbs and the Bosnian Muslims. The later uses of force in Goražde and Bihać represented responses to what were perceived as Serb attempts to alter the military balance decisively in their favor. But the threat and the use of force in Goražde and Bihać were of only limited military value and were not accompanied by a serious effort to extract any larger political concessions from the Serbs. Their net effect, if any, appears to have been to deepen divisions within NATO over the use of force and erode the effectiveness of any future threat to do so.

The divisions within the alliance that followed the limited use of force against the Serbs at Bihać in November 1994 led U.S. policymakers to adopt a more comprehensive approach to ending the conflict in Bosnia. They concluded that the use of force alone was futile, that the Serbs had to be given incentives to accept a settlement, and that if force was to be used it had to support a political settlement. They entered into direct negotiations with both Milošević and the Bosnian Serbs and prepared to back up their negotiating positions with a more credible threat of force. The establishment of a credible threat required intensive diplomatic efforts with NATO allies and

Russia. These were carried out in the context of the Contact Group. Most important, it also required the continuation of ongoing efforts to shift the military balance on the ground in Bosnia against the Serbs. In order to exercise control over negotiations with the target(s) of coercion, the United States had to shift negotiations over a political settlement away from the ICFY and to the Contact Group. It also had to alter the very nature of those negotiations, replacing mediated exchanges among the warring parties in search of a mutually acceptable solution with exchanges among the Contact Group powers in search of a solution they all could accept and then impose on the warring parties. The United States can thus be said to have laid the basis for a strategy of coercive diplomacy in Bosnia in late 1994. But it was not until July 1995 that policymakers appear self-consciously to have committed themselves to such a strategy.

The resort to coercive diplomacy by the United States in Bosnia in 1995 was driven for the most part by concern on the part of U.S. policymakers that U.S. troops would be drawn into a potentially costly operation to evacuate UN forces, including those of the NATO allies. According to Richard Holbrooke, following the fall of the Muslim-held enclaves of Srebrenica and Žepa in eastern Bosnia to the Serbs in July 1995 and the realization that the UN operation was heading for failure, "the President saw the degree to which involvement was now inevitable, and how much better it would be to have involvement built on success rather than failure."[4] The resort to coercive diplomacy in 1995 was thus driven by a clear sense of national interest in avoiding a potential military catastrophe that might threaten the survival of the NATO alliance. But policymakers in the Clinton administration, including the president, also turned to coercive diplomacy out of a narrower sense of political self-interest—an interest in resolving the Bosnian issue in time to prevent the presumed Republican candidate for president from using it against the administration in the 1996 election. A journalistic account of the policy debates in June and July makes clear the intensity with which policymakers felt these concerns.[5] Thus, domestic political considerations reinforced the inclination of U.S. policymakers to embark on an exercise in coercive diplomacy in Bosnia.

Unlike the earlier uses of force in Bosnia outlined above, the decision to resort to coercive diplomacy in 1995 was directed toward a broader, more comprehensive goal: achieving an agreement that would put an end to the fighting. This was a goal shared by the United States and its allies, who also were concerned about the consequences of a collapse of the UN mission for their troops on the ground. This shared interest in avoiding catastrophe made the management of alliance politics over Bosnia more tractable in the period July–October 1995 than it had been at any point in the previous three years. The actions of the United States combined the "flexible diplomacy" described by Alexander George as including "accommodation" of the interests of the target(s) of coercion with a "quite limited" use of force.[6] Because coercive diplomacy was being applied to multiple actors in 1995, the threats, inducements, and actual force applied by the coercing party (the United States) varied with respect to each actor over the course of the effort, as well as from actor to actor at any given moment.

The success of coercive diplomacy in Bosnia in 1995 was built first on the foundation of changes in the military situation on the ground in the direction of a stalemate or standoff between the parties. In the literature on conflict resolution, the emergence of such a stalemate is seen as "ripening" and is characterized as "hurting" when each party is assumed to be neither willing or capable of enduring it nor able to overcome it. However, Shoup and I have demonstrated that, contrary to the spontaneous process posited in the literature, the "ripening" process in Bosnia was manufactured or engineered by the coercing power. U.S. support for the development of the regular Croatian army and its war-fighting capacity began more than a year earlier, before coercive diplomacy was adopted as a strategy. Moreover, the stalemate in Bosnia was clearly not "hurting"; it was a stalemate enforced by the United States, which was determined not to allow the strategic balance between Croatia and Serbia that was essential to regional stability to be tipped in favor of Croatia. It should be noted that a major role in establishing the conditions for this stalemate was played by the tragedies in Srebrenica and Žepa, which involved genocidal killing of Muslims by Serbs but which were greeted by some U.S. officials as events that eliminated heretofore thorny "map problems."

The second factor contributing to the success of coercive diplomacy in Bosnia also involved a change in the U.S. political position from one-sided support for the Bosnian Muslims (and Bosnian Croats, to the extent that these two parties could be kept in agreement) to recognition of the need to address the real and often conflicting interests of all sides, including the outside actors, Serbia (Milošević) and Croatia (Tudjman). A December 1994 NATO declaration calling for "equitable and balanced arrangements" signaled the onset of this transformation. It was completed by the de facto recognition of "Republika Srpska" and partition of Bosnia incorporated in a September 1 agreement negotiated by Holbrooke with Milošević and the Bosnian Serbs, which provided the general framework for the later Dayton settlement.

The key to securing Milošević's cooperation from this point on, including his dramatic role at Dayton, appears to have been the combination of a credible threat that the Bosnian Serbs would be defeated on the battlefield, thereby tipping the larger balance of power in the region against Serbia, and the positive inducements of recognition for the Bosnian Serb republic and a promise to lift sanctions against Serbia (formally, the Federal Republic of Yugoslavia, or FRY, which includes the republic of Montenegro). The threat was made credible by the successes of the Croatian army and by the application of limited but significant U.S. and NATO airpower. Milošević's interest in lifting sanctions had been clear since 1993, and he had been pursuing that interest in intensive negotiations in May and June 1995 with the U.S. diplomat then responsible for Bosnia, Robert Frasure. Milošević's cooperation at Dayton, secured in an apparent deal with Holbrooke in exchange for sanctions lifting, is actually the beginning of the overlapping story of intervention in Kosovo, to which we will return later.

The third factor in the successful application of coercive diplomacy to ending the war in Bosnia, of course, was the use of airpower. These words are often followed by the phrase "against the Serbs." But the story in Bosnia, at least, was more subtle; airpower was used not only to pressure the Serbs into specific action on the ground—primarily a withdrawal from around Sarajevo—but also to pressure the Muslims into accepting the emerging partition of Bosnia; and it was the end of bombing that opened the door to a cease-fire agreement and all-party nego-

tiations, not vice versa. The agreement on "basic constitutional principles" for Bosnia, signed by the foreign ministers of Croatia, Serbia,
and Bosnia on September 8 in Geneva, was reached while the bombing was still in progress. But the bombing did not, in fact, "bring the
Serbs to the negotiating table." Milošević was already moving in early
August toward establishing control over the Bosnian Serbs so as to
bring them to the negotiating table, and he had completed his moves
before the bombing began. It was the Bosnian Muslims who were
brought to the negotiating table by the bombing or, more accurately, by
the threat that it would be ended if they did not agree to the U.S. settlement. The initial decision to "suspend" the bombing on September
14 came in exchange for an agreement by the Bosnian Serbs to withdraw their heavy weapons from the exclusion zone around Sarajevo and
end the siege of that city.

At the same time, the United States did not allow the combined
Croatian-Muslim offensive in western Bosnia that followed the ouster
of the Krajina Serbs to inflict too great a defeat on the Bosnian Serbs.
To have done so might have drawn Serbia into the conflict directly and
threatened the strategic balance in the region. The bombing in Bosnia
constituted the "exemplary use of quite limited force to persuade the
opponent to back down" consistent with the concept of coercive diplomacy. George defines "exemplary" as "the use of just enough force of
an appropriate kind to demonstrate resolution to protect one's interests
and to establish the credibility of one's determination to use more force
if necessary."[7] A military analyst points out that the total bombing effort
in Bosnia "equated to just about a busy day's sorties count for coalition
air forces during the Gulf War" and characterizes it as "a strategically
limited, tactically intense, high-technology, coalition air campaign, conducted under tight restraints of time and permissible collateral damage
. . . aimed at coercing political and military compliance from a regional
opponent who had no airpower."[8] The United States and its NATO allies
were careful not to use so much force as to lead either side to believe
that all was won or lost, thereby creating real incentives to accept the
U.S.-brokered settlement.

To a certain extent, the "balancing act" carried out by U.S. diplomats—led by Richard Holbrooke—in their relations with the Serbs,

Croats, and Muslims during the bombing was necessitated by the
pressures exerted by the British, French, and Russians. The British
and the French refused to "wage war on behalf of the Muslim-led government,"[9] while the Russians continued to oppose the bombing.
However, "balancing" reflected to a far greater extent the difficulties
of applying the techniques of coercive diplomacy to the behaviors of
multiple parties with conflicting interests. This is a far more difficult
task than attempting to affect the behavior of a single opponent. By
facilitating the emergence of a Croatian ground army and using airpower against the Bosnian Serb army, the United States encouraged
the political and territorial ambitions of the Croats and the Muslims.
The United States, therefore, did not prevent the Bosnian Serbs from
using artillery withdrawn from Sarajevo, and Serbian airpower, to stop
the Croatian and Muslim advance in western Bosnia. Whereas Holbrooke had blamed the Serbs for the difficulties of negotiations in
August and September, for example, by October he was blaming the
Muslims for blocking the conclusion of a cease-fire agreement. On
October 4 Holbrooke cautioned Bosnian president Alija Izetbegović
that he was "playing craps with the destiny of his country" by refusing to agree to a cease-fire and warned him that "[i]f you want to let
the fighting go on, that is your right, but do not expect the United
States to be your air force."[10] Despite this threat, the Bosnian Muslims
refused to agree to a cease-fire until they had extracted a commitment
from the United States to provide them with military assistance. Thus,
the coercing power (the United States) was compelled to supply positive inducements to cooperation to all the targets of its coercive actions
(the Bosnian Muslims, Serbs, and Croats; and both Croatia/Tudjman
and Serbia/Milošević).

Milošević's cooperation was the direct result of the coercive diplomacy—the combination of threats, inducements, and actual use of
force—exercised by the United States. That cooperation hastened the
end of the fighting in Bosnia. Thus, coercive diplomacy in Bosnia in
the summer and fall of 1995 achieved its immediate goal and should
be considered a success. But the importance of Milošević's cooperation to secure an end to the fighting, an agreement at Dayton, and
its (partial) implementation made it more difficult for the United

States and its NATO allies to achieve a similar success with respect to the conflict in Kosovo.

KOSOVO IN LIGHT OF BOSNIA: DRAWING THE WRONG LESSONS

Both U.S. policymakers and the primary target of their attention in Kosovo, Slobodan Milošević, seem to have learned only some of the lessons of the Bosnian endgame, or to have learned the wrong lessons. One of the most important lessons of Bosnia could be summarized as "the longer a violent conflict is allowed to go on, the more difficult it is to end." Western policymakers simply waited too long to act in Kosovo. Earlier action might have avoided the need for coercive diplomacy.

U.S. and other Western policymakers also seem to have erred in precisely the way Alexander George suggests is likely in "cases in which some version of an ultimatum proved to be effective." George warns that it is "incorrect" to conclude from such cases "that resort to the strong variant of coercive diplomacy was the sole or primary factor contributing to its success." He reiterates that "[c]risis bargaining can use persuasion, coercion, and/or accommodation" and argues that "the policymaker must decide *what combination* of these three elements to employ *and in what sequence*" (George's emphasis).[11] Clearly, finding a viable combination of these elements was even more difficult in Kosovo than in Bosnia; but given timely action, it appears not to have been impossible. The United States was able to turn negotiation of a settlement in Bosnia into a non-zero-sum game. In Kosovo, by the time policymakers turned their attention to the conflict, it had also become three-sided—involving the independence-minded and militant Kosova Liberation Army (KLA); the more moderate nationalist political movement, the Democratic League of Kosova (LDK); and Milošević—and had turned into a decidedly zero-sum game.

Confronted with the irreconcilable positions of the three parties, U.S. policymakers turned to what Alexander George calls "the starkest variant" of coercive diplomacy: "a full-fledged ultimatum."[12] However, that ultimatum was deficient in two critical respects. The demands finally settled upon by the coercing power (the United States), as defined at Rambouillet, were impossible for the opponent

(Milošević or any other Serbian leadership) to accept in the absence of powerful positive inducements. The threat lacked credibility and, when carried out, proved insufficiently potent to achieve compellence. In attempting to formulate a credible threat to back up their demands, U.S. policymakers neglected the critical role of Croatian ground forces in the Bosnian endgame. The singular emphasis on airpower in Kosovo, and the belief among some senior U.S. policymakers that all it would take would be a few days of bombing, appears to have been based on a faulty interpretation of the events surrounding the endgame in Bosnia. This conviction, as well as concerns about the domestic political costs of committing ground troops, led U.S. policymakers to take even the possibility of deploying ground forces "off the table" and thus to weaken the coercive threat they were attempting to construct.

There is little concrete evidence concerning the policy calculations of the opponent. If the behavior of Milošević conforms to George's assumption of "pure rationality," then we can infer certain calculations from his actions. On this basis we can say that in constructing his response to the coercive diplomacy being brought to bear against him in the fall of 1998, Milošević also seems to have misread the relevant lessons to be drawn from the Bosnian experience. Milošević clearly failed to understand the singular importance of Srebrenica, the powerful emotive force of the specter of genocide for Western policymakers, and the effect this would have on decisions about the level of force to be used against him. In effect, Milošević chose to escalate the crisis on the ground in Kosovo—to use George and William Simons's terms, "to initiate war himself rather than accept the demand."[13] Milošević's escalatory response appears to have been based on a calculation that failed to take into account the impact of genocidal killing and the flight of massive numbers of refugees on the calculations of U.S. and NATO policymakers.

KOSOVO: THE NARROWING OF WESTERN OPTIONS

The conflict between Albanians and Serbs over control of the Kosovo region has its roots in the overlapping historical claims of the two peoples to territories in which important events in their respective national histories unfolded. For Serbs, Kosovo encompasses the historical birthplace of their nation, as well as the site of the single most important event in their national historical mythology. At the same time, however, Kosovo encompasses territories long inhabited by a substantial ethnically Albanian population, which Albanians view as a natural part of a greater Albanian state.

Although it could be said that the disintegration of Yugoslavia began in Kosovo in 1981, the West excluded Kosovo from its efforts to negotiate an end to the crisis in the former Yugoslavia. The Conference on Yugoslavia established by the European Community (EC) in August 1991 focused negotiations on redefining relations among the federal republics of the soon-to-be-former Yugoslavia. Kosovo, as part of Serbia, was relegated to secondary status. While the Badinter Commission, established by the EC to arbitrate disputes associated with the dissolution of former Yugoslavia, granted recognition to the republics, it denied the petition of the Kosovar Albanians, as well as a similar petition from the Krajina Serbs of Croatia, for recognition as a distinct entity in the wake of the "dissolution" of the former Yugoslavia. The conference proposed instead that minority-populated regions be granted "a special status of autonomy" that would allow for extensive local self-government under "permanent" international monitoring,[14] a proposal rejected by Serbia because it granted too much to the Kosovar Albanians and by the Kosovar Albanians because it granted them too little.

With the outbreak of war in Bosnia, Western negotiations focused on bringing the fighting in that republic to an end, although efforts were undertaken to find a solution to the Kosovo problem as a means of preventing the spread of fighting from Bosnia to neighboring areas. The United States issued what has become known as the "Christmas warning" in December 1992, declaring that the United States would act against Serbia if violence broke out in Kosovo and could be attributed to the Serbs. But despite awareness of the importance of Kosovo to establishing peace in the former Yugoslavia and the southern Balkans more generally, the Americans later rebuffed efforts by the Kosovar Albanians to be included in the Dayton negotiations. U.S. negotiators were dependent on Milošević's cooperation in imposing a settlement on the Bosnian Serbs and were therefore disinclined to recognize the demands of the Kosovar Albanians.

For many Kosovar Albanians, the message from Dayton was clear: force was the only means by which to secure group interests in the former Yugoslav space, and the escalation that results from the use of force was the only means by which to draw the United States into the conflict and thereby internationalize it.[15] Indeed, the KLA made its first public appearance within a few months. This began the transformation of the Albanian nationalist movement in Kosovo from a peaceful resistance to an armed insurgency. The rapid shift in support among the Kosovars from the LDK, which had been waging a peaceful campaign of political resistance to Serbian rule since the 1980s, to the KLA ended any pretense that the struggle in Kosovo was about securing minority rights in Serbia or even Yugoslavia. By this time, however, Western policy options had been reduced to precisely the pursuit of minority rights for the Albanians of Kosovo, because in Bosnia the West had committed itself to opposing secessionism and partition as solutions to ethnic conflicts within states and to opposing the consolidation of ethnic irredenta with their national states.

MEDIATION: A MISSED OPPORTUNITY?

The appearance of the KLA changed the political dynamic of the conflict in Kosovo. Up to then, the vast power differential between the LDK and the Serbs, the naive insistence by LDK leader Ibrahim Rugova on independence as the only acceptable solution,[16] and the willingness of the Serbian leadership around Milošević to rule by force and repression, all contributed to the failure of the two sides to enter into serious negotiations. But the rise of the KLA threatened the hold of the LDK over the population and undermined Rugova's personal leadership. As the KLA began to demonstrate that armed resistance was possible, it rapidly gained the support of an increasing proportion of the Kosovar Albanian population. The LDK began to splinter. This gave Rugova, and those elements in the LDK leadership either loyal to him or committed to finding a peaceful solution, a powerful new incentive to negotiate. A negotiated agreement with Serbia held the promise of improved material well-being and enhanced security for the Albanians of Kosovo, as well as affirmation and reinforcement of their own political status and power against the emerging threat of the KLA.

In the wake of Dayton, Milošević and the Serbs also had new incentives to negotiate. The principal motivation for Milošević's support for Dayton had been the lifting of sanctions against Serbia. But the conclusion of the Dayton Peace Accords produced only a partial lifting of sanctions. Milošević now had to achieve progress on Kosovo in order to achieve the lifting of the remaining sanctions (the "outer wall" of sanctions).[17] Progress on Kosovo also was required if Milošević was to achieve the recognition and reintegration of "rump" Yugoslavia (that is, Serbia and Montenegro, formally the FRY) into international organizations, including international financial institutions.

The interests of Rugova and Milošević were thus converging in September 1996 when they concluded the so-called school pact, or education agreement. The pact, signed by both leaders, called for "normalization" of the educational system of Kosovo.[18] Shkelzen Maliqi reported at the time that "[s]ources in Prishtina claim [the negotiations] have also produced agreement in principle for the gradual solution of a host of concrete political and other questions." Maliqi suggested that "[t]he agreement indicates that both sides have adopted the principle of a gradual solution of the Kosova problem."[19] Significantly, the school pact was made possible only through the efforts of a nongovernmental third party, the Community of Sant'Egidio of Rome, an organization devoted to the peaceful resolution of conflicts. Implementation of the pact seemed to require interested outside actors to bring both pressure and resources to bear on the issue. But there was little immediate interest in the West, especially not in the United States, in supporting this agreement, not even as a first step toward "normalization" of conditions in the province. Implementation of the agreement held out the promise for the Western actors of reducing the immediate threat to peace in Kosovo, establishing a precedent for peacefully resolving interethnic issues in neighboring Macedonia, and reinforcing Dayton. But it also might have helped solidify the rule of Milošević, who was at that moment facing mounting popular opposition from within Serbia. The latter represented a powerful disincentive for Western, particularly U.S., policymakers to act in support of the pact. Nonetheless, the failure to support the school pact may constitute a missed opportunity to resolve the conflict without resorting to coercive diplomacy.

Despite difficulties implementing the school pact agreement, both the Kosovar and Serbian sides continued to show real interest in negotiations. In April 1997 a roundtable organized by another non-governmental organization, the Project on Ethnic Relations, brought prominent Serbian and Kosovar Albanian political figures together in New York for two days of frank discussions.[20] The course of the meeting reflected the depth of the divisions between Serbs and Albanians, but the participants also made a genuine effort to find common ground from which both sides could move toward negotiations. However, existing incentives to cooperation on both sides were not strong enough to overcome their conflicting interests or accumulated animosities. A senior German diplomat reported to the author in March 2000 that he had been negotiating behind the scenes from fall of 1997 until summer of 1998 with the conflict parties on behalf of Chancellor Helmut Kohl. The German approach, he reported, consisted of an effort to get Yugoslavia under a European umbrella by making it a cooperative partner, and then an associate and then putting it on a long-term track to membership, with economic assistance from the European Union (EU). These steps would be taken in exchange for Yugoslav actions, including withdrawal of forces from Kosovo and verification on the ground, but no military action. In George's terms, this represented an effort to provide carrots without sticks, and it appears to have been directed toward only one side of the conflict. It is therefore not surprising that this approach failed.

The absence of efforts by the West to provide Milošević with incentives in the form of both positive inducements to negotiate with the Kosovar Albanians and threats of punishment if he failed to reach agreement with them can be attributed, first, to the fact that Milošević's support remained essential for implementation of the Dayton agreement and especially for imposing political changes in the Bosnian Serb republic ("Republika Srpska"). During the most promising period of Kosovar-Serbian contact and communication, policymakers in the United States appear to have been preoccupied with developments in Bosnia. Dependence on Milošević also blinded Western policymakers to opportunities for change in Serbia that not only might have hastened a negotiated settlement in Kosovo but also might have contributed to stabilizing peace throughout the region.

Although the Contact Group had called for dialogue in September 1997, there was no concerted U.S. diplomatic effort to address the conflict until rising violence in the province compelled the United States to encourage dialogue between Milošević and the LDK in early 1998. Special Representative Robert Gelbard traveled to Belgrade and Priština in January and February and urged Milošević to begin implementing the 1996 school pact as a first step toward establishing such a dialogue—a tacit acknowledgment that a real opportunity had been missed. He called for dialogue between the government of Yugoslavia and "the responsible democratic Kosovar Albanian leadership," without any preconditions. He emphasized the need for "extremely rapid movement toward the development of some concrete actions, which would also have important psychological benefits, to build confidence and lessen tensions" and again singled out implementation of the education agreement as a means by which this might be achieved.[21] LDK and Serbian government negotiators reached further agreement in spring of 1998 on several steps to begin implementing the school pact,[22] and on May 15, under pressure from the United States, Milošević and Rugova met in Belgrade to open the way for talks about talks and confidence-building measures. These began a week later in Priština. But these positive steps were too little, too late.

By February 1998 the KLA already presented a serious challenge to Serbian control of Kosovo. Special Representative Gelbard, in his Priština press conference on February 22, rightly attributed "the great majority" of the violence to the Serbian police. But he also condemned the violence perpetrated by the KLA. "I consider these to be terrorist actions," he declared, "and it is the strong and firm policy of the United States to fully oppose all terrorist actions and all terrorist organizations." He expanded upon this comment at his press conference in Belgrade the next day:

The great majority of this violence we attribute to the police, but we are tremendously disturbed and also condemn very strongly the unacceptable violence done by terrorist groups in Kosovo and particularly the UCK—the Kosovo Liberation Army. This is without any question a terrorist group. I refuse to accept any kind of excuses. Having worked for years on counterterrorist activity I know very well that to look at a terrorist group, to define it, you strip away the rhetoric and just look at actions. And the actions of this group speak for themselves.[23]

Gelbard called upon "the responsible, democratic Kosovar Albanian leaders to condemn this terrorism and to show which side they are on." But this was impossible. For Rugova and the LDK to have done so would have accelerated their loss of popular support. By March 1998 "dissatisfaction" with and "antagonism" toward Rugova were evident in the actions of some prominent Kosovar Albanian political figures and in mass street demonstrations, leading one Albanian commentator for the local Helsinki Committee to conclude that "the belligerent option is gaining more followers, at the expense of the peaceful one."[24]

TOWARD COERCIVE DIPLOMACY

The characterization of the KLA as "terrorists" reflected the U.S. preference for the more peaceful approach of Rugova and the hope that negotiations between the Serbs and the LDK might bear fruit. The Contact Group called in March 1998 for an end to violence against civilians and the withdrawal of special police units from the province while also condemning terrorism; for the granting of greater autonomy and self-administration for the province while continuing to support the territorial integrity of the Federal Republic of Yugoslavia; and for dialogue, expressing support for the efforts of Sant'Egidio and pledging to identify resources to assist in its efforts. The Contact Group adopted relatively mild negative incentives, including an arms embargo, visa restrictions, and the cutting-off of financial assistance to the Yugoslav government. These were strengthened in April by the freezing of Yugoslav funds held abroad. The Contact Group actions gained international authority through their incorporation in UN Security Council Resolution 1160, adopted March 31, 1998, which condemned both the excessive use of force by the government and all acts of terrorism by the KLA.

Some evidence suggests that U.S. policymakers considered and then rejected the use of air strikes against Serb forces in Kosovo as early as May 1998.[25] But the White House was distracted from action on Kosovo at this time by the mounting domestic political crisis over impeachment. A "political adviser" to the president, in commenting on this period in a later press report, said, "I hardly remember Kosovo in political discussions. It was all impeachment, impeachment, impeachment. There was nothing else."[26] Media sources reported in June 1998 that British officials were also pressing U.S. and other NATO leaders to consider military action, going so far as to circulate a draft Security Council resolution in June calling for the use of "all necessary measures."[27] Nonetheless, the two-track U.S. strategy of sanctions and negotiation remained in place, and the White House dispatched Richard Holbrooke in May 1998 to encourage Milošević and Rugova to engage in negotiations. This produced the May 15 meeting between Milošević and Rugova but little substantive progress.[28]

Those who sought to end the crisis through negotiations confronted two unresolved dilemmas: first, how to reconcile greater autonomy and self-administration for Kosovo with the territorial integrity of Yugoslavia, two seemingly contradictory goals; and second, how to prevent KLA violence from undermining the negotiation effort. By spring of 1998 the Serbs would settle for nothing less than reaffirmation of Kosovo as an integral part of Serbia, not just Yugoslavia, while Kosovar Albanians would settle for nothing less than independence.

The United States and the other members of the Contact Group also found it difficult to balance condemnation of the KLA for violence with efforts to gain its accession to negotiations.[29] The Contact Group concluded that the KLA would have to be represented in any negotiations, despite the fact that the KLA was unprepared to compromise on methods and goals that were completely incompatible with the diplomatic/political approach adopted by U.S. policymakers. This made the KLA a natural competitor rather than a partner to the LDK, and an enemy of the Serbs. Indeed, the apparent success of

KLA military actions in spring of 1998 produced a split within the ranks of the LDK leadership, weakening its credibility as a negotiating partner. Nonetheless, U.S. diplomats continued to seek inclusion of both LDK and KLA representatives on the Kosovar team negotiating a draft agreement with State Department representatives.[30]

While U.S. diplomats were expanding their contacts with the KLA, it was engaged in increasingly violent confrontations with the Yugoslav military and police in Kosovo. The United States was thus entering into a triangular zero-sum game for which the tools of diplomacy and even coercive diplomacy seemed inappropriate. Note that George's model addresses a bilateral relationship between coercer and coerced. In Bosnia the United States and its allies also faced multiple actors with conflicting interests, but in Bosnia the United States enjoyed direct or, in the case of the Bosnian Serbs, indirect leverage over all the parties. In Kosovo, in contrast, the coercing party exercised no leverage over the KLA and rapidly declining leverage over the LDK and Milošević.

A KLA offensive in spring and early summer of 1998 gained control of some 40 percent of the province. A Serbian counteroffensive in late summer and early fall of 1998 employed disproportionate levels of force, directed not only against the KLA itself but also against the civilian populations of villages and towns in areas of KLA activity, displacing more than 230,000 Kosovar Albanians from their homes.[31] The resulting flow of refugees into neighboring and Western European countries, the increasing number of internally displaced persons and the rapid deterioration of humanitarian conditions in Kosovo, and the "excessive and indiscriminate use of force by Serbian security forces and the Yugoslav Army" led the UN Security Council to adopt Resolution 1199 (September 23, 1998). The resolution called for "all parties, groups and individuals [to] immediately cease hostilities and maintain a ceasefire," and for the Yugoslav government and Kosovo Albanian leadership to "take immediate steps to improve the humanitarian situation" and "enter immediately into a meaningful dialogue without preconditions and with international involvement, and . . . a clear timetable, leading to an end of the crisis and to a negotiated political solution to the issue of Kosovo." The next day, the NATO allies backed up the demand for an immediate end to the fighting by adopting an "activation warning" for an air campaign against Yugoslavia. But Resolution 1199 did not authorize the use of force, and the "activation warning" constituted only, in the words of NATO secretary-general Javier Solana, "an important political signal of NATO's readiness to use force if it becomes necessary to do so,"[32] rather than a threat to use force. The elements of a strategy of coercive diplomacy were thus not yet in place.

By fall of 1998 neither Milošević nor the LDK leadership had even the limited freedom to bargain they appeared to have earlier. The emergence of the KLA made it impossible for the LDK to settle for anything less than independence. At the same time, the increasing authority of the KLA relative to the LDK and the apparent likelihood that the KLA would quickly gain power in a self-governing Kosovo made it impossible for the Serbian side even to restore the autonomies that had existed in the province prior to 1989. That restoration was the starting point, not the goal, of LDK negotiators in September and October 1998. Details of a draft document prepared by U.S. State Department negotiators and submitted to LDK negotiators for discussion in September were leaked in the Kosovar press, severely criticized, and rejected by leaders from the LDK, the KLA, and others.[33] Veton Surroi, editor of *Koha Ditore*, suggested that the international community now faced only two options: "to impose their own solution and seal this with the NATO presence, same as in Bosnia, or to continue for an indefinite time drafting versions between two irreconcilable stands, the Kosovar independentist and the Serb anexionist [sic]."[34]

A massacre of twenty-one civilians in Gornji Obrinje in late September 1998,[35] only days after the NATO activation warning, prompted a simultaneous escalation of threat and diplomacy. This was the context in which Richard Holbrooke returned to Belgrade in October 1998 in an effort to end the conflict by negotiating once again with Milošević. The Contact Group demanded that Milošević comply with Resolution 1199,[36] backed up by an escalation of the NATO threat to use force against Yugoslavia in the event of noncompliance. On October 12 NATO adopted an "activation order" authorizing the military to carry out the attacks but delayed its implementation for ninety-six hours in order to allow Milošević to demonstrate compliance.[37] This action came in the absence of an explicit Security Council authorization to use force and can be seen as effort to sidestep Russia's opposition to the use of force and willingness to employ its veto to prevent the council from authorizing the use of force.

The October 1998 negotiations produced what appeared to be an agreement to comply with Resolution 1199 and the demands of the Contact Group.[38] The October agreements established an Organization for Security and Cooperation in Europe (OSCE) verification mission on the ground in Kosovo and called for OSCE-supervised elections within nine months.[39] The Yugoslavs also accepted the provisions of a Contact Group paper of October 2—very likely the document leaked and criticized by *Koha Ditore*—as the "core elements" for a political settlement to be concluded by November 2.[40] However, the language and tone of the Yugoslav description of the October agreement, contained in a letter to the president of the Security Council, make it clear that the Serbian leadership still refused to accept anything more than cosmetic changes in the basic political status of the province and its subordination to Serbia.[41]

The initial October agreement thus had all the makings of a successful exercise in coercive diplomacy: demands that could be accepted, backed up by a credible threat of force that remained in effect until acceptance of the demands and the reversal of objectionable actions, followed by restraint in the use of force. On the surface it looked very much like the February 1994 NATO ultimatum in Bosnia, and State Department officials tried to characterize it as such. Spokesperson James Rubin insisted, for example, that the only "quid pro quo" for the Serbs was "avoiding air strikes.[42] Implementation of the NATO activation order was further delayed, but the order was not rescinded. There is, however, some evidence that the escalation of threat embodied in the October 12 NATO activation order came after, rather than before, Milošević's decision to comply with the demands presented by Holbrooke. A senior U.S. diplomat, cited in a media report only a few days later, characterized the NATO action as "a product of 'momentum' within the alliance. . . . Not so much a lever in the . . . bargaining with Milosevic as the final act of a carefully scripted play that called for a public display of NATO strength after months of inaction."[43] Nonetheless, it seems reasonable to conclude, as British foreign secretary Robin Cook did on

October 13, that Milošević would not "have gone into these arrangements, and gone so far, if he had not been convinced that NATO meant business."[44]

The October demands were limited and did not challenge fundamental interests of the Serbian side. Similarly, the threat to Milošević was limited: in the midst of the October talks, U.S. national security adviser Sandy Berger publicly downplayed the prospect of deploying U.S. troops and Senate Majority Leader Trent Lott warned of public opposition to such deployment, making it clear that the threat of a NATO invasion, if it existed, was a distant one.[45]

But compliance with the October agreement was acceptable to Milošević and the Serbs only as long as it did not result in gains for the KLA. The Serb counteroffensive in Kosovo in summer and fall had reduced the KLA military and political threat significantly. This was a view shared by some U.S. officials, who reportedly now viewed the KLA as "of little relevance to the negotiations."[46] The field reports of international observers on the ground in Kosovo make it clear that the Serbs, in fact, did carry out the reductions and withdrawals called for by the agreement. U.S. secretary of state Albright declared on October 27 that the Serbs were "in very substantial compliance with Security Council Resolution 1199, and that this compliance is sufficient to justify not launching any strikes at this time."[47]

The October 1998 agreement negotiated by Holbrooke seemed to suggest that, if the KLA could have been contained, Milošević might have been persuaded to reach a compromise with the Rugova leadership in Kosovo. A November 1998 U.S. intelligence analysis, cited in an April 1999 media analysis of the U.S. decision to resort to force, concluded that "the October agreement indicates that Milosevic is susceptible to outside pressure. He will eventually accept a number of outcomes, from autonomy to provisional status with final resolution to be determined, as long as he remains the undisputed leader in Belgrade." Such outcomes fell well within the parameters of U.S. policy as it stood as late as January 1999. According to the April analysis, a classified U.S. strategy paper defined the "fundamental strategic objectives" of the Clinton administration in Kosovo as "promote regional stability and protect our inestment in Bosnia; prevent resumption of hostilities in Kosovo and renewed humanitarian crisis; preserve U.S. and NATO credibility."[48]

Unlike the agreements negotiated in Bosnia in September 1995 that provided the basis for the later Dayton agreement, however, the agreements negotiated in Belgrade in October did not define a settlement acceptable to both the Serbs and the Kosovar Albanians and especially not to the KLA. One analyst has suggested that NATO military and U.S. diplomatic officials assured Milošević during the October meetings that NATO would control the KLA.[49] However, a U.S. participant in the October meetings has reported to the author that no such assurance was given, because "I would not have made such an assertion as we knew too little about the KLA to begin with. We only began to get some sense of the structure, leadership and size of the KLA after the so-called cease-fire went into effect. None of us, including [General Wesley] Clark, were in a position to make such claims and all of us, including Clark, knew that." This U.S. diplomat pointed out to the author that negotiating team members who met with Milošević in October "all knew the October agreement was a huge risk as KVM [the Kosovo Verification Mission] had no enforcement mechanism and the KLA was not party to it. I spent the next five months trying to persuade the KLA to honor something it did not sign or was consulted on. We all knew the agreement was shot full of holes. There was no alternative to open war, however. So we signed, took a deep breath, and did our best."[50]

Despite these efforts, the KLA did, in fact, exploit the Serb pullback. According to reports of the verification mission, skirmishing continued, with periodic attacks by the KLA on police and Serb civilians. The KLA attitude toward the cease-fire, the observers reported, was that it was merely a means by which to secure Yugoslav army withdrawal. The KLA expanded its visible presence in areas from which the Serbs withdrew and increased its provocations, becoming more overt and assertive in its efforts to exploit the advantage offered by Serb withdrawals.[51] Western governments openly criticized the KLA for violating the cease-fire established by the October agreement, even though the KLA was not formally a party to the agreement. British foreign secretary Cook, for example, noted in late November that "we cannot hope to secure a settlement in Kosovo if only one side stops fighting; and that is why we have repeatedly condemned breaches of the cease-fire by the Kosovo Liberation Army."[52] The KLA actions surprised no one. At the time of the October agreements, Veton Surroi noted that because "the KLA has not been included in this process . . . the Serbs can rightfully say that if they withdraw, the KLA will come down from the hills into the towns. Of course they will."[53] But Western governments did not have the capacity, perceived no compelling interest, and almost certainly did not have the inclination to oppose the KLA on the ground. Western leaders continued to recognize this as a fundamental problem even as they moved toward coercion in January 1999,[54] but they took no action to address it.

The resurgence of the KLA in the wake of the October agreement posed a direct threat to Milošević's leadership in Belgrade. Paradoxically, therefore, Milošević might have been far better served if he had himself insisted on an armed international presence in Kosovo as part of the October 1998 agreement, to serve as a barrier to the resurgence of the KLA at a time when the international community was still committed to preserving the territorial integrity of Yugoslavia. Instead, the Serbian response appears to have been to put in place a plan to "cleanse" the province by force. A *Washington Post* analysis published in April 1999 suggested that the plan, identified as "Operation Horseshoe," was put in place in November 1998, after the post-October agreement resurgence of the KLA, with internal Yugoslav troop movements and other operations associated with the plan beginning in December.[55] The CIA was reported to have "privately warned senior administration officials that the Yugoslav government was planning a possible crackdown by Serbian forces on ethnic Albanians."[56] International observers on the ground in Kosovo noted in December that violence was increasing in the province, including some highly publicized incidents, and reported later in the month that the Yugoslav army was undertaking offensive operations and meeting KLA resistance.[57]

To at least some of those engaged in the effort to find a political solution acceptable to both sides, it was clear by the end of 1998 that negotiations were futile. U.S. officials reported at the time that "key players in the Kosovo conflict are all still confident that they know best, that others are at a larger disadvantage and that the international community in the end will force their opponents to yield more ground." As a result, "neither side is ready for a deal right now." According to another official, "neither side understands that the other side has a point of view. They each say that you [the United States] have to just tell the other side what to do." The Kosovar Albanian negotiators, for example, finally rejected U.S. efforts to draft a compromise solution that would have given Kosovo extensive autonomy but not independence.[58]

FROM COERCIVE DIPLOMACY TO COERCION

The U.S. response to the escalating conflict in Kosovo was formulated in the context of a mounting domestic political crisis. The U.S. House of Representatives was moving in the fall of 1998 toward a vote to impeach President Clinton. That vote was cast in mid-December. The Senate trial of the president took place in early 1999. One consequence of this crisis appears to have been a significant increase in the influence of the secretary of state over U.S. responses to developments in Kosovo. During the Bosnia crisis, then ambassador Albright had been a clear advocate of the use of force, even when its use appeared likely to involve great costs. By the time of the Kosovo crisis, some more cautious actors were gone from the administration, as in the case of Chairman of the Joint Chiefs of Staff General Colin Powell, or removed from the foreign policymaking apparatus to bolster the president's effort to defend himself against impeachment, as in the case of Greg Craig, who left as director of the State Department Policy Planning Staff to join the White House legal defense team in mid-September 1998. Thus, as the conflict on the ground in Kosovo grew more violent and efforts to negotiate grew more difficult, the relative influence of the primary advocate of the use of force grew more powerful.

George argues that "both the objective of coercive diplomacy and the means employed on its behalf are likely to be sensitive to the type of relationship the coercing power hopes to have with the opponent after the crisis is over."[59] There is little evidence that U.S. policymakers hoped to have a constructive relationship with Milošević after the Kosovo crisis. They appear to have been motivated largely by a desire to punish him for his actions in Kosovo, and in no small part by a desire to atone for what some felt to have been their failure to act early enough in Bosnia or even in 1991, when former Yugoslavia collapsed. Animus toward Milošević had continued to mount in the period since Dayton. For Secretary Albright and others, use of force offered an opportunity to pay Milošević back for Bosnia, as well as for Kosovo. In March 1998 Secretary Albright had pressed the Contact Group foreign ministers to act by arguing that "history is watching us, and we have an opportunity to make up for the mistakes that had been made four or five years ago."[60] But as one participant in a December 1998 discussion argued, "as long as there were no atrocities committed in Kosovo that might conjure up memories of ethnic cleansing in Bosnia, the West would not intervene."[61]

By perpetrating the brutal massacre of forty-five civilians in the Kosovo village of Račak January 1999, the Serbs appear to have crossed that perceptual threshold, conjuring up images and memories of Bosnia and diverting attention away from the actions of the KLA. The Račak massacre thus provided the emotional impetus for policy-makers to abandon what appears to have been a White House strategy of negotiating with Milošević, as embodied in the Holbrooke missions of May and October, for the strategy of coercion embodied in a plan put forward by Secretary Albright. According to "confidants" of Secretary Albright, quoted in an April 1999 media analysis of the decision to use force, Albright "realized that the galvanizing force of the atrocity would not last long. 'Whatever threat of force you don't get in the next two weeks you're never getting,' one advisor told her, 'at least until the next Racak.'"[62]

According to one participant in the Clinton administration's deliber-ations, quoted in an April media analysis, the massacre at Račak led U.S. policymakers to adopt a strategy consisting of four elements: a demand that the conflicting parties attend a meeting; presentation at the meeting of demands—including deployment of a NATO implemen-tation force in Kosovo—decided upon in advance by the Contact Group, including Russia; nonnegotiability of these demands; and a credible threat of military force to back up the demands.[63] These elements correspond almost precisely to George's definition of "a full-fledged ultimatum." According to George, "[a] classic ultimatum has three components: (1) a demand on the opponent; (2) a time limit or sense of urgency for compliance with the demand; and (3) a threat of punishment for noncompliance that is both credible to the opponent and sufficiently potent to impress upon him that compliance is preferable."[64]

George's model of coercive diplomacy suggests that whether an ultimatum will succeed depends heavily on the relative interests at stake for each actor. For the United States, the articulated interests were, for the most part, abstract. Secretary Albright defined these in a key public speech before the United States Institute of Peace in early February 1999.[65] They included peace and stability in Southern Europe, strengthening institutions that keep the peace, preserving Bosnia's progress toward peace, and strengthening democratic principles and practices in the region. Secretary Albright also identified three more compelling interests. The first of these, preventing a flood of refugees and creation of havens for international terrorists, drug traffickers, and criminals, was, however, an interest that appeared to be of more immediate concern to the European allies than to the United States.[66] The second and third were interrelated: preventing the spread of conflict to Albania and Macedonia and the involvement of Greece and Turkey, and preserving NATO's credibility as the guarantor of peace and stability in Europe. Unlike with the situation in Bosnia in 1995, however, there were as yet no allied troops on the ground and at risk in Kosovo. The threat to alliance cohesion and the survival of NATO was thus not yet as pronounced in Kosovo as it had been in Bosnia in 1995. President Clinton, in a radio talk later in February 1999, underscored the importance of preventing both spillover of the conflict and a massive refugee crisis in the middle of Europe.[67] But these interests represented relatively distant concerns for the United States. For Milošević, in contrast, it was clear that the territorial integrity of his country was at risk. However, the overriding interest at stake in the conflict for him appears to have been his own personal power.

George warns that "if the coercing power pursues ambitious objectives that go beyond its own vital or important interests, and if its demands infringe on vital or important interests of the adversary, then the asymmetry of interests and balance of motivation will favor the adversary and make successful application of coercive diplomacy much more difficult."[68] In the case of Kosovo the interests at stake appear, at least at the outset, to have been relatively greater for Milošević than for U.S. policymakers. Thus, in George's terms, the asymmetry of interests and motivations seem to have favored the adversary. This asymmetry appears to have been reinforced in Kosovo by the fact that the demands placed on Milošević proved unacceptable, and the threat behind the ultimatum lacked, from Milošević's perspective, sufficient credibility or potency (or both) to require compliance.

DEMANDS AND THREATS

By late January 1999 the United States and its NATO allies had agreed on a combination of demands and threats. The substantive demands were advanced through the Contact Group, which included the Russians. But because the Russians were not willing to endorse the use of force, the threat of force was advanced through NATO, which excluded the Russians. On January 29 the Contact Group, after acknowledging that "both Belgrade's security forces and the Kosovo Liberation Army (KLA) are responsible" for "the escalation in violence," demanded that Yugoslavia stop all offensive actions/repression in Kosovo; comply fully with the October agreements; cooperate with the Verification Mission and the International Tribunal, including full investigation of the Račak massacre; and promote the safe return of refugees and displaced persons and the delivery of humanitarian aid to the people of Kosovo. These, for the most part, reiterated already-articulated demands. The Contact Group also called upon the Kosovo Albanians to comply with all relevant Security Council resolutions and condemned KLA "provocations." The Contact Group called on "both sides . . . to commit themselves to a process of negotiation leading to a political settlement." It "insisted" on acceptance of the principles set out by the Contact Group and "summoned" representatives of the Kosovo Albanians and Yugoslavia/Serbia to negotiations at Rambouillet, with "the direct involvement of the Contact Group," to be based on a revised version of the draft developed by negotiators but rejected by both sides in late 1998. It set a deadline of seven days for conclusion of an agreement but allowed for the possibility of an extension of "less than one week," if justified.[69]

The Contact Group demands and call for talks on January 29 were backed up by an explicit NATO threat, adopted by the North Atlantic Council on January 30, to "take whatever measures are necessary in the light of both parties' compliance with international commitments and requirements, including in particular assessment by the Contact Group of the response to its demands, to avert a humanitarian catastrophe, by compelling compliance with the demands of the international community and the achievement of a political settlement." The council empowered the NATO secretary-general to "authorize air strikes against targets on FRY territory." But cognizant of the fact that the conflict in Kosovo had become (at least) three-sided, the council noted that the NATO secretary-general "will take full account of the position and actions of the Kosovar leadership and all Kosovar armed elements in and around Kosovo in reaching his decision on military action. NATO will take all appropriate measures in case of a failure by the Kosovar Albanian side to comply with the demands of the international community."[70] Although no UN Security Council resolution authorized NATO's use of force, UN secretary-general Kofi Annan, speaking at NATO headquarters in Brussels on January 28, emphasized "combination of force and diplomacy" as "the key to peace in the Balkans" and observed that "[t]he bloody wars of the last decade have left us with no illusions about the difficulty of halting internal conflicts—by reason or by force—particularly against the wishes of the government of a sovereign state. But nor have they left us with any illusions about the need to use force, when all other means have failed." He then declared, "We may be reaching that limit, once again, in the former Yugoslavia."[71] This represented a clear, and unprecedented, endorsement of the NATO threat to use force. Thus, the strategy adopted by the United States and its allies in January 1999 had all the characteristics of an ultimatum, directed against Milošević and the Serbs, but contingent on cooperation by the Kosovar Albanians, including the KLA.

The Contact Group then promulgated a list of "non-negotiable principles/basic elements for a settlement."[72] Prominent among these was the requirement to establish "a mechanism for final settlement after an interim period of three years." Marc Weller reports that Western negotiators presented a draft agreement to the parties at the outset of the conference on February 6. Unlike with the Dayton conference that ended the Bosnian war, there is little evidence that either side had agreed to the basic principles or concepts of an agreement. Indeed, as we have noted, there is abundant evidence that both sides had already in late 1998 rejected the approach adopted by negotiators. Nonetheless, the Albanian delegation at Rambouillet, which included a cross section of Kosovar Albanian political leaders including representatives of the KLA, responded constructively to the proposal. The Yugoslav/Serbian delegation remained unresponsive. The British press reported at the time that some European diplomats "close to the Kosovo talks" had warned the United States to "stop treating Serbia like Iraq" and told the KLA that it must drop its demands for independence.[73] Nonetheless, a controversial trip to Belgrade by the chief U.S. negotiator, Ambassador Christopher Hill, to deal directly with Milošević in an effort to overcome Serb resistance to the proposed settlement produced instead a Serbian response that consisted of an almost complete rejection of the proposal. According to Weller, negotiators then attempted to meet Serbian objections by altering the proposed draft without at the same time consulting the Albanian delegation. When it became apparent that neither the Serbs nor the Albanians could or would agree to the revised draft, Weller reports, more intensive negotiations in the form of "genuine proximity talks" got under way. The Albanian delegation, unhappy with the effort of negotiators to accommodate the Serbs, was persuaded to accept the proposed agreement only under intense pressure from the United States.

Secretary Albright traveled to Rambouillet to lobby the Kosovar Albanian delegation or, in the words of her press spokesman, James Rubin, "help to push the Kosovar Albanians across the finish line so that they can agree to the combined political and military package."[74] At a press conference in Rambouillet Secretary Albright made her argument public. She explained that

[i]f we have a yes from both sides, we will have an implementation force. If the talks crater because the Serbs do not say yes, we will have bombing. If the talks crater because the Albanians have not said yes, we will not be able to support them, and in fact we will have to cut off whatever help they are getting from the outside. If it fails because both parties say no, there will not be bombing of Serbia and we will try to figure out ways to continue trying to deal with both sides.[75]

NATO air strikes against the Serbs were thus explicitly contingent on Kosovar Albanian acquiescence to the Rambouillet accord in much the same way that air strikes against the Serbs in Bosnia had been made contingent on Bosnian Muslim acquiescence to the agreements that later were incorporated in the Dayton Peace Accords. This represented both a positive and a negative inducement to cooperation. The Kosovar Albanians were also offered a more clearly positive inducement to cooperate in the form of incorporation of "the will of the people" into the mechanism for determining a final settlement—manifest in a referendum of the people of Kosovo. For the Albanians, this provision established what appeared to be a road map to independence. For the Serbs, however, there appear to have been few, if any, positive inducements to cooperate. This made it impossible for U.S. negotiators to find a formula that could accommodate both the Kosovar Albanians and the Serbs and ended the Rambouillet process. There is little support in the publicly available documents, however, for the contention of a senior U.S. official, reported in the press after two weeks of bombing, that the proposed agreement "walked right up to the edge of appeasement" of Milošević.[76]

The proposed settlement put on the table by the United States at the meeting at Rambouillet may be viewed as a valid peace plan, a flawed peace plan that nonetheless represented a genuine effort to reach a settlement, or a "turn-down" proposal. From the latter perspective, the events at Rambouillet are seen not as an effort actually to negotiate a settlement, as had been the case at Dayton, but as an effort to gain support for and legitimate the use of force by presenting an ultimatum known in advance to be unacceptable to the Serbs so as to frame the Kosovo conflict as one in which the Serbs "rejected peace." U.S. policymakers understood at the outset that there was, in the words of Ambassador Hill, "zero point zero" chance of the Serbs accepting the proposed settlement.[77] Secretary Albright, as we have seen, publicly linked the use of force to Kosovar Albanian acceptance and Serb rejection of the proposal. She also acknowledged in a later interview with the *New York Times* that Rambouillet was crucial for "getting [the Europeans] to agree to the use of force."[78] But there is insufficient evidence to support this view, and the fact that the last phase of the Rambouillet process involved an effort by U.S. negotiators to meet Serb objections argues against it.

Secretary Albright's apparent eagerness to turn to force was matched, nonetheless, by Milošević's willingness to accept bombing by NATO rather than sign the agreement. Developments following the October 1998 agreements had made it clear that the withdrawal of Yugoslav forces called for in the implementation provisions would quickly be exploited by the KLA. In Kosovo the coercing power could not control or even influence the KLA as effectively as it had been able to do with respect to the warring parties in Bosnia. The Bosnian Serb and Bosnian Croat forces had been under the effective control of Serbia and Croatia, each of which had broader interests that were better served by peace in Bosnia than by further war, and to which U.S. negotiators could appeal. The KLA was not under their control and was subject to only limited influence by any outside actor. Its medium- and long-term interests were not served by peace and certainly not by any arrangements that preserved a Serbian presence in and sovereignty over Kosovo. Although represented at Rambouillet, the KLA was not a party to the negotiations over the draft proposal leading up to the meeting and remained a competitor or even adversary to the coercing power's main negotiating partner in Kosovo, the LDK. There was little reason to believe that the KLA would comply with the disarmament provisions of the Rambouillet proposal. Acceptance of Rambouillet therefore raised the specter, from Milošević's perspective, of the occupation of Kosovo by foreign troops and the takeover of power in Kosovo by the KLA.

George cautions that, in formulating a strategy of coercive diplomacy, "the coercing power . . . must leave the opponent with a way

out of the crisis that enables him at least to save face and avoid humiliation."[79] George's description of the impact of the U.S. oil embargo
on Japan seems to apply equally well to the consequences of the Rambouillet proposal for Milošević and the Serbs:

> Backed into a corner and given no acceptable diplomatic way out, and
> confronted by the humiliating demand that they give up their imperi-
> alistic achievements and aspirations, Japan's desperate leaders felt
> they were left with no acceptable alternative but to initiate what they
> knew to be a highly risky war against a militarily and economically
> stronger opponent.[80]

For Milošević, initiating war in Kosovo entailed enduring a threatened air attack by NATO while carrying out plans to eliminate the
KLA and expel a large proportion of the ethnically Albanian population from Kosovo by force.

The NATO threat failed to compel Milošević to comply with the
Contact Group demands or to deter him from initiating war. George
cautions that with respect to the effectiveness of a threat, it is not the
coercing party's commitments and beliefs that are crucial; "[r]ather, it
is the target's estimate of the credibility and potency of the threat that
is critical."[81] A NATO threat of air strikes against Yugoslavia had been
an important element in the successful exercise of coercive diplomacy
in October 1998. At that time, General Klaus Naumann explained
later to a U.S. Senate committee, "we were sent to Belgrade with a
clear stick in our hip pocket, the ultimatum." By January 1999, he
argued, "this stick had been transformed into a rubber baton since
our threat was not as credible as it used to be in October. We had
threatened too often and hadn't done anything."[82]

The credibility of the coercive threat mounted by the United States
and its NATO allies also was weakened by Russian and Chinese diplomatic opposition to Security Council authorization of the use of force,
which heretofore had been an essential step in the establishment of
credibility. On several occasions in September and October 1998
Russian and Chinese officials warned publicly against any use of force
against Yugoslavia. Both Russia and China abstained from voting
even for UN Security Council Resolution 1203 (October 24, 1998),

which endorsed the October agreements, despite the fact that the resolution did not provide authorization for any military action by NATO. While there can be no doubt that a humanitarian disaster was developing in Kosovo at the time, it appears that Western diplomatic and political rhetoric shifted to "humanitarian disaster" as justification for the threat and, later, use of force because Russian and Chinese opposition to the use of force made it unlikely that NATO could secure Security Council authorization.

Milošević's estimate of the probable potency of the NATO threat was likely to have taken into account the relatively limited air campaign conducted in Bosnia in 1995 and the similarly limited action taken by the United States and Britain against Iraq in December 1997. Ivo Daalder and Michael O'Hanlon argue that that action "demonstrated that air strikes designed to 'degrade' an opponent's military capability—even that of an opponent as feared and loathed as Saddam Hussein, ruling a country in a region of critical interest to the United States, and possessing the capacity to produce weapons of mass destruction—would likely last only a few days."[83] Knowledge that some senior U.S. policymakers were, in fact, operating on the assumption that "Milosevic would probably back down after a few visible targets were hit"[84] may also have contributed to lowering his estimate of the NATO threat. Secretary Albright stated publicly at the outset of the bombing that "I don't see this as a long-term operation. . . . I think this is something. achievable within a relatively short period of time."[85] Senior British and French defense officials reported in interviews conducted by Robert Art in June and July 2000 that this view was widely shared among the allies.

It is almost certainly the case that the absence of any threat of a ground assault also lowered Milošević's estimate of the potency of the NATO threat. The central lesson of the endgame in Bosnia for U.S. policymakers should have been that the creation and deployment of a credible ground force—in the case of Bosnia, the army of Croatia and its operations to expel the Serbs from the Krajina region and take control of much of western Bosnia—was critical to the success of coercive diplomacy. Nonetheless, resistance to the use of ground forces on the part of some U.S. policymakers was a matter of public record. This resistance can be attributed to continuing opposition from within the U.S. military,[86] the absence of a viable military plan of action,[87] concern about divisions with Congress[88] and among NATO allies,[89] and opinion polls indicating that the U.S. public believed no U.S. interests were at stake and no U.S. troops should be involved.[90]

Given the reasonable expectation that NATO air strikes would be limited in duration and scope as in Bosnia and Iraq, and the absence of any immediate threat of a ground invasion, the potency of the NATO threat of force was insufficient to either compel or deter Milošević. However, any expectation on Milošević's part that the United States and NATO would not be able to sustain the bombing and that, as in Bosnia, the United States would negotiate with him while the bombing unfolded and accommodate at least some of his real interests proved misplaced. The motivations of U.S. policymakers were quite different now. Within ten days of the start of the bombing, U.S. and European policymakers were considering adding the removal of Milošević from power to the list of NATO objectives, making it "a condition for stopping the war," and Secretary of State Albright was asking publicly whether it was "going to be possible to deal with somebody that [sic] is behind all this."[91] When the motivation for the use of force is punishment, there are likely to be few constraints on its use, and few incentives to be flexible in diplomacy or to accommodate the interests of one's opponent—key factors contributing to the success of coercive diplomacy in Bosnia. When the motivation for the use of force is, in fact, to oust the opponent from power, the coercing actor may have every incentive to put forward unacceptable demands so as to compel the target to resist, thereby legitimating the use of force against him.

USE OF FORCE AND ASYMMETRICAL RESPONSE

As we have noted, several sources warned of the probability that Milošević would respond to bombing by initiating a massive expulsion of the Albanian population from Kosovo. Policymakers appear neither to have heard these warnings nor to have been given pause by actions by Milošević that clearly signaled a hardening of his position. During the "final run-up" to the bombing, Secretary of State Albright had asked her policy planning staff to "look for unpleasant scenarios" that might develop as NATO moved closer to a bombing campaign. Among the several possibilities suggested by the staff was "'a massive offensive by the Serbs' touched off by the start of NATO bombing.'" Despite all the evidence suggesting not only that this would be the case but also that such an offensive might already be under way, this appears to have been considered the least likely development.[92] As the Rambouillet process was reaching deadlock in early March 1999, however, Milošević made this threat explicit, warning German foreign minister Joschka Fischer "that he could empty Kosovo within a week."[93] In the same period, observers of the Verification Mission on the ground in Kosovo were reporting heavy fighting associated with "sweep operations" by augmented Serb forces aimed against the KLA, but also emptying or destroying Albanian villages and producing thousands of displaced persons.[94] This was evidence consistent with earlier reports of the existence of Operation Horseshoe.

President Clinton, in his speech announcing the start of air strikes, stated that one of the three goals of the operation was "to deter President Milosevic from continuing and escalating his attacks on helpless civilians by imposing a price for those attacks."[95] As Kelly Greenhill has demonstrated, however, the scale, tempo, and geographic sources of forced expulsions from Kosovo escalated after NATO initiated its air campaign.[96] Milošević's escalation of ethnic cleansing created the incentives necessary for Western policymakers to carry out a strategy of coercion. It increased the humanitarian costs of the crisis; undermined the already weak Serbian claim to "victimhood"; provided a concrete threat to the stability of neighboring states and, in the long run, threatened to create a refugee crisis affecting the national interests of states in the West; provoked political splits among NATO states that raised the political cost of failure; and posed a direct challenge to the prestige of the United States and senior U.S. policymakers. These provided the countervailing concrete interests and motivations required to keep policymakers committed to the bombing, to intensify it, and to remain steadfast in their demands. By the April NATO summit, it was clear that the leading NATO countries perceived the challenge posed by Milošević

as what one NATO spokesman called "a defining moment for the future
of the alliance,"[97] if not an outright threat to its survival. As in the case
of Bosnia, preservation of the NATO alliance was a powerful motivation
for the use of force to ensure success and reinforced the shift among
U.S. policymakers from a strategy of coercive diplomacy to straightforward coercion. In terms of George's analytical framework, Milošević's escalatory response shifted the asymmetry of motivations in
favor of the United States and its allies to impose a settlement.

Milošević's response thus transformed the relationship between
him and the coercing power into a zero-sum game for the United
States. Under these circumstances, Milošević's failure to cave in after
only a few days of bombing left U.S. policymakers with no choice but
to escalate. As Robert Art suggests in the introduction to this volume,
the use of large-scale force in this manner to compel an adversary to
change his behavior signals the failure of coercive diplomacy and a
resort to simple coercion. Thus, the bombing campaign and its outcome, despite minor concessions to Milošević and the Serbs that were
part of the diplomatic endgame, represents a case of war and coercion,
not coercive diplomacy.

THE CAPITULATION

Although the demands placed on Milošević and the Yugoslavs by the
United States and its NATO allies changed in certain significant respects,
Yugoslav acceptance in June 1999 of the terms conveyed by Finnish
president Martti Ahtisaari (on behalf of the EU) and Russian special
envoy Viktor Chernomyrdin nonetheless represented an almost complete capitulation. Unlike in the case of Bosnia, with respect to which
we have direct testimonies of participants on the calculations that led to
Milošević's decision to cooperate and the course of negotiations that
shaped the outcome, we have as yet no such direct testimonies in the
case of Kosovo. We can only infer Milošević's reasoning from the known
facts of the external structure of the situation he faced and our less-
certain understanding of the internal situation in Yugoslavia. Working
within these constraints, we can explain Milošević's capitulation in
terms of four factors:

1. *The escalation of NATO bombing.* Escalation of the air campaign disabled power-generating stations and the power grid, which had the effect of cutting both electrical power and the water supply to many areas. This reinforced the accumulating effects of bombing roads, bridges, and other infrastructure, as well as factories, refineries, and other economic targets. These were affecting not only the Yugoslav military but also large segments of the urban civilian population.[98] The domestic political impact of the bombing was clearly on the rise, which may have made peace a more attractive option than continued war. The indictment of Milošević for war crimes in late May seemed to reduce the constraints on Western action against him. The potential negative political consequences of further escalation for Western policymakers, including shifts in public opinion and open discussion of whether the escalated bombing constituted war crimes, were insignificant in comparison. Thus, the negative inducements to cooperation—in this case, capitulation—were increasing for Milošević.

2. *The threat of a ground offensive by NATO.* In a media account published in September 1999, long after the end of the bombing campaign, President Clinton is reported to have decided "shortly before" the April NATO summit in Washington to send in U.S. troops if the bombing failed. According to this account, President Clinton "agreed to allow NATO to update old contingency plans," and U.S. military planners in Europe "started work on a top secret invasion plan."[99] On the eve of the NATO summit, however, both French president Jacques Chirac and Italian foreign minister Lamberto Dini were reported in the European press to have expressed their opposition to the use of ground troops.[100] Moreover, senior U.S. policymakers in the White House and the Pentagon continued to resist implementation of any such plans. And according to the *Washington Post*, all NATO officials who spoke publicly at the summit in Washington asserted that there was "unanimity in the alliance not to send troops into a 'nonpermissive environment.'"[101] By mid-May the NATO allies were deeply divided over the use of ground troops. The British were pressing for deployment in preparation for an invasion in the event Yugoslav forces began to retreat to escape the bombing. But German

chancellor Gerhard Schroeder dismissed even the idea of a NATO invasion as "unthinkable." Italian prime minister Massimo D'Alema also spoke out against the use of troops.[102] At a late May meeting in Bonn of Secretary of Defense William Cohen and the defense ministers from Britain, Germany, France, and Italy, the British pledged fifty thousand troops to a joint ground force, but the Germans and the Italians demurred. The French argued there was not enough time to prepare an invasion before winter. Cohen concluded, according to a *Washington Post* account, "that it was safer to stick with the air campaign than to risk division over ground troops."[103]

U.S. domestic political support for the air campaign was beginning to erode by early May. Both houses of Congress were showing signs of internal divisions over the air war and the prospect of a ground campaign.[104] Public opinion polls were showing a steady erosion of popular support for the air war, with 40 percent in April and 47 percent in May declaring it a "mistake." Opinion was about evenly divided over sending U.S. troops to participate in a peacekeeping force once an agreement had been reached in Kosovo.[105] Such developments made it seem increasingly unlikely that U.S. policymakers in fact would implement any plans for a ground war. Nonetheless, a media analysis on June 2, 1999, reported that a decision to use ground troops was only a few days or a week away.[106] Although preparations for the invasion could not have been completed before September 1999, formal approval by the president for them to begin was only days away when Milošević agreed to the NATO-EU-Russian demands for ending the war.[107]

Thus, the threat of a NATO ground invasion was, at the time of the capitulation, still a distant threat, and the Yugoslav capacity to make such an invasion costly was still substantial. Despite public assertions during and after the bombing campaign of extensive destruction of Serbian military assets in Kosovo by NATO military and Western political leaders, there is clear evidence that at the moment of capitulation the Yugoslav military retained substantial fighting capacity on the ground in Kosovo.[108] Although a NATO invasion would undoubtedly have succeeded, NATO forces could have met significant resistance, at least at the outset, and incurred politically significant casualties.

This suggests that the intensifying air campaign and its domestic social and potentially political consequences represented a more significant factor in Milošević's calculations at the moment of his capitulation than the threat of a NATO ground invasion.

It is sometimes asserted that military action by the KLA inside Kosovo played an important role in pressuring Milošević to capitulate because this compelled Yugoslav forces to mass for attack or counterattack, making them more vulnerable to air attack by NATO and thus increasing Yugoslav losses. Reports surrounding one apparent battle in the last days of the air campaign are central to this argument. KLA action on Mount Pastrik is alleged to have drawn Yugoslav forces out into the open, exposing them to bombing by NATO B-52s.[109] However, NATO air reconnaissance could find no evidence of such Yugoslav losses, and Milošević had already capitulated before the B-52 bombing.[110] Thus, the argument that it was a coordinated KLA-NATO offensive that forced Milošević to capitulate in Kosovo is not persuasive.

3. Evidence of allied interest in a negotiated settlement, and a concomitant change in the Russian position, from support for Yugoslavia to cooperation with the West. At a press conference on the first day of the air campaign, Secretary of State Albright insisted that Milošević had to "embrace the framework of Rambouillet." The Rambouillet accords as signed by the Kosovar Albanians, she insisted, were nonnegotiable.[111] European Union leaders, meeting in Berlin on the day the air strikes began, insisted that "Milosevic must stop Serb aggression in Kosovo and sign the Rambouillet Accords, which include a NATO-led implementation force."[112] These statements represented what might be characterized as demands that Milošević and the Serbs simply capitulate to the demands they had previously rejected and were consistent with the ultimatum strategy adopted by the allies.

By the time NATO leaders convened in Brussels on April 12, however, there were clear signals that the bombing could be ended by a negotiated settlement that included at least some limited concessions that might allow Milošević and the Serbs to "save face and avoid

humiliation." French foreign minister Hubert Vedrine suggested that
NATO was "starting to consider a political settlement . . . and that
Russia had an essential role in negotiating a deal." He also raised the
possibility that instead of the NATO-only peacekeeping force and
NATO-led administration replacing Yugoslav forces and government
institutions as called for at Rambouillet, the Russians might participate in a peacekeeping force under a UN-led administration in a
postconflict Kosovo.[113] The formal statement issued by NATO foreign
ministers on April 12 demanded that Milošević "agree to the stationing in Kosovo of an international military presence" rather than a
NATO force. The statement also created the appearance of some
diplomatic flexibility by demanding that Milošević "provide credible
assurance of his willingness to work on the basis of the Rambouillet
Accords in the establishment of a political framework agreement for
Kosovo" rather than demanding that he accept the accords themselves.[114] On April 14 the German government advanced a proposal,
endorsed the same day by EU leaders, for a Security Council resolution outlining the steps to peace. It included a cease-fire, withdrawal
of Yugoslav forces, disarming and demilitarizing the KLA, establishment of an international peace force and transitional civilian administration authorized by the United Nations, and return of refugees. The
German proposal called for a twenty-four-hour suspension of air strikes
once withdrawal of Yugoslav forces began, to be extended as long as
withdrawal continued and made permanent if withdrawal were completed within a specified time period.[115] One EU diplomat remarked
that "whatever comes out won't be very pretty for Milosevic, but if it is
dressed up in U.N. clothes it would be tidier for everyone."[116]

These initiatives opened the door to Russian participation in a
search for a negotiated end to the bombing. The role of Russia seems
far more immediate a factor for understanding Milošević's decision to
capitulate than the anticipation of a NATO ground invasion. Russia
had at once opposed the bombing, proposing a Security Council resolution on March 26 calling for an immediate halt to the bombing.
That resolution, supported by China, was rejected by a vote of 12 to
3.[117] NATO's April 12 call for an "international military presence"
in Kosovo was a response to Russia's continued opposition to the

deployment of NATO forces in Kosovo as part of a settlement. An April 13 meeting between Secretary Albright and Russian foreign minister Igor Ivanov, however, revealed that differences remained significant: Ivanov called for an end to air strikes as a first step, so as to allow withdrawal of troops and repatriation of refugees. Albright, however, insisted that Belgrade had to make the first move. The Russians also supported Belgrade's rejection of a NATO occupation force for Kosovo, citing the need for additional talks to determine "acceptable forms of an international presence."[118] On April 21 Secretary Albright reported to Congress that she and Foreign Minister Ivanov continued to differ "over the kind of international presence required." She called for a force that was credible, "which requires that its core must come from NATO."[119]

A change in the Russian position appears to have begun with the appointment of Viktor Chernomyrdin as special envoy on April 14, displacing Prime Minister Yevgeny Primakov as the Russian diplomatic point man on Yugoslavia. From the outset, Chernomyrdin appeared more intent on achieving cooperation with the West than on defending Milošević's and therefore more in line with the views of Russian president Boris Yeltsin. Indeed, Yeltsin removed Primakov as prime minister in May. Chernomyrdin's appointment initiated a period of intense, direct East-West diplomacy over ending the war.[120] Chernomyrdin, after meeting with Milošević in Belgrade, announced on April 22 that Milošević would accept an "international presence" in Kosovo under UN auspices.[121] But there was no agreement between NATO, Russia, and Milošević on the nature of that presence.[122] By the Washington summit, NATO had defined the "international military force" that would be deployed to Kosovo as "multinational in character with contributions from non-NATO countries," but with NATO forming its "core."[123] The Yugoslavs continued to insist on an unarmed, civilian mission.[124] As late as May 4 the Russians were still calling for only a partial withdrawal of Yugoslav forces, an international force limited to side arms rather than a more robust military force, and a halt to the bombing to allow withdrawal rather than withdrawal as a precondition for a bombing halt.[125] By May 6, however, Russia had agreed to the deployment of an "effective international civil and security presence . . . capable of guaranteeing . . . the common objectives." This formulation, contained in the May 6 G-8 statement, represented diplomatic code for armed, NATO forces.[126] According to one report, the Western powers agreed to include affirmation of the sovereignty and territorial integrity of Yugoslavia in exchange for this Russian concession.[127] But such an affirmation had already been included in the Rambouillet drafts and Security Council documents. The G-8 statement also called for "withdrawal from Kosovo of military, police and paramilitary forces," rather than *all* such forces, and establishment of a UN interim administration for Kosovo.[128] These represented genuine concessions to the Russians (and Yugoslavs). A month later, however, the Russians agreed to a withdrawal of all Yugoslav forces as part of a joint agreement with the United States and the EU.[129] This shift in Russian position significantly reduced any prospect of the NATO allies fracturing over future escalation of the war. Perhaps more significant, Chernomyrdin is also reported to have advised Milošević that the threat of an eventual NATO ground invasion was, in fact, real and that Russia would not help Milošević resist such an invasion.[130] This left Milošević and the Yugoslavs diplomatically and militarily isolated and is likely to have made the distant threat of an invasion politically more immediate and the NATO-EU-Russian demands more attractive.[131] This shift, conveyed to Milošević and the Yugoslavs by Chernomyrdin in Belgrade on June 2, in the presence of EU envoy Martti Ahtisaari,[132] produced capitulation in the form of a Yugoslav parliamentary endorsement of the NATO-EU-Russian demands on June 3.[133] These were later incorporated in Security Council Resolution 1244 (June 10, 1999), ending the war.

Explanations for the Russian change in position vary. Some analysts attribute it to a decision by President Yeltsin that Russia had to resolve its differences with NATO over Kosovo in advance of the G-8 meeting scheduled for mid-June so as to maximize his chance to secure economic assistance from the West.[134] Some suggest the change may have been prompted by an agreement among U.S., European, and Russian negotiators to "partition" Kosovo into occupation zones, with the northeast assigned to Russian occupation. Zbigniew Brzezinski attributes Milošević's capitulation to "a desperate double-cross attempt engineered jointly by Belgrade and Moscow" to establish a Russian zone of occupation over NATO's objections.[135] Two U.S. intelligence officials suggested privately to the author that there was a U.S.-Russian agreement to establish "occupation zones" in Kosovo and to assign one of these zones to the Russians, but that this was an agreement on which the Americans later reneged. The reasons for the Russian change are, however, less important for explaining Milošević's capitulation than the fact of the change and its consequences for the Yugoslav calculation of costs.

4. *Two concessions to Yugoslav interests.* The interest of the NATO allies in securing Russian agreement created a positive incentive for Milošević to capitulate in the form of two significant concessions to Yugoslav interests. One of the concessions offered the Serbs in May was elimination of the three-year limit on the transitional period included in the Rambouillet document, which seemed to establish a road map to secession and independence for Kosovo. The NATO-EU-Russian "principles" for resolution of the crisis accepted by Milošević on June 2 and incorporated as annex 2 to Resolution 1244 included "establishment of an interim administration . . . under which the people of Kosovo can enjoy substantial autonomy within the Federal Republic of Yugoslavia to be decided by the Security Council of the United Nations." The interim administration would oversee "development of provisional democratic self-governing institutions to insure conditions for a peaceful and normal life for all inhabitants of Kosovo." The establishment of such institutions should not be delayed or disrupted by "negotiations between the parties for a settlement." This formulation seemed to negate the three-year transitional period and eliminate the referendum incorporated in the Rambouillet document. It also reintroduced the UN Security Council into the process of authorizing and legitimating arrangements for the administration of Kosovo in the (undefined) postconflict transitional period and, more important, adoption of a long-term "solution." This created a Russian, and/or Chinese, roadblock to independence for Kosovo without the accommodation of Serbian/Yugoslav interests.

CONCLUSION

The success of coercive diplomacy in Bosnia, and its contrasting failure and displacement by a strategy of ultimatum in Kosovo, highlight some of the limitations of coercive diplomacy and underscore the importance of certain propositions for its conduct advanced by Alexander George. Both the Bosnian and Kosovo cases suggest the difficulty of employing coercive diplomacy in a conflict involving multiple actors: a threat or inducement aimed at affecting the behavior of one target actor also affects the behaviors of others. Threats or coercion applied against one in order to encourage that party to negotiate or comply may make another less willing to negotiate or comply, or may even be exploited to another's advantage, thereby potentially worsening the situation rather than moving it toward a solution. In Bosnia the United States and its allies faced multiple actors with conflicting interests. But the United States also enjoyed direct or, in the case of the Bosnian Serbs, indirect leverage over all the parties. In Kosovo, in contrast, the coercing party exercised no leverage over the KLA and rapidly declining leverage over the LDK and Milošević. This absence of leverage over the conflicting parties undermined the October 1998 agreement, which initially had all the makings of a successful exercise in coercive diplomacy. The October 1998 Belgrade agreement looked very much like the coercive diplomacy exercised by NATO in summer 1993 and February 1994 in Bosnia that led to pullbacks of the Bosnian Serbs around Sarajevo. But it is important to recall that one key to securing Bosnian Serb compliance with the NATO ultimatums was preventing the Serbs' adversary—the Bosnian Muslims—from taking advantage of their withdrawals. Similarly, compliance with the October 1998 Belgrade agreement was acceptable to Milošević and the Serbs only as long as it did not result in gains for the KLA. The resurgence of the KLA in the wake of the October agreement posed a direct threat to Milošević's leadership in Belgrade and demonstrated the inability of the United States and its allies to contain the KLA threat in the way they had earlier contained the Bosnian Muslims.

The Bosnian and Kosovo cases involve repeated efforts by the United States and its allies to persuade, induce, and even compel compliance in ending an armed conflict. In both cases these efforts remained inadequate—that is, they did not include all the elements of coercive diplomacy or an ultimatum strategy—until the United States and its European allies finally achieved a clear unity of purpose. This did not occur until both U.S. and European policymakers shared the perception of a real threat to their national and common interests. The resort to coercive diplomacy by the United States in Bosnia in 1995 was driven for the most part by a clear sense of national interest in avoiding a potential military catastrophe that could prove costly to the United States and threaten the survival of the NATO alliance. This national interest was reinforced by a sense of political self-interest on the part of the Clinton administration in resolving the Bosnian issue well before the 1996 presidential election campaign. The Europeans were concerned about the consequences of a collapse of the UN mission for their troops on the ground, as well as the implications of unrestrained warfare on their southern flank. This shared interest in avoiding catastrophe made the management of alliance politics over Bosnia more tractable in the period July–October 1995 than it had been at any point in the previous three years. Similarly, in the case of Kosovo it was clear by the April 1999 NATO summit that European and U.S. policymakers perceived the challenge posed by Milošević as a potential threat to the coherence, if not the survival, of the alliance. As in the case of Bosnia, preservation of the NATO alliance was a powerful motivation for the use of force to ensure success and reinforced the commitment of U.S. and European policymakers to a strategy of coercion.

In the Bosnian case the balance of interests and motivations central to George's model of coercive diplomacy favored Milošević and the Bosnian Serbs until late 1994/early 1995. At that point, the balance shifted quickly in favor of the United States and its European allies, for the reasons suggested earlier and because Milošević's interests began to diverge sharply from those of the Bosnian Serbs. That divergence can be attributed to the positive inducement of U.S. promises to lift sanctions on Serbia (Yugoslavia) in exchange for cooperation in ending the Bosnian war. At the same time, concessions to the Bosnian Serbs in the form of de facto partition of Bosnia and establishment of the Bosnian Serb Republic as a constituent part of the

Bosnian state acted as strong positive inducements to Bosnian Serb cooperation. The Bosnian Muslims, too, were offered a significant positive inducement to cooperate: the promise of military assistance from the United States. They were also subjected to a threat: abandonment. The Bosnian case thus provides clear evidence of the importance of positive inducements to a successful strategy of coercive diplomacy.

In the Kosovo case the interests at stake appear, at least at the outset, to have been relatively greater for Milošević than for U.S. policymakers. Those interests all favored resisting the NATO ultimatum. George warns that "if the coercing power pursues ambitious objectives that go beyond its own vital or important interests, and if its demands infringe on vital or important interests of the adversary, then the asymmetry of interests and balance of motivation will favor the adversary and make successful application of coercive diplomacy much more difficult."[136] Thus, in George's terms, the asymmetry of interests and motivations seems to have favored Milošević at the outset of the NATO bombing campaign. This asymmetry was reinforced by the fact that there were few positive inducements for Milošević to cooperate once the KLA reemerged after the October 1998 agreements and that the threat behind the NATO ultimatum lacked, from Milošević's perspective, sufficient credibility or potency (or both) to command compliance. This asymmetry appears to have been an important factor leading Milošević to adopt an asymmetrical response to the NATO ultimatum—escalation in the form of ethnic cleansing and mass expulsions of the Kosovar Albanians. In terms of George's analytical framework, however, Milošević's escalatory response shifted the asymmetry of motivations in favor of the United States and its allies, making it easier for them to sustain the ultimatum strategy and engage in an escalation of their own.

George argues that "both the objective of coercive diplomacy and the means employed on its behalf are likely to be sensitive to the type of relationship the coercing power hopes to have with the opponent after the crisis is over."[137] In Bosnia it was clear that the West would have to continue to deal with Milošević in order to secure the settlement in Bosnia and resolve other outstanding issues, including Kosovo. But in the case of Kosovo, in contrast, there is little evidence that U.S. policy-makers hoped to have a constructive relationship with Milošević after the crisis. As we have seen, U.S. policymakers appear to have been motivated largely by a desire to punish Milošević for his actions in Kosovo and in Bosnia. When the motivation for the use of force is pun-ishment, there are likely to be few constraints on its use against the tar-get, and few incentives to be flexible in diplomacy or to accommodate the interests of the adversary. The actions of the United States and its allies in Bosnia thus combined the "flexible diplomacy" described by Alexander George as including "accommodation" of the interests of the target(s) of coercion with a "quite limited" use of force.[138] These were key factors contributing to the success of coercive diplomacy in Bosnia, and their absence in Kosovo led inevitably to adoption of the ultima-tum strategy by U.S. policymakers. As we have seen, within ten days of the start of the bombing, U.S. and European policymakers were con-sidering adding the removal of Milošević from power to the list of NATO objectives. In late May Milošević was indicted for war crimes by The Hague Tribunal, with substantial support from the United States. When the motivation for the use of force is, in fact, to oust the oppo-nent from power, the constraints on the use of force and the incentives to be flexible for the coercing actor are even weaker, thereby legitimat-ing the escalation of force against him.

Escalation of the air campaign against Milošević and Yugoslavia was consistent with the full-fledged ultimatum strategy on which the United States and the European allies embarked in January 1999. In the absence of negotiation, however, escalation can end only with the military defeat of the adversary. This was an outcome that far exceeded the goals of NATO in Kosovo, raised even greater problems for the alliance than the conflict in Kosovo, and contradicted the allies' own interests. According to then U.S. deputy national security adviser James Steinberg, speaking in May 1999, "A ground war in Kosovo . . . could lead to a split in the NATO alliance or a rupture with Russia that would threaten U.S. interests and European stability in ways reaching far beyond the Balkans."[139] In order to end the war in a manner consistent with their own interest in avoiding a ground war and the inevitable need to defeat and occupy Serbia, the coercing power(s) were required to move from the pure strategy of coercion, or ultimatum, upon which the bombing was initiated, to a strategy involving at least limited, mediated negotiations with the target of their actions. As we have seen, Russian participation was crucial to the success of this effort. As a result, Western and particularly U.S. actions moved somewhat closer to the model of coercive diplomacy outlined by Alexander George, in which "signaling, bargaining, and negotiating are important dimensions . . . though their roles vary in different crises."[140] In the Kosovo case we can say that the role of bargaining was far more limited than it was in Bosnia, but its reintroduction reflected the inherent limits of the full-fledged ultimatum strategy.

NOTES

1. Steven L. Burg and Paul S. Shoup, *The War in Bosnia-Herzegovina: Ethnic Conflict and International Intervention* (Armonk, N.Y.: M. E. Sharpe, 1999).

2. Alexander L. George, *Forceful Persuasion: Coercive Diplomacy as an Alternative to War* (Washington, D.C.: United States Institute of Peace Press, 1991).

3. Madeleine Albright, quoted in Burg and Shoup, *The War in Bosnia-Herzegovina*, 291.

4. Richard Holbrooke, quoted in Burg and Shoup, *The War in Bosnia-Herzegovina*, 325.

5. Bob Woodward, *The Choice* (New York: Simon and Schuster, 1996), 253–270.

6. For an assessment of the bombing, see Colonel Robert C. Owen, "The Balkans Air Campaign Study," part 1 and part 2, *Airpower Journal* 11, nos. 2 and 3 (summer 1997 and fall 1997): 4–24 and 6–25.

7. George, *Forceful Persuasion*, 5.

8. Owen, "The Balkans Air Campaign Study," part 2, 8, 20.

9. Woodward, *The Choice*, 357.

10. Richard Holbrooke, quoted in Woodward, *The Choice*, 359.

11. George, *Forceful Persuasion*, 73.

12. Ibid., 7.

13. Alexander L. George and William Simons, "Findings and Conclu-

sions," in *The Limits of Coercive Diplomacy*, ed. Alexander L. George and William E. Simons, 2d ed. (Boulder, Colo.: Westview Press, 1994), 277.

14. European Community Conference on Yugoslavia, "Treaty Provisions for the Convention," Article 2c. Corrected version (November 4, 1991).

15. See, for example, Veton Surroi, "The Albanian National Question: The Post Dayton Pay-Off," in *War Report* 41 (May 1996), www.iwpr.net.

16. See Shkelzen Maliqi, *Kosova: Separate Worlds–Reflections and Analyses, 1989–1998* (Priština: MM Society and Dukagjini PH, 1998), 34; and Stefan Troebst, "Conflict in Kosovo: Failure of Prevention? An Analytical Documentation, 1992–1998," *ECMI Working Paper*, no. 1 (European Center for Minority Issues, May 1998), www.ecmi.de/publications/working-papers.htm#ECMI Working Papers.

17. For indications of Serbian–and Kosovar Albanian–interest in negotiations in late 1995, see "The Field Mission," in *Toward Comprehensive Peace in Southeast Europe*, Report of the South Balkans Working Group of the Council on Foreign Relations Center for Preventive Action, ed. Barnett R. Rubin (New York: Twentieth Century Fund Press, 1996).

18. Troebst presents two English-language versions of the pact in "Conflict in Kosovo."

19. Shkelzen Maliqi, "Toward 'Autonomy Plus,'" *War Report* 46 (October 1996), www.iwpr.net; reprinted in Maliqi, *Kosova: Separate Worlds*, 172.

20. Project on Ethnic Relations, *The New York Roundtable: Toward Peaceful Accommodation in Kosovo* (Princeton, N.J.: Project on Ethnic Relations, 1997).

21. Special Representative Robert Gelbard, press conference, Priština, Serbia and Montenegro (February 22, 1998), and press conference, Belgrade, Serbia and Montenegro (February 23, 1998), www.state.gov.

22. Text of the agreement published by RadioB92 (Belgrade), moumee. calstatela.edu; also reported in United Nations Security Council document S/1998/470 (June 4, 1998).

23. Gelbard, press conference, February 23, 1998.

24. Behlul Begaj, "'Drenica' Homogenization of Albanians," *Helsinki Charter* (March 1998); reprinted in Helsinki Committee for Human Rights in Serbia, *Helsinki Charter*, special English edition on Kosovo (Belgrade, January 1999), 4–5.

25. *New York Times*, April 18, 1999, 1.

26. Ibid.

27. *Washington Post*, June 6, 1998, A1, www.washingtonpost.com.

28. *Washington Post*, May 16, 1998, A20, www.washingtonpost.com.

29. See, for example, text of Contact Group statement in United Nations Security Council document S/1998/657 (July 16, 1998).

30. House Committee on International Relations, statement by Robert S. Gelbard, July 23, 1998, www.state.gov.

31. United Nations Security Council document S/1998/834 (September 4, 1998), 2.

32. *Statement to the Press*, Villamoura, September 24, 1998, www.nato.int.

33. Kosova Information Center, "FOCUS: U.S. Plan Published, Kosovars Slam It Unacceptable, Pro-Serb" and "Utterly Negative Response from Kosovars," *Kosova Daily Report*, no. 1556 (September 18, 1998).

34. "American Draft Document" and Veton Surroi, "One, Mistaken, Step Forward," *Koha Ditore*, October 7, 1998, www.kohaditore.com/ARTA/Archive (October 10, 1998).

35. For contemporary news reports, see *New York Times*, September 30, 1998, A1; and *Washington Post*, September 30, 1998, A1, www.washingtonpost.com. For a more detailed, later analysis, see Human Rights Watch, *A Week of Terror in Drenica* (New York: Human Rights Watch, 1999).

36. Foreign and Commonwealth Office, "Contact Group Discussions on Kosovo," London, October 8, 1998, www.fco.gov.uk.

37. *Statement to the Press of the Secretary-General*, NATO HQ, October 13, 1998, www.nato.int.

38. For an overview of the October agreements, see Tim Youngs, *Kosovo: The Diplomatic and Military Options*, Research Paper 98/93 (London: House of Commons Library, October 27, 1998), 15–19.

39. U.S. Department of State, *Ambassador Richard Holbrooke, Special Envoy, and Ambassador William Walker, Director of the OSCE Kosovo Verification Mission, on the Record Briefing*, released by the Office of the Spokesman, U.S. Department of State: Washington, D.C., October 28, 1999, www.state.gov.

40. UN Security Council document S/1998/953 *(Letter dated 14 October 1998 from the Chargé d'Affaires . . . of Yugoslavia . . . to the President of the Security Council)* (October 14, 1998).

41. Ibid.

42. James P. Rubin, "Excerpt from the Daily Press Briefing," Washington, D.C., October 13, 1998, released by the Office of the Spokesman, U.S. Department of State.

43. *Washington Post*, October 15, 1998, A32, www.washingtonpost.com.

44. "Milosevic Backs Down on Kosovo," press conference by the foreign secretary, October 13, 1998, www.fco.gov.uk.

45. *Washington Post*, October 12, 1998, A14, www.washingtonpost.com.

46. *Washington Post*, September 3, 1998, A48, www.washingtonpost.com.

47. Secretary of State Madeleine K. Albright, "Remarks on Kosovo," Washington, D.C., October 27, 1998, released by the Office of the Spokesperson, U.S. Department of State.

48. *Washington Post*, April 18, 1999, A1, www.washingtonpost.com.

49. Ivo Daalder and Michael E. O'Hanlon, *Winning Ugly: NATO's War to Save Kosovo* (Washington, D.C.: Brookings Institution, 2000), 58.

50. Shaun Byrnes, personal communication to author, August 25, 2001.

51. For reports of KLA activity, see Kosovo Diplomatic Observer Mission (KDOM) reports of October 31 and November 2, 3, and 4, 1998, as posted on the U.S. State Department's website, special section on Kosovo, www.state.gov/regions/eur; United Nations Security Council document S/1998/1068 (November 12, 1998), paras. 13–17; *Washington Post*, November 18, 1998, A1, www.washingtonpost.com; and *New York Times*, December 8, 1998, A3.

52. Foreign and Commonwealth Office, *Edited Transcript of a Press Conference by the Foreign Secretary, Mr. Robin Cook, Ljubljana, Slovenia, Monday 23 November 1998*, www.fco.uk/news.

53. Veton Surroi, quoted in Youngs, *Kosovo*, 22.

54. *Washington Post*, April 19, 1999, www.washingtonpost.com.

55. *Washington Post*, April 11, 1999, A1, www.washingtonpost.com. For a less detailed analysis that nonetheless argues that the campaign was well organized in advance, see *New York Times*, May 29, 1999, A1.

56. *Washington Post*, March 5, 1998, A23, www.washingtonpost.com.

57. See KDOM reports of December 12, 14, 16, 18, 19, 20, 21, 22, and 27, 1998.

58. *Washington Post*, December 30, 1998, A16, www.washingtonpost.com.

59. George, *Forceful Persuasion*, 71.

60. *Washington Post*, April 18, 1999, www.washingtonpost.com.

61. Steven L. Burg, "The Failure of Early Warning in Kosovo," in *The Application of Prevention*, Report of the Center for Preventive Action's Fifth

Annual Conference (New York: Council on Foreign Relations, December 11, 1998), 8.

62. *Washington Post*, April 18, 1999, A1, www.washingtonpost.com; and *New York Times*, April 18, 1999, 13.

63. *Washington Post*, April 18, 1999, www.washingtonpost.com.

64. George, *Forceful Persuasion*, 7.

65. Secretary of State Madeleine K. Albright, "Remarks at the U.S. Institute of Peace," Washington, D.C., February 4, 1999, released by the Office of the Spokesman, U.S. Department of State, secretary.state.gov/www/statements/1999.

66. See, for example, *Guardian* (London), April 6, 1999, www.newsunlimited.co.uk.

67. President Bill Clinton, "Radio Address to the Nation," released by the Office of the Press Secretary, Washington, D.C., February 13, 1999.

68. Alexander L. George, "Theory and Practice," in *The Limits of Coercive Diplomacy*, 15.

69. The Contact Group statement of January 29, 1999, is contained in United Nations Security Council document S/1999/96 (January 29, 1999).

70. North Atlantic Council, *Statement by the North Atlantic Council on Kosovo* (Brussels: North Atlantic Council, January 30, 1999).

71. United Nations, *Secretary-General Calls for Unconditional Respect for Human Rights of Kosovo Citizens, in Statement to North Atlantic Treaty Organization*, United Nations Press Release SG/SM/6878 (January 28, 1999). The subtitle of the press release *(Kofi Annan Stresses Peaceful Negotiation Only Way to Resolve Kosovo Conflict)* contradicts the substance of Annan's remarks and may represent an attempt by UN staff to distance the organization from the NATO threat.

72. These are reproduced in Marc Weller, "The Rambouillet Conference on Kosovo," *International Affairs* 75, no. 2 (1999): 225–256.

73. *Times* (London), February 18, 1999, www.thetimes.co.uk.

74. James P. Rubin, *Press Briefing on the Kosovo Peace Talks*, Rambouillet, France, February 21, 1999, released by the Office of the Spokesman (Paris), U.S. Department of State, secretary.state.gov/www/statements/1999.

75. Secretary of State Madeleine K. Albright, *Press Availability on the Kosovo Peace Talks*, Rambouillet, France, February 21, 1999, released by the Office of the Spokesman (Paris), U.S. Department of State, secretary.state.gov/www/statements/1999.

76. *Washington Post*, April 7, 1999, A1, www.washingtonpost.com.

77. *Washington Post*, March 27, 1999, A15, www.washingtonpost.com.

78. *New York Times*, April 18, 1999, 13.

79. Alexander George, "The Role of Force in Diplomacy: A Continuing Dilemma for U.S. Foreign Policy" (paper prepared for the Dedication Conference of the George Bush School of Government and Public Service, Texas A&M University, College Station, September 9–10, 1997), 42.

80. Alexander L. George and William Simons, "Findings and Conclusions," in *The Limits of Coercive Diplomacy*, 275.

81. George, *Forceful Persuasion*, 14.

82. U.S. Senate Committee on Armed Services, *Hearing on Operation Allied Force and Relief Operations in Kosovo*, November 3, 1999, as published by Federal Document Clearing House on CIS Congressional Universe (Lexis-Nexis).

83. Daalder and O'Hanlon, *Winning Ugly*, 95.

84. *Washington Post*, April 7, 1999, A1, www.washingtonpost.com.

85. *Washington Post*, April 8, 1999, A26, www.washingtonpost.com.

86. In late January 1999, while the British were advocating the use of troops (including U.S. troops), the military and civilian leaderships of the Pentagon were reported "firmly opposed" to sending U.S. ground forces. *Washington Post*, January 23, 1999, A1, www.washingtonpost.com. In early February, the secretary of defense was telling Congress that U.S. troops "would go to Kosovo only if a peace agreement is reached." *Washington Post*, February 4, 1999, A21, www.washingtonpost.com.

87. A senior officer from NATO's Southern Command told the author in October 1998 that, although military planners had developed numerous plans for Kosovo, "none of them worked." The scale of the operation that might have been required to ensure success also raised certain political problems for policymakers. According to one later account, military planners estimated that as many as two hundred thousand troops would have been needed. *New York Times*, April 18, 1999, 1. Several administration officials reported that "that number was instantly viewed as a deal killer. . . . It was a complete eye-roller." *Washington Post*, April 1, 1999, A1, www.washingtonpost.com.

88. A later analysis of the U.S. decision to use force, for example, argues that it was "for fear of a divisive congressional and allied debate" that President Clinton accompanied announcement of the bombing with the declaration that "I do not intend to put our troops in Kosovo to fight a war." *Washington Post*, April 18, 1999, A1, www.washingtonpost.com.

89. President Clinton's national security adviser, Sandy Berger, suggested in a May 1999 interview with the *Washington Post* that "[i]f Clinton had pushed a ground option, . . . 'We would have been paralyzed by a debate in NATO, and paralyzed, in my judgment, by a debate in this country by what was at that point a hypothetical, distant option,'" *Washington Post*, May 16, 1999, A1, www.washingtonpost.com. For additional evidence of divided elite opinion at the outset of the bombing, see the Associated Press report, "US Mulls Reasons for Kosovo Strike," March 24, 1999, www. washingtonpost.com.

90. As the bombing began, a CNN/USA Today/Gallup poll reported that only 50 percent of those polled favored U.S. involvement in NATO air strikes, and 39 percent opposed it. CNN/USA Today/Gallup poll, March 25, 1999, www.cnn.com. Nonetheless, while only 43 percent believed U.S. interests were at stake and 50 percent believed no U.S. interests were involved, 64 percent believed the United States had a moral obligation to keep the peace. A few days later, a Pew public opinion poll reported that 60 percent of the U.S. public approved of the bombing and believed that NATO had a responsibility to act. Pew Research Center, "Support for NATO Air Strikes with Plenty of Buts," *NEWS Release*, March 29, 1999. After two weeks, a Pew poll revealed that support for the air strikes had risen to 62 percent, but concerns about potential involvement of U.S. troops, casualties, and the cost of the war also were beginning to rise. The public was evenly divided over the use of U.S. ground forces "if the air strikes do not stop Serbian military attacks in Kosovo," with 48 percent opposed and 47 percent in favor. CNN/USA Today/Gallup had reported at the outset of the campaign that 65 percent had been opposed. Thus, opposition to the use of troops seemed to be declining. The Pew poll showed that support for the use of ground troops was higher, 51 percent, when the question was phrased in terms of trying "to end the conflict"; but support was significantly lower in response to questions that linked deployment to "a combat situation" (40 percent), to being "in Serbia for more than a year" (39 percent), or "forcing the Serbians to accept a U.S. sponsored peace deal" (29 percent). The U.S. public also was less sanguine about the effects of the bombing than the Clinton administration professed to be: 53 percent said the bombing was making the Serbs "less likely to agree to peace," and 52 percent thought the bombing would not make them agree to peace. Only 19 percent thought air strikes would "be enough to make Yugoslav president Milosevic comply fully with the peace plan," while 65 percent thought that NATO ground forces would be required. Pew Research Center, "Continued Public Support for Kosovo, but Worries Grow," *NEWS Release*, April 21, 1999. A Washington Post/ABC News poll on April 5 found that support for the bombing had

risen to 68 percent. But at the same time, 68 percent of respondents thought air strikes would not achieve NATO goals and ground troops would be required. *Washington Post*, April 6, 1999, A1, www.washingtonpost.com. For separate discussion of the impact of wording on the responses to questions about the use of ground troops, see Pew Research Center, "Poll Analysis: May 13, 1999," *NEWS Release*, May 13, 1999. Significantly, British public opinion seems to have been more favorable from the outset toward both bombing and the use of ground troops. See, for example, *Guardian*, April 2, 1999, www.newsunlimited.co.uk. But despite the fact that after almost two weeks of bombing two-thirds of those polled recognized "a moral obligation to establish peace in Kosovo," and that 57 percent favored the use of ground troops if the bombing failed "to force Milosevic to the peace table," "[a]bout half of all Americans [responding to a Washington Post-ABC News poll on April 5 and 6] said they [were] unwilling to lose any American soldiers to help bring peace to Kosovo. Even a third of those who favored sending in ground troops would reconsider if it meant Americans would die. . . . Only three in 10 would be willing to accept the loss of 100 U.S. soldiers to win the peace." *Washington Post*, April 8, 1999, A26, www.washingtonpost.com.

91. *Washington Post*, April 5, 1999, A12, www.washingtonpost.com.

92. *Washington Post*, April 18, 1999, A1, www.washingtonpost.com.

93. *Irish Times*, March 25, 2000, quoted in Kelly M. Greenhill, "The Use of Refugees as Political and Military Weapons in the Kosovo Conflict," in *Yugoslavia Unraveled: Sovereignty, Self-Determination, and Intervention*, ed. Raju G. C. Thomas (Lanham, Md.: Lexington Books, forthcoming).

94. See "Kosovo Update" reports based on Kosovo Verification Mission reports, dated March 10, 11, and 12, 1999, www.state.gov/regions.

95. "Full Text of President Clinton's Statement," www.cnn.com, March 24, 1999. For the European statement of goals, which fails to mention the NATO air strikes, see *Guardian*, March 24, 1999, www.newsunlimited.co.uk.

96. Greenhill, "People Pressure." See also the map and time line of expulsions in *New York Times*, May 29, 1999, A4, A5.

97. Ibid.

98. See, for example, the report in *Washington Post*, May 4, 1999, A1, www.washingtonpost.com.

99. See the three-part series entitled "The Commanders' War," *Washington Post*, September 19, 20, and 21, 1999, www.washingtonpost.com. The material quoted here is from the September 19 article.

100. *Guardian*, April 23, 1999, www.newsunlimited.uk.co.

101. *Washington Post*, April 23, 1999, A1, www.washingtonpost.com.

102. See the reports on divisions in NATO in *Washington Post*, May 18, 1999, A15; May 19, 1999, A1; and May 20, 1999, A1, www.washingtonpost.com; and *Guardian*, May 19, 1999, www.newsunlimited.co.uk. For coverage of the renewed British pressure to use ground troops and German chancellor Schroeder's unequivocal public opposition, see *New York Times*, May 19, 1999, A1, A8, and May 20, 1999, A1, A4.

103. *Washington Post*, September 19, 1999, A1, www.washingtonpost.com.

104. *Washington Post*, May 9, 1999, A22; May 23, 1999, A23; and May 28, 1999, A32, www.washingtonpost.com.

105. *Washington Post*, June 7, 1999, A16, www.washingtonpost.com.

106. *New York Times*, June 2, 1999, A12.

107. *New York Times*, June 2, 1999, A12, and November 7, 1999, 4.

108. NATO and Pentagon officials reported that "the units that withdrew from Kosovo a week ago were clearly not as hobbled as they had believed." NATO counted the withdrawal of hundreds of tanks, armored personnel carriers, artillery batteries, and other vehicles and trucks loaded with military equipment, as well as forty-seven thousand troops and police, "several thousand more than intelligence reports showed at the height of Mr. Milosevic's campaign." *New York Times*, June 28, 1999, A8. According to a September 1999 *Washington Post* report, "NATO commanders were surprised to see the robust columns that eventually withdrew from Kosovo, and they concluded that the Yugoslav Third Army could have held out for weeks or even months." *Washington Post*, September 19, 1999, A1, www.washingtonpost.com. *Newsweek* reported in May 2000 that U.S. and British intelligence experts concluded in November 1999 that the bombing destroyed only "a tiny fraction" of the mobile military targets claimed, and "that the Yugoslav Army after the war was only marginally smaller than it had been before." John Barry and Evan Thomas, "The Kosovo Cover-Up," *Newsweek*, May 15, 2000, 22.

109. See, for example, the account in *Washington Post*, June 6, 1999, A1, www.washingtonpost.com.

110. See *Washington Post*, September 19, 1999, A1, www.washingtonpost.com. For an earlier, contemporary account that assigns decidedly less significance to the KLA, see *Washington Post*, June 2, 1999, www.washingtonpost.com.

111. Secretary of State Madeleine K. Albright, *Press Conference on "Kosovo,"* Washington, D.C., March 25, 1999, released by the Office of the Spokesman, U.S. Department of State, secretary.state.gov/www/statements.

112. "Official Text of EU Declaration on Kosovo," *Guardian*, May 24, 1999, www.newsunlimited.co.uk.

113. *Washington Post*, April 12, 1999, A1, www.washingtonpost.com.

114. "The Situation in and around Kosovo," *Statement Issued at the Extraordinary Ministerial Meeting of the North Atlantic Council Held at NATO Headquarters, Brussels, on 12th April 1999*, press release M-NAC-1(99)51, April 12, 1999, www.nato.int.

115. For the text, see United Nations Security Council document S/1999/428 (April 15, 1999).

116. "EU Summit Backs U.N. Peace Plan for Kosovo," April 14, 1999, www.washingtonpost.com.

117. "Security Council Rejects Russian Call to Halt Bombing," March 26, 1999, www.cnn.com.

118. *Washington Post*, April 14, 1999, A23, www.washingtonpost.com.

119. Secretary of State Madeleine K. Albright, *Statement before the House International Relations Committee*, Washington, D.C., April 21, 1999, released by the Office of the Spokesman, U.S. Department of State.

120. *New York Times*, June 8, 1999, A13A, A13B (Northeast edition).

121. *Washington Post*, April 23, 1999, A1, www.washingtonpost.com.

122. *Washington Post*, April 28, 1999, A21, www.washingtonpost.com.

123. *Statement on Kosovo Issued by the Heads of State and Government Participating in the Meeting of the North Atlantic Council in Washington, D.C. on 23rd and 24th April 1999*, press release S-1(99)62, April 23, 1999, www.nato.int.

124. *Washington Post*, May 1, 1999, A1, www.washingtonpost.com.

125. *Washington Post*, May 4, 1999, A1, www.washingtonpost.com.

126. "Peace Plan Draws in Russia," *Guardian*, May 7, 1999, www.newsunlimited.co.uk.

127. *Washington Post*, May 7, 1999, A1, www.washingtonpost.com.

128. "Text of the Statement on Kosovo from the G-8 Foreign Ministers," May 6, 1999, www.cnn.com.

129. *Washington Post*, June 6, 1999, A1, www.washingtonpost.com.

130. *New York Times*, November 7, 1999, 4.

131. Some sources suggest that a British businessman with close ties to the Russian government may also have played a role in convincing Milošević to accept the demands. See, for example, *New York Times*, June 13, 1999, A15.

132. One account of the meeting suggests Chernomyrdin merely remained "silent" while Ahtisaari articulated the threat. See *New York Times*, June 8, 1999, A13A, A13B (Northeast edition).

133. Associated Press, "Text of the Kosovo Peace Plan," June 3, 1999, www.washingtonpost.com.

134. *Washington Post*, June 4, 1999, A1, and June 6, 1999, A1, www.washingtonpost.com.

135. Zbigniew Brzezinski, "Why Milosevic Capitulated in Kosovo," *New Leader* (October 7, 1999).

136. George, "Theory and Practice," 15.

137. George, *Forceful Persuasion*, 71.

138. For an assessment of the bombing, see Owen, "The Balkans Air Campaign Study."

139. *Washington Post*, May 16, 1999, A1, www.washingtonpost.com.

140. George, *Forceful Persuasion*, 6.

4

The Delicate Balance between Coercion and Diplomacy

The Case of Haiti, 1994

ROBERT A. PASTOR

F REDERICK THE GREAT WROTE: "Diplomacy without force is like an orchestra without a score." This is the first principle learned by students of international diplomacy. After stumbling on the problem of Haiti for his first eighteen months in office, President Bill Clinton seemed to have finally mastered this lesson in September 1994 when he dispatched the nation's most skillful orchestra, former U.S. president Jimmy Carter, Senator Sam Nunn, and former chairman of the Joint Chiefs of Staff General Colin Powell, with background music provided by twenty-five thousand U.S. troops. The agreement that they negotiated was the direct result, according to the president, of "the clear imminence of military action by the United States." National security adviser Anthony Lake agreed that the policy succeeded because of "diplomacy backed by power."[1]

A closer analysis of the Haiti case suggests that it was hardly a textbook example of the adept combination of diplomacy backed by a credible threat. For nearly three years the United States practiced diplomacy with empty threats. Then it chose to use force without considering diplomacy. And then, within hours of the president saying that all diplomatic options were exhausted, he decided to try again. The negotiations came within a knife-edge of failing because at a delicate moment soon

119

after the negotiators had persuaded the Haitian military to accept U.S. intervention, the Haitians learned that an invasion was under way, and they ended the talks. Only a clever tactic and the persistence of unusually independent negotiators made an agreement possible, but the United States had to pay a higher price to secure the agreement than it would have if an invasion had not begun. (The price: the agreement had to be completed with the provisional president, rather than the military, and that enraged the actual president, Jean-Bertrand Aristide, and almost precluded the agreement.) The case demonstrated, among other lessons, that the credible threat of force can be constructive when used by skillful negotiators, but in the critical psychological moment when the protagonist begins to drop his opposition to an agreement, the actual use of force can be counterproductive. It turns out that Haiti is a superb case study, not of how to combine diplomacy with force, but why it is so difficult to do so, particularly for a democracy.

An intensive analysis of the case also shows why "coercive diplomacy" is easier to conceptualize than to execute. In Alexander George's typology of "coercive diplomacy," the Haitian case would be "type C," an effort to persuade an opponent to make changes in its government.[2] Indeed, this was the toughest case because the United States and the international community were trying to convince the Haitian military junta and the de facto government installed by the junta to give up and transfer power to their archenemy, President Aristide. Given the difficulty of accomplishing the objective, it is not at all surprising that the full gamut of instruments was used by the United States and the international community during a three-year period. The manner in which the instruments were used, however, offers some useful lessons to consider in future cases. Before offering some conclusions on the Haiti case, this chapter will examine briefly a similar case—the U.S. invasion of Panama in 1989—to try to understand better the difficulty of deploying coercive diplomacy effectively.

BACKGROUND TO THE HAITIAN CASE

On December 16, 1990, Haiti held its first and only election that was judged free and fair by all its political parties and the international community.[3] A young, multilingual priest, Jean-Bertrand Aristide, won two-thirds of the vote in a race for the presidency against twelve other candidates. Aristide took office in February 1991, when democracy seemed to reach a crest in the hemisphere. In June foreign ministers of all members of the Organization of American States (OAS) met in Santiago, Chile, at a General Assembly session to discuss new ways to strengthen democracy in the hemisphere. They approved unanimously a resolution that called for an emergency OAS meeting in the event of an unconstitutional change of government. The emergency meeting would then decide on specific actions to persuade coup plotters to return power to constitutionally elected leaders.

For a region that had opposed any interference in its internal affairs, the Santiago Resolution was a watershed event—a bold collective initiative to prevent any unconstitutional changes of government. It is well to recall that the principle of nonintervention was first enunciated by Latin diplomats at the dawn of the twentieth century in reaction to U.S. interventions, and it was repeated at regular intervals whenever the United States threatened force. In the Cold War the United States justified its interventions on behalf of democracy, but many governments in Latin America doubted the motives and insisted on nonintervention. The Santiago Resolution of democratic solidarity became *possible* only after all the members of the OAS had free elections; and it became *necessary* because few governments felt that their democracies were firmly rooted. The fear that a coup d'état in one country might spill over and lead to coups in other countries compelled the region to modify its position on nonintervention and seek new collective measures to defend all of their democracies.

From the United States' standpoint, the Santiago Resolution was a godsend; it meant there would be collective support for one of its core objectives in the hemisphere: democracy.[4] Since the turn of the century, the United States had been worried that instability in the region could be exploited by one of its rivals to gain a foothold and threaten U.S. interests. The best way to avoid such instability was through a democratic process of peaceful political change, so when Latin America accepted the Santiago Resolution, the U.S. government applauded the initiative.[5]

On September 30, 1991, the military overthrew Aristide, and Haiti, a country with almost no experience in democracy, became the hemisphere's first test of its commitment to restore it. Haiti was the second independent nation in the hemisphere and the first black republic in the world. Stirred by the spirit of the French Revolution, Haitian slaves rose up in 1791 and in a brutal war defeated Napoleon and the world's greatest army. But Haiti's declaration of independence in 1804 was not an announcement of freedom. It represented an exchange of masters. No people in the hemisphere have suffered as much as Haitians, with less freedom and poverty and more isolation from the international community. Indeed, it is not far from the truth to say that the only democracy Haiti ever enjoyed was the six months before the coup on September 30, 1991.

Few of the OAS foreign ministers, who met in emergency session in Washington after news of the coup, knew even that much of Haiti's history, yet they were filled with the spirit of the Santiago Resolution and determined to restore democracy to the island. Secretary of State James A. Baker III described the coup as a "test" for the hemisphere "to stand united as a community of democracies," and he declared emphatically: "This coup must not and will not succeed."[6] The foreign ministers passed a resolution condemning the coup in the strongest terms, demanding the restoration of democracy, and dispatching several foreign ministers to Port-au-Prince to negotiate Aristide's return. This exercise in multilateral diplomacy proved to be a disaster. The new military leaders handled the diplomats' arrival with the ineptitude that one would expect from a group that was desperate to find a legitimate purpose for its coup and looked to the interlopers to provide a nationalistic excuse. The Haitian generals treated the mediators with disrespect, and the foreign ministers returned the compliment in Washington. They passed an OAS resolution on October 8, 1991, urging member states to impose a trade and oil embargo on the military government. On October 11 the UN General Assembly condemned the coup and declared the regime illegal.[7]

Why did this first effort at resolving the conflict fail? OAS foreign ministers viewed their role more as judges than as problem solvers. They judged the coup a violation of the Santiago Resolution, and they arrived in Haiti to present their conclusions and order the military to step down. In the words of one foreign minister, "To the extent that there was a negotiating strategy, it was cobbled together during the flight. . . . It was agreed that we would remain adamant in our objective [to reconstitute democracy in Haiti] with no fallback position."[8] It is not clear that another approach would have worked, but it is hard to imagine a less effective one than this. The embargo was symbolically important, but it was voluntary and thus "porous from the start," a fact demonstrated a month later by the arrival in Port-au-Prince of a Colombian oil tanker.[9]

Although rumors circulated that the United States backed the coup, the opposite is true. President Aristide owed his life to the intervention of the U.S. and French ambassadors, and the U.S. government immediately suspended all U.S. assistance to Haiti. At the OAS meeting Baker told the other foreign ministers: "We do not and we will not recognize this outlaw regime. Until President Aristide's government is restored, this junta will be treated as a pariah throughout this hemisphere—without assistance, without friends, and without a future."[10] In exile Aristide embarked on a global effort to marshal support for his return. The Caribbean states, led by Jamaican prime minister Michael Manley, realized that a diplomatic effort without a credible threat of force would not succeed. Manley approached Baker in December 1991 with a proposal for a multinational force, not unlike the one that intervened in Grenada in October 1983.[11] Some in the first Bush administration took Manley's proposal seriously and consulted with several governments in the hemisphere, but they encountered two problems. First, the Pentagon opposed an invasion, and second, the other governments wanted some legitimization, but they doubted the OAS would ever sanction the use of force.[12]

The administration supported Aristide, but many questioned his stability, and most thought it unwise to invade when, in the words of Baker, "the security of our country or the safety of our citizens was not at risk." Therefore, Baker concluded, "no serious consideration was given to the use of such force to restore Aristide to power in Haiti."[13] The Haitian military suspected that the United States had decided not to use force, and that may explain why the military never implemented the Washington Protocol, an agreement signed by Aristide and the military on February 23, 1992.

The administration was also concerned about the increasing number of refugees fleeing the island, but that became less of a problem when George Bush decided to return them to Haiti. Presidential candidate Bill Clinton criticized this policy as inconsistent with U.S. tradition and international law, but soon after his election, intelligence reports of a new wave of refugees led Clinton to adopt the same policy. With African Americans as a core base of his political constituency, however, an antirefugee policy was not sustainable for Clinton without a clear pledge to restore Aristide to power. Clinton made such a pledge in a conversation with Aristide on January 13, 1993, and he later affirmed publicly his determination to see Aristide restored.[14]

It took eighteen months for Clinton to come to grips with the implications of that promise. In the fall of 1992 the OAS secretary-general asked Manley, who had recently resigned from his position as Jamaican prime minister because of poor health, to be a special envoy to negotiate the return of Aristide, but Manley still believed that the negotiations would be futile without a credible threat. After consultations with Carter Center staff in November 1992, Manley decided to ask the UN secretary-general to appoint former president Carter as the UN envoy and jointly negotiate U.S.-Caribbean military support for an enhanced mediation effort.[15] Manley, UN secretary-general Boutros Boutros-Ghali, Carter, and staff met in Atlanta in December 1992. During these talks Carter spoke with President-elect Clinton and Venezuelan president Carlos Andrés Pérez, a close friend of Manley's and Carter's, who threw his support behind the arrangement. Everything seemed in order, but then Boutros-Ghali returned to New York and appointed a former Argentine foreign minister as his special envoy. Manley, feeling betrayed, resigned from his position as OAS special envoy.

Why did this effort not bear fruit? First, Clinton was not willing to commit himself to a policy or to Carter at that time, and second, some of Boutros-Ghali's UN advisers were ideologically opposed to the idea of using a former U.S. president as a UN mediator.[16] This was the second missed opportunity. Even if the new envoys had not solved the problem, they would have probably abbreviated the time needed to learn the conditions necessary for success.

During the next eighteen months, the United Nations and the United States pursued a number of diplomatic options. The principal one culminated in the Governors Island Agreement, signed on July 4, 1993, with the first step being the lifting of UN sanctions against Haiti as a positive inducement to completing the agreement. Similar in substance to the Washington Protocol, the agreement would begin with the appointment of a new prime minister by consensus. Then it would proceed with a proclamation of amnesty for the military, some power-sharing arrangements, the arrival of UN police advisers, and, finally, the return of Aristide on October 30, 1993. Each time the Haitians dragged their feet, Washington threatened the reimposition of sanctions.[17] Finally, on October 11, 1993, the UN police advisers, who were supposed to serve as a bridge to a change in government, sailed to Port-au-Prince on the USS *Harlan County*. The timing was bad, coming right after the gruesome murder of U.S. troops in the chaos surrounding the U.S.-UN intervention in Somalia. When Haitian thugs, orchestrated by the regime, threatened the police advisers if they landed, the ship was withdrawn. The U.S. bluff was called.[18]

The withdrawal proved so embarrassing that some of the president's counselors advised him to intervene.[19] He wisely chose not to do so then, when there was so little support in the United States or internationally, but this event must have weighed heavily on his mind. The decision was criticized harshly by those who favored the return of Aristide, including U.S. diplomats in Port-au-Prince, and those who opposed the president's policy, including some U.S. military and CIA officials.[20] In response, the United States promoted tougher UN sanctions, and the president ordered six destroyers to enforce the sanctions, prevent the departure of large numbers of refugees, and "press for the restoration of democracy."[21] The tightened embargo had a complicated effect on Haiti: the poor became much poorer, the Haitian military High Command grew richer from smuggling, and the wealthy families began to withdraw their support from the military.[22]

By early May 1994 it became clear that the embargo would not be sufficient to solve the problem. President Clinton's credibility was being questioned, and the Congressional Black Caucus, which had adopted Aristide and Haiti as its priorities, was applying considerable pressure on him to act. Clinton appointed William Gray III, who had been chairman of the Congressional Black Caucus, as his envoy to the Haiti negotiations, and administration officials began threatening force if the Haitian military leaders did not give up power. Haiti was not moved, and even the president's U.S. supporters thought he was bluffing. Randall Robinson, the leader of TransAfrica, a nongovernmental organization dedicated to helping the Caribbean and Africa, began a hunger strike, and Senator Tom Harkin (D-Iowa) urged the administration "to get some steel in its spine and stop equivocating."[23]

The administration then pressed the UN Security Council in July 1994 to approve Resolution 940, which called on member states "to use all necessary means to facilitate the departure from Haiti of the military leadership."[24] This was an unprecedented and historic statement by the international community; it was the first time that the United Nations legitimized the use of force in the internal affairs of a country in defense of democracy. In the summer, the administration began to openly discuss invasion plans, but public opinion in the United States was not in favor of using military force, and opposition to its use began to coalesce from different sources.[25] Conservative Republicans viewed Aristide as a leftist, if not a communist, and did not want him returned to power. Some moderates believed that the United States should employ force only when its vital interests were threatened, and they did not believe that the restoration of democracy in Haiti constituted a vital interest of the United States.

THE CARTER CONNECTION

Although rebuffed by the Clinton administration in the winter of 1992, Jimmy Carter and Carter Center staff continued to monitor the Haiti issue. The center's involvement in Haiti had begun a year after Jean-Claude Duvalier had fled Haiti in February 1986. In the fall of 1987, just after the assassination of a leading candidate for president, leaders from various nongovernmental organizations invited Carter to Haiti. Carter invited George Price, the prime minister of Belize, to join him. Price was a member of the Council of Freely Elected Heads of Government (the council), a group of presidents and prime ministers of the Americas that was established at a meeting of the Carter Center in October 1986. Carter's trip stabilized the situation but only for a moment; the presidential elections were aborted two months later by the military.

In the summer of 1990 the provisional president of Haiti, Ertha Pascal-Trouillot, invited Carter's council to observe the elections scheduled in December, and the council worked with the National Democratic Institute for International Affairs (NDI), a nongovernmental group associated with the U.S. Democratic Party that assists democracy abroad. Through trial and error, the Carter Center had learned that passively observing elections in a country with little or no experience in democracy was not a sufficient strategy to assure a free and fair election. Instead, the center adopted a more active approach of "election mediation," in which it worked with all parties contesting an election to make sure that the rules of the game were judged fair by all. This meant that Carter and his colleagues made numerous trips to Haiti beginning in the summer of 1990 and continuing through the inauguration of the new president in February 1991.[26] On each trip council members listened to the political parties' complaints about the electoral process and advised the Election Commission, which was responsible for conducting the election, on ways to respond positively. By the eve of the election, the council had gained the trust of the parties and the candidates, and they accepted the legitimacy of the process. The Carter Center also worked closely with the military and especially with Chief of Staff General Herard Abraham and Colonel Raoul Cedras, who was the officer charged with assuring public order on election day.

The election of Aristide turned the power pyramid of Haiti upside down, putting the champion of the masses on top and in the Presidential Palace and relegating the elite to the margins of political power. It was a delicate transition, and the elite and the soldiers became fearful as rumors spread that Aristide was going to abolish the military and replace it with his own police force. Aristide sparked further alarm when he gave a speech that was interpreted as encouraging his fol-

lowers to use "necklaces" of burning tires on the necks of people who
opposed him. In the summer of 1991 Aristide replaced Abraham, a
mistake that Aristide himself later acknowledged,[27] with Cedras, who
was weaker but also more popular among the rank and file. When soldiers rebelled against Aristide in September 1991, the General Staff
pushed Cedras in front of the movement, and after Aristide went into
exile, Cedras became general and commander in chief.

   In July 1993 Cedras's aide passed a message to Carter, inviting him
to Haiti and indicating that "Cedras has complete confidence in President Carter's objectiveness and world perspective."[28] That occurred at
a tense moment in the negotiations between the United Nations and
the Haitians, and Carter did not pursue it. Carter also had plenty of
contact with Aristide, who visited the Carter Center several times dur-
ing this period and joined the Council of Freely Elected Heads of
Government. Carter continued to offer ideas to President Clinton on
Haiti policy, writing detailed memoranda to him on several occasions.
Then on August 6, less than one week after the passage of the UN
Security Council resolution sanctioning an invasion of Haiti, Robert
Novak conducted a CNN interview in Port-au-Prince with Cedras.
Novak asked Cedras whether he would welcome mediation by Carter.
Cedras responded positively: "I met Mr. Carter in 1990 when I was in
charge of security for the election of 1990. He did good work in Haiti.
I am open to dialogue with all those who come to understand the
Haitian problem."

   Novak's interview precipitated speculation of a Carter trip to Haiti,
and the de facto foreign minister and Cedras's brother contacted
Carter Center staff to invite Carter to Haiti. On September 12 national
security adviser Anthony Lake warned Cedras that the invasion clock
would strike midnight in "minutes, not hours." After so many threats,
it was obvious that Lake's watch had not been synchronized by Swiss
craftsmen. The only question was whether the watch was a Timex that
would keep on ticking after midnight, or whether time was really running out. When Carter returned from a trip to Africa the next day, he
began talks with Cedras and with President Clinton.

   Carter invited Senator Sam Nunn into the discussions, and Nunn
suggested including General Colin Powell. Both Nunn and Powell said

that they would consider going to Haiti only if President Clinton authorized the visit. Clinton then phoned Powell and told him: "Jimmy Carter is sometimes a wild card, but I took a chance on him in North Korea, and that didn't turn out too badly." The president wanted to make sure that Powell understood that if they went, the only purpose was to negotiate "how, not if, our troops would go ashore."[29]

That evening, on September 15, the president addressed the American people on television. He defined U.S. goals in Haiti, said that all diplomatic options had been tried and failed, and warned the Haitian generals to leave power. In fact, there had been no diplomatic initiatives for at least six months; the U.S. embassy had been prohibited from contacting Cedras or the provisional government. A few hours later, the president phoned Carter and tentatively approved the mission.

THE TWENTY-FOUR-HOUR SOLUTION

The next afternoon, Friday, September 16, at 5:00 P.M., President Clinton finally authorized Carter, Nunn, and Powell to leave the next morning at 7:00 A.M. Carter asked me to accompany and advise the group. The Carter-Nunn-Powell team understood its objectives but intended to approach the Haitian military in a manner very different from the way that the Clinton administration preferred. This is not surprising. The administration had already moved to a war footing. The three-day countdown to an invasion had begun, although neither the negotiators nor the public was aware of the fact. (The team thought that if its mission failed, there would be time to discuss the next steps with the president before any military action was taken.) In the early evening, before the team's departure, National Security Council officials sent "talking points." Carter was instructed to threaten to "drive you [Cedras] from power if you do not depart." Many of the points assured Cedras of a safe haven, free of extradition, and the use of funds that the administration assumed he had outside the country. After reviewing the paper with me, Carter phoned the president, who agreed that the talking points did not need to be used. The negotiators would have more flexibility.

The members of the mediation team approached the negotiations with the benefit of distinct but complementary backgrounds. As someone who had traveled to Haiti many times, knew Cedras, and had mediated a host of Third World conflicts, Carter not only brought the stature of a former president but also familiarity with the specific case. His skills in mediation derived from a combination of a politician's charm, a democrat's empathy, a technician's mastery of detail, and a winner's focus on the finishing line.[30] Sam Nunn was then chairman of the Senate Armed Service Committee and the single most respected individual in the Senate and, to most informed individuals, in the country on national security issues. Carter had great respect for his judgment, and Nunn brought a cool, calm wisdom to the deliberations and a keen lawyer's eye to the text of the agreement. A few days before the trip, Nunn spoke on the Senate floor against an invasion, which impressed the Haitians and gave him greater credibility when he delivered the hard message that he would support an invasion when it came.

General Colin Powell had been chairman of the Joint Chiefs of Staff under Presidents Bush and Clinton. The victor of Desert Storm, Powell was being touted in the United States as the "Eisenhower of the 1990s," but his reputation in Haiti and the Caribbean derived from widespread knowledge and pride that he was a son of Jamaican immigrants who had risen to the highest military office in the United States.

In the United States Powell and Nunn had reputations as tough, defense-minded leaders, and their involvement sent a clear message to Americans that the president was serious. While Carter was viewed in the United States as softer and more liberal, in Haiti Carter was better known for his tough negotiations during the 1990 elections. At the negotiating table he was not only primus inter pares, he was also the strongest voice. Powell, whose views of Carter were not that different from the general public's, admitted publicly on his return from Haiti that he was surprised at Carter's strength and courage.

All three negotiators were skeptical about a U.S. invasion if not opposed to one. Carter believed that negotiations would make an invasion unnecessary, and Nunn and Powell were not convinced that vital U.S. security interests were at stake. Nonetheless, they all understood the president's position and saw their job as using the leverage provided by him to persuade the Haitian generals to leave power peacefully. From years of experience they also understood that they would have to listen closely to the Haitians, to get into their shoes if they were to get the Haitians to march out of office.

Soon after their arrival, they met with the former Haitian army commander in chief General Herard Abraham, one of the shrewdest political actors in the country. Abraham said that the delegation would have to pay its respects to the provisional government and not insist that the General Staff go into exile—astute comments as it turned out. Then, disregarding the objections of administration officials, the group met the de facto government's foreign minister, who had invited them. He also urged them to meet with the provisional president—a wise recommendation that proved useful in breaking the impasse at the end of the talks.

The next stop—at 2:00 P.M.—was the National Military Command Center for the first meeting with General Cedras, General Philippe Biamby, and the General Staff. After an exchange of courtesies, Carter and his colleagues explained to the generals in a straightforward and firm manner that an invasion would occur if the negotiations to restore President Aristide failed. It was clear by the look on their faces and their stated reactions that until that moment, the Haitian military had not believed that the United States would invade. There had been too many bluffs. All three said they were against an invasion, but the American people would support it, as would they, when it occurred. When Powell described in extraordinarily vivid detail exactly how it would happen, any question about the willingness of Clinton to use force that remained in the minds of the Haitian generals dissolved. After putting the threat on the table, the three Americans put it aside, never to use it again in the negotiations. This did not mean that the threat was no longer relevant to the talks, only that the negotiators understood that continued reference to the threat could have a counterproductive effect. Instead, they listened and worked through a series of points that together made up the final agreement. But there was no doubt that the three had delivered the message as effectively and credibly as was possible, and that it concentrated the minds of the Haitians.

The General Staff was coming from a direction that was different from what the administration had anticipated. The administration thought the generals would be concerned only with securing access to their offshore bank accounts and obtaining exile in a desirable location, but the military never once raised either issue. Rather, members of the General Staff saw themselves as representing, in effect, the ancien régime, protecting the country against a demagogic leader whose return would bring chaos. They suspected that the Americans did not know Aristide as they did and tried to explain why they thought he was the devil. General Cedras alone spoke for the entire General Staff. If there were divisions among the General Staff, they were never evident in the negotiations. Cedras spoke of the nation's history in fighting for its independence against Napoleon's imperial army and then resisting every form of foreign interference after that. The world had never recognized or respected Haiti, but no one could conquer its spirit, and they were determined to show the Americans that they were the guarantors of that history. These were intelligent and articulate individuals who understood that they would be overwhelmingly defeated by a U.S. invasion, but Haiti had faced worse odds in its history and had suffered many defeats. Haitians were quite capable of resisting agreements that seemed obvious to the outside world.

General Powell empathized and discussed how a new Haitian-U.S. military agreement not only would assure stability during the transition but also would permit a renewal and modernization of the armed forces. Senator Nunn said that he would be prepared to support such an aid program in Congress. Carter said that amnesty was possible, but he returned to the central point of the talks: UN forces would arrive in war or in peace; Aristide would return; and General Cedras would have to step down and, following the administration's instructions, go into exile.

The Haitians made very clear that they were *not* prepared to consider exile, as it was unconstitutional to banish a Haitian, and that they did not want the United Nations involved. They were willing to consider a new relationship with only U.S. forces, but the delegation had to pay respects to the provisional government of Émile Jonassaint. That was the opening. Even more significant, at the end of the first round of talks at 5:45 P.M. Cedras pleaded with Carter: "You cannot leave Haiti without a solution. Speak to others. We have great respect for you, but you don't have the right to leave the country knowing your mission could be a failure."

After the meeting, Carter, Nunn, Powell, and I retired to Carter's suite to review his draft proposal. We went through three drafts and then returned to the National Military Command Center for a meeting that began at 10:50 P.M. and ended at 2:00 A.M. Carter put the main elements of the proposal before the military—the arrival of U.S. forces, the military's stepping down, Aristide's return. These were discussed at some length, and the military asked for time to consider them. We agreed to meet the next morning.

The team was supposed to have breakfast at the U.S. ambassador's residence with a group of Aristide's principal supporters, but only the mayor of Port-au-Prince, Evans Paul, arrived the next morning. It was an ominous sign that we failed to recognize at the time, believing that Aristide's other supporters were simply afraid of traveling because of the state of fear in the city. In fact, Aristide was very upset by the negotiation and had probably told his people not to attend.

The team then went to see Cedras and his family at his home. A Haitian businessman had alerted us to the strong influence that Cedras's wife had on him, and when Carter phoned his own wife that first evening, she also recommended that they visit his house. Cedras's wife was a resolute and dominant figure. Both her father and grandfather had been commanders in chief of the army, and while Cedras sat quietly with a dazed look, she explained forcefully that the entire family had made a pact the night before that they would die together in the house when the invasion occurred. It was obvious why Cedras felt he had so little room for maneuver; she was prepared for an invasion and believed the military had no choice but to fight. Carter and Nunn argued for alternatives, but the key figure was Colin Powell, whom she admired. He explained with passion that the honorable path for a soldier was to reach agreement with the United States.

Following this emotional meeting, the team returned to the military headquarters, but only after stopping to see the provisional president, Jonassaint, who pulled Powell aside after the meeting and asked him to return to help rebuild the military just as MacArthur had done in Japan!

The High Command had worked through the night on its paper, which took a few elements from the proposal of Carter, Nunn, and Powell (CNP), including the main one permitting U.S. forces to enter Haiti. But the High Command's paper, presented in English, posed conditions on the arrival and operation of U.S. forces that were unacceptable to the United States. The real negotiations began. After about ninety minutes, a few minutes beyond the deadline, the Haitians accepted compromises from CNP that permitted the Americans to report to the president that they had achieved the principal goal—getting approval of the entry of U.S. forces and flexibility on their operations—but they needed more time to set a deadline for Aristide's return and the generals' departure.

The negotiations were occurring not only between the three Americans and the Haitian military, but also between the three and President Clinton and, in Washington, between the administration and President Aristide, who was proving very difficult. Aristide's aides later confided to their friends in the United States and to journalists that they had hoped for an invasion to destroy the military.[31] Aristide wanted it both ways: he wanted an invasion, but he did not want to invite or endorse it so that he would not have to take responsibility for any civilian deaths. He also was afraid that President Clinton might retreat at the last moment and not use force; this fear might have been shared by some of the president's advisers and might partly explain their negative reaction to his last-minute decision to send Carter. It might also explain why the countdown to the invasion began while CNP were in Haiti and why they were not informed of it by the administration.

CNP were asked to incorporate some important issues and some minor details into the text. All were reasonable proposals, but none of them took into account the delicate psychology of the bargaining. Members of the Haitian military were already feeling as if they had given up more than they should have, and each new item grew more difficult, not less, for them to accept. Washington was also uncertain about its negotiators. When the White House received the faxed proposal, some U.S. officials thought it was CNP's and insisted on rewriting it completely, not realizing that the proposal represented the military's rewriting of the original CNP proposal. The administration therefore sent a different proposal at about 1:00 P.M. CNP decided to try to insert the important points of the administration's proposal rather than shift texts.

Two hours after the deadline, by 2:00 P.M. on Sunday, September 18, the U.S. invasion checklist was advanced. General Hugh Shelton, the commander of the operation and subsequently chairman of the Joint Chiefs of Staff, was on the aircraft carrier offshore that was responsible for the first wave of troops and planes. Later he said that every time his officers checked a major item on their list, they would turn on CNN and see the team walk into another meeting, and they would all scream at the TV: "Get out of there!"

The tension in President Clinton's voice grew with each conversation with the team; he insisted that the team leave and then allowed some more time. Finally, at 4:00 P.M., General Philippe Biamby, who was number two in the Haitian military forces, burst into the talks and said that he had information that the Eighty-second Airborne was getting its parachutes and was about to depart for an invasion. He said that the Americans had betrayed them and that the negotiations were over. He was taking General Cedras, the commander in chief, to prepare the nation's defenses. The talks would end. He grabbed Cedras and began to leave. Carter stepped between them and made a fervent case to sign the agreement. It was a very tense moment. Carter then asked them to remain while he went into the next room to speak privately to President Clinton.

When Carter returned, he asked the foreign minister to call Émile Jonassaint for a meeting with CNP and Cedras. It was a brilliant move because Cedras could not reject the request from the civilian authorities. In the earlier meeting Jonassaint had left the impression that he was ready for the agreement. So Carter, Nunn, and Powell took Cedras with them to the Presidential Palace.

Jonassaint was a tall, distinguished eighty-one-year-old who had been chief justice before the military asked him to be provisional president in May 1994. Clinton administration officials viewed him as a puppet of the military and refused to deal with him, but the Carter team found him dignified and his own man, a man who appeared to want to use this moment at the conclusion of a long career to take charge of the country. He pivoted and asked Cedras bluntly: "Can you defend us against attack?" Cedras sat erect but passive. After a long pause, he said no. Jonassaint responded: "In that case, I'm signing this agreement." The minister of defense announced his resignation, and Cedras would not sign the agreement. Powell asked Cedras twice whether he would uphold the agreement; Cedras was silent at first but then said he would follow his president's instructions. It wasn't clear whether the rest of his General Staff would do so. It was also not clear whether President Clinton would authorize Carter to sign it because Aristide would not accept Jonaissant's signature on the document. President Clinton spoke individually with Carter, Nunn, and Powell while the agreement was being translated. He finally authorized Carter to sign it, which he did. Soon after, Secretary of State Warren Christopher raised some concerns, but it was too late.

Carter, Nunn, and Powell returned to Washington. I was asked to remain in Port-au-Prince to brief the ambassador and the Joint Chiefs, who had not participated in any of the negotiations, and to set up the proposed meetings the next day between the U.S. military and the Haitian military that would permit the entry of U.S. forces peacefully. The problem was that the U.S. embassy and the U.S. military did not believe that the agreement would work. They postponed, but did not cancel, the invasion until the next morning.

It was very hard to reach Cedras to arrange a meeting because he and the General Staff had gone into a secret command center, fearful that U.S. forces might try to assassinate them. The next morning, with barely ninety minutes before the troops would land, I finally persuaded Cedras's wife to arrange a meeting with him, General Jared Bates from the Joint Chiefs, Ambassador Bill Swing, and me. I told her that he had to meet us in fifteen minutes as 3,500 U.S. troops were going to land at the airport in twenty helicopter gunships. During the meeting both sides were able to discuss details for cooperation and the terms of engagement between the two forces. We then raced to the airport just as the helicopters were landing. General Shelton had the courage and the foresight to understand the situation, and despite advice he received from some of his aides, he came to town to meet with Cedras and work out arrangements that ensured both U.S. and

Haitian forces would work with each other to guarantee the peace. After a long dinner and discussion the next evening, Cedras gave me a letter confirming his adherence and that of the General Staff to the accord signed by Carter and Jonassaint.

Based in part on previous agreements that had been abandoned by the Haitian military, there was considerable skepticism in the press, as well as among U.S. diplomats, about whether the accord would be implemented.[32] But the central elements of the agreement were implemented. The Haitian military cooperated with the U.S. forces, and there was not a single casualty. On October 15, as defined in the agreement, President Aristide returned to Haiti. A few days before, Cedras and Biamby decided to go into exile in Panama. Contrary to reports that he had great wealth in overseas accounts, Cedras said that virtually all of his wealth was tied up in his home, and he requested Carter's help in renting the home in order to secure enough income to live in Panama. Carter worked out a modest rental of his home with the U.S. embassy.

THE SHADOW BETWEEN CREDIBLE COERCION AND DETERMINED DIPLOMACY

For three frustrating years, between the military overthrow of Haitian president Aristide on September 30, 1991, and his return to power on October 15, 1994, the United States and the international community wrestled with the "problem" of Haiti. An assortment of mediators/negotiators were deployed with a quiver of weapons, including international condemnation, diplomatic isolation, repeated negotiations, economic and financial sanctions, threats, and finally the use of force. All but the last mediating effort by Carter, Nunn, and Powell failed to achieve the objective.

What could be learned from the case that would contribute to the theory and practice of conflict resolution and coercive diplomacy? The literature on conflict resolution extends back at least to World War I, and it has passed through a number of phases—from an analysis of conflicts to the collection of data, from realist-based game theories and strategies of bargaining to human relations theory, from abstract modeling to workshops and guides for practitioners.[33] Much of the literature deals with alternatives to the use of force, but it is the rare analyst who denies the effectiveness of an approach that connects diplomacy with a credible threat. The proper equation can compel leaders to recalculate their options and choose a different course than they would have in the absence of adept diplomats backed by force. Much depends on the message and the way that it is delivered, but the issue is not whether diplomacy backed by force is a good idea; the far more interesting question is why it is so hard to execute. That question has two parts: first, why is it so difficult to back up diplomatic threats with force, and, second, why is it so difficult to connect force with diplomacy?

The answer to the first part of the question is that democratic leaders are reluctant to put their country's soldiers in harm's way unless vital interests are threatened. As long as public opinion is either opposed or not supportive and there is vocal opposition to the use of force, as there was by Republicans on Haiti, the president's threats are unlikely to be taken very seriously by those he is trying to influence. Acts inconsistent with the threats—such as an ineffectual embargo or an abortive attempt to deploy police advisers—further impugn the president's credibility. President Harry Truman could try to "scare the hell" out of the American people in 1947 in order to get Congress to approve aid to Europe, but Clinton did not have that option on Haiti.

It is possible that some in the Clinton administration conveyed threats confidentially to the press in order to put the president in a position in which he was compelled to use force, but it is understandable why the president was reluctant. He expected American lives would be lost, and while no one doubted that U.S. troops would prevail over the ragtag Haitian army, the overall operation could fail in any number of ways—by tragic accidents, by Haitian sabotage or snipers, or by the difficulty of installing democracy in a country that had never really had it. Any of these problems would jeopardize his capacity to lead both at home and abroad. He was therefore not ready to cross that Rubicon and invade Haiti until he realized that his prestige and power were at risk *for failing to deliver on his repeated pledge* to restore Aristide to power. The Congressional Black Caucus and other liberal groups exerted important influence. Clinton knew that they would constantly remind him of his promise, and they were among his most reliable supporters.

The Founding Fathers deliberately imposed constraints on the president's war-making powers precisely because they did not want him to make war as the European monarchs did—on a whim or to acquire territory. Those constraints inhibited but did not preclude presidential action. *However, in the post–Cold War era when the sole superpower is needed to catalyze the international community on behalf of humanitarian goals, the president's inability to credibly threaten pariah regimes may mean, paradoxically, that force is needed more often and with more intensity than if his threats were taken seriously.*[34]

Why, after the decision is made to use force, do democracies have so much difficulty negotiating? Why, for a six-month period preceding the entry of U.S. troops, would the United States not talk with the Haitian military or Jonassaint? If the answer to the first part of the question resides in the democratic system, then the answer to the second can be found in the "logic of war." As a nation moves closer to war, its leaders demonize the adversary. The reason is obvious: it is hard to persuade a nation to risk its children's lives and murder others unless the other side is evil. This dilemma is neither new nor unique to democracies, but modern democracies obviously are more responsive to and constrained by public opinion. Once a people are convinced that they face a heinous enemy, it is hard to pursue serious negotiations without being accused of granting recognition to the illegitimate, and of course the Jonaissant regime *was illegitimate*. In fact, this was the main criticism leveled at Clinton and Carter for the mission. "There is much that is troubling in the agreement," wrote Jim Hoagland of the *Washington Post*. "Its promise of amnesty for Haiti's illegal military-police command is hard to square with the accusations of butchery and unique evil the president leveled against the junta Thursday."[35] To understand just how difficult serious negotiations are with an enemy that is viewed as ghastly or depraved, imagine Israel negotiating with Hamas after the suicide bombings. Or the United States negotiating with Libya. In both cases some people would criticize negotiations as immoral and/or impractical. The democratic connection, in brief, is both solution and problem on this issue.

The issue for policymakers, then, is how to mobilize a populace for war while retaining the space to negotiate. This is easier, though rarely easy, for a dictatorship; it is far harder but not impossible for a democracy. The solution must be found in the political process. The president has to build a critical mass of support in the U.S. Congress, and once he feels he enjoys the support to threaten credibly, he should identify the people who can best deliver the message.

Not every person can be a good mediator or negotiator, and not every good negotiator can be effective in all circumstances. The right person should have experience in the country (or plenty of time and access to learn), credibility with the key actors, and a mediator's special skills to listen to the other side (and convince the other side that one is listening). This latter quality is especially hard to find—indeed, it has become one of the clichés of conflict resolution to ask why so few people can listen effectively. The answer is that many politicians and experienced statesmen are asked to speak so often that their listening skills atrophy. George Mitchell, who negotiated the agreement in Northern Ireland, and Jimmy Carter are two exceptions, but people without diplomatic experience rarely have the patience or restraint to listen for hours to those who make war not only with weapons but with their language and gestures. The protagonists of a conflict are usually quite provocative; the test of a good mediator/negotiator is to sidestep provocations and return the discussion to the most important points to be negotiated.

In the case of Haiti, President Clinton selected three negotiators who understood intuitively that they needed to show respect to their interlocutors if they were to accomplish their task. This is more easily grasped in the abstract than it is in the confines of a tropical room when hundreds of people are screaming at you from outside, but the three were experienced enough to avoid the temptation to get under the skin of their adversaries. Rather, they sought ways to get into their shoes. By choosing negotiators of great political stature such as Carter, Nunn, and Powell, the president also took a serious risk, because they had autonomous power. No doubt that was why Clinton contemplated that option for so long before choosing it. It turns out that he chose wisely, and the nation benefited, but he also paid a political price with both the

State Department, which opposed the mission, and many outside who wrote that Carter had pulled Clinton's chestnuts out of the fire.

All negotiators understand the importance of an ultimatum and a deadline. The interesting question is why both sides resist setting them for so long. The answer is that up until the critical moments of a negotiation, both sides have powerful reasons for not making the decision they need to make—in Haiti, for the military to give up power, and for President Clinton, to use force or to retreat. Both sides try to force the other to make the decision. Clinton and his administration's officials kept telling the Haitian generals to leave to save themselves the agony of using force. The risk of setting a deadline is that if it passes without action, one side or the other loses credibility, which is, of course, what happened in Haiti. So many deadlines had passed that when the president finally made the decision to invade, his advisers and Aristide insisted that he not retreat, despite the fact that he put his three negotiators in a very dangerous position. That is why it is so difficult to set a deadline and to know when to relax it once it is set.

There is a certain dynamic in any tough negotiation. When one side makes the major concession, time is often needed to reduce the humiliation before a second point is accepted. Sometimes, a symbolic gesture can help. In the case of the Haitian talks, the military conceded the entry of U.S. troops, but at that moment the administration insisted on other demands—for example, an October 15 deadline for the return of President Aristide—which were reasonable, though not essential. (Once the U.S. troops were on the ground, as Powell said, they would set the deadline.) More time was needed to negotiate such points. Having achieved the principal goal, the negotiators should have received an extension of, say, twelve hours to wrap up a satisfactory agreement.

A successful negotiator is one who knows how to close a deal. This is one of Carter's strengths. He has a way of focusing on the principal goal and not allowing anything to divert him, and Nunn and Powell, possessing the same strength, reinforced Carter. In addition to having the personal skill to complete an agreement, a negotiator needs to have the political leverage to deliver an agreement. That is always problematic either because the president wants to reserve the option to make the final decision or because Congress might have the final say.

Sealing an agreement often requires a symbolic concession, which might come back to haunt the negotiators. To close the agreement, Carter told Cedras: "If you cannot accept the agreement, I can assure you that there is no way to stop the invasion. If you can accept the agreement, that will be an honorable decision, and I can assure you that I will be at your side and will express my gratitude and admiration for your decision." After the events, Carter was criticized for being too complimentary of Cedras, but this was part of what Carter felt was necessary to complete the agreement. Similarly, Powell told Cedras that if he stepped down, Powell would make sure that the general received full military honors. Again, that proved arduous to implement when Aristide returned, but it was helpful to complete the negotiations.

The need to formulate an "exit strategy" before entering a tough negotiation is often noted but rarely fulfilled. Carter, Nunn, and Powell departed the United States without the administration ever asking what they would say publicly on their return if the talks failed. As a result, the administration found itself in an awkward position as the deadline approached. If the three mediators had announced they had reached an agreement, but the administration rejected it, would Congress and the American people have accepted a war? Doubtful. If exit strategies are so important, why are they so rarely developed? It might be that the highest levels of government are so focused on their internal debate and the next step that they do not have the time or the temper to think of the long term.

Perhaps the most important lesson of this case centers on a critical distinction between the threat and the use of force. The credible threat of force facilitated an agreement; the actual decision to use force came within a hair of scuttling the talks and, in the end, created a new problem for the United States. General Biamby shut down the negotiations upon learning that the invasion was under way. Of all the generals, he was probably least interested in reaching an agreement. When he learned that the United States had been, in his mind, duplicitous in negotiating and marshaling its forces at the same time, he was pushed over the edge. Only Carter's quick decision to change the negotiating venue from Military Headquarters to the Presidential Palace kept the talks going. But that move created serious problems for Aristide and the administration, both of whom did not recognize the provisional government and refused to deal with it.

Throughout most of its history, Haiti has been uniquely isolated from the world, either because the Western world feared the implications of an independent black republic or because its local oppressors preferred to keep the world away from Haiti. To a country used to being isolated, the international community's initial approach of condemning the regime and imposing an embargo was nothing new. The literature on sanctions draws some clear lessons. Sanctions are most effective when they are comprehensive, effectively enforced, and aimed at changing a specific policy. They are almost always ineffective if they are porous and aimed at changing the regime,[36] as was the case in Haiti. It is far easier, for example, to induce a government to adopt a new policy or alter an existing one than it is to compel a government to renounce power.

Why, then, were sanctions the weapon of choice for the international community for three years? The alternatives—to do nothing or to intervene—were more costly. Also, sanctions can be viewed as small steps on the road to more serious decisions that signal to both the target and the home audience an escalation in tensions. It was only when the sanctions proved so ineffective in restoring democracy yet so debilitating to the population that decision makers were embarrassed enough to consider more costly alternatives. But at this point U.S. leadership was divided, as the president and the Congressional Black Caucus leaned toward intervention and many Republicans and moderates preferred disengagement.

To move the Haitian military out of power, the United States needed to alter the terms of its decision. In Bosnia Richard Holbrooke was able to change empty threats into real ones and use them effectively, but later threats failed to prevent Yugoslav president Slobodan Milosevic from trying to "cleanse" Kosovo. In the Persian Gulf, in 1998 Saddam Hussein finally realized that the United States was serious and conceded enough to the UN secretary-general to compel the United States to postpone its attack, but Saddam's subsequent reversal ensured that the United States would act. Each case shows the difficulty in executing the precise connection between threat and force.

THE PANAMANIAN INTERVENTION OF 1989

One other case deserves attention because it shares many similarities with Haiti, although there are two key differences: President George Bush's decision in December 1989 to invade Panama. As for the similarities, first, the clash in Panama, like that in Haiti, was between a U.S. president and an oppressive military dictator. Second, the United States had a history of deep involvement in the country's affairs, including extended periods of military occupation. Third, the asymmetry in the relationship was overpowering, which meant that it was harder for the president to accept obstinacy on important issues like drug trafficking without looking weak. Fourth, diplomacy was tried over an extended period through many bilateral and multilateral channels. Fifth, diplomacy failed because General Manuel Antonio Noriega, like Cedras, viewed the U.S. government as divided and Latin America as resistant to any military intervention. In other words, Noriega viewed U.S. threats as a bluff, and he didn't take them seriously. Sixth, the president finally decided to invade only after a long and frustrating period of failed negotiations.

As for the two key differences between the cases, *first, unlike Clinton, when Bush decided to use force, he did not try to use that leverage for one final negotiation.* In the biggest military operation since Vietnam and the largest parachute drop since World War II, twenty-six thousand U.S. soldiers attacked the Panamanian Defense Force on December 20, 1989. At least 314 Panamanian soldiers and 500 to 1,000 Panamanian civilians were killed. Twenty-three U.S. soldiers and 3 U.S. civilians were killed, and 124 were wounded.[37] In spite of repeated threats against him by two U.S. presidents over a two-year period, Noriega was completely surprised by the invasion as well as its timing. When the invasion began, he was drunk and with a prostitute at a hotel near the airport. He fled to, of all places, the Vatican embassy, until he was compelled to leave. DEA agents flew him to Miami, where he was convicted of drug trafficking and sentenced to forty years in prison.[38]

The second important difference was that the U.S. intervention in Panama was unilateral—in fact, the first unilateral military intervention by the United States in the hemisphere since U.S. forces invaded Nicaragua in 1926. President Bush did not try to gain the approval of the international community—either through the Organization of American States or the United Nations—and, indeed, both organizations condemned the invasion in one-sided votes.

As with Haiti, the Panamanian case involved two sides so unequal in power that a skillful display of coercive diplomacy should have obviated the need for a forceful invasion. That was the conclusion of Michael Kozak, deputy assistant secretary of state, who was the principal negotiator with Noriega. In a memo to Secretary of State James Baker on April 14, 1989, Kozak wrote: "While we don't think U.S. military force would be necessary, the President must be prepared to use force as a last resort. The credible threat represented by our willingness to use force opens other options and is the only wedge which will separate Noriega from the Panama Defense Forces." The "other options" began with negotiations, which he thought could work if the U.S. government spoke with one voice on behalf of one strategy. If that didn't work, then he advocated promoting a coup in the armed forces, and if that failed, the United States should either "snatch" Noriega or invade.[39]

The history of U.S. relations with Noriega has been related in considerable detail in the memoirs of the main actors—Presidents Ronald Reagan and George Bush, Secretaries of State George Shultz and James Baker, and Noriega—and in other articles and books.[40] As the chief of military intelligence when Omar Torrijos was head of government (1968–81), Manuel Noriega established relations with the CIA and U.S. military intelligence, which he continued and expanded when he took over the government shortly after Torrijos died in a plane crash. Unlike Torrijos, Noriega had a nasty streak and was responsible for having a political rival beheaded, forcing two of Panama's presidents to resign, and engaging in drug trafficking. In February 1988 two federal grand juries in Florida indicted him for the latter crime, and at this point, the Reagan administration decided to seduce or push him from power. But each time that the State Department or the White House threatened Noriega, the Pentagon or the Treasury Department, under James Baker, would say that force was not an option. Sanctions were imposed, but the administration could

not even decide whether to trade the indictments for Noriega's departure. President Reagan was strongly in favor of the trade, but he
was practically alone. In one telling comment at a National Security
Council meeting, Reagan protested: "None of you has shaken me a
bit as to the rightness or the wrongness of this." Then he pointed to
Kozak in jest and told him to tell Noriega that "we're a bunch of jerks
who can't make up our minds." Secretary of State George Shultz later
acknowledged that the negotiations could have succeeded "if President Reagan had been supported in his decisions and if the execution of his decisions had been firm and accelerated."[41]

George Bush opposed the trade, but after his election he reconsidered his position. In the meantime he kept up the pressure. His
spokesman made clear in December 1988 that "Noriega must go."
Bush authorized covert operations to support the opposition and
encourage the military to try to overthrow Noriega. Jimmy Carter and
his council observed Panama's elections on May 9, and their "quick
count" revealed that the opposition had won. The next day, Noriega
tried to manipulate the results, and Carter denounced the election as
a fraud and urged the OAS to condemn him. Bush supported OAS
action but also announced a seven-point plan designed to remove
Noriega through a combination of incentives as well as threats,
including the dispatch of U.S. troops to the Panama Canal area, but
on the same day the secretary of defense said on television that the
United States would not intervene in Panama.[42]

The OAS debated whether to criticize Noriega by name, a telling sign
that it was not ready to apply the kind of pressure necessary to compel
the Panamanian to give up power. Instead, the OAS appointed a three-
member team to negotiate. Noriega insisted on another election, and
the OAS team seriously considered it, even though the Bush administration correctly rejected the idea. Instead of using U.S. pressure to
move Noriega, the OAS team began to criticize U.S. policy. The negotiations petered out.

Within the administration, the chairman of the Joint Chiefs of Staff
and the commander of Southern Command both opposed military
intervention, but in late September they were replaced by General Colin
Powell and General Max Thurman. Both Powell and Thurman were

willing to consider force. At that very time, members of Noriega's inner circle passed messages to the U.S. embassy that they were planning a coup and needed help. The administration thought it might be a trap and were slow to respond. By the time the United States decided to support the effort, it was doomed, and Noriega murdered the plotters. The criticism of the Bush administration by members of Congress across the political spectrum was humiliating. Senator Jesse Helms called the administration "a bunch of Keystone Kops." Democratic congressman Dave McCurdy ridiculed "a resurgence of the wimp factor."[43] The gap between Bush's threats and his hesitation had begun to impugn his credibility.

The embarrassment that Bush suffered in October 1989 for failing to come to the support of officers trying to overthrow Noriega was comparable to what Clinton felt after he withdrew the USS *Harlan County* from Port-au-Prince four years later. General Colin Powell, who was involved in both cases, agreed that neither Bush nor Clinton wanted to repeat that mistake.[44] Noriega and Haitian general Raoul Cedras, however, drew a conclusion opposite to that of the two presidents. Both thought that since the president had shown weakness once, he would show it again.

In fact, each time Noriega survived an encounter like the coup, he felt less vulnerable, and the United States felt more frustrated. That dynamic led Bush to ask his secretary of defense and chairman of the Joint Chiefs of Staff to prepare a plan to defeat the Panamanian Defense Force. On December 15, 1989, the Panamanian National Assembly appointed Noriega chief of government and declared Panama to be in a state of war with the United States. On the same day Panamanian soldiers stopped a U.S. military patrol car and held the police officer at gunpoint. The next day they fired at a U.S. car and killed a marine. A navy officer and his wife who witnessed the shooting were arrested and beaten, and the woman was sexually assaulted. On December 17 Bush approved the invasion plan, believing that if the United States did not act soon, other Americans would be at risk in Panama.

Months before, Bush had changed his position on whether to lift the indictments against Noriega if he left power, but that offer proved insufficient to persuade Noriega. Kozak believed that "if Noriega were convinced that force was definite, he would have re-calculated his options" and would probably have accepted the deal. So the obvious question is why the administration didn't use the threat, which was credible for the first time, before using force. Assistant Secretary of State Bernard Aronson acknowledged that the administration had "never thought to attach a diplomatic component" at that time, and the reason was the fear that any delay would jeopardize the lives of Americans. Kozak said the decisive factor was that "the Department of Defense did not want to warn Noriega. They wanted the advantage of surprise."[45]

Noriega was certainly surprised, but the option of coercive diplomacy, premised on a *credible* threat, was never used. Up until December 17 every threat was an empty one, and Noriega thought that he had outfoxed the United States and that his allies in certain parts of the U.S. government would prevent the use of force against him. Indeed, in his memoirs Noriega writes that the invasion would never have happened if William Casey, Reagan's CIA director, had still been alive.[46] Noriega was not paying attention to the change in the actors in Washington, nor was he wise enough to understand that each of his "victories" raised the price of inaction in the United States. Unlike Cedras, who seemed to be carrying the weight of Haitian history on his shoulders, Noriega was the supreme opportunist, a high-risk taker but also a survivor. A deal, in brief, was possible, but it would have involved a risk for the Bush administration of alerting Noriega. Weighed against the certainty that lives would be lost in the invasion, as they were, a detached actor might have chosen to try to negotiate one last time. But by the time of decision, Bush also had his prestige on the line. He could no longer afford to show any sign of weakness, and one more negotiating initiative could have conveyed that message.

CONCLUSION

The world is not a laboratory that will hold still while a social scientist changes one variable to see if that will produce a different result. But the Haiti negotiation was as close to a hothouse laboratory as one is likely to find, and the outcome sat on a knife-edge and almost went wrong several times.

There were three critical moments. The first was at deadline—at Sunday noon. It is hard to imagine a different set of negotiators standing up to the president at that moment and insisting that they be permitted to stay. Within a few hours, Powell learned that an invasion was under way and, at a discreet moment, told the others. And yet none of them flinched.

The second moment occurred when General Biamby burst into the room and insisted on stopping the talks—a perfect example of the counterproductive use of force in a delicate negotiation. By shifting the venue to the Presidential Palace, Carter saved the talks, but they dragged on because the administration and Aristide were reluctant to conclude an agreement with the de facto government.

The third moment occurred the next morning. Only two hours before an invasion, the Haitian forces were not on alert, but the prospects of some violence, either deliberate or accidental, were high in the absence of clear instructions from the High Command to soldiers in the field. That occurred only after the meeting was arranged with U.S. ambassador Swing and the U.S. military. On the way to that meeting, a senior U.S. military officer described to me in great detail the devastation that would have struck Port-au-Prince and the estimated number of casualties had the negotiations failed. Many Haitians would have died, and some Americans as well. The healing challenge that faced Aristide was simply nothing when compared with what would have happened had there been a violent invasion.

The Haitian case, in brief, explains why the simple lessons of conflict resolution and coercive diplomacy are easier to state than to apply. Some of these lessons suggest that democracy is both the solution and part of the problem, and that we need to develop new mechanisms that will permit democracies and the international community to threaten and negotiate more effectively. Threats of force can change a decision, but only if the threats are credible and conveyed in a manner that offers a face-saving exit for the target.

Although the United States did succeed in achieving its immediate objectives in Panama and Haiti, in both cases the United States had to deploy more coercion—indeed, military intervention—than diplomacy. That seems incongruous given that the vast difference in power that separated the United States from its two adversaries, Why, then, did the United States fail to accomplish its goals with a credible threat and without force? First, the U.S. government was maladroit and divided; the adversary thought such division would inhibit action, and Washington's continuous bluffing reinforced that view. Second, the asymmetry in interests and power wowrked against the United States.[47] Although U.S. power eclipsed that of Panama and Haiti, U.S. vital interests were not at play. In contrast, the survival of the weaker nation's regime was directly threatened. This meant that the United States had to be more adept and credible, and it was neither.

We can never know for sure what led the Haitian military to change its position and permit the return of Aristide. There was some information that the military was divided or that the FRAPH, a right-wing paramilitary group, was trying to control the military. But the military spoke with a united voice during the negotiations and made clear that it could deliver the FRAPH and its leader. Had the sanctions encouraged agreement? That seems very unlikely; the Haitian generals seemed unaffected or enriched by the sanctions, and the business community was still not ready to allow Aristide to return even though the community understood that was a prerequisite for lifting the sanctions.

A threat of force is necessary but not sufficient. It can compel the pariah regime—or actors in it—to alter its calculations. Such regimes, however, are often defiant or out of touch. The Haitian military, like Saddam Hussein, would have fought a losing battle. *The reason the military did not fight is that the negotiators concentrated their minds with a credible threat and then provided the psychological reassurance that transformed Haitian defiance into accommodation.* As for Noriega, he did not believe that he faced the final battle yet.

The path toward a successful use of coercive diplomacy is, in brief, never straight, and it is rarely short. To reach the end of the path, the challenger—in this case, the United States—needs to be credible and effective in the target country. And the target—the Haitian military—must be at the point where it is prepared to consider changing its position. In the end the difference between a successful and a failed use of coercive diplomacy can be as simple as a decision to change the venue or an assurance by a respected leader. Just as it is so hard for the United States to believe that President Kennedy met his end at the hands of a single demented fanatic, it is also hard to realize that a conflict can be the result of mistaken communication, or that peace can emerge from the ingenuity of an exhausted negotiator. But the truth is sometimes that simple.

NOTES

The author is especially grateful to Robert Art, Michael Desch, Patrick Cronin, and Alexander George for thoughtful and detailed comments, and to Bernard Aronson and the participants in the United States Institute of Peace Conference for their critiques. The author assumes responsibility for any remaining flaws.

Some of the issues developed in this essay were first sketched in the author's "More and Less Than It Seemed: The Carter-Nunn-Powell Mediation in Haiti, 1994," in *Herding Cats: Multiparty Mediation in a Complex World*, ed. Chester A. Crocker, Fen Osler Hampson, and Pamela Aall (Washington, D.C.: United States Institute of Peace Press, 1999), 505–525.

1. For President Clinton's statement, see White House Press Release, September 19, 1994, reprinted in *Foreign Policy Bulletin: Documentary Record of U.S. Foreign Policy* 5, no. 3 (November-December 1994): 23, 19; for Anthony Lake's, see Anthony Lewis, "Reward for a Job Well Done," *New York Times*, October 7, 1994, 5.

2. See Alexander George, "Coercive Diplomacy: Definition and Characteristics," in *The Limits of Coercive Diplomacy*, ed. Alexander L. George and William E. Simons (Boulder, Colo.: Westview Press, 1994).

3. This followed years of mediation among the political parties conducted by the Carter Center–based Council of Freely Elected Heads of Government, the National Democratic Institute for International Affairs (NDI), the United Nations, and the Organization of American States (OAS). See the reports of these organizations, including The Carter Center/NDI, *The 1990 General Elections in Haiti* (Washington, D.C.: NDI, 1991).

4. For a full development of this theme, see Robert A. Pastor, *Exiting the Whirlpool: U.S. Foreign Policy toward Latin America and the Caribbean* (Boulder, Colo.: Westview Press, 2001), esp. chap. 11, "Promoting Democracy: Pushing on the Pendulum," and chap. 13, "The Redefinition of Sovereignty: The Nicaraguan Precedent and the Mexican Model."

5. It is true that the United States did not always support democracies, and in a few notable cases (Guatemala, 1954; Chile, 1970–73) the U.S. government undermined democracies. These were unfortunate exceptions. Secretary of State James Baker described overall U.S. policy well in explaining why the administration supported Aristide despite what he called "his erratic behavior and mixed reputation." He wrote: "My position was simple: if you support democracy, you support what democracy brings you, so long as the process is free and fair, and the victors are not clearly bent on using the electoral process simply to gain power and then in effect destroy democracy by establishing authoritarian rule." James A. Baker III, *The Politics of Diplomacy* (New York: G. P. Putnam's Sons, 1995), 601.

6. U.S. Department of State, "Statement by the Hon. James A. Baker III to the OAS Meeting of Foreign Ministers on the Situation in Haiti," October 2, 1991, 1, 3.

7. For a review of the negotiations and decisions by the international community, see Robert Maguire et al., *Haiti Held Hostage: International Responses to the Quest for Nationhood, 1986 to 1996*, Occasional Paper No. 23 (Providence, R.I.: Thomas J. Watson Institute for International Studies, 1996); and Ian Martin, "Haiti: Mangled Multilateralism," *Foreign Policy* 95 (summer 1994): 72–89.

8. See Barbara McDougall, "Haiti: Canada's Role in the OAS," in *Herding Cats*, ed. Crocker, Hampson, and Aall, 393.

9. Maguire, *Haiti Held Hostage*, 33.

10. Baker, *The Politics of Diplomacy*, 601.

11. Former prime minister Michael Manley, interview with author, Atlanta, Georgia, December 1992.

12. Hon. Bernard Aronson, assistant secretary of state for inter-American affairs (1989–93), interview with author, Washington, D.C., March 30, 2000.

13. See Baker, *The Politics of Diplomacy*, 601–602.

14. I was with Aristide when Clinton phoned him.

15. I was the Carter Center staff member involved.

16. White House officials and senior UN officials, confidential interviews with author.

17. For a good survey of the talks leading up to the agreement, see James Morrell, *The Governors Island Accord on Haiti*, International Policy Report (Washington, D.C.: Center for International Policy, September 1993).

18. Ian Martin quotes Emmanuel Constant, the leader of the demonstration: "My people kept wanting to run away. But I took the game and urged them to stay. Then the Americans pulled out! We were astonished. That was the day FRAPH [a right-wing paramilitary group] was born. Before, everyone said we were crazy, suicidal, that we would all be burned if Aristide returned. But now we know he is never going to return." Martin, "Haiti," 72–73.

19. White House staff, confidential interview with author.

20. John M. Goshko, "Blacks Criticize Clinton on Haiti: Multilateral Military Action to Return Aristide Suggested," *Washington Post*, November 11, 1993; and Howard W. French, "U.S. Move Angers Diplomats in Haiti," *New York Times*, October 14, 1993.

21. "Presidential News Conference: Clinton Says Haiti Must Put 'Democracy Back on Track,'" *Congressional Quarterly*, October 23, 1993, 2907.

22. Elizabeth D. Gibbons, *Sanctions in Haiti: Human Rights and Democracy under Assault* (Westport, Conn.: Praeger, 1999).

23. Senator Tom Harkin, quoted in Carroll J. Doherty, "President Broadly Criticized for Talk of Military Action: Conservatives Warn of Somalia-like Fiasco; Liberals Fear Clinton Is Bluffing," *Congressional Quarterly*, May 7, 1994, 1134.

24. United Nations Resolution 940 was reprinted in the *New York Times*, August 1, 1994, 6.

25. "Should We Invade Haiti? A Botched Refugee Policy Has Left Clinton in a Bind and Preparing to Invade," *Newsweek*, July 18, 1994, 40–43. The article describes the administration's invasion plans, the increasing threats by the administration that it will invade, and the public opinion surveys that show a lack of public support.

26. Robert A. Pastor, "Mediating Elections," *Journal of Democracy* 9 (January 1998): 154–163.

27. Aristide acknowledged the mistake at a Carter Center conference in Atlanta, Georgia, on January 14, 1992.

28. Darryl Reaves, military assistant to General Cedras, letter to the Hon. Jimmy Carter, July 7, 1993.

29. Colin Powell and Joseph E. Persico, *My American Journey* (New York: Random House, 1995), 597–602.

30. For the definitive work on Carter's postpresidency, see Douglas Brinkley, *The Unfinished Presidency: Jimmy Carter's Journey beyond the White House* (New York: Viking, 1998), esp. chap. 21, on Haiti.

31. This explains why several of the aides were probably responsible for graffiti on the walls of Port-au-Prince on the eve of a visit in February 1995 by Carter, Nunn, and Powell to throw their support behind Aristide.

32. See, for example, Michael Wines, "As Three Emissaries Claim Victory, Doubts Remain," *New York Times*, September 20, 1994, 1, 10; and David S. Broder, "Hostage to Haiti," and Charles Krauthammer, "Our Partner, Gen. Cedras," *Washington Post*, September 20, 1994. Broder predicted that U.S. troops would soon find themselves "caught in an ongoing civil war," and Krauthammer projected that Haiti would prove "more problematic than Somalia."

33. For reviews of the literature, see the following, all published by the United States Institute of Peace Press in Washington, D.C.: Lewis Kreisberg, "The Development of the Conflict Resolution Field," and Jacob Bercovitch, "Mediation in International Conflict: An Overview of Theory, a Review of Practice," in *Peacemaking in International Conflict: Methods and Techniques*, ed. I. William Zartman and J. Lewis Rasmussen (1997); *Herding Cats*, chaps. 1, 2; and Fen Osler Hampson, *Nurturing Peace: Why Peace Settlements Succeed or Fail* (1996). See also George and Simons, eds., *The Limits of Coercive Diplomacy*.

34. See Robert A. Pastor, ed., *A Century's Journey: How the Great Powers Shape the World* (New York: Basic Books, 1999).

35. Jim Hoagland, "Big Deal, Bigger Questions," *Washington Post*, September 20, 1994. See also Jack Nelson, "Criticism over Crisis Handling Erupts in Capital," *Los Angeles Times*, September 20, 1994.

36. Gary Clyde Hufbauer, Jeffrey J. Schott, and Kimberly Ann Elliot, *Economic Sanctions Reconsidered: History and Current Policy*, 2d ed. (Washington, D.C.: Institute for International Economics, 1990); and Robert A. Pape, "Why Economic Sanctions Do Not Work," *International Security* 22 (fall 1997).

37. Margaret E. Scranton, *The Noriega Years: U.S.-Panamanian Relations, 1981–1990* (Boulder, Colo.: Lynne Rienner Publishers, 1991), 202-205.

38. Manuel Noriega and Peter Eisner, *The Memoirs of Manuel Noriega: America's Prisoner* (New York: Random House, 1997). See also my review of the book in the *Washington Monthly* (June 1997): 43–45.

39. Michael Kozak, memo quoted in Baker, *The Politics of Diplomacy*, 181. Kozak related his views to me in an interview in Alexandria, Virginia, on March 30, 2000.

40. For a good summary of the case, see Eytan Gilboa, "The Panama Invasion Revisited: Lessons for the Use of Force in the Post–Cold War Era," in *The New American Interventionism: Lessons from Successes and Failures*, ed. Demetrios James Caraley (New York: Columbia University Press, 1999),

89–112. See also Scranton, *The Noriega Years;* Frederick Kempe, *Divorcing the Dictator: America's Bungled Affair with Noriega* (New York: G. P. Putnam's Sons, 1990); and Kevin Buckley, *Panama: The Whole Story* (New York: Simon and Schuster, 1991).

41. George Shultz, *Turmoil and Triumph* (New York: Charles Scribner's Sons, 1993), 1074–1079.

42. Gilboa, "The Panama Invasion Revisited," 102–104.

43. Congressman Dave McCurdy, quoted in Gilboa, "The Panama Invasion Revisited," 105.

44. Retired General Colin Powell, letter to author, March 16, 2000, and interview with author, February 25, 1995.

45. Bernard Aronson and Michael Kozak, interviews with author, March 30, 2000.

46. Noriega and Eisner, *The Memoirs of Manuel Noriega*, 66. Shultz acknowledges in his memoirs Casey's special relationship with Noriega and confirms that Casey had encouraged Noriega to go to Cuba "as our representative" during the moment of the U.S. invasion of Grenada in October 1983. Shultz was incredulous. Shultz, *Turmoil and Triumph*, 337.

47. I am indebted to Michael Desch for this point.

5

Nuclear Weapons and North Korea

Who's Coercing Whom?

WILLIAM M. DRENNAN

T HE UNITED STATES CAME PERILOUSLY CLOSE TO WAR with the Democratic People's Republic of Korea (DPRK, or North Korea) in 1994 over the North's initial quest for nuclear weapons. U.S. intelligence had been tracking the North's effort for years, and by the late 1980s there was little doubt in the minds of U.S. policymakers that the North had a comprehensive clandestine plutonium-based nuclear weapons program centered at Yongbyon, sixty miles north of Pyongyang, the capital of the DPRK. What little comfort North Korea's membership in the International Atomic Energy Agency (IAEA) and the Nuclear Nonproliferation Treaty (NPT) may have given the outside world had been swept away in the aftermath of the Persian Gulf War; Iraq, too, had been a "member in good standing" of the IAEA and the NPT, yet UN inspectors were stunned after the war to discover the extent and sophistication of Iraq's weapons of mass destruction programs.

In the early 1990s, as now, North Korea's acquisition of nuclear weapons would fundamentally alter the strategic balance in Northeast Asia, vastly complicate the defense of the Republic of Korea (ROK, or South Korea), and threaten the strategic position of the United States in a region vitally important to Washington. The stakes could not have been much higher for the United States and its allies, but as the Cold War drew to a close there was reason for cautious optimism.

The end of the Cold War renewed hope that relations between South and North Korea might improve at last. By the end of 1991 that hope seemed to have been realized when the two signed a comprehensive set of agreements—including an agreement to keep the Korean peninsula free of nuclear weapons—designed to ease tensions and foster reconciliation. Relations between the United States and North Korea improved as a result, and with the North appearing to cooperate with both the IAEA and South Korea on nuclear matters, there was reason to believe that the threat posed by the North's nascent nuclear weapons program might be on the road to resolution.

Those hopes were dashed in early 1993, igniting a crisis that lasted well into the next year, a crisis that was not defused before the peninsula stood on the brink of war. In the aftermath of the crisis, senior American officials would portray the outcome as a triumph of U.S. leadership and resolve, suggesting that toughness at the negotiating table, backed by the might of the U.S. military, the threat of UN sanctions, and the full support of Washington's allies had compelled North Korea to give up its nuclear weapons ambitions. "We negotiated from a position of strength," declared Secretary of State Warren Christopher, ascribing the outcome to "a consistent policy . . . supported by successful diplomacy at the United Nations and evident military readiness on the ground."[1] Secretary of Defense William Perry asserted that "[t]he resolve and determination of the United States and South Korea and Japan forced North Korea to shut down this dangerous nuclear program."[2] The president's national security adviser, Anthony Lake, claimed the administration had "confronted the North Korean nuclear threat and . . . stopped it dead in its tracks."[3]

Not exactly.

This chapter argues that both North Korea and the United States attempted to employ strategies of coercive diplomacy. The North emphasized "coercion" through the use of brinkmanship tactics, the creation of deadlines, and threats of the use of force (with the implied promise of a peaceful resolution to all outstanding bilateral matters if the United States would "do the right thing"). The United States emphasized "diplomacy" in the form of inducements and concessions (with the threat of future UN sanctions and ultimately the use of force if North Korea would not accept benefits in exchange for its nuclear weapons program). In the end both strategies failed, creating a highly combustible situation that, in the judgment of those closest to the action, was almost certain to result in a major war that neither side wanted but appeared unable to stop. This "Guns of August" situation was prevented from descending into a new Korean war only by the unprecedented (and unauthorized) intervention of former president Jimmy Carter, who essentially hijacked U.S. policy, remade it to his liking in meetings with North Korea's supreme leader, negotiated terms to end the crisis, and then presented the U.S. administration with a fait accompli.

While North Korea had been building its nuclear capability for years, the heart of the first Korean nuclear crisis corresponds closely with the opening seventeen months of President Bill Clinton's first term—from January 1993 to June 1994, when Carter visited Pyongyang and struck the deal with North Korea's leader, Kim Il Sung, that stopped the march to war and led in October 1994 to the U.S.-DPRK Agreed Framework—the bargain intended, by the United States at least, to freeze and eventually dismantle the North Korean nuclear program. But the Agreed Framework was not the result of a successful strategy of coercive diplomacy by either the United States or North Korea. There would have been no Agreed Framework had it not been for Jimmy Carter.

This chapter consists of three main parts. The first is a narrative history that explains the uniqueness of the Korea case, provides background material, and summarizes "the story"; the second part is an analysis of the attempts by the United States and North Korea to employ strategies of coercive diplomacy; and the third part is devoted to observations and conclusions.

NARRATIVE

Uniqueness of the Case

Coercion is inherently difficult, even for the most determined and powerful of state actors. As the number of "players" increases, the degree of difficulty goes up considerably. In 1993–94 the United States, the world's sole remaining superpower, found itself facing a highly dangerous and complex nuclear challenge from North Korea: dangerous for the simple reason that the combination of North Korea and nuclear weapons was (and remains) a nightmare scenario for the United States, on a par with, or even exceeding, the specter of Saddam Hussein's Iraq "going nuclear"; complex in that the United States could not go it alone in confronting the North, one of the world's few remaining rogue states. As a result, the United States had to try to balance the often conflicting interests of allies and other regional states, as well as international organizations—the United Nations and the International Atomic Energy Agency—in addition to trying to uphold the NPT, the foundation of the nonproliferation "system" that had emerged during the Cold War.

The Korea case also has aspects that put it in a different category from the other cases examined in this volume. With the possible exception of terrorism, none of the others involved the vital interests of the United States. Indeed, most of the others address humanitarian crises, some of them horrific, but all of them instances in which U.S. intervention was optional. Only the Korea case involved a threat of nuclear proliferation. Finally, none of the other cases entailed a risk of large-scale warfare, possibly including the use of weapons of mass destruction. In that regard, Korea's is the only "worst-case scenario" in which a great number of Americans—civilians as well as military personnel—would have died.

Military Aspects. Every U.S. president since Harry Truman has had to contend with the dangers North Korea poses to U.S. interests. For four decades following the signing of the Korean War Armistice Agreement in 1953, U.S. policy toward the DPRK was one of containing and deterring an aggressive and unpredictable North Korea and of being prepared, in partnership with its ally South Korea, to win a renewed war should deterrence fail.

But deterrence did not fail, and for forty years, until the nuclear crisis of 1993–94, deterrence alone was sufficient. The U.S. commitment to the defense of the ROK dates from the signing of the Mutual Defense Treaty in 1953,[4] and U.S. troops have been deployed in South Korea ever since. They remain primarily because the Korean War has never officially ended. The Armistice Agreement is essentially a cease-fire agreement between opposing military commanders, not a permanent political resolution to the war.[5] The absence of a formal declaration of war in 1950 notwithstanding, the United States was, and remains, a belligerent in the unresolved Korean War.[6]

While the U.S. military commitment to the ROK has remained firm, the size of the U.S. military presence has diminished over time as ROK forces have become more capable. In the early 1990s approximately thirty-six thousand GIs remained in the South, the bulk of them ground troops deployed between Seoul, the capital of the ROK, and the Demilitarized Zone (DMZ), only thirty miles to the north. They, and others from the U.S. Air Force, Navy, and Marine Corps, compose United States Forces Korea (USFK) and are under the command of a U.S. Army four-star general. That general has other duties—in military jargon, he wears other "hats"—the most important of which is commander in chief of the U.S.-ROK Combined Forces Command (CINCCFC).[7] In a command structure unique to Korea, CINCCFC serves two masters, the "National Command and Military Authorities" of both the United States and the Republic of Korea.[8] As the "warfighter," CINCCFC would prosecute any renewed war with those South Korean and U.S. forces allocated to him by their governments.[9]

The defense of the ROK is thus a responsibility shared by the United States and South Korea. In the event of a military crisis on the Korean peninsula, the United States would not have the luxury of deciding whether or not to intervene. That decision was made long ago, and North Korea knows that if it were to attack the South again, U.S. involvement would be "automatic"—U.S. troops would be under fire with the opening salvo of the war, triggering massive U.S. reinforcements.

Deterrence of North Korean aggression depends in large measure on U.S. troops being placed at risk, and there are fewer places more risky than the Korean peninsula, where more than a million soldiers face each other across the DMZ. But while deterrence in Korea is enhanced by the forward deployment of large numbers of U.S. military personnel, their presence in South Korea vastly complicates any attempt by the United States to employ a strategy of coercive diplomacy against North Korea, since such a strategy relies on the threat and/or exemplary use of force. Deterring the use of force by North Korea is one thing. The use of force to coerce North Korea is something entirely different. The risk of uncontrolled escalation is seen as simply too great, not only to U.S. forces but also to the forces and citizens of South Korea, whose territory would be a battleground in a renewed war.[10]

With forces twice the size of those of the U.S. military, the bulk of them deployed near the DMZ, North Korea has long posed a significant conventional military challenge to allied defense planners, but the prospect of its acquiring nuclear weapons fundamentally altered the nature of the threat. While necessary, conventional deterrence alone was no longer sufficient to address a threat that was on the verge of metastasizing into an enemy armed with nuclear weapons. "Deterrence plus" was needed in the light of these dramatically altered circumstances. Arriving at the "plus" would prove frustratingly difficult for the United States, South Korea, and the region as a whole. Before the crisis was finally defused, the United States seriously contemplated a preemptive strike to destroy North Korea's nuclear facilities, knowing that such an attack would in all likelihood trigger a war, but fearing that the North might lash out first with everything in its formidable arsenal, before the United States was ready to act.[11]

Regional Actors. U.S. relations with the ROK, marked by longstanding sensitivities in Seoul regarding any real or perceived diminution of U.S. support for the ROK, make the prospect of direct, bilateral interaction between Washington and Pyongyang a difficult alliance management problem for the United States. Washington must take into account the interests of Seoul, interests that are not necessarily identical (or, on occasion, compatible) with those of the United States. Policy coordination, even when the allies agree on overall objectives—keeping the peninsula free of nuclear weapons, for example—can be difficult. The zero-sum nature of South-North competition restricts U.S. freedom of movement and forecloses options that might exist were U.S.-DPRK interaction solely a two-player game. The imperative for the allies to present a united front to Pyong-yang has on occasion given Seoul a de facto veto over U.S. policy preferences.

The United States' room to maneuver vis-à-vis North Korea is further constrained by the interests of Japan, China, and Russia, the other major regional powers whose interests intersect (and have often clashed) on the Korean peninsula. Japan, also a treaty ally of the United States, is home to military bases essential to the defense of the ROK, making Japan a potential target for North Korea in the event of war. China shares a long border with North Korea and, despite a somewhat contentious relationship with the North since the end of the Cold War, remains the DPRK's closest ally, putting China in the position of potential spoiler in any attempt to coerce Pyongyang. While Russian influence in North Korea has waned since the breakup of the Soviet Union, Moscow nonetheless has a stake in the future of the peninsula. While Russia has largely been sidelined on Korean issues owing to its own domestic problems, its views cannot be ignored.[12]

Background to the Crisis

The IAEA and the NPT. Established in 1957, the International Atomic Energy Agency (IAEA) is an "independent intergovernmental, science and technology-based organization, in the United Nations family, that serves as the global focal point for nuclear cooperation."[13] It develops and promotes nuclear safety and assists member states in planning for and using nuclear power for peaceful purposes, such as the generation of electricity.

With the promulgation of the Nuclear Nonproliferation Treaty in 1970, the IAEA assumed the responsibility of verifying member states' compliance with the treaty's provisions.[14] To help ensure that nuclear materials are not diverted for military purposes, an agreement known as the IAEA Safeguards Framework Agreement (INFCIRC/153) for nonnuclear-weapons states (NNWS) was negotiated concurrently with the NPT. This Full-Scope Safeguards (FSS) agreement requires that all nuclear material be declared and placed under safeguards.[15]

The principal means by which the IAEA tries to guard against diversion of nuclear material is through a system of on-site inspections,[16] of which there are three types: ad hoc, routine, and special inspections. Should the IAEA suspect that a party to the NPT has not declared all its nuclear sites, it can "request" a special inspection. The request, which cannot legally be denied, has been described as a "nuclear hunting license."[17] Needless to say, special inspections have rarely been conducted, principally because, before the discovery after the Gulf War of the extent of Iraqi cheating, there was an assumption of honesty and complete disclosure on the part of member states.[18]

The IAEA has no indigenous intelligence capability and little ability to detect undeclared nuclear sites on its own. It is heavily dependent upon member states for information about suspected violations by other members.[19] Special inspections may be a hunting license, but the license is not unrestricted—the agency needs to know where to look. The IAEA also lacks both the mandate and the means to enforce compliance with the terms of IAEA and NPT membership. The agency cannot prevent noncompliance by a member state determined to cheat, and its inspectors "cannot shoot their way in" if a state refuses to provide access to a suspect site.[20] However, by the early 1990s, seared by its failure to detect cheating by Iraq, the IAEA was determined not to be fooled again.

North Korea's Nuclear Weapons Program. The North Korean nuclear program dates from the mid-1950s when the USSR and the DPRK signed two agreements to cooperate on nuclear research. In 1974 the North joined the IAEA, apparently to receive the technical assistance that membership affords. There are indications that in the late 1970s North Korea's supreme leader, Kim Il Sung, secretly directed that the North develop both an indigenous weapons capability and associated delivery systems. By early 1986 North Korea had brought a 30-megawatt (30MW[t])[21] experimental reactor on line at Yongbyon and was two years into the construction of a 200MW(t) reactor, with a completion date estimated at 1995. In 1987 the North began construction of a massive reprocessing plant—which it called a "radio-chemical laboratory"—capable of reprocessing two hundred tons of spent fuel a year. In addition, a 600–800MW(t) reactor was under construction at Taechon in the northwest of the DPRK, scheduled to be completed in 1998.[22]

At the urging of the United States, the Soviet Union, which shared U.S. concern over nuclear proliferation, persuaded the North to join the NPT in late 1985. States have eighteen months from the date of NPT entry to complete an IAEA FSS agreement. It would be over six years, though, before North Korea finally signed the required IAEA INFCIRC/153 safeguards agreement, which obligated the North to the ad hoc, routine, and special inspections that are standard provisions of such an agreement.[23]

In 1989 North Korea shut down the 30MW(t) Yongbyon reactor for an estimated one hundred days.[24] U.S. intelligence concluded that the refueling operation conducted during that period provided the North with enough plutonium for one to two nuclear weapons.[25] The 1989 refueling, along with the steady expansion of North Korea's nuclear infrastructure, the delay in signing the safeguards agreement, and data from "national technical means" (i.e., satellites and reconnaissance aircraft) convinced U.S. officials that North Korea was intent on secretly acquiring an indigenous, self-contained nuclear weapons capability. All the pieces were in place: domestically mined uranium; Soviet-trained technicians; a small, operational graphite-moderated reactor; spent fuel from which plutonium could already have been extracted; larger reactors in varying stages of completion; a huge reprocessing plant under construction to extract weapons-grade material from the spent fuel; a program to develop the high-explosive capability necessary to trigger a nuclear weapon; and a complementary program of increasingly sophisticated missiles designed to carry nuclear warheads.[26]

Nuclear Diplomacy. Information about the North Korean program became public in the summer of 1989. Following a highly classified briefing by U.S. officials, the ROK government leaked the news to the South Korean media, and the story was promptly picked up by the U.S. and international press.[27] Nuclear diplomacy from then on would play out under the watchful eye of the media.

Despite the long-standing U.S. policy to "neither confirm nor deny" (NCND) the existence of nuclear weapons in specific locations, it had been an open secret for years that U.S. forces in Korea had ready access to tactical nuclear weapons.[28] With the end of the Cold War, however, the Bush administration decided to dramatically reduce the number of nuclear weapons deployed worldwide, including in the ROK.[29] The removal of U.S. nuclear weapons, coupled with U.S. "negative security assurances," met two of North Korea's long-standing demands and helped foster a dramatic, albeit temporary, improvement in North Korean relations with the ROK and the United States.[30]

Following a series of high-level meetings in 1991, the ROK and the DPRK signed the Agreement on Reconciliation, Non-Aggression, and Exchanges and Cooperation between South and North Korea (known as the Basic Agreement), followed by the Joint Declaration for Denuclearization of the Korean Peninsula, which bans the development or possession of nuclear weapons, reprocessing facilities, and uranium-enrichment technology. The two sides established a Joint Nuclear Control Commission (JNCC) to implement the agreement, including inspections of each other's nuclear facilities.[31] On January 7, 1992, Seoul, with the concurrence of Washington, announced the cancellation of the annual ROK-U.S. Team Spirit military exercise. In return the North immediately announced that it would sign a safeguards agreement with the IAEA.[32]

In this improved environment the Bush administration agreed to a one-time meeting at the senior political level with North Korean representatives.[33] The North's nuclear weapons program was at the center of U.S. concerns. The U.S. representative, Under Secretary of State Arnold Kanter, made it clear that any improvement in U.S.-DPRK relations was conditioned on the North's implementation of IAEA safeguards *and* the South-North reciprocal nuclear inspections regime.[34]

Surprisingly, North Korea's initial declaration to the IAEA on May 4—mandatory under the safeguards agreement—was more detailed than required, including an admission that it had reprocessed ninety grams of plutonium in the past. In all, North Korea declared seven nuclear sites.[35] By the spring of 1992, the architecture to dismantle and eliminate the North Korean nuclear weapons program was in place.[36] The trick, as always in dealing with the North, was to get the DPRK to abide by its agreements.

The DPRK vs. the IAEA. Things began well enough. Shortly after receiving the DPRK's initial report, the IAEA began a series of ad hoc inspections to verify the accuracy and completeness of the North's declaration. Initially the North was cooperative, even allowing the inspectors to visit sites not included in its declaration—in essence, acceding to "special inspections."[37] However, given the nature of the regime in North Korea—and with the IAEA's credibility on the line following the Iraq debacle—IAEA inspectors proceeded aggressively on the assumption that North Korea was cheating, that it was hiding evidence of additional plutonium and undeclared facilities.

IAEA inspection teams visited North Korea six times between May 1992 and February 1993. The IAEA "requested" access to conduct special inspections of two undeclared facilities at Yongbyon suspected of being nuclear waste storage sites. The North had gone to considerable effort to disguise the size and purpose of the two facilities and refused to allow access to them, claiming they were military facilities unrelated to nuclear activities. North Korea's recalcitrance only fueled suspicions that it had something to hide, suspicions that were largely confirmed when laboratory analysis of evidence gathered during the ad hoc inspections revealed that North Korea had lied when it claimed it had processed only a small amount of plutonium for research purposes in 1989.[38] Scientific evidence showed that the North had produced plutonium in 1989, 1990, and 1991, strongly suggesting that the North had more weapons material than it had declared, perhaps enough for one or two crude nuclear weapons.[39]

On February 9, 1993, the director general of the IAEA, Hans Blix, again requested access to the two suspected waste sites and, in a show of the IAEA's post–Desert Storm determination not to be deceived again, gave the North ten days to respond, after which he would refer the matter to the agency's Board of Governors. The North refused, setting the stage for a confrontation with the board on February 21. Armed with highly classified satellite photos provided by the United States, Blix stunned the North Korean representative and the members of the board with compelling evidence of Pyongyang's clandestine nuclear program.[40] Following the briefing, the board gave Pyongyang one month to accede to inspections or the matter would be referred to the UN Security Council, which had the power to impose sanctions for failure to comply.[41]

Faced with the prospect of sanctions imposed by the United Nations (under whose flag sixteen nations had fought the North in the Korean War) and with evidence against it supplied by the United States (its principal adversary in the war and since), North Korea responded to the IAEA ultimatum with brinkmanship of its own. On March 12 Pyongyang, citing its "supreme interests" and warning that sanctions would be an act of war, announced its withdrawal from the NPT, effective upon the expiration of the required three months' notice.[42]

Nuclear Crisis

Summer 1993. In announcing its withdrawal from the NPT, North Korea had taken the world by surprise on an issue—the threat of nuclear proliferation—for which the stakes could hardly have been higher, with little time to respond.[43] North Korea had seized the initiative from the IAEA, as well as from Seoul (and Washington); it would retain the initiative for the duration on the crisis.

Pyongyang had moved the focus away from technical issues that few people other than experts understood—IAEA Full-Scope Safeguards, special inspections, the amount of plutonium that could be extracted from X amount of nuclear fuel given various equipment and techniques, and so on—and onto the imperative of keeping North Korea in the NPT. And by hinting that it might be willing to remain in the NPT and allow IAEA inspections if *the United States* met certain conditions, Pyongyang maneuvered Washington into doing what it had long refused to do: enter into a bilateral diplomatic process with North Korea. Only weeks after announcing its withdrawal from the NPT, Pyongyang accepted the Clinton administration's offer, in what came to be known as the "step-by-step approach," to hold bilateral talks aimed at keeping North Korea in the NPT.[44]

The first high-level U.S.-DPRK talks since January 1992 convened in New York in early June 1993. Late on June 11, only hours before its withdrawal from the NPT was to take effect, North Korea and the United States issued a joint statement in which they agreed to the principles of assurance against the threat and use of force, including the use of nuclear weapons; peace and security in a nuclear-free Korean peninsula, including impartial application of Full-Scope Safeguards; mutual respect for each other's sovereignty, and noninterference in each other's internal affairs; and support for the peaceful reunification of Korea.

In exchange for continued dialogue with the United States, North Korea agreed "unilaterally to suspend as long as it considers necessary the effectuation of its withdrawal" from the NPT.[45] There was no mention of IAEA special inspections, the subject that had sparked the crisis in the first place. In what would become a leitmotif of the crisis in the months ahead, brinkmanship had paid off for Pyongyang. "If North Korea's objective had been to seize the attention of Washington and to force it to negotiate seriously on a bilateral basis, its strategy had succeeded brilliantly."[46]

After a second round of talks in Geneva a month later, the two sides issued another statement in which the United States announced that it was "prepared to support the introduction of LWRs [light-water–moderated reactors, to replace North Korea's more proliferation-prone graphite-moderated reactors] and to explore with the DPRK ways in which the LWRs could be obtained." For its part North Korea agreed to "begin consultations with the IAEA on outstanding safeguards and other issues as soon as possible" and "to begin the North-South talks as soon as possible, on bilateral issues, including the nuclear issue." Once again, there was no mention of special inspections.

At the conclusion of the second round of talks, the chief U.S. negotiator, Robert L. Gallucci, issued a statement that the United States "would not expect to begin a third round . . . with the DPRK unless serious discussions with the IAEA and the ROK were underway."[47] Pyongyang had allowed the IAEA to maintain a presence in North Korea since the crisis erupted but had not allowed the agency to conduct inspections of any kind, which the North held hostage to progress in bilateral relations with the United States.[48]

In mid-September, with the North stonewalling the IAEA and the ROK, the United States attempted to turn up the heat on Pyongyang by announcing the indefinite postponement of the third round of U.S.-DPRK talks unless its conditions were met.[49] By that time the

IAEA was increasingly concerned about the degradation of its ability to monitor the seven facilities previously placed under safeguards. North Korea offered only limited access for "maintaining continuity of safeguards information."[50] Washington, hoping to avoid a confrontation between North Korea and the IAEA that would further complicate its own diplomacy with Pyongyang, urged the IAEA to accept the offer, but Blix refused, declaring that "[s]afeguards are not something you have à la carte, where a customer orders hors d'oeuvres and dessert. It is a whole menu."[51] Washington, which had rested its hopes for resolving the crisis on the IAEA and South Korea only six months earlier, was now discovering the difficulties of trying to reconcile its own agenda with that of the IAEA. It would soon discover similar problems with South Korea.

Fall 1993. In October North Korea, while steadfastly refusing to allow inspections or to engage the South, once again took the initiative, privately proposing a "package deal" with the United States rather than continuing the step-by-step approach begun in the spring. Specifically, Pyongyang proposed linking IAEA special inspections with the lifting of U.S. economic sanctions against the North, negotiations on diplomatic recognition, and the cancellation of Team Spirit.[52] With the United States slow to respond, the North repeated its "package deal" proposal publicly on November 11.[53]

Five days later, admitting that its approach to the North Korean nuclear challenge had failed, the United States abruptly shifted policy and notified North Korea that it would agree to convene the third round of high-level talks and cancel Team Spirit in return for a resumption of South-North dialogue and IAEA ad hoc inspections at declared facilities. And in a momentous decision whose ramifications were not fully understood at the time, special inspections of the two suspect waste sites would now be deferred under this new "comprehensive" approach, presumably to be negotiated between Washington and Pyongyang during the third round of talks. What had earlier been a precondition for a third round was now a U.S. agenda item to be addressed during the round.[54] "We've put the special inspections on the back burner for now," an administration spokesman said, "just to get the talks going again."[55] And on the back burner they would stay.

The administration was particularly concerned that the IAEA would declare the "continuity of safeguards" broken, triggering a crisis the administration was anxious to avoid.[56] Agency inspectors had not been allowed to conduct inspections of any kind since February 1993, and the batteries and film in the monitoring equipment installed at the seven declared sites needed to be replaced. An IAEA declaration of a break in continuity would move the locus of the crisis from Washington to the UN Security Council. As noted earlier, the Security Council had the authority to impose sanctions on the North, a step that Pyongyang had warned would be tantamount to a declaration of war. While officially the United States continued to brandish the threat of UN sanctions in an effort to pressure North Korea, by the fall of 1993 it was clear that the administration (as well as the South Korean and Japanese governments) wanted to avoid such a move for fear that the "wrong kind of pressure on the isolated North Korean government could cause it to lash out."[57] By agreeing to a package deal, Washington hoped that it would be able to persuade North Korea to allow IAEA inspectors to replace batteries and film before Blix felt compelled to declare what many believed already to be the case—that the continuity of safeguards was indeed broken.[58]

The U.S. "comprehensive approach," unveiled on November 16 in response to North Korea's call for a package deal, lasted exactly one week, a casualty not of the IAEA but of U.S. ally South Korea. At a meeting in the Oval Office on November 23, ROK president Kim Young Sam, heavily criticized at home for being a spectator as Seoul's archenemy negotiated the future of the peninsula with Seoul's only ally, blindsided his U.S. host, refusing to agree to any "package deal" or "comprehensive approach" between the United States and North Korea that was not preceded by the North's fulfilling its IAEA obligations and making progress in South-North dialogue.[59]

At a joint press briefing following the Oval Office ambush, President Clinton attempted to put the best face on the situation, saying that he and Kim had agreed to adopt a "thorough and broad" approach to North Korea. However, neither the two presidents nor their aides were able to describe what the term meant.[60] Kim went home boasting that "[t]he [South] Korean government will have final say on issues affecting the peninsula."[61]

At that moment the United States no longer had a policy, only a slogan. "Thorough and broad" was a bumper sticker without a bumper. According to Mitchell Reiss, "The administration had changed course but did not know where it was going or how to get there."[62] North Korea had continued to defy the United States, and Washington's relations with both Seoul and the IAEA were increasingly strained.

Winter 1993–94. As the administration cast about for a new approach, the safeguards system at Yongbyon continued to deteriorate. Director General Blix was edging ever closer to declaring that the IAEA could not certify that nuclear material had not been diverted for military purposes, and the United States continued to pressure him to avoid taking that step, although "[v]irtually all of the cameras and other surveillance equipment installed . . . [had] now run out of film and battery power."[63] For the next ten weeks the United States continued a working-level dialogue with North Korea over U.S. concessions in return for some degree of IAEA access. At the end of December, the United States apparently agreed to a limited, one-time inspection of the North's seven declared sites to replace batteries and film, reestablishing the safeguards system.[64] The IAEA balked again at this "à la carte" approach but eventually agreed.[65] Negotiations on the details, however, dragged on to the middle of February 1994. Finally, as Blix was about to report formally to the IAEA Board of Governors that the continuity of safeguards was indeed broken, the agency and Pyongyang agreed in principle on limited access to Yongbyon. By early March that opening had been expanded to include resumption of South-North talks in exchange for the cancellation of Team Spirit, followed by the opening of the long-delayed third round of U.S.–North Korea high-level talks on March 21.[66] There was optimism in Washington and Seoul that things were back on the right track.[67]

Spring 1994. The optimism was short-lived. In early March North Korea again prevented IAEA inspectors from taking samples that would help reveal the North's past reprocessing activities. But the inspectors had seen enough to determine that the North was continuing to expand its nuclear infrastructure, including its ability to reprocess spent fuel.[68] Then, two days before the third round of U.S.-DPRK talks was to begin, South-North talks collapsed in mutual recrimination, with the head of the North Korean delegation angrily declaring that North Korea would turn Seoul into a "sea of fire" in the event of war. The United States canceled the third round, rescheduled Team Spirit, announced the shipment of Patriot missile batteries to South Korea, and began trying to line up support for UN sanctions. South Korean armed forces were put on heightened alert, and the IAEA Board of Governors voted overwhelmingly to refer the matter to the UN Security Council. Diplomacy was dead in the water, replaced by threats of sanctions and warnings of war.[69]

On April 1 North Korea sharply escalated the crisis by shutting down the 30MW(t) reactor in preparation for a refueling operation.[70] The United States' shift away from special inspections, designed to determine what the North may have done in the past (a shift begun six months earlier with the stillborn "comprehensive approach"), was now virtually complete as Washington focused on preventing Pyongyang from reprocessing the spent fuel and adding to the one or two bombs' worth of plutonium it was suspected of already having. The United States was "faced with the highly dangerous prospect that North Korea could, within months, have five or six nuclear bombs and an active weapons program."[71]

In this increasingly high-stakes game of chicken, the allies once again flinched first. In the middle of April Seoul dropped its objections to a third round of U.S.-DPRK talks that was not preceded by South-North exchange of senior-level envoys, an objection that had contributed to the failure of South-North talks just a month earlier. A few days later the defense ministers of the United States and the ROK reversed their March decision on Team Spirit, offering once again to cancel the exercise if North Korea would agree to inspections.[72] The North ignored the offer.

The situation deteriorated rapidly in May. Pyongyang informed the IAEA early in the month that it was about to refuel the reactor and that the agency would be allowed to observe the procedure and count the spent fuel rods as they were extracted. However, asserting its "unique" status with regard to the NPT (neither fully in nor fully out), the North refused to allow the IAEA to follow its normal procedures of making detailed measurements from the rods, procedures that would help clear up questions about earlier refuelings and plutonium production.[73] The IAEA rejected the conditions.[74]

On May 2 and again on May 5, the United States threatened the future of high-level talks if the reactor were unloaded without the IAEA present to select and store fuel rods for further evaluation. The North responded on May 12 by informing the IAEA that it had already begun removing the spent fuel. On May 20, with about 5 percent of the rods removed and in cooling ponds, Washington again reversed course and offered to go to a third round in early June in exchange for what the IAEA had rejected earlier in the month—observing the removal and storage of the (remaining) spent fuel, with later access to be negotiated. Pyongyang's response was to stall. It agreed to meet with the IAEA; it also accelerated the pace of the unmonitored defueling operation, so that by the end of May the IAEA was on the verge of losing forever its ability to reconstruct North Korea's "nuclear past."[75] And on May 27 Pyongyang turned the tables on Washington, rejecting the U.S. offer of a third round of high-level talks.[76]

At a loss to explain Pyongyang's actions, and with its efforts to "induce North Korea to live up to its IAEA and North-South dialogue commitments" a failure, the administration at last prepared to go to the Security Council to push for UN sanctions, with the North reiterating its warning that "sanctions mean war, and there is no mercy in war."[77] On June 10 the IAEA imposed its own minor sanctions by terminating technical aid to North Korea, a largely symbolic action that nonetheless helped pave the way for UN sanctions as it was coupled with the IAEA's report to the Security Council that it could not guarantee the continuity of safeguards nor verify that North Korea was not diverting and reprocessing spent fuel.[78] On June 13 the crisis reached the boiling point when the North announced its immediate withdrawal from the IAEA and the expulsion of the last remaining IAEA personnel. While Pyongyang stopped short of completing its withdrawal from the NPT, without an IAEA presence at Yongbyon there would be no way of knowing whether the North was violating the treaty or not.[79]

On June 16, following a two-day review of the military plan for the defense of South Korea, the secretary of defense, William Perry, and the chairman of the Joint Chiefs of Staff, General John Shalikashvili, went to the White House to present the president with "a choice between a disastrous option—allowing North Korea to get a nuclear arsenal, which we might have to face someday—and an unpalatable option, blocking this development, but thereby risking a destructive non-nuclear war."[80]

The secretary of defense had publicly warned earlier in the spring that, even at the risk of a North Korean attack, the United States would not allow Pyongyang to build a nuclear arsenal. "We are going to stop them from doing that," he said at the end of March.[81] In early May he again warned that, while "we will not initiate [nor] provoke a war by rash action . . . we will not invite a war by neglecting appropriate defense preparations."[82] On June 16, with the understanding that "we were poised on the brink of a war that might involve weapons of mass destruction,"[83] the secretary presented the president with three options for the reinforcement of U.S. troops in Korea, "one of them by a very considerable increment," knowing that any such deployments might trigger a preemptive strike by North Korea.[84]

According to the secretary of defense, the president was within minutes of making a decision on which "flexible deterrent option" to order when the meeting was interrupted by an aide announcing that former president Jimmy Carter was on the phone from Pyongyang.[85]

Enter Jimmy Carter

Carter had arrived in Pyongyang the previous day on what was ostensibly a private visit.[86] In fact it was the latest mission in Carter's post–White House career as "diplo-evangelist."[87] Carter, who had been watching events on the peninsula with increasing concern in the spring of 1994, had been approached by an old friend from Atlanta, James Laney, the U.S. ambassador to Seoul, who convinced him that events on the peninsula were on the verge of spinning out of control.[88]

Anxious to halt what he saw as an inexorable march to war, Laney urged Carter in May to accept a standing invitation from Kim Il Sung to visit North Korea.

Carter did not enjoy the full trust of the White House or the Blue House (the South Korean presidential mansion); neither welcomed his intrusion into the crisis, but neither tried to block him.[89] So, after getting a "yellow light" from the White House (and a frosty reception in Seoul),[90] Carter and his small entourage headed north through the DMZ, beginning a mission tailor-made for Carter as global peacemaker specializing in dealing with international rogues and answerable only to a higher power.[91]

If Carter's intrusion was unwelcome in Washington and Seoul, it received just the opposite reaction in Pyongyang. Eager to make contact with the only U.S. president to advocate the withdrawal of U.S. forces from South Korea, Kim Il Sung had written a series of letters to Carter, beginning during the transition following Carter's victory in the 1976 election. In the early 1990s Kim had invited Carter several times to visit North Korea.[92] Having a former president as his guest would give Kim tremendous face both domestically and internationally, something that had eluded him for decades.[93] Kim certainly did not treat Carter as a "private citizen," nor did Carter conduct himself as such, immediately setting about negotiating an end to the crisis, remaking U.S. policy in the process.

Carter found a willing partner in Kim Il Sung, and the two quickly struck a deal. Carter committed the United States to a resumption of bilateral talks in return for Kim's agreeing to freeze his nuclear program under IAEA monitoring for the duration of the talks and "to consider a permanent freeze if their aged reactors could be replaced with modern and safer ones." Carter then called the White House, interrupting the council of war, and briefed Robert Gallucci, the president's point man for North Korea, on the terms of his and Kim's agreement. Having thus informed the White House, Carter next informed the world in an interview on CNN International.[94]

The following day Carter announced to Kim—again with the CNN camera rolling—something he knew to be false, that the White House had ceased all sanctions activity in the United Nations.[95] The administration immediately denied Carter's claim, but for all intents and purposes, sanctions were dead. Whatever support may have existed among Washington's regional allies and in the Security Council for sanctions evaporated with Carter's televised announcement of his breakthrough with Kim Il Sung.[96] Carter had always opposed sanctions, seeing them as an insult to North Korea and its "Great Leader" and the road to war.[97] Over the next several days, as the administration struggled to regain control over policy, the president and his lieutenants asserted that "nothing has changed" in their quest for sanctions as they attempted to verify and toughen the terms of the deal Carter had struck. The receipt of an official letter from North Korea acknowledging the terms of the agreement put the final nail in the sanctions coffin.[98]

Carter had gone to Pyongyang determined to kill sanctions, and he had succeeded.[99] In doing so he had effectively ended the crisis and created a new reality in which diplomacy would finally have a chance. The United States and North Korea quickly agreed to convene the long-delayed third round of talks. Even South Korean president Kim Young Sam, still adamantly opposed to U.S.–North Korean diplomacy at the expense of South-North interaction, was mollified by news from Carter that Kim Il Sung had agreed to meet him for an unprecedented South-North summit, scheduled for late July.[100]

Upon his return to the United States on June 19, Carter declared that the crisis was over, a pronouncement met with deep skepticism by the administration. But Carter was right. Despite the death of Kim Il Sung on July 8—the day the third round of talks convened—the two sides were able over the next few months to craft the Agreed Framework between the United States of America and the Democratic People's Republic of Korea, the formal capstone to Jimmy Carter's unprecedented diplomacy with Kim Il Sung.[101]

ANALYSIS

The North Korean Challenge

Only two weeks after North Korea announced its intention to withdraw from the NPT, its brinkmanship began to pay off. The new Clinton administration, agreeing with the new ROK government that "pressure alone will not work," signaled its willingness to offer a package of benefits in return for Pyongyang meeting its NPT and IAEA obligations.[102] A week before the first round of "high-level" talks in early June 1993, the head of the U.S. delegation—while insisting that the nuclear issue had to be resolved "on its merits" and that North Korea would have to "meet our objectives"—testified that the administration was "prepared to . . . address concerns that we regard as legitimate concerns that [the North Koreans] have raised."[103]

However, there was no mention of IAEA special inspections (and only boilerplate "support" for the South-North denuclearization agreement) in the joint statements issued at the conclusion of the bilateral talks in June and July 1993. Having agreed to "speak to" North Korean demands in the spring of 1993, the United States found itself stuck uncomfortably halfway between the old policy of low-level contact with the North in neutral settings and Pyongyang's insistence on full engagement with Washington as the key to resolving the nuclear issue. Having been maneuvered between North Korea and the IAEA, as well as between the two Koreas, Washington was unwilling or unable to go the full distance and impose its own policy preferences on either the IAEA or Seoul, limiting U.S. courses of action in confronting North Korea's nuclear challenge.

Pyongyang had fared considerably better. Four months after triggering the crisis, North Korea had successfully defied the international community on special inspections. It had attained its long-sought goal of an ongoing diplomatic dialogue with Washington, in the process relegating U.S. ally South Korea to the sidelines. It had marginalized the IAEA by transferring the matter of special inspections from a DPRK-IAEA context and onto the DPRK-U.S. negotiating agenda, where the United States was now "responsible" for resolving the crisis. Furthermore, having merely "suspended" its withdrawal from the NPT, North Korea now asserted its "unique status" within the treaty, neither fully in nor fully out, in effect making itself the arbiter of which treaty provisions applied to the DPRK.[104] Finally, having established a bilateral relationship with Washington, Pyongyang was positioned to play the United States, South Korea, and the IAEA off against one another on the nuclear issue, which it would do to great effect in the months ahead.[105]

North Korea quickly learned that its coercive tactics worked: it created problems with the IAEA and then argued (successfully) that these could be resolved only bilaterally with the United States. It was particularly adept at creating artificial "deadlines" (withdrawing from the NPT, refusing to allow IAEA film and batteries to be replaced at declared nuclear sites, and defueling the 30MW[t] reactor without IAEA supervision and sampling) to which the United States felt compelled to respond to keep the situation from deteriorating further. North Korea seized the initiative early and never relinquished it throughout the course of the crisis. How had an impoverished, isolated country of twenty-two million frustrated the international community in general and the United States in particular? In reality, North Korea was not nearly as weak as the sorry state of its economy may have suggested. Pyongyang enjoyed several distinct advantages in the contest of who could coerce whom in the 1993–94 nuclear crisis.

To begin with, the United States had simply been dealt a tougher hand than North Korea had been.[106] The United States was trying to play by the rules of the international system. Nonproliferation and the structures erected over the years to foster it (the NPT, the IAEA) were valued by the United States. The United States also valued its allies, partners in the Cold War and important sources of regional stability in the post–Cold War environment. The United States was never a unilateral actor in the Korean nuclear crisis; its actions were always influenced (and often restrained) by the requirement to protect international agreements and to factor in the positions and stakes of its international partners.

North Korea, in contrast, confronted the outside world with a singleness of purpose not enjoyed by the United States with its global responsibilities. While North Korea's nuclear aspirations were a clear challenge to vital U.S. interests, the survival of the United States was never in question. The survival of the regime in Pyongyang, however, *was* potentially at risk in its confrontation with the United States, and it devoted its resources accordingly. Moreover, North Korea played by the rules of the international system only on those rare occasions when doing so afforded it some immediate tangible benefit.[107] It had never had a real stake in the system, nor, by the early 1990s, did it have any reliable allies or friends. Self-consciously a "guerrilla nation" whose survival in an increasingly hostile world required unconventional methods, North Korea was relatively unconstrained in its choice of tactics throughout the crisis.[108]

North Korea enjoyed another advantage in the competition in risk taking—the mismatch in information available to the two sides. North Korea was an intelligence nightmare, "America's longest running intelligence failure" in the words of CIA veteran and former ambassador to South Korea Donald Gregg.[109] The United States had few independent resources other than satellites, spy planes, and electronic intercepts with which to gather information on the most closed society on earth. Other sources were significantly flawed. Information made available by the North was tightly controlled by the regime. The few foreigners allowed to visit were carefully selected and closely monitored, with no freedom of movement. North Korean defectors were few in number and hardly representative of the population at large.[110] What little information defectors could provide to the United States was subject to filtering by a South Korean intelligence system that was not always as forthcoming as Washington would have liked. The dearth of reliable information contributed to serious splits among U.S. intelligence analysts, further compounding an already difficult policymaking process.[111]

In this information vacuum, it was difficult for U.S. officials to get beyond the image of the North's leadership as irrational at worst, terrorists at best, of North Koreans as "wild people."[112] The lack of reliable intelligence tended to reinforce preconceived notions of the nature of the regime, complicating the ability of policymakers to gauge the seriousness of Pyongyang's harsh rhetoric, giving the North's threats perhaps more credibility than was warranted.[113] North Korea's image as a dangerous, unpredictable rogue state—well established by decades of the most egregious behavior—also contributed to the U.S. reluctance to engage at a senior political level.

On the other hand, the nature of U.S. society meant that the new president and his administration were an open book. Media critiques of the administration's performance during the period of the nuclear crisis were often harsh and highly personal, focusing as much on the president's perceived leadership deficiencies as on his administration's policies. Nowhere was this more true than in the realm of foreign and national security policy.[114]

The "image" of the United States created since the Korean War also may have worked against U.S. efforts at coercion. While the U.S. guarantee of South Korea's security had prevented the re-ignition of the Korean War, U.S. leadership of the allies' combined defense arrangement had also acted as a brake on South Korean desires to retaliate for Pyongyang's periodic attacks on South Korean (and U.S.) interests. The pattern of U.S. restraint since the war—in the face of often brutal provocations—may have contributed to a sense in North Korea that the United States was willing to accept any action short of another invasion, unintentionally reinforcing Pyongyang's penchant for brinkmanship.[115] To the extent that the North Korean leadership shared this image of the United States, Washington's reaction to Pyongyang's nuclear challenge through the spring of 1994 could only have emboldened it.

Dealing with the IAEA and with Allies

Concerns about the IAEA's record in dealing with Iraq's nuclear program notwithstanding, the Clinton administration, like its predecessor, had hoped that the burden of confronting North Korea's nuclear challenge could be borne by international organizations (principally the IAEA) and allies (principally South Korea). The North's refusal to cooperate with either soon dashed this hope, and Pyongyang's announcement of its withdrawal from the NPT convinced the administration it had little choice but to take the lead. Rather than go it alone, though, and risk damaging relations with both the IAEA and the ROK, the administration tried to split the difference, engaging the North directly, but largely in the name of, or as proxy for, the "international community" in general but especially for the IAEA and South Korea. The administration insisted that Pyongyang cooperate fully on IAEA safeguards and inspections as well as fulfill its obligations under the South-North joint denuclearization agreement as preconditions for progress in relations with the United States.

The administration discovered that tying itself to the IAEA and the ROK would bedevil its diplomacy and often put it at odds with its two "partners." Strains in the relationships quickly developed when the United States remained engaged with the North in the summer of 1993 despite Pyongyang's failure to satisfy U.S. preconditions. When the United States made commitments to the North, they were often on issues that required performance by, or at least the acquiescence of, the IAEA, the ROK, or both, cooperation that was not always forthcoming.[116]

The IAEA, smarting from its failure to detect Iraq's clandestine nuclear weapons program, was determined to reestablish its reputation and reassert its prerogatives—its "right of special inspections"—in North Korea.[117] It refused to recognize North Korea's claim to a "unique status" in the NPT, insisting on full compliance with all inspection requirements—ad hoc and routine, as well as special. It strongly protested any deviation from the North's Full-Scope Safeguards agreement worked out between Pyongyang and Washington, telling the Board of Governors in December 1993 that safeguards "are not subject to the course of discussions with other parties."[118] The IAEA was anxious to protect the global nonproliferation regime against a rogue member of the NPT and was wary of being seen as subordinate to, or dependent on, the United States as it attempted to fulfill its mandate.[119]

U.S. policy in the fall and winter of 1993 was a muddle. The administration was trying to regain control but was stuck uncomfortably between focusing on the past (IAEA special inspections to determine how much plutonium Pyongyang had produced between 1989 and 1991—the State Department's preference) and concentrating on the future (freezing the North Korean nuclear program so that it could not produce any more plutonium, while deferring special inspections—the Pentagon's preference).[120] The administration was also anxious to head off a declaration by the IAEA that it could offer no assurances that nuclear material had not been diverted for military purposes, a step that would trigger Security Council consideration of sanctions. With no one in the administration clearly in charge to force decisions and impose them on the bureaucracy, the administration found itself by the winter of 1993–94 in an uncomfortable straddle, signaling to the North its agreement to an unprecedented "one-time" inspection to (re)establish the continuity of safeguards, but then, in the face of a firestorm of criticism for giving in to the North, asserting that the number, type, and extent of inspections were matters for the IAEA to determine.[121]

While certainly not immune from international politics, the agency itself is not a political organization. With regard to the NPT, its mission is to uphold the provisions of the treaty; it has no authority to negotiate exceptions to, or deviations from, provisions of the treaty. The U.S. government, on the other hand, while desiring to uphold the treaty specifically and the norm against the spread of nuclear weapons generally, operates—unilaterally or as a representative of the "international community"—at the higher level of international diplomacy and security on issues ultimately dealing with war and peace. Effectiveness in the international system requires more flexibility than the narrow, technical orientation of the IAEA would allow.

To their mutual disadvantage, the United States and the IAEA never were able fully to reconcile their differences. Neither were the United States and the ROK. The problem for the administration in dealing with the IAEA was one of consistency—the agency's insistence on strict compliance with all NPT and Full-Scope Safeguards requirements. The problem in dealing with the ROK was its *lack* of consistency—Seoul's tendency to shift its stance at any given point to the opposite of Washington's.

When the crisis erupted in the spring of 1993, ROK president Kim Young Sam, worried that the United States might adopt an overly confrontational approach, dispatched his foreign minister to Washington to press successfully for a policy of engaging the North and offering a "package deal" of incentives to persuade it to remain in the NPT.[122] However, sensitive at being cut out of a direct role in the ensuing U.S.-DPRK meetings, Kim soon reversed course out of concern that the bilateral talks were conferring too great a degree of legitimacy on his rival in the North. In July, only three months after advocating a policy emphasizing "carrots" over "sticks," Kim began counseling toughness, complaining that the United States was being led on by a North Korean regime bent on acquiring nuclear weapons and warning that "time is running short" to stop the North from acquiring more plutonium.[123]

By the fall of 1993, however, Seoul was anxious to avoid the UN channel, concerned that Security Council action might trigger an attack by Pyongyang. That concern, though, did not stop Kim from scuttling Clinton's proposed "comprehensive approach" during the November 1993 Oval Office meeting, an approach designed to resolve the nuclear question in return for normalization of diplomatic and trade relations between the United States and North Korea.[124] Clinton's deference to Kim transcended policy coordination among allies; rather, it gave Kim a de facto veto over U.S. policy.

By the spring of 1994 Kim had reverted to a tougher stance. His insistence that progress in South-North dialogue precede resumption of U.S.-DPRK talks contributed to the cancellation of the March 21 third round, and it took Kim's approval before the Clinton administration would renew its offer to meet in April as the crisis escalated.[125] However, while Kim was publicly insisting on firmness—at least on South-North dialogue as a precondition for U.S.-DPRK talks—he was working behind the scenes against any sanctions initiative that the Clinton administration might attempt in the Security Council.[126]

Washington was experiencing difficulties with its other regional ally, Japan, as well. Relations with Tokyo, already in "dismal shape" as a result of the administration's "Japan bashing" over trade imbalances and other economic issues, were further strained over North Korea policy.[127] Concerned with the Clinton administration's handling of the nuclear crisis, Japan in the spring of 1994 began backing a Russian proposal for an eight-party international conference to seek a "balanced" approach to the Korea problem.[128] And, like the ROK, Japan was increasingly uncomfortable with the United States' threat of UN sanctions.[129]

Lack of High-Level Engagement

These U.S. disadvantages were exacerbated by the fact that Korea policy was an orphan for almost the entire duration of the crisis. North Korea had no domestic U.S. constituency, and senior officials in the new administration perceived little political payoff for dealing with one of the world's worst rogue states. North Korea was initially seen by the top ranks of government as "a nuisance, not a foreign policy priority." The secretary of defense (first Les Aspin and later William

Perry) and his staff were exceptions, but the rest of the government tended to think of the North Korean nuclear program as primarily a proliferation issue rather than a regional security challenge, which meant the State Department should have the lead. The "Seventh Floor" was not actively engaged, however, and for the duration of the crisis, the administration simply was not organized to deal with North Korea in a sustained, coherent manner.[130]

The new administration generally had difficulty finding its footing on foreign affairs, with both friends and foes around the world openly questioning Washington's management of an unruly post–Cold War world. As the Korea crisis escalated in the spring of 1994, Clinton was reportedly having second thoughts about the wisdom of sanctions and was becoming increasingly unhappy with his top national security aides. But the president was not engaged on a sustained basis, and he did nothing about sanctions or his staff.[131]

With no one in charge, getting decisions, and getting them to stick, was difficult. By October 1993 some officials were beginning to question the wisdom of backing the IAEA's demand for special inspections as a precondition for further talks with the North. The Pentagon had been uncomfortable with the position from the start. Demanding, and getting, special inspections would buttress the international norm against nuclear proliferation and help the IAEA regain some of its credibility, but inspections alone would not address the larger security threat posed by North Korea's weapons program; only freezing and eliminating the program could do that, which meant Washington would have to deal with Pyongyang.[132] But, complained one Pentagon official, "It was such a dysfunctional N.S.C. system at that time that nothing could get done."[133] The Pentagon's preference to defer special inspections, toward which the administration had begun edging in the fall of 1993 when it put special inspections on the "back burner, just to get . . . talks going again," was not fully adopted until the next spring, and at that point Pyongyang appeared to have stopped listening.

The Sanctions Threat

From the opening days of the crisis in March 1993, the administration attempted to wield two "sticks" in an effort to coerce North Korea into abandoning its quest for nuclear weapons: an explicit threat to seek UN sanctions and a thinly veiled threat, if all else failed, to use military force to prevent North Korea from proceeding further down the path to acquiring a nuclear weapons capability.[134] The credibility of the administration's threats eroded over time, however, so that by late spring of 1994, there were reasons for North Korea to question the administration's ability to deliver on either threat, which only added to the danger.

From the beginning of the nuclear crisis, there were actually two sanctions initiatives running parallel to each other, seemingly unrelated but in fact closely linked. The first concerned the Clinton administration's warnings of UN sanctions should North Korea fail to allow special inspections. At the same time, the administration was pondering what to do about renewing Most Favored Nation (MFN) trading status for the People's Republic of China. Candidate Clinton had criticized President Bush for "coddling" China in the aftermath of the Tiananmen massacre, suggesting that he would be tougher on China if elected.[135] On May 28, 1993, five days before the opening of the first round of high-level talks with North Korea, Clinton seemed to make good on his campaign promise by signing an executive order extending MFN status for one year but tying renewal in 1994 to China's making "significant overall progress" on human rights, prison labor, and nuclear nonproliferation.[136]

By the end of 1993, though, as Beijing continued to defy Washington on human rights, it was an open secret that the administration was looking for a way not to do what the president's executive order said it would do—revoke China's MFN status if it failed to meet the administration's conditions.[137] China had been confident all along that the 1993 executive order was a bluff, that the president had established criteria that in the end he would be unwilling to enforce.[138] China chose to call the president's bluff, administering a "diplomatic mugging" to the U.S. secretary of state during his visit to Beijing in March 1994 to press for compliance with the conditions codified in the president's order. China also cracked down harshly on human rights and democracy advocates, daring the administration to sacrifice the China market on the altar of human rights.[139]

In the end China prevailed. On May 27, 1994—the same day North Korea rejected the administration's offer to convene the third round of talks despite Pyongyang's unmonitored defueling of the Yongbyon reactor—the president abandoned his executive order, eliminating the link between trade and human rights and granting China permanent MFN status. It was a humiliating climb-down for the president, and he paid a high price in terms of credibility precisely when he needed it most—the moment of truth over North Korea's nuclear challenge.[140]

But the sanctions threat against North Korea was problematic even before the humiliation over China's MFN status. Sanctions raised three questions for which there were few good answers. First, could the United States make good on its threat? The administration hoped that if forced to make a choice, the other members of the Permanent Five would support, or at least not oppose, a sanctions resolution.[141] But China consistently signaled its opposition to sanctions and, with a veto in the Security Council, was positioned to block such a move.[142] UN sanctions rested on the assumption—the hope—that at worst China would abstain, but there was little evidence to support that hope; China had consistently declared its opposition to UN sanctions from the outset of the crisis.[143]

Second, in the event China chose not to block the resolution, would UN sanctions be effective? Even senior administration officials were skeptical, including the secretary of state, who questioned the efficacy of sanctions at the very moment the administration was trying to rally support for them in the Security Council in June 1994.[144]

Third, how would North Korea react if UN sanctions were imposed? North Korea's ability to "out-threaten" the United States was nowhere more clearly on display than in its reaction to the possible imposition of sanctions. Given the reputation of North Korea, its threat to treat sanctions as an act of war could not be dismissed as a bluff by the administration.[145] Simply stated, Pyongyang's threats were more credible than were Washington's. The fear that the "irrational" North might lash out militarily was never far from the minds of U.S. (or ROK and Japanese) officials, even among those who were confident of ultimate victory in a renewed war. The price of allied victory was seen as too great, and the North knew it, allowing Pyongyang to dominate the competition in risk taking.[146]

Years later Ambassador Gallucci stated there was no expectation that sanctions would have been effective.[147] So why sanctions? One critic has charged that the administration "did not want to be seen giving any inducements to North Korea for doing what any signatory was obliged to do under the Nonproliferation Treaty. It clung to sanctions as a shield against accusations of appeasement."[148] But the administration's policy from the beginning emphasized inducements over threats, offering North Korea incentives "for doing what any signatory was obliged to do under the Nonproliferation Treaty." Sanctions had always been held in reserve, with the administration's concerns about the possible consequences more prominently on display than were concerns that may have existed in Pyongyang over the impact of sanctions.

As had been the case with China and MFN status, it was clear by the fall of 1993 that the administration wanted to avoid having to act on its threat out of concern that North Korea might make good on its counterthreat to treat sanctions as an act of war. U.S. ambivalence made sanctions, already a tough sell to the "international community," that much harder. China's opposition was the biggest obstacle, but South Korea and Japan (as well as Russia) were also reluctant to endorse sanctions. Perhaps as a consequence of this resistance, the administration did not begin seriously trying to round up support for sanctions in the Security Council until early June 1994 and even then seemed not to have a clear vision of exactly how to proceed.[149]

But once the drive for sanctions had begun, the administration was determined to push ahead. Should the use of force become necessary, the administration felt that it first had to be seen by the international community as having exhausted all nonmilitary means of resolving the crisis. By June 1994 the administration was not merely posturing. Sanctions were intended to force Pyongyang to make a political choice. "Sanctions were a step back to the negotiating table if the North Koreans wanted to avoid them, or a step to war, one or the other. . . . I think the [North] Koreans understood that."[150]

It is not clear, however, that the North Koreans *did* understand the administration's resolve. From the beginning the administration had suffered a series of embarrassing foreign policy setbacks. It had been successfully defied in the Balkans, Somalia, Haiti, and most recently China. Each setback had taken a toll on the administration's credibility, and the history of U.S. concessions throughout the course of the Korean nuclear crisis only added to the perception of an administration easily thwarted. China had correctly read the administration's MFN threat as a bluff. North Korea, confronting the United States with an infinitely more serious challenge, appeared to misread the administration's UN sanctions threat as a bluff as well, a mistake with potentially devastating consequences.[151] North Korea's defiance in the spring of 1994 strongly suggests that the leadership in Pyongyang did not understand that, at the end of the day, the United States was determined to prevent it from acquiring a nuclear weapons capability, by force if necessary.

War in '94?

No one will ever know how close the United States and North Korea came to war in the summer of 1994, but, as Don Oberdorfer points out, people "closest to the decisions are among those who, in retrospect, rate the chances for hostilities to have been the highest."[152] And for good reason. Gallucci and others were concerned that they were witnessing the unfolding of a "Guns of August" scenario.

By the middle of June the North Korean strategy of coercion, which up to that point had worked so well, had finally failed: the DPRK was about to cross the one line in the sand drawn by the United States—the prohibition against the North acquiring any additional plutonium, something the United States was determined to prevent, by force if all else failed. North Korea had taken the first step on the slippery slope to war with its unmonitored refueling of the Yongbyon reactor. The United States responded by moving away from its failed strategy of emphasizing "carrots" over "sticks" to one of pure coercion—a drive for sanctions backed by threats to use force if necessary.

On June 16, as U.S. officials were beginning the push for sanctions in the Security Council, the president was being asked by the secretary of defense and the chairman of the Joint Chiefs of Staff to choose among three options to reinforce South Korea. The U.S. ambassador to the ROK has stated that as soon as he was informed of a presidential decision to send U.S. reinforcements, he would have ordered the evacuation of U.S. civilians from South Korea, an action that would have triggered the exodus of other foreigners as well.[153] Reinforcements and the evacuation of foreign noncombatants were simultaneously prudent and highly provocative.[154] U.S. reinforcements pouring in and U.S. and other foreign civilians pouring out were unlikely to be interpreted in Pyongyang as defensive moves.[155] North Korea had long warned that it would view sanctions as an act of war; moreover, senior U.S. military officers were worried that the North Korean leadership had learned from the Persian Gulf War that "if you plan to go to war with the United States, strike before they have built up their forces."[156]

One obvious way to avoid war was for North Korea to accede to special inspections. Less satisfactory but adequate in the short term would have been for Pyongyang to agree to convene the third round of talks with the United States. But North Korea had never wavered in its refusal to allow special inspections; moreover, the defueling of the 30MW(t) reactor was done in such a way as to all but destroy other means by which questions regarding past plutonium production could be addressed. All other roads seemed to lead to war:

- North Korea may well have acted on its threat to treat the imposition of sanctions as an act of war.

- Even if it did not, prudence required that sanctions be accompanied by U.S. reinforcements to enhance allied defense capability. But reinforcements would have triggered the mass evacuation of foreign civilians, and North Korea was unlikely to have interpreted reinforcements and civilian evacuations as deterrent moves. On the contrary, reasonably prudent decision makers in Pyongyang could have been expected to conclude that the United States and its allies were preparing to attack, giving the North huge—possibly irresistible—incentives to launch a preemptive strike.

- If the North did not launch a preemptive strike, the United States likely would have attacked the North's nuclear facilities before the fuel rods were moved from the cooling pond to the reprocessing center rather than allow North Korea to acquire an ever-greater nuclear weapons capability.[157]

The danger of war was very real, and no one understood it better than CINCCFC, General Gary E. Luck. Luck knew that a war on the peninsula would not be like Operation Desert Storm, with its quick victory and minimal allied casualties.[158] "I can win a war," he cautioned Washington; "I just can't do it right away."[159] And the cost of winning was potentially enormous. The Pentagon estimated that in the first three months of war there would be more than fifty thousand U.S. and nearly five hundred thousand ROK military casualties, an untold number of civilian casualties, and destruction of property running into the tens of billions of dollars, devastating the economies of South Korea and the entire region.[160] In addition, in the words of Luck's predecessor, "Seoul will be destroyed almost totally in less than a week. . . . I think everyone knows that."[161]

The Carter Mission

The administration had no one above the desk officer level working on the Korea problem full-time until Laney forced the issue with White House chief of staff Thomas "Mack" McLarty at the end of March 1994.[162] The idea of naming a senior envoy for North Korea attracted some interest within the administration. Certainly Laney and Perry favored the idea (as had Aspin before them, only to have the idea rejected by Lake);[163] Clinton, too, also showed some interest, taking advantage of a January 1994 visit to Pyongyang by the Reverend Billy Graham to send a message to Kim Il Sung. Nothing came of the gesture.[164] In May 1994 Clinton agreed to a Laney/Perry proposal to send Senators Sam Nunn and Richard Lugar as official envoys, but North Korea refused the trip.[165] Clinton had not sought out Jimmy Carter, but he posed no objections when informed of Carter's intention to go to Pyongyang. But perhaps because of his thinly veiled disdain for the former president, Clinton made no attempt to leverage the potential of Carter's quasi-official status as a former chief executive to establish a link to the only person in North Korea who really mattered, Kim Il Sung. Carter, on the other hand, with his affinity for the world's rogues and outcasts, seemed to understand instinctively that the only hope for resolving the crisis peacefully was to deal directly with North Korea's "Great Leader."

Given Carter's history since leaving the White House, Clinton and his top aides perhaps should have been more wary. From the beginning Carter had been "obsessed with being useful" to the new Democratic administration and desperate to be included in managing the world's trouble spots.[166] Clinton and his team, eager to avoid being linked in the public's mind with the failed Carter presidency, largely ignored him, seeming not to realize what Carter was capable of in his postpresidential career as a self-appointed crisis intervener, the "Saint Paul of conflict resolution."[167] While "many in the administration thought it disastrous for Carter to go" to North Korea,[168] Clinton nonetheless had had officials brief him[169] and detailed a Korean-speaking foreign service officer to serve as his interpreter. But there was no expectation that Carter would have any impact.[170] At the very moment the sitting president was being asked by his top defense officials to reinforce South Korea—by far the most important decision he would be asked to make in the entire crisis up to that point—the former president was meeting with the man those reinforcements were targeted against, with no apparent thought given in the White House that perhaps the two meetings might have some connection.

In his own words, Carter had departed for Korea "without any clear instructions or official endorsement."[171] Administration officials had not vetted the talking points Carter planned to use in his discussions with Kim Il Sung,[172] nor did they know that Carter had a CNN crew with him until minutes before he appeared live to announce the details of the agreement he had struck over the heads of the elected U.S. government.[173] "White House officials found themselves bystanders, gathered around the television like everyone else as Carter spoke by satellite to CNN White House correspondent Wolf Blitzer, only a few yards away on the White House lawn."[174] Administration officials were furious at becoming little more than spectators to what many thought was a North Korean ruse sold to a naïve, out-of-control do-gooder.[175] "'It looked as if we were contracting out our foreign policy, like we were bystanders . . . and had totally lost control of it,' a White House official later recalled."[176]

The second part of the statement was true enough. In an episode unique in the annals of U.S. diplomacy, the former president had not only embarrassed the incumbent president already under attack for his "feckless" foreign policy but also gutted the sanctions threat, the centerpiece of the administration's constricted set of options for contending with the North Korean nuclear challenge.[177] Once again, the White House was left scrambling to regain its footing and reestablish control over policy.[178]

CONCLUSION

In many ways the Korean nuclear crisis is a textbook example of coercive diplomacy—its strengths as well as the risks inherent in such a strategy. Of the two sides, North Korea succeeded in seizing and retaining the initiative, using threats and other forms of brinkmanship, manufacturing deadlines, and displaying a degree of consistency unmatched by the other side. The United States chose to employ inducements in an effort to persuade North Korea to meet its NPT and IAEA obligations, holding out the prospect of even greater rewards ("joining the community of nations"), but also holding in reserve the prospect of punishment in the form of UN sanctions and, if all else failed, military force to prevent North Korea from "going nuclear."

But the deficiencies of the administration in its first two years, partially revealed in other foreign policy crises, were on full view in dealing with the fundamental challenge to U.S. vital interests posed by North Korea's quest for nuclear weapons. In crisis after crisis the administration had waffled, wavered, and backtracked, squandering the essential element of coercive diplomacy, credibility. The new president and his administration inspired little fear or respect during the period of the North Korean nuclear crisis. None of the other crises confounding the administration had threatened the vital interests of the United States or endangered the lives of tens of thousands of its citizens, not to mention those of its allies. Yet each of these other challenges had extracted a price in terms of the image and reputation of the new administration, and the cumulative effect by the spring of 1994 was undeniable: U.S. credibility in Seoul, Tokyo, Beijing, Moscow, and especially Pyongyang had reached worrisome levels in a situation where the stakes were immense.

As had been the case in other crises, the Clinton administration's approach to the North Korea nuclear challenge was tactical and ad hoc. The administration had a "posture, not a policy," a desired outcome to the North Korean nuclear challenge.[179] But at crucial times, especially in November 1993, March 1994, and May 1994, the administration's preferred path had been unexpectedly blocked, leaving it with no compass, no map to get to its desired outcome, and vulnerable to the further manipulations of others—not just North Korea, but South Korea, the IAEA, and China as well.

Coercion had worked for the "extremely tough characters" in Pyongyang; in fact, it had worked too well, apparently blinding North Korea to the fact that it was about to cross the only real "red line" that the United States had—preventing North Korea from acquiring additional nuclear weapons capability.[180] At the end of the day, Kim Il Sung surely did not want war, but his penchant for brinkmanship tactics (which had been so effective) and the Clinton administration's penchant for offering incentives (which appeared endless) had finally reached their limits.[181] Bill Clinton surely did not want war either, but his inexperience, indecisiveness, disinterest in foreign policy, lack of a strategy, and mishandling of other crises appeared finally to have caught up with him.

Neither side had even attempted high-level diplomacy to achieve its goals. The president's point man, a career civil servant serving as an assistant secretary of state—the fourth level in the department's bureaucracy—had met with his North Korean counterpart only twice, in June and July 1993. For the next eleven months, on an issue that had a high probability of igniting a catastrophic war, the most senior U.S. officials in regular contact with North Korean representatives were a deputy assistant secretary and career officers from the State Department's Office of Korean Affairs.

In this diplomatic vacuum the two sides were prevented from falling over the edge only by the unexpected—and unprecedented—intrusion of Jimmy Carter into the crisis. Carter, appalled that Clinton had not sent a senior envoy to North Korea,[182] was uniquely qualified to fill the void. The only living former Democratic president, Carter was also a former nuclear submariner with a detailed understanding of nuclear technology. Moreover, he had had a relationship, albeit episodic and long-distance, with Kim Il Sung for years and, most important, he had an open invitation to visit North Korea. Finally, while Carter had shown little regard for the prerogatives of his successors, his antipathy for Bill Clinton was particularly strong and personal.[183] It does not appear that he hesitated long before launching the mission that would resolve the nuclear crisis.

Carter's actions were as outrageous as they were essential. It is hard to imagine Carter's doing what he did under any other administration; it is equally difficult to imagine his intervention being necessary under any other administration. Sensing danger, Carter had seen the smallest of openings and seized the opportunity, meeting with Kim Il Sung face-to-face and crafting a solution to his liking over the head of the administration. By killing sanctions, Carter stopped the march to war and created an environment conducive to real diplomacy. But the resulting Agreed Framework between the United States and North Korea did not end the crisis—Jimmy Carter did. There would have been no Agreed Framework had Carter not gone to Pyongyang.

The Agreed Framework, signed on October 21, 1994, was (and remains) highly controversial, but it was seen as good enough to satisfy both the Clinton administration and Pyongyang in the immediate aftermath of Carter's trip. The administration got enough on nonproliferation up front (a verifiable freeze on known nuclear activity in the North), with the promise of getting it all in the future (special inspections to "resolve the nuclear past" and a dismantling of the North's weapons program). Perhaps most important for the administration, the Agreed Framework got the issue off the president's desk.

North Korea got enough up front to save face (direct engagement with the United States) as well as heavy fuel oil for immediate energy needs, with the promise of the future provision of light-water reactors and the easing of economic sanctions, increased aid and trade, and diplomatic recognition from Washington. Perhaps most important for the regime in Pyongyang, the crisis, Carter's visit, and the Agreed Framework together buttressed the central myth—in this case, the reality—upon which the Kim Il Sung system, and hence the DPRK, rests: the ability, unique in the long history of Korea, of the "Great Leader" to stand up to outside powers.

Dealing with North Korea has always been a difficult, unappealing, and frustrating task. At no time was this more true than in the 1993–94 nuclear crisis. The new U.S. administration tried to engage the North, offering inducements in an effort to resolve peacefully the challenge posed by its nuclear weapons program while holding in reserve the stick of United Nations sanctions, and the even bigger stick of military action, should inducements and pressure both fail. Ultimately, the administration was willing to go to war rather than allow North Korea to progress further toward a nuclear weapons capability. In the end, coercive diplomacy had failed for both North Korea and the United States. War was prevented only by the most unlikely of factors, the intervention of former president Jimmy Carter.

AFTERWORD

Critics of the Agreed Framework have charged that it sets a dangerous precedent by giving in to nuclear blackmail and rewarding the bad behavior of an inherently untrustworthy regime. Its defenders have countered that the Agreed Framework is not based on trust but on a series of reciprocal and verifiable steps that, among other things, ensures that North Korea will not receive the critical components of the light-water reactors unless and until it satisfactorily resolves questions about its past nuclear weapons activities and dismantles its graphite-moderated reactors and related facilities. Moreover, critics were initially assured sotto voce that North Korea—in dire economic straits, unable to adequately feed its citizens, and under the leadership of a supposedly sick and erratic Kim Jong Il[184]—would collapse before the provisions of the Agreed Framework would have to be met.[185]

However, as time wore on—and in the absence of North Korea's collapse and any clear evidence of nuclear cheating on Pyongyang's part—the Agreed Framework became the foundation for a U.S. policy of engaging the DPRK. Up to the fall of 2002, the agreement had withstood a number of mini-crises,[186] a change of administrations in South Korea, and a 1999 review of U.S. policy toward North Korea by the outgoing Clinton administration, followed by a similar review at the outset of the Bush administration.[187]

While North Korea remained a rogue state in the eyes of much of the world, as of the early fall of 2002 its nuclear weapons ambitions were thought to be contained by a structure of international agreements. Of these, the Agreed Framework with the United States was arguably the cornerstone. Its major feature was to freeze North Korea's plutonium-based nuclear weapons program, but it also envisioned "an overall resolution of the nuclear issue" on the peninsula by creating a link to the South-North joint denuclearization agreement of February 19, 1992, in which the North pledged not to "test, manufacture, produce, receive, possess, store, deploy or use nuclear weapons" or "to possess nuclear reprocessing and *uranium enrichment* facilities."[188] In addition, North Korea was still a member of the Nonproliferation Treaty.[189] And, while the North remained formally outside the IAEA, it continued to allow IAEA monitoring personnel to remain at Yongbyon in accordance with the Agreed Framework; moreover, the North's IAEA safeguards agreement was still in force.[190]

In early October 2002 North Korean officials surprised the United States and the rest of the world by admitting, in the face of evidence gathered by U.S. intelligence, to having a clandestine nuclear weapons program based on highly enriched uranium (HEU). The program, reportedly begun in 1997, is a clear violation of all four of these international agreements and potentially undermines the entire structure of engagement that the United States, South Korea, Japan, the European Union, and others have constructed since 1994.

For the second time in a decade, North Korea had been caught cheating, and again it reverted to brinkmanship, warning that, in addition to its new nuclear weapons program, it has "more powerful things as well."[191] Several weeks after its "confession," though, North Korean officials, describing themselves as "stunned" by the Bush administration's suspension of its offer to engage Pyongyang and its attempts to increase international pressure on Pyongyang, suggested that it might be willing to negotiate away its HEU program in return for a nonaggression pact and security guarantees from Washington.[192]

As of February 2003, the United States, while repeating its desire to resolve the new nuclear crisis in a peaceful manner, was insisting that North Korea make the first move by visibly and verifiably dismantling its HEU program. On the basis that North Korea had much more to lose in 2003 than it had had in 1994, Washington has tried to work with allies and friends (including China) to present North Korea with a united front. Its initial efforts in that regard appeared successful; on November 14 the executive board of the Korea Peninsula Energy Development Organization (KEDO, the international consortium created to implement the provisions of the Agreed Framework), condemned North Korea for its pursuit of nuclear weapons, voted unanimously to suspend delivery of heavy fuel oil, and, in an apparent reference to LWRs, warned that it would "review other KEDO activities with North Korea."[193] North Korea, however, responded by expelling IAEA inspectors, withdrawing from the NPT, and unfreezing the facilities at Yongbyon.

The Agreed Framework now appears to be a dead letter. Political support for the agreement all but disappeared in the United States and diminished elsewhere in light of North Korea's cheating and subsequent escalatory steps. But the facilities and material at Yongbyon are still the quickest means for North Korea to add to its nuclear arsenal, and North Korea's moves to do exactly that have once again plunged the peninsula into crisis.

Coercive diplomacy failed in the first nuclear crisis. Will it succeed in the second? There are different leaders in Washington and Pyongyang this time, each attempting to impose his will on the other. The international context is also very different. In the aftermath of the terrorist attacks of September 11, 2001, the U.S. president declared that North Korea was part of a new "axis of evil" and warned that "the United States of America will not permit the world's most dangerous regimes to threaten us with the world's most destructive weapons."[194]

The president's rhetoric, and his tough initial response to North Korea's HEU program, is clearly designed to coerce Pyongyang to give up its nuclear weapons ambitions. If the North does not comply, President Bush will then be confronted with starker choices even than those faced by his predecessor. To paraphrase the words of the secretary of defense in 1994, President Bush will have to choose between a disastrous option—allowing North Korea to get an ever-larger nuclear arsenal, which we might have to face someday—and an unpalatable option—blocking this development, but thereby risking a destructive war in which nuclear as well as chemical and biological weapons may be used.

NOTES

The views expressed herein are the author's and do not necessarily represent those of the United States Institute of Peace. The author would like to thank Robert Art, Patrick Cronin, Richard Solomon, Paul Stares, Jim Cornelius, Dan Snodderly, and Nigel Quinney, without whose support this chapter would not have been completed. In addition, the author owes a debt of gratitude to the following individuals, all of whom made indispensable substantive contributions (and none of whom is responsible for any errors of fact or interpretation): Robert Gallucci, Charles Kartman, James Laney, Stephen Linton, Gary Luck, William McKinney, William Pendley, and Robert Sennewald.

1. Warren Christopher, quoted in Leon V. Sigal, *Disarming Strangers: Nuclear Diplomacy with North Korea* (Princeton, N.J.: Princeton University Press, 1998), 198–199.

2. William J. Perry, speech before the Council on U.S.-Korean Security Studies, Washington, D.C., October 26, 1995.

3. Anthony Lake, "A Year of Decision: Arms Control and Nonproliferation in 1995," *Nonproliferation Review* (winter 1995): 57.

4. The treaty was signed on October 1, 1953, and entered into force on November 17, 1954.

5. The Armistice Agreement was signed on July 27, 1953, by U.S. general Mark Clark in his capacity as commander in chief of United Nations Command; Marshall Kim Il Sung, supreme commander of the (North) Korean People's Army; and General Peng Teh-Huai, commander of the Chinese People's Volunteers. The Armistice Agreement was to stay in effect until "an appropriate agreement for a peaceful settlement at a political level" formally ended the war.

6. See Patrick M. Norton, "Ending the Korean Armistice Agreement: The Legal Issues," Northeast Asia Peace and Security Network, Virtual Forum #2, March 1997, www.nautilus.org/fora/security/2a_armisticelegal _norton.html.

7. In the period examined in this chapter, CINCCFC, in addition to being the commander of USFK, had five other "hats": commander in chief,

United Nations Command (CINCUNC); commanding general, Eighth U.S. Army; commander of the ground component commands of both CFC and UNC; and a position known as Senior U.S. Military Officer Assigned to Korea, which enabled the incumbent to represent the chairman of the Joint Chiefs of Staff in certain bilateral meetings. "Command Relations Briefing," 1993, Headquarters U.S.-ROK Combined Forces Command, copy in author's possession.

8. The U.S.-ROK National Command and Military Authorities are the president and secretary of defense of the United States and the president and the minister of national defense of the ROK.

9. It is often asserted—erroneously—that a U.S. general (CINCCFC) "commands" the armed forces of the ROK (e.g., Sigal, *Disarming Strangers*, 44). Correctly stated, CINCCFC exercises "operational control" over those forces—U.S. as well as ROK—assigned to him at the discretion of the National Command and Military Authorities of the two nations. Under normal armistice conditions ("peacetime" in Korea), CINCCFC has but a handful of troops under his operational control.

10. Steven Greenhouse, "Administration Defends North Korea Pact," *New York Times*, January 25, 1995, A6.

11. North Korea, with a population of only twenty-two million, has the world's fourth-largest military.

12. Alexander Zhebin, "Russia and North Korea: An Emerging, Uneasy Partnership," *Asian Survey* 35, no. 8 (1995): 726–739; and Stephen Blank, "Russian Policy and the Changing Korean Question," *Asian Survey* 35, no. 8 (1995): 711–725.

13. IAEA Mission Statement, www.iaea.org. As of 1992, 110 countries were members of the IAEA. Tai Ming Cheung, "Ready for Inspection," *Far Eastern Economic Review* (June 4, 1992): 25.

14. Membership in the IAEA and NPT is voluntary. States are free to join one, both, or neither.

15. "Director General's Statement to the Board of Governors on the Democratic People's Republic of Korea," June 7, 1994, www.fas.org/news/un/dprk/dgbg1994n01.html; and Wolfgang Fischer and Gotthard Stein, "On-Site Inspections: Experiences from Nuclear Safeguarding," *Disarmament Forum* 3 (1999): 46.

16. Mohamed IlBaradei, "Special Comment," *Disarmament Forum* 3 (1999): 3–5.

17. While there are technical differences between the two, ad hoc and routine inspections are similar. The main difference is whether the site to be

inspected is covered by a "facility attachment agreement" between the state and the IAEA. If it is not, the inspection is ad hoc; if it is, the inspection is routine. Fischer and Stein, "On-Site Inspections"; and Mitchell Reiss, *Bridled Ambition: Why Countries Constrain Their Nuclear Capabilities* (Washington, D.C.: Woodrow Wilson Center Press, 1995), 241–242, 294 n. 35.

18. The number of special inspections conducted by the IAEA since its creation is not clear. Some experts assert that none have ever been performed; others suggest one or two (conducted with the full cooperation of the member state). What is clear is that "adversarial" special inspections—when the IAEA demands access to undeclared sites suspected of being nuclear weapons related—is a product of the post–Desert Storm revelations in Iraq. See Paul Lewis, "U.N. Maps Plan to Nab Atomic Cheats," *New York Times*, October 11, 1991, A10; and "Statement of IAEA Director General regarding DPRK at Informal Briefing of UN Security Council," April 6, 1993, www.fas.org/news/un/dprk/dgsp1993n10.html. Before the Gulf War, lesser-developed nonnuclear weapons states (NNWS) such as Iraq, with modest declared nuclear capabilities, received relatively little scrutiny from the IAEA, which unwittingly contributed to an environment where threats to the nonproliferation regime could emerge from within the ranks of NPT members. IlBaradei, "Special Comment," 5; and Sigal, *Disarming Strangers*, 18.

19. IlBaradei, "Special Comment"; Sigal, *Disarming Strangers*, 18; and Rich Hooper, "The IAEA's Additional Protocol," *Disarmament Forum* 3 (1999): 12.

20. Hans Blix, interview, *Arms Control Today* (November 1991): 4. There are no international legal prohibitions against a state's acquiring nuclear weapons; ironically, membership in the IAEA and the NPT could be a "fast track" to nuclear weapons for a state determined to acquire them. Member states receive technical assistance from the IAEA for help in the peaceful uses of nuclear power. In a program that began before, and continued throughout the duration of the nuclear crisis, IAEA personnel were teaching North Koreans how to locate and mine indigenous uranium deposits. John J. Fialka, "North Korea May Be Developing Ability to Build Nuclear Weapons," *Wall Street Journal*, July 19, 1989. Furthermore, there is nothing in the NPT charter that precludes stockpiling plutonium. The nightmare scenario is that a state would join the IAEA and the NPT, receive assistance with its supposedly peaceful nuclear program, extract plutonium from spent fuel rods under IAEA supervision, stockpile as much plutonium as it wished, then quit the NPT and proceed to make nuclear weapons—all within the letter, if not the spirit, of the IAEA and the NPT. Leonard S. Spector and Jacqueline R. Smith, "North Korea: The Next Nuclear Nightmare?" *Arms Control Today* (March 1991): 10;

Andrew Mack, "North Korea and the Bomb," *Foreign Policy* 83 (1991): 96; Andrew Mack, "The Nuclear Crisis on the Korean Peninsula," *Asian Survey* 33, no. 4 (1993): 346–347; Ronald F. Lehman, "Some Considerations on Resolving the North Korean Nuclear Question," *Korean Journal of Defense Analysis* 6, no. 2 (1994): 22; Leonard S. Spector, "Kim Il Sung's Legal Loophole," *Far Eastern Economic Review* (July 7, 1994): 30; and Bruce E. Nelan, "Diplomacy," *Time*, July 4, 1994, www.time.com/time/magazine/archive/1994/940704.diplomacy.html.

21. Since there are no power lines connected to the reactor, this chapter will follow the helpful example of Mitchell Reiss, who has pointed out that "[a]ll nuclear reactors can be described in terms of either their thermal (t) or their electrical (e) capacity. The Yongbyon reactor has been characterized as either a 30 MW(t) or a 5 MW(e) reactor; this has sometimes given rise to confusion. Since its purpose was not to generate electrical power, it will be referred to as a 30 MW(t) reactor." Reiss, *Bridled Ambition*, 289 n. 3. For the same reason, the reactors under construction in North Korea during the events described in this chapter have been identified as 200MW(t) and 600–800MW(t) reactors, respectively.

22. Alexandre Y. Mansourov, "The Origins, Evolution, and Current Politics of the North Korean Nuclear Program," *Nonproliferation Review* (spring-summer 1995): 25–27; Kongdan Oh and Ralph C. Hassig, "North Korea's Nuclear Program," in *Korea and the World: Beyond the Cold War*, ed. Young Whan Kihl (Boulder, Colo.: Westview Press, 1994), 234–235; Young Whan Kihl, "Confrontation or Compromise on the Korean Peninsula: The North Korean Nuclear Issue," *Korean Journal of Defense Analysis* 6, no. 2 (1994): 107; Reiss, *Bridled Ambition*, 234; Don Oberdorfer, *The Two Koreas: A Contemporary History* (Reading, Mass.: Addison-Wesley, 1997), 253. Kim Il Sung may have been motivated to seek a nuclear weapons capability in part by the discovery of a similar effort by the ROK earlier in the decade, an effort uncovered—and stopped—by the United States. For background on the South Korean program, see Mitchell Reiss, *Without the Bomb: The Politics of Nuclear Nonproliferation* (New York: Columbia University Press, 1988), 78–108; and Michael J. Engelhardt, "Rewarding Nonproliferation: The South and North Korean Cases," *Nonproliferation Review* (spring-summer 1996): 31–33. If completed, the 200MW(t) and 800MW(t) reactors together could produce plutonium sufficient for up to forty-five nuclear weapons a year, giving North Korea the capacity of "turning out plutonium like sausages." Under Secretary of Defense Walter Slocombe, quoted in Kongdan Oh and Ralph C. Hassig, *North Korea through the Looking Glass* (Washington, D.C.: Brookings Institution Press, 2000), 203.

23. A bureaucratic snafu—the IAEA initially sent North Korea the wrong form—contributed to the delay. The main reason, however, was the North's insistence on two preconditions: that U.S. tactical nuclear weapons be removed from the ROK and that the United States provide a "negative security assurance" that it would not use nuclear weapons against the North. Don Oberdorfer and T. R. Reid, "North Korea Issues Demand for Mutual Nuclear Inspections," *Washington Post*, June 21, 1991, A19; Mack, "North Korea and the Bomb," 90; and Reiss, *Bridled Ambition*, 236, 294 n. 35.

24. Robert S. Greenberger and Steve Glain, "How U.S., North Korea Went from Promise to Peril in Two Years," *Wall Street Journal*, June 8, 1994, A1.

25. R. Jeffrey Smith, "N. Korea and the Bomb: High-Tech Hide and Seek," *Washington Post*, April 27, 1993, A1. Eight to ten kilograms of plutonium are required to produce a weapon.

26. Reiss, *Bridled Ambition*, 234.

27. Fialka, "North Korea May Be Developing Ability to Build Nuclear Weapons"; Don Oberdorfer, "North Koreans Pursue Nuclear Arms," *Washington Post*, July 29, 1989, A9; and Oberdorfer, *Two Koreas*, 256.

28. During a public hearing in 1974 Senator Stuart Symington revealed that the United States had nuclear weapons stationed in the ROK. Nine months later the secretary of defense confirmed this in a press conference. Reiss, *Without the Bomb*, 292 n. 16.

29. David E. Rosenbaum, "U.S. to Pull A-Bombs from South Korea," *New York Times*, October 20, 1991, A3. On December 18, 1991, South Korean president Roh announced that there were no nuclear weapons in the ROK. At a press conference in Seoul the next month, President Bush, while unwilling explicitly to deviate from the NCND policy, said he was "not about to argue" with Roh. Sigal, *Disarming Strangers*, 30; and Byung Chul Koh, "Confrontation and Cooperation on the Korean Peninsula: The Politics of Nuclear Proliferation," *Korean Journal of Defense Analysis* 6, no. 2 (1994): 58.

30. North Korea sought a formal commitment that the United States would not use nuclear weapons against it (a pledge the United States had made to all NNWS members of the NPT). See George Bunn, "The Legal Status of U.S. Negative Security Assurances to Non-Nuclear Weapon States," *Nonproliferation Review* (spring-summer 1997): 1–17.

31. Shim Jae Hoon, "Unity of Purpose," *Far Eastern Economic Review* (January 9, 1992): 10; and Oberdorfer, *Two Koreas*, 264. The Joint Declaration "went further than any other arms control agreement in history and far exceeded what was required by the NPT and IAEA safeguards agreement." Reiss, *Bridled Ambition*, 239.

32. North Korea signed the agreement on January 30, and it was ratified by the rubber-stamp Supreme People's Assembly on April 9. Sigal, *Disarming Strangers*, 31, 32; and Oberdorfer, *Two Koreas*, 267. Article 73 of the agreement specifies that "the Agency may make special inspections . . . if the Agency considers that information made available by the Democratic People's Republic of Korea . . . is not adequate for the Agency to fulfill its responsibilities under this Agreement." For the text of the agreement, see www.fas.org/news/un/dprk/inf403.html.

33. The meeting was held on January 22, 1992.

34. Reiss, *Bridled Ambition*, 239; and Sigal, *Disarming Strangers*, 37.

35. The North's inventory of nuclear facilities included the 30MW(t) reactor, the "radio-chemical laboratory," the 200MW(t) and 600–800MW(t) reactors under construction, a nuclear fuel rod fabrication and storage plant, uranium mines, and plans for three additional reactors. Koh, "Confrontation and Cooperation on the Korean Peninsula," 59; Sigal, *Disarming Strangers*, 39; Reiss, *Bridled Ambition*, 242; and Smith, "N. Korea and the Bomb."

36. Lehman, "Some Considerations on Resolving the North Korean Nuclear Question," 12.

37. Reiss, *Bridled Ambition*, 241–242, 245.

38. "The plutonium declared and analyzed and the nuclear waste declared and analyzed are like two gloves which didn't match. There should be two more gloves to match the pair which we have seen and analyzed." "Statement of IAEA Director General regarding DPRK at Informal Briefing of UN Security Council."

39. Workers had attempted to make one facility at Yongbyon—a two-story structure connected to the "radio-chemical laboratory" by underground pipes—appear to be a one-story building by piling dirt around the walls up to the second floor. IAEA inspectors had been allowed to visit the top floor in September 1992 (their North Korean escorts denied that there was another floor below). Requests for return visits were denied. The other suspect facility had been completely buried and the surface landscaped with trees and other plants, all of which quickly died, presumably from contamination from nuclear waste stored within. Smith, "N. Korea and the Bomb"; Don Oberdorfer, "Gates Remains Suspicious of N. Korea," *Washington Post*, January 12, 1993, A17; and R. Jeffrey Smith, "West Watching Reactor for Sign of N. Korea's Nuclear Intentions," *Washington Post*, December 12, 1993, A49. See also Reiss, *Bridled Ambition*, 246; Sigal, *Disarming Strangers*, 19, 33; Kihl, "Confrontation or Compromise on the Korean Peninsula," 107–109; and Oberdorfer, *Two Koreas*, 267.

40. Smith, "N. Korea and the Bomb." While the CIA had long provided the IAEA with satellite photographs, it had refused to allow the IAEA to show them to the Board of Governors, whose thirty-five members included states unfriendly to the United States. After a debate with both the outgoing Bush administration and the incoming Clinton administration, the CIA eventually provided the IAEA with high-quality photos of Yongbyon to use at the February 21 briefing (the resolution of the photos was slightly distorted to avoid revealing the full extent of U.S. spy satellite capabilities).

41. Reiss, *Bridled Ambition*, 249–250; Mack, "Nuclear Crisis," 339; and Sigal, *Disarming Strangers*, 49.

42. Mack, "Nuclear Crisis," 339; and Koh, "Confrontation and Cooperation on the Korean Peninsula," 60.

43. Oberdorfer points out that North Korea's decision to withdraw from the NPT should not have been a surprise, that North Korea had signaled for some time that it might withdraw. Oberdorfer, *Two Koreas*, 280. See also Mack, "North Korea and the Bomb," 91.

44. Reiss, *Bridled Ambition*, 251–253. North Korea conditioned meeting its IAEA and NPT obligations on security assurances from the United States, inspection of U.S. military bases in South Korea, and the cancellation of Team Spirit.

45. Reiss, *Bridled Ambition*, 254; and Koh, "Confrontation and Cooperation on the Korean Peninsula," 61. For the text of the statement, see Sigal, *Disarming Strangers*, 260.

46. Oberdorfer, *Two Koreas*, 287.

47. Quoted in Sigal, *Disarming Strangers*, 70.

48. Ibid., 65–66. IAEA inspectors did visit Yongbyon in August, but just once, at night, the facilities illuminated only by the inspectors' flashlights. They were permitted to replace only some of the batteries and film in the monitoring equipment installed during the 1992 ad hoc inspections. John J. Fialka, "Check of North Korean Nuclear Sites Won't Provide Comfort Clinton Wants," *Wall Street Journal*, January 31, 1994, A14. And despite its July pledge, the North also refused to discuss the nuclear issue in the South-North Joint Nuclear Control Commission. The JNCC met eleven times between March 19 and November 27, 1992. Nothing substantive was accomplished at any of the meetings, and no inspections of nuclear facilities were ever conducted. Center for Nonproliferation Studies, "North Korean Nuclear Developments: An Updated Chronology 1992," cns.miis.edu/research/korea/nuc/chr92.htm.

49. Reiss, *Bridled Ambition*, 255.

50. The history of the North Korean nuclear crisis is replete with use of the term "continuity of safeguards," but the term does not appear in either the NPT or the standard IAEA Safeguards Framework Agreement (INFCIRC/153). INFCIRC/153 does address "continuity of knowledge" regarding "the flow and inventory of nuclear material" (something that, as of this writing, has never been established in North Korea). The origin of "continuity of safeguards" is not clear. The IAEA asserts that it is an invention of the Clinton administration. Administration officials deny this, with one key participant claiming that the concept was "completely fabricated by the IAEA to help [the U.S.] out." Robert L. Gallucci, interview with author, June 4, 2002. All parties to the nuclear crisis—with the exception of the IAEA—have used the term, but since it lacks a standard definition, its meaning is subject to differing interpretations. According to the Congressional Research Service, both the DPRK and the United States seem to agree that maintaining the continuity of safeguards does not necessarily require IAEA special inspections. Beyond that, the two parties diverge: the United States stresses a level of IAEA activity that would provide assurances that no reprocessing has occurred, whereas the North asserts a narrower interpretation that would limit IAEA access only to cameras and seals installed at declared sites. Larry Niksch, "North Korean Nuclear Controversy: Defining Treaties, Agreements, and Terms," *Congressional Research Service*, September 16, 1994, 3–4; Oberdorfer, *Two Koreas*, 292; and Reiss, *Bridled Ambition*, 256.

51. Blix, quoted in Reiss, *Bridled Ambition*, 256.

52. Oberdorfer, *Two Koreas*, 293; and Reiss, *Bridled Ambition*, 257.

53. David E. Sanger, "Seoul's Big Fear: Pushing North Koreans Too Far," *New York Times*, November 7, 1993, A16; James Adams and Jon Swain, "U.S. Targets Cruise Missiles at Korea," *Sunday Times* (London), November 7, 1993; and R. Jeffrey Smith, "North Korea Deal Urged by State Dept.," *Washington Post*, November 15, 1993, A15.

54. R. Jeffrey Smith, "U.S. Weighs N. Korean Incentives," *Washington Post*, November 7, 1993, A31.

55. Quoted in David E. Sanger, "U.S. Revising North Korea Strategy," *New York Times*, November 22, 1993, A5. See also Sanger, "Seoul's Big Fear"; Reiss, *Bridled Ambition*, 260–263; Oberdorfer, *Two Koreas*, 295; and Sigal, *Disarming Strangers*, 82–84.

56. Sanger, "U.S. Revising North Korea Strategy."

57. Sanger, "Seoul's Big Fear"; David E. Sanger, "U.S. Delay Urged on Korea Sanction," *New York Times*, November 4, 1993, A9; T. R. Reid, "Aspin Prods, Warns North Korea," *Washington Post*, November 5, 1993, A29; and Sanger, "U.S. Revising North Korea Strategy."

58. Sanger, "U.S. Revising North Korea Strategy"; and Michael R. Gordon, "Pentagon Studies Plans to Bolster U.S.-Korea Forces," *New York Times*, December 2, 1993, A1.

59. Ruth Marcus and R. Jeffrey Smith, "U.S., South Korea Shift Strategy on North," *Washington Post*, November 24, 1993, A12. See also Thomas L. Friedman, "U.S. and Seoul Differ on Appeal to North Korea on Nuclear Sites," *New York Times*, November 24, 1993, A16; Reiss, *Bridled Ambition*, 262; and Sigal, *Disarming Strangers*, 88. ROK officials had made their objections to a "package deal" known to their U.S. counterparts before November 16, but the administration was confident that "at the end of the day we'll be able to work something out." Sigal, *Disarming Strangers*, 86; and Douglas Jehl, "U.S. May Dilute Earlier Threats to North Korea," *New York Times*, November 23, 1993, A6.

60. Greenberger and Glain, "How the U.S., North Korea Went from Promise to Peril in Two Years"; and Reiss, *Bridled Ambition*, 280.

61. Kim Young Sam, quoted in Robert D. Novak, "Package Deal on Korea," *Washington Post*, June 20, 1994, A15.

62. Reiss, *Bridled Ambition*, 262.

63. David E. Sanger, "U.N. Agency Finds No Assurance on North Korean Atomic Program," *New York Times*, December 3, 1993, A8; Gordon, "Pentagon Studies Plans to Bolster U.S.-Korea Forces"; and R. Jeffrey Smith, "U.S. Analysts Are Pessimistic on Korea Nuclear Inspection," *Washington Post*, December 3, 1993, A1. IAEA officials were increasingly worried that further delays in declaring that the "continuity of safeguards" had been broken would undermine the agency's credibility. Smith, "West Watching Reactor for Sign of N. Korea's Nuclear Intentions."

64. Steven Greenhouse, "U.S. Now Seeks Just One Survey of North Korea," *New York Times*, January 5, 1994, A1.

65. The record is not clear on this "one-time" inspection agreement, which was reached in a telephone conversation between midlevel U.S. and North Korean diplomats on December 29, 1993. The State Department initially confirmed, then denied, agreeing to a single "continuity of safeguards" inspection, saying that details on inspections were for North Korea and the IAEA to work out. The weight of evidence suggests, though, that the administration gave at least tacit approval to the North's proposal. See Larry A. Niksch, "North Korea's Nuclear Weapons Program," Congressional Research Service, November 23, 1994, 4; Richard Cronin, "North Korea's Nuclear Weapons Program: U.S. Policy Options," Congressional Research Service, June 1, 1994, 7; and Sigal, *Disarming Strangers*, 100–101. For criticism of the administration's actions, see Charles Krauthammer, "Capitulation in Korea: Clinton's Cave-in Makes a Joke of the NPT," *Washington Post*, January 7, 1994, A19. For the administration's response, see Lynn Davis, "Korea: No Capitulation," *Washington Post*, January 26, 1994, A21. See also Reiss, *Bridled Ambition*, 307–308 n. 129.

66. Reiss, *Bridled Ambition*, 263–267; and Sigal, *Disarming Strangers*, 104–107.

67. Robert L. Gallucci, remarks made at Georgetown University, Washington, D.C., April 5, 2000.

68. R. Jeffrey Smith, "N. Korean Conduct in Inspections Draws Criticism of U.S. Officials," *Washington Post*, March 10, 1994, A34; David E. Sanger, "North Korea Said to Block Taking of Radioactive Samples from Site," *New York Times*, March 16, 1994, A1; and R. Jeffrey Smith, "N. Korea Adds Arms Capacity," *Washington Post*, April 2, 1994, A1.

69. Smith, "N. Korea Adds Arms Capacity"; R. Jeffrey Smith and Ann Devroy, "Clinton Orders Patriot Missiles to South Korea," *Washington Post*, March 22, 1994, A1; T. R. Reid, "North Korea Warns of 'Brink of War,'" *Washington Post*, March 23, 1994, A23; Steven Greenhouse, "Christopher Says U.S. Stays Firm on Korea but Pledges Diplomacy," *New York Times*, March 23, 1994, A12; and R. Jeffrey Smith, "Perry Sharply Warns North Korea," *Washington Post*, March 31, 1994, A1.

70. The shutdown, while unwelcome, was not unexpected. "We understand that the technology and the operating history of the 25-megawatt [*sic*] reactor make it technically necessary to do this refueling very soon. But at the same time it is our top priority to be sure that this refueling does not lead to diversion of the spent fuel to reprocessing into weapons grade plutonium. It is equally important that this not become a source of new uncertainty about the use of spent fuel." William J. Perry, "U.S. Security Policy in Korea" (address before the Asia Society, Washington, D.C., May 3, 1994, fas.org/news/dprk/1994/940509-dprk-usia.htm); Oberdorfer, "Gates Remains Suspicious of N. Korea"; and Smith, "West Watching Reactor for Sign of N. Korea's Nuclear Intentions" and "N. Korea Adds Arms Capacity."

71. William J. Perry, "Standing at the Brink in North Korea: The Counterproliferation Imperative," in Ashton B. Carter and William J. Perry, *Preventive Defense: A New Security for America* (Washington, D.C.: Brookings Institution Press, 1999), 128.

72. Reiss, *Bridled Ambition*, 268; and Gallucci, interview with author.

73. Measuring radioactive emissions of the fuel rods as they were removed would show how long they had been in the reactor, giving inspectors a good sense of how much fuel had been removed in 1989–91, and therefore how much plutonium the North may have manufactured in the past. Smith, "West Watching Reactor for Sign of N. Korea's Nuclear Intention."

74. David Albright, "How Much Plutonium Does North Korea Have?" *Bulletin of the Atomic Scientists* (September/October 1994), www.thebulletin.org/issues/1994/so94/Albright.html.

75. Michael R. Gordon, "Korea Speeds Nuclear Fuel Removal, Impeding Inspection," *New York Times*, May 28, 1993, A3; and R. Jeffrey Smith and Julia Preston, "Nuclear Watchdog Says N. Korea Steps Up Fuel Rod Withdrawal," *Washington Post*, May 28, 1994, A25.

76. Smith and Preston, "Nuclear Watchdog Says N. Korea Steps Up Fuel Rod Withdrawal"; Reiss, *Bridled Ambition*, 268–269; and Sigal, *Disarming Strangers*, 115–118.

77. Reiss, *Bridled Ambition*, 269. "The fact of the matter is," said one U.S. official, "we don't really understand what they are doing." David E. Sanger, "North Korea Foils Efforts to Halt Its Nuclear Plans," *New York Times*, May 29, 1994, A1. See also Reiss, *Bridled Ambition*, 311 n. 155. On June 3 the United States withdrew its (already rejected) offer to go to the third round of talks. Sigal, *Disarming Strangers*, 118. Quotations are from Perry, "U.S. Security Policy in Korea"; and Douglas Brinkley, *The Unfinished Presidency: Jimmy Carter's Journey beyond the White House* (New York: Viking, 1998), 397.

78. The IAEA suspended $250,000 in nonmedical technical assistance. Robert S. Greenberger, "North Korea Has New Threat in Nuclear Issue—Nation Says It Will Quit IAEA, Expel Officials; U.S. Pursues Sanctions," *Wall Street Journal*, June 4, 1994, A11; David E. Sanger, "North Korea Quits Atom Agency in Wider Rift with U.S. and U.N.," *New York Times*, June 14, 1994, A1; R. Jeffrey Smith and T. R. Reid, "North Korea Quits U.N. Nuclear Body," *Washington Post*, June 14, 1994, A1; Koh, "Confrontation and Compromise on the Korean Peninsula," 69; Kihl, "Confrontation or Compromise on the Korean Peninsula," 105; and Matthias Dembinski, "North Korea, IAEA Special Inspections, and the Future of the Nonproliferation Regime," *Nonproliferation Review* (winter 1995): 36.

79. Greenberger, "North Korea Has New Threat in Nuclear Issue"; Smith and Reid, "North Korea Quits U.N. Nuclear Body"; and Sanger, "North Korea Quits Atomic Agency in Wider Rift with U.S. and U.N."

80. Perry, "Standing at the Brink in North Korea," 123–124, 129. Perry incorrectly states that CINCCFC, General Gary Luck, participated in the

June 14–15 review of the plan to defend South Korea as well as the June 16 briefing to the president. In fact, Luck remained at his post in Seoul, unaware that "his" war plan was being reviewed in the Pentagon and that the secretary of defense planned to recommend that the president accept the advice of the chairman of the Joint Chiefs of Staff on a specific reinforcement "package." General Luck and the U.S. ambassador to Seoul, James T. Laney, were informed of the briefing to the president only hours before it began. Ret. General Gary E. Luck, telephone interview with author, June 19, 2002; James T. Laney, interview with author, February 11, 2002; Ret. Colonel William McKinney (U.S. defense attaché in Seoul, 1990–96), telephone interview with author, April 4, 2002; and Oberdorfer, *Two Koreas*, 326.

81. Smith, "Perry Sharply Warns North Korea." Secretary of Defense Perry echoed the sentiments of former national security adviser Brent Scowcroft, who had written in February 1994, "If the situation is serious enough that they are contemplating an attack, it is better that we find that out before, rather than after, they have nuclear weapons." Michael R. Gordon and David E. Sanger, "North Korea's Huge Military Spurs New Strategy in South," *New York Times*, February 6, 1994, A1.

82. Perry, "U.S. Security Policy in Korea."

83. The U.S. military expected North Korea to use chemical, and possibly biological, weapons in the event of war. To CINCCFC, these weapons were more worrisome in some respects than the one or two nuclear weapons the CIA thought might be in the North's possession. Perry, "Standing at the Brink in North Korea," 130–131.

84. Perry, "Standing at the Brink in North Korea," 131; James T. Laney and Gary E. Luck, remarks at Georgetown University, April 5, 2000; and Laney, interview with author. Option 1 called for the dispatch of two thousand troops to prepare the way for larger numbers. Option 2 entailed deploying several battalions of combat troops to South Korea as well as stationing additional air force fighter and bomber units and a second aircraft carrier near the peninsula—approximately ten thousand troops in all. Option 3 would have added even more combat aircraft and tens of thousands of ground troops. Oberdorfer, *Two Koreas*, 324–325; and Michael R. Gordon, "Clinton May Add G.I.'s in Korea While Remaining Open to Talks," *New York Times*, June 17, 1994, A1.

85. Perry, "Standing at the Brink in North Korea," 131. Another participant has said that the president had already decided on Option 2 when Carter's call came through. Gallucci, interview with author. See also Leon V. Sigal, "Jimmy Carter Makes a Deal," *Bulletin of the Atomic Scientists* (January-February 1998): 43.

86. "Jimmy Carter to Visit South Korea and North Korea," fas.org/news/dprk/1994/940610-dprk-usia.htm; and Brinkley, *The Unfinished Presidency*, 398.

87. R. Jeffrey Smith and Ann Devroy, "Carter's Call from N. Korea Offered Option," *Washington Post*, June 26, 1994, A1.

88. Laney, interview with author. See also Smith and Devroy, "Carter's Call from N. Korea Offered Option"; and Sigal, *Disarming Strangers*, 151. Before being named ambassador to the ROK, Laney had been president of Emory University, home to the Carter Center.

89. Brinkley, *The Unfinished Presidency*, 398–399; and Sigal, *Disarming Strangers*, 151. Clinton had long been openly disdainful of Carter's performance as president and, with the exception of his national security adviser, Anthony Lake, had barred any Carter administration veterans from positions in his White House. For the difficult Carter-Clinton relationship, see Brinkley, *The Unfinished Presidency*, 355–356, 366; Elizabeth Drew, *On the Edge: The Clinton Presidency* (New York: Simon and Schuster, 1994), 28–29, 130; David Gergen, *Eyewitness to Power: The Essence of Leadership, Nixon to Clinton* (New York: Simon and Schuster, 2000), 259; and David Halberstam, *War in a Time of Peace: Clinton and the Generals* (New York: Charles Scribner's Sons, 2001), 175. South Koreans remained suspicious of Carter for his attempt as president to pull U.S. forces out of South Korea and for his public criticism of South Korea's human rights record. R. Jeffrey Smith and Ruth Marcus, "Carter Trip May Offer 'Opening,'" *Washington Post*, June 20, 1994, A1; Smith and Devroy, "Carter's Call from N. Korea Offered Option"; Brinkley, *The Unfinished Presidency*, 393; William H. Gleysteen, Jr., *Massive Entanglement, Marginal Influence: Carter and Korea in Crisis* (Washington, D.C.: Brookings Institution Press, 1999), 17–52; and William H. Gleysteen, Jr., "Korea: A Special Target of American Concern," in *The Diplomacy of Human Rights*, ed. David D. Newsom (Lanham, Md.: University Press of America, 1986), 85–99.

90. Laney, interview with author; and Oberdorfer, *Two Koreas*, 322–323.

91. Brinkley, *The Unfinished Presidency*, 372, 382, 407, 456.

92. On three separate occasions in 1992–93 the Bush and Clinton State Departments had persuaded Carter not to accept Kim's invitations. The offer, however, remained open. Brinkley, *The Unfinished Presidency*, 389–390, 392–393, 395, 398; Oberdorfer, *Two Koreas*, 317; and Smith and Marcus, "Carter Trip May Offer 'Opening.'"

93. T. R. Reid, "Respect Has Eluded Kim Il Sung," *Washington Post*, June 21, 1994, A1.

94. Sigal, *Disarming Strangers*, 156–157.

95. Brinkley, *The Unfinished Presidency*, 406–407. Carter knew from having talked by telephone with national security adviser Lake between his first and second meetings with Kim Il Sung that the administration was continuing to lobby Security Council members to support its quest for sanctions, yet he told Kim Il Sung, "I would like to inform you that they [in the United States] have stopped the sanctions activity in the United Nations." R. Jeffrey Smith and Bradley Graham, "White House Disputes Carter on North Korea," *Washington Post*, June 18, 1994, A1. Oberdorfer (*Two Koreas*, 333) ascribes Carter's false statement to fatigue. Other authoritative accounts assert that the former president, who adamantly disagreed with the administration's approach on sanctions, purposely made the statement in a (successful) effort to undercut the president's policy. Sigal, *Disarming Strangers*, 158, 160–162. See also David E. Sanger, "Two Koreas Plan Summit Talks on Nuclear Issue," *New York Times*, June 19, 1994, 1.

96. R. Jeffrey Smith, "'Promising' Signs Seen in N. Korea," *Washington Post*, June 17, 1994, A1; Sanger, "Two Koreas Plan Summit"; and Douglas Jehl, "Carter, His Own Emissary, Outpaces White House," *New York Times*, June 20, 1994, A3.

97. Smith and Devroy, "Carter's Call from N. Korea Offered Option"; and Sigal, *Disarming Strangers*, 152.

98. In a letter to his North Korean counterpart, First Vice Foreign Minister Kang Sok Ju, Ambassador Gallucci asked for formal confirmation from the North that it would not refuel the 30MW(t) reactor nor reprocess the spent fuel. In his reply dated June 21, 1994, Kang confirmed North Korea's oral pledge to Carter that it would do neither as long as U.S.-DPRK talks proceeded. North Korea also promised that IAEA inspectors and monitoring equipment would be allowed to remain at Yongbyon. Ruth Marcus and R. Jeffrey Smith, "North Korea Confirms Freeze; U.S. Agrees to Resume Talks," *Washington Post*, June 23, 1994, A1.

99. Marcus and Smith, "North Korea Confirms Freeze"; R. Jeffrey Smith and Ann Devroy, "U.S. Debates Shift on North Korea," *Washington Post*, June 21, 1994, A1; Sigal, *Disarming Strangers*, 158–162; Brinkley, *The Unfinished Presidency*, 407; Reiss, *Bridled Ambition*, 272; and Shim Jae Hoon and Ted Morella, "Not All Smiles," *Far Eastern Economic Review*, June 30, 1994, 16.

100. Laney, interview with author; and Oberdorfer, *Two Koreas*, 334.

101. The Agreed Framework was signed on October 21, 1994. For the text of the agreement, see www.armscontrol.org/documents/af.asp.

102. Don Oberdorfer, "South Korean: U.S. Agrees to Plan to Pressure North," *Washington Post*, March 30, 1993, A14. Clinton had been in office seven weeks when North Korea announced its withdrawal; ROK president Kim Young Sam, only two.

103. U.S. objectives were that North Korea adhere to the NPT, fully implement the South-North joint denuclearization agreement, and fulfill its IAEA obligations, including allowing special inspections. The North's "legitimate concerns" included U.S. security assurances, cancellation of Team Spirit, and further U.S.-DPRK talks on political and economic issues. R. Jeffrey Smith, "U.S., North Korea Set High-Level Meeting on Nuclear Program," *Washington Post*, May 25, 1993, A14; R. Jeffrey Smith, "U.S. Outlines Compromise on Korea Talks," *Washington Post*, May 27, 1993, A43; and Douglas Jehl, "U.S. May Bargain with Korea on Atom Issue," *New York Times*, May 27, 1993, A6.

104. North Korea further claimed that suspending its withdrawal did not reset the three-month "clock" specified in Article X of the NPT; rather, the North asserted that, having suspended its withdrawal at the eighty-nine-day point, it was only one day away from leaving the treaty.

105. Reiss, *Bridled Ambition*, 253, 254; and Oberdorfer, *Two Koreas*, 292.

106. Reiss, *Bridled Ambition*, 281.

107. North Korea's joining the NPT, for instance, "was intended to remove the nuclear threats of the United States against the DPRK, never to sacrifice its sovereignty and security for someone's benefit." Statement of the Government of the Democratic People's Republic of Korea, March 12, 1993. Reproduced as Annex 7 to IAEA INFCIRC/419, www.fax.org/news/un/dprk/inf419.html#annex3.

108. See Adrian Buzo, *The Guerrilla Dynasty: Politics and Leadership in North Korea* (Boulder, Colo.: Westview Press, 1999), 194, 197, 204–205, 244, 245; and Oh and Hassig, *North Korea through the Looking Glass*, 182–183, 191.

109. "Compared to North Korea, the former [*sic*] Soviet Union was a duck-soup intelligence target," notes a Pentagon analyst. "Here we just don't know much." Jill Smolowe, "What If . . . War Breaks Out in Korea?" *Time*, June 13, 1994, www.time.com/time/magazine/archive/1994/940613/940613.cover.war.html.

110. See Helen-Louise Hunter, *Kim Il Sung's North Korea* (Westport, Conn.: Praeger, 1999), xv.

111. Generally the Defense Intelligence Agency was the most pessimistic regarding North Korea's nuclear capabilities, the State Department's Bureau of Intelligence and Research the most optimistic. Smith, "U.S. Analysts Are Pessimistic on Korea Nuclear Inspection." President Carter was particularly dissatisfied with the quality of the intelligence information he was given before his departure for Pyongyang, challenging the briefers, "Have you ever been to North Korea? How do you know?" Jimmy Carter, quoted in Sigal, *Disarming Strangers*, 153.

112. The description is that of Deputy National Security Adviser William Hyland, in the aftermath of the 1976 ax murders of two U.S. army officers in the DMZ.

113. Stewart Stogel and Paul Bedard, "U.S. Proposes Arms Embargo on North Korea," *Washington Post*, June 16, 1994, A1; and Reiss, *Bridled Ambition*, 281.

114. See, for example, Michael Duffy, "That Sinking Feeling," *Time*, June 7, 1993, 23–29; David Broder, "Big Talk, Weak Hand," *Washington Post*, July 25, 1993, C7; Krauthammer, "Capitulation in Korea"; Jim Hoagland, "More Donald Trump Than John Wayne," *Washington Post*, January 13, 1994, A27; Gerald F. Seib, "In North Korea, Trouble Starts in Credibility Gap," *Wall Street Journal*, June 15, 1994, A20; and William Drozdiak, "Machiavelli He Isn't: Clinton Wants to Be Liked, Not Feared," *Washington Post*, July 10, 1994, A23.

115. The most serious of the thousands of armistice violations committed by North Korea since 1953 include assassination attempts against ROK presidents in 1968, 1974 (resulting in the murder of the first lady), and 1983 (the Rangoon bombing in which seventeen senior ROK officials traveling with the president were killed), the seizure of the USS *Pueblo* in 1968, the shoot-down of a U.S. EC-121 aircraft in 1969, the ax murders of two U.S. Army officers in the DMZ in 1976, and the destruction of Korean Airlines flight 858 in 1987 (in which 115 ROK citizens were killed).

116. Sigal, *Disarming Strangers*, 8.

117. "Statement of IAEA Director General regarding DPRK at Informal Briefing of UN Security Council"; Michael R. Gordon, "U.N. Agency Rejects Offer by North Korea," *New York Times*, December 7, 1993, A6; Smith, "West Watching Reactor for Sign of N. Korea's Nuclear Intentions"; and Oberdorfer, *Two Koreas*, 310. The IAEA resented that the United States pushed adherence to the South-North joint denuclearization agreement, with its rigorous inspection provisions, precisely because of the agency's failures in Iraq before the Gulf War. Sigal, *Disarming Strangers*, 42. (During Operation Desert Shield, an IAEA official described Iraq's cooperation with the agency up to that point as "exemplary." Leonard Weiss, "Perspectives: Tighten Up on Nuclear Cheaters," *Bulletin of the Atomic Scientists* [May 1991], www.thebulletin.org/issues/1991/may91/may91persp.html#anchor705535). The secretary of defense in a 1992 interview said, "[W]e've discovered . . . in the area of nuclear weapons, that the inspection regime of the [IAEA] is not as good as we had hoped, because even though Iraq was a party to the Nonproliferation Treaty—allowed periodic inspections of their facilities—they still had a very aggressive program underway to develop nuclear weapons. The treaty was not adequate. The inspection regime was not adequate." "Cheney: U.S. Sees North Korea as Threat for Many Reasons," interview, May 4, 1992, www.fas.org/news/dprk/ 1992/920504-dprk-usia.htm. Beyond questions of turf, the IAEA was concerned that inspections under the Joint Denuclearization Agreement would be both inadequate *and* seen as an acceptable substitute for IAEA safeguards. David Albright and Mark Hibbs, "North Korea's Plutonium Puzzle," *Bulletin of the Atomic Scientists* (November 1992): 37.

118. IAEA, quoted in Sigal, *Disarming Strangers*, 96.

119. Smith, "West Watching Reactor for Sign of N. Korea's Nuclear Intentions."

120. Perry, "Standing at the Brink in North Korea," 127.

121. Davis, "Korea: No Capitulation." See also Sigal, *Disarming Strangers*, 100.

122. Oberdorfer, "South Korean."

123. David E. Sanger, "Seoul's Leader Says North Is Manipulating U.S. on Nuclear Issue," *New York Times*, July 2, 1993, A3.

124. Novak, "Package Deal on Korea."

125. Gallucci, interview with author.

126. During a visit to China, Kim said that with regard to sanctions and negotiations, he and Chinese president Jiang Zemin "had 'confirmed a common position' on the North Korea issue and that they would 'cooperate closely' in dealing with it." Paul Lewis, "China Shields North Korea on Atom Issue," *New York Times*, March 30, 1994, A10. See also David E. Sanger, "Squeezing North Korea: Getting Blood from a Stone," *New York Times*, March 23, 1994, A12; and Greenhouse, "Christopher Says U.S. Stays Firm on Korea but Pledges Diplomacy."

127. Don Oberdorfer, "The Remilitarized Zone," *Washington Post*, May 1, 1994, C1. See also Susumu Awanohara, "Uphill Battle: Japan Finds Few Friends in Clinton White House," and "Golden Opportunity," *Far Eastern Economic Review*, June 2 and July 21, 1994, 30–31 and 24–25, respectively.

128. Moscow envisioned Russia, China, Japan, the United States, South Korea, and North Korea participating, along with representatives from the United Nations and the IAEA. Fred Hiatt, "Moscow Proposes Conference to Deal with North Korea," *Washington Post*, March 25, 1994, A25. See also Oberdorfer, "The Remilitarized Zone"; Michael R. Gordon, "White House

Asks Global Sanctions on North Korea," *New York Times*, June 3, 1994, A1; and Charles Smith, "Ifs and Buts of Sanctions," *Far Eastern Economic Review*, June 16, 1994, 16.

129. David E. Sanger, "Tokyo Reluctant to Levy Sanctions on North Koreans," *New York Times*, June 9, 1994, A1; and David E. Sanger, "North Korea Threatens Japan over Backing U.S.-Led Sanctions," *New York Times*, June 10, 1994, A11.

130. Laney, interview with author; Charles Kartman, interview with author, March 26, 2002; Reiss, *Bridled Ambition*, 260; and Sigal, *Disarming Strangers*, 53, 55, 59–60.

131. Drew, *On the Edge*, 335, 359; Reiss, *Bridled Ambition*, 271; and Paul Bedard, "President Talks Tough on Haiti, North Korea," *Washington Times*, November 8, 1993, A1. Clinton did cashier his first secretary of defense, Les Aspin, in December 1993, but Aspin's firing was in response to the October 1993 firefight in Mogadishu that cost the lives of eighteen U.S. servicemen, not dissatisfaction with North Korea policy.

132. Perry, "Standing at the Brink in North Korea," 127; and Sigal, *Disarming Strangers*, 60–61.

133. Ashton B. Carter, quoted in Sigal, *Disarming Strangers*, 80.

134. Oberdorfer, "South Korean."

135. Keith Bradsher, "China Trade: Cash or Care?" *New York Times*, May 14, 1993, A6; and Keith Bradsher, "Clinton Aides Propose Renewal of China's Favored Trade Status," *New York Times*, May 25, 1993, A1.

136. Steven Greenhouse, "Renewal Backed for China Trade," *New York Times*, May 28, 1993, A5.

137. Elaine Sciolino (with Thomas L. Friedman and Patrick E. Tyler), "Clinton and China: How Promise Self-Destructed," *New York Times*, May 29, 1994, A1.

138. U.S. intelligence experts warned early on that the executive order lacked credibility in Beijing. Daniel Williams and Ann Devroy, "China's Disbelief of Rights Threat Sank Clinton Ploy," *Washington Post*, May 28, 1994, A1. See also E. J. Dionne, Jr., "Goodbye to Human Rights?" *Washington Post*, May 31, 1994, A17.

139. Patrick E. Tyler, "Chinese Puzzle: After Months of Dialogue on Human Rights, Beijing Takes Harder Line toward the U.S.," *New York Times*, March 14, 1994, A1; and Elaine Sciolino, "China Rejects Call from Christopher for Rights Gains," *New York Times*, March 13, 1994, A1.

140. The China MFN debacle's impact on the crisis with North Korea was obvious. Warned a *New York Times* columnist: "The surrender at Beijing will make it impossible for friend or foe to trust his foreign policy word—even when he writes it into law himself. When friends cannot trust a Presidential word, alliances erode. When foes do not believe a President, the risk is war by miscalculation, as in Korea." A. M. Rosenthal, "Bill Clinton's Teachings," *New York Times*, May 27, 1994, A27. The *Nation* of Bangkok added, "After climbing down so dramatically after a year of issuing tough ultimatums, it is hard to see why tyrants anywhere in the world, let alone Pyongyang, will pay much attention to U.S. pressure"—quoted in William Branigin, "Asians Welcome China Decision; Retreat Seen as Stamp of Clinton's Waffling Foreign Policy," *Washington Post*, May 29, 1994, A49.

141. "[A] U.N. resolution . . . has the weight of international law." Julia Preston, "U.N. Bows to China, Issues Mild Call to N. Korea to Permit Nuclear Checks," *Washington Post*, April 1, 1994, A27.

142. Oberdorfer, "South Korean"; Greenhouse, "Christopher Says U.S. Stays Firm on Korea but Pledges Diplomacy"; Steven Greenhouse, "Christopher Presses Policy of Engagement with Asia," *New York Times*, May 28, 1994, A5; and Preston "U.N. Bows to China."

143. Oberdorfer, "South Korean"; Oberdorfer, "The Remilitarized Zone"; Sanger, "Tokyo Reluctant to Levy Sanctions on North Koreans"; Patrick E. Tyler, "China Tells Why It Opposes Korea Sanctions," *New York Times*, June 13, 1994 , A5; and Gordon, "Clinton May Add G.I.'s in Korea While Remaining Open to U.N. Talks."

144. Greenberger and Glain, "How the U.S., North Korea Went from Promise to Peril in Two Years." Among the skeptics was the U.S. intelligence community. Gordon, "White House Asks Global Sanctions on North Korea." See also Thomas W. Lippman, "North Korea Could Prove Sanction-Proof," *Washington Post*, December 25, 1993, A30; Sanger, "Squeezing North Korea"; Sanger, "U.S. Delay Urged on Korea Sanction"; and Reid, "Aspin Prods, Warns North Korea."

145. Gordon, "Pentagon Studies Plans to Bolster U.S.-Korea Forces"; Sanger, "U.N. Agency Finds No Assurance on North Korean Atomic Program"; and Perry, "Standing at the Brink in North Korea," 129.

146. "[T]he imperative to stop a battle of nerves from erupting into hostilities underscores every discussion of U.S. options to limit North Korea's nuclear program, according to senior officials. Not only does this caution rule out preemptive use of force, akin to Israel's 1981 surprise air attack on an Iraqi nuclear facility, but it also has dampened enthusiasm even for aggressive economic sanctions." Barton Gellman, "Trepidation at Root of

U.S. Korea Policy; Conventional War Seen Catastrophic for South," *Washington Post*, December 12, 1993, A1.

147. "Could we have stopped the North Korean program with sanctions? Nobody in the administration or out thought we could then or now." Robert Gallucci, Arms Control Association press conference, March 23, 2001, transcript at www.nautilus.org/nukepolicy/Text_Files/010301ArmsControlAssociation.txt.

148. Sigal, *Disarming Strangers*, 162.

149. On June 3, 1994, the U.S. ambassador to the United Nations, Madeleine Albright, said that "the United States was now ready to start consulting with other [Security] Council members 'regarding the timing, the objectives and the substance of sanctions.'" Paul Lewis, "U.N. Told North Korea's Nuclear Record Can't Be Retrieved," *New York Times*, June 4, 1994, A1. See also Gordon, "White House Asks Global Sanctions on North Korea"; and "ROK Official Discusses Sanctions with Security Council," June 6, 1994, www.fas.org/ news/dprk/1994/940606-dprk-usia.htm.

150. Gallucci, interview with author.

151. Even the sanctions proposed by the United States may have inadvertently conveyed weakness rather than resolve. Following a thirty-day grace period, during which Pyongyang would supposedly contemplate the error of its ways, symbolic sanctions—such as cutting off scientific and cultural exchanges and UN development assistance—would be imposed. In the next phase, Japan would be asked to block remittances to Pyongyang from its ethnic Korean population. Only later stages contemplated measures with real bite, including embargoes on oil and arms, enforced by a naval blockade. Sanger, "North Korea Quits Atomic Agency in Wider Rift with U.S. and U.N."; Greenberger, "North Korea Has New Threat in Nuclear Issue"; Stogel and Bedard, "U.S. Proposes Arms Embargo on North Korea"; and Oberdorfer, *Two Koreas*, 318.

152. Oberdorfer, *Two Koreas*, 335.

153. James T. Laney, remarks at Georgetown University, April 5, 2000. A "Noncombatant Evacuation Operation" would have affected as many as eighty thousand U.S. civilians—military dependents, embassy families and nonessential staff, businesspeople and their families, tourists, students, and so on. Laney estimates the number of other foreigners expected to leave in conjunction with an evacuation of Americans would have increased the number to two hundred fifty thousand.

154. The National Intelligence Officer for Warning briefed the president that North Korea would view reinforcements as escalatory. The secretary of defense and the JCS chairman acknowledged that possibility, but they saw even greater risks in *not* reinforcing. Gallucci, interview with author; see also Sigal, *Disarming Strangers*, 155.

155. "[H]ere the US announces a massive buildup in Korea and begins evacuating noncombatants. Doesn't that sound like war? [T]he point was, [North Korea's leaders] are not going to sit there and be a patsy." Laney, interview with author. "If we thought we could build up forces in South Korea and Japan under the rubric of deterrence and have that accepted [by North Korea], we're dreaming." Gary E. Luck, remarks at Georgetown University, April 5, 2000.

156. Brinkley, *The Unfinished Presidency*, 401. In May 1994 a North Korean colonel seemed to confirm this, telling a U.S. officer, "We're not going to let you do a build-up." Quoted in Oberdorfer, *Two Koreas*, 325–326 (see also 329).

157. Gallucci, interview with author.

158. Gordon, "Pentagon Studies Plans to Bolster U.S.-Korea Forces." Luck is a combat veteran of both the Vietnam War and the Persian Gulf War, where he commanded the XVIII Corps in the famous "left hook" that swept across the desert in four days and ended the war with Iraq.

159. Gary E. Luck, quoted in Gellman, "Trepidation at Root of U.S. Korea Policy."

160. Smith, "North Korea Deal Urged by State Dept."; Reiss, *Bridled Ambition*, 259; Oberdorfer, *Two Koreas*, 315, 324; and Luck, interview with author. General Luck, while emphasizing the tremendous loss of life and property destruction in a new Korean war, nevertheless disputes the fifty thousand U.S. casualty figure as too high.

161. General Robert RisCassi (CINCCFC 1990–93), quoted in Smolowe, "What If . . . War Breaks Out in Korea?" See also Gordon, "Pentagon Studies Plans to Bolster U.S.-Korea Forces"; Gellman, "Trepidation at Root of U.S. Korea Policy"; Gordon and Sanger, "North Korea's Huge Military Spurs New Strategy in South." Seoul—located no farther from the DMZ than Washington, D.C., is from Dulles International Airport and within range of more than eleven thousand North Korean artillery pieces and rocket launchers— is home to a quarter of the ROK population (forty-four million in 1993) and is the political, financial, educational, and cultural heart of South Korea.

162. Laney met with McLarty in the White House on March 30, 1994. "I remember the shock that Mack expressed, when he said 'Well, you've got to realize that this is a very unpolitical . . . this won't play well domestically. We don't want to get involved again in Korea.' I said, 'How do you think fifty thousand body bags are going to play?'" That afternoon Gallucci was relieved of his responsibilities running the State Department's bureau of political-military affairs and named ambassador-at-large for Korea. Laney, interview with author; and Gallucci, interview with author.

163. Sigal, *Disarming Strangers*, 82, 96–97; and Oberdorfer, *Two Koreas*, 317.

164. It has been erroneously reported (Sigal, *Disarming Strangers*, 134; and Brinkley, *The Unfinished Presidency*, 395) that Graham delivered a letter from Clinton to Kim Il Sung. There was no letter; rather, Clinton's message—described as little more than a presidential courtesy—was conveyed orally by Graham. Kim responded by asking Graham to convey Kim's personal invitation to Clinton to visit North Korea. Interview with someone having personal knowledge of the Graham-Kim meeting who wishes to remain anonymous, March 4, 2002.

165. Brinkley, *The Unfinished Presidency*, 397; and Oberdorfer, *Two Koreas*, 317.

166. Brinkley, *The Unfinished Presidency*, 371, 373. See also Halberstam, *War in Times of Peace*, 175.

167. Brinkley, *The Unfinished Presidency*, 382. For example, on the eve of the Gulf War, in a move that infuriated President Bush, Carter wrote to the members of the UN Security Council, urging them not to vote for the resolution sought by the Bush administration authorizing the use of force against Iraq. Carter objected to what he perceived as the lack of "good faith talks" to resolve the situation peacefully. Douglas Brinkley, "Jimmy Carter's Modest Quest for Global Peace," *Foreign Affairs* (November-December 1995): 95–96; and Maureen Dowd, "Mission to Haiti: The Diplomat; Despite Role as Negotiator, Carter Feels Unappreciated," *New York Times*, September 21, 1994, A1.

168. Robert Gallucci, quoted in Brinkley, *The Unfinished Presidency*, 399; and Russell Watson, "A Stooge or a Savior?" *Newsweek*, June 27, 1994, 38.

169. Gallucci had briefed Carter in Plains, Georgia, on June 5, 1994. Rather than reassuring Carter, the briefing left him convinced that sanctions would be dangerously counterproductive and distressed that "we were approaching the possibility of a major confrontation [with] no avenue of communication that I could ascertain that might have led to resolution." Jimmy Carter, quoted in Smith and Marcus, "Carter Trip May Offer 'Opening.'" Carter came to Washington on June 10 for additional briefings by Lake (who told Carter he had no authority to speak for the United States) as well as by intelligence officials. Sigal, *Disarming Strangers*, 151–152.

170. "[I]t was a shot in the dark. We didn't have any idea he was going to be able to break through. That's why it was so stunning. . . . No one thought it would succeed." Laney, interview with author. "I don't think we thought much would come of it." Gallucci, interview with author. Carter himself thought "the chances of success were minimal because so much momentum had built up on both sides on the sanctions issue." Carter, quoted in Oberdorfer, *Two Koreas*, 326.

171. Carter, quoted in Sigal, *Disarming Strangers*, 152. "We had our own policy [i.e., UN sanctions] we were mobilizing behind." Gallucci, quoted in Brinkley, *The Unfinished Presidency*, 399.

172. During a stop on his way to Korea, Carter had read his talking points over the phone to Gallucci, who suggested only minor changes. But Gallucci did not inform anyone else in the government of the conversation. Once in Pyongyang, Carter, speaking from his talking points, indicated to Kim Il Sung that the United States had no objection to the reprocessing of the spent fuel removed from the Yongbyon reactor in May, a statement Carter later had to correct with his North Korean host. Sigal, *Disarming Strangers*, 153, 157; and Smith and Devroy, "Carter's Call from N. Korea Offered Option."

173. White House officials would later complain that they had not been told that Carter had taken a CNN crew with him to North Korea. Brinkley, *The Unfinished Presidency*, 400, 403. But it was hardly a secret. See Seib, "In North Korea, Trouble Starts in Credibility Gap."

174. Brinkley, *The Unfinished Presidency*, 404.

175. Ibid., 405.

176. Smith and Devroy, "Carter's Call from N. Korea Offered Option."

177. Brinkley, *The Unfinished Presidency*, 403.

178. Smith and Graham, "White House Disputes Carter on North Korea"; Michael R. Gordon, "A Shift on North Korea," *New York Times*, June 18, 1994, A1; Sanger, "Two Koreas Plan Summit Talks on Nuclear Issue"; Jehl, "Carter, His Own Emissary, Outpaces White House"; Smith and Marcus, "Carter Trip May Offer 'Opening'"; Jehl, "Clinton Is Hopeful"; Smith and Devroy, "U.S. Debates Shift on North Korea"; Ann Devroy and T. R. Reid, "U.S. Awaits Word on North Korea's Intentions," *Washington Post*, June 22, 1994, A15; and Smith and Devroy, "Carter's Call from N. Korea Offered Option."

179. Sigal, *Disarming Strangers*, 53.

180. The characterization of North Korea's leadership is Paul Wolfowitz's. See R. Jeffrey Smith, "N. Korean Strongman: 'Crazy' or Canny?" *Washington Post*, September 26, 1993, A1.

181. Administration officials have cited the quickness with which North Korea agreed not to reprocess the fuel rods and not to refuel the 30MW(t) reactor—"raising the bar," in administration parlance—as evidence that they retained control over policy in the immediate aftermath of the Carter mission. Gallucci, interview with author. But there is nothing to suggest that either of these agreements would have been possible had Carter not struck his deal with Kim Il Sung.

182. Jehl, "Carter, His Own Emissary, Outpaces White House."

183. "[Carter] was going to have his way on CNN and was going to make Clinton pay as well." Gallucci, interview with author.

184. Kim Jong Il had replaced his father, Kim Il Sung, as supreme leader of the DPRK on the latter's death in July 1994.

185. Both the secretary of defense and the director of Central Intelligence publicly predicted the near-term collapse of North Korea, a view shared by many Korea analysts in the mid-1990s.

186. Major incidents included the hunt in 1996 for North Korean commandos who had infiltrated the ROK via submarine, suspicions voiced in August 1988 over a mysterious underground construction site at Kumchangni in North Korea, the launch of a Taepodong ballistic missile over Japan (also in August 1998), and deadly clashes between North and South naval units in the Yellow ("West") Sea in 1999 and 2002.

187. The 1999 review, mandated by Congress and conducted by former secretary of defense William Perry, recommended a two-path strategy. The preferred path would supplement the Agreed Framework, seeking "complete and verifiable assurances that the DPRK does not have a nuclear weapons program," the "complete and verifiable cessation" of all aspects of the DPRK missile program that exceed the parameters of the Missile Technology Control Regime, and the complete cessation of exports of missiles and related equipment and technology. In return, the United States and its allies would reduce pressures that the North found threatening and move to normalize relations. Should the North reject the preferred path, the United States and its allies would "take . . . steps to assure their security and contain the threat." "Review of United States Policy toward North Korea: Findings and Recommendations, October 12, 1999," www.state.gov/www/regions/eap/991012_northkorea_rpt.html. The Bush administration's review resulted in a policy of undertaking discussions with North Korea on improved implementation of the Agreed Framework, and verifiable constraints on missile programs and a ban on exports; in addition, it added the North's conventional military posture to the discussion agenda. "Text: Bush

Statement on Undertaking Talks with North Korea," White House, June 6, 2001. http:// www.usembassy.state.gov/tokyo/wwwhse0193.html.

188. "Joint Declaration on the Denuclearization of the Korean Peninsula," February 19, 1992. Text at www.fas.org/news/dprk/1992/920219-D4129.html. Emphasis added.

189. North Korea, however, maintains that it is only a day away from completing its withdrawal, having "unilaterally suspended" its withdrawal in June 1993, on the eighty-ninth day of the required ninety-day notification period.

190. The Agreed Framework states that the North need not come into full compliance until "a significant portion of the LWR project is completed, but before delivery of key nuclear components." Agreed Framework between the United States of America and the Democratic People's Republic of Korea, October 21, 1994, Section IV, 3.

191. Quoted in David E. Sanger, "North Korea Says It Has a Program on Nuclear Arms," *New York Times*, October 17, 2002, A1. In admitting to the HEU program, North Korea declared the Agreed Framework "nullified," a description that it changed to "hanging by a thread" a few weeks later. Don Kirk, "North Korea Softens Its Tone on Nuclear Arms Agreement," *New York Times*, November 7, 2002, A18.

192. Philip Shenon, "North Korea Says Nuclear Program Can Be Negotiated," *New York Times*, November 3, 2002, A1. The initial U.S. response was dismissive: "We bought that horse one time before," said Assistant Secretary of State James Kelly in an interview on "The NewsHour with Jim Lehrer," November 5, 2002, available at www.pbs.org/newshour/bb/military/july-dec02/nuclear_11-5.html.

193. "Statement by KEDO Executive Board (November 14, 2002)." The Executive Board is made up of representatives of the United States, the Republic of Korea, Japan, and the European Union.

194. The president's State of the Union Address, January 29, 2002. www.whitehouse.gov/news/releases/2002/01/print/20020129-11.html.

6

The 1995–96 Taiwan Strait Confrontation

Coercion, Credibility, and Use of Force

ROBERT S. ROSS

O N MAY 22, 1995, the White House approved a visa for Lee Teng-hui to visit the United States in early June to attend his graduate school reunion at Cornell University. This decision to allow Taiwan's most senior leader to enter the United States reversed more than thirty years of U.S. diplomatic precedent and challenged Clinton administration public policy statements and private reassurances to Chinese leaders that such a visit was contrary to U.S. policy. Equally important, the visa decision followed a three-year evolution of U.S. policy toward Taiwan. In 1992 the Bush administration, in violation of its pledge in the 1982 U.S.-China arms sales communiqué to reduce the quantity of U.S. arms sales to Taiwan, sold Taiwan 150 F-16 warplanes. In 1994 the Clinton administration revised upward the protocol rules regarding U.S. "unofficial" treatment of Taiwan diplomats, which had for the most part been in effect since 1981. Then, the next year it allowed Lee Teng-hui to visit the United States. From China's perspective, the United States seemed determined to continue revising its Taiwan policy and, in so doing, encourage Taiwan's leaders to seek formal sovereign independence for Taiwan. Should Taiwan declare sovereign independence, it would likely lead to war, given China's credible forty-five-year commitment to use force in retaliation against Taiwan independence.

During the ten months following Lee's visit to Cornell, the United States and China reopened their difficult negotiations over U.S. policy toward Taiwan. These negotiations reached a climax in March 1996, when China displayed a dramatic show of force with missile tests targeted near Taiwan and when the United States responded with an equally dramatic deployment of two carrier battle groups. The 1996 Taiwan Strait confrontation was the closest the United States and China had come to a crisis since the early 1960s. It was a critical turning point in post–Cold War U.S.-China relations and in the development of the post–Cold War East Asian regional order. The confrontation continues to influence Chinese and U.S. security policies and the bilateral relationships among all three of the actors in U.S.-China-Taiwan relations.

Many scholars have argued that Chinese use of force coerced the Clinton administration to reverse the trend of improving U.S.-Taiwan relations and to oppose Taiwan independence. They argue that the lesson of 1996 is that the United States needs to adopt a stronger posture against Chinese policy.[1] This chapter challenges this view. It argues that China did not coerce the United States to adopt policy that harmed U.S. interests but that both China and the United States achieved their interests.

The best way to address the U.S.-China confrontation is to focus on the distinct strategic objectives of the United States and China. The confrontation reflected the interaction of Chinese coercive diplomacy and U.S. deterrence diplomacy. China used coercive diplomacy to threaten costs until the United States and Taiwan changed their respective policies.[2] The United States, on the other hand, used deterrence diplomacy to communicate to Chinese leaders and regional leaders the credibility of its strategic commitments. It sought reputational objectives by influencing perceptions of U.S. resolve.[3]

China's objective was to coerce the United States into ending the recent trend of its indirect yet increasingly significant support for Taiwan independence by adopting a new position on U.S.-Taiwan relations and Taiwan's role in international politics. China also aimed to coerce Taiwan into abandoning its effort to redefine the "one-China" principle and Taiwan's status in international politics. Use of force was a crucial element in China's coercive diplomacy. Its large-scale military exercises and missile tests were intended to signal the United States and Taiwan the great risks inherent in their policies.[4] This use of force made the potential costs of U.S. and Taiwan policy more credible and China's coercive diplomacy more effective.[5]

The Clinton administration did not use force to defend U.S. policy against Chinese coercion. On the contrary, as will be discussed, the administration had opposed Lee's visit to Cornell, and National Security Council (NSC) officials understood that Chinese use of force might help to curtail Taiwan's independence diplomacy. The administration's purpose was to bolster the credibility of its deterrence posture to discourage future Chinese military action and to influence the behavior of its allies. China's missile tests had challenged Washington's commitment to impose costs on any attempt to resolve the Taiwan issue with force and to defend its strategic partners from future military threats. Washington believed that its commitments were "interdependent." The United States thus used force to deter prospective challenges to its interests and to maintain its reputation for loyalty to its security partners.[6]

Because China and the United States pursued two different types of strategic objectives, each was able to achieve its purpose. China influenced Taiwan's assessment of the costs of independence. It also succeeded in curtailing the evolution of U.S. policy toward Taiwan, thus reestablishing U.S. constraint on Taiwan's independence diplomacy. For its part, the United States secured its reputational objectives. Following U.S. deployment of two carrier battle groups, China, Taiwan, and U.S. regional allies concluded that the United States remained committed to the defense of Taiwan and to using its military power to maintain the East Asian strategic order. The United States thus succeeded in maintaining its preconfrontation reputation so that the credibility of U.S. deterrence was intact.[7]

The first section of this chapter addresses the origins of the U.S.-China confrontation. It examines why China considered Lee Teng-hui's 1995 visit to the United States a major challenge to its interests and its initial efforts to affect U.S. and Taiwan behavior. The second section examines the March 1996 confrontation. It explains why each side used force to achieve its objectives. The third section examines the consequences of the confrontation, including the costs and benefits for U.S. and Chinese interests and for U.S.-China relations. The conclusion argues that because both the United States and China achieved their objectives and were content with the restoration of the status quo before Lee Teng-hui's visit to the United States, the confrontation itself was unnecessary and avoidable. Both countries could have achieved their interests without putting their relationship under such intense pressure. The lesson of 1996 is not that the United States requires a tougher China policy, but that policymaking must avoid the mistakes of 1995 to prevent future similar costly and unnecessary confrontations.

FROM ITHACA TO NEW YORK CITY

Between May 1995, when Lee Teng-hui received his visa, and October 1995, when President Bill Clinton and President Jiang Zemin met in New York for an unofficial summit, Washington and Beijing negotiated restoration of the pre-visa agenda of U.S.-China relations. Beijing pressed Washington to affirm its opposition to Taiwan independence and to reassure Chinese leaders that there would be no further erosion of U.S. policy toward Taiwan, as agreed to in the three U.S.-China communiqués.[8] Washington resisted Chinese pressure. After offering China informal and ambiguous assurances, it insisted that U.S.-Taiwan relations were no longer at issue and that China should refocus on the prior agenda of U.S.-China relations, that is, trade, human rights policies, and U.S. opposition to Chinese arms proliferation. This period ended with China's failure to achieve its objectives through diplomatic persuasion.

China's Response to Lee Teng-hui's Visit to Cornell

President Clinton's decision to issue a visa to Lee Teng-hui reflected not considered analysis of U.S. interests but rather White House acquiescence to congressional pressure. In April 1995 Secretary of State Warren Christopher told Foreign Minister Qian Qichen that a visa for Lee Teng-hui would be "inconsistent with an unofficial relationship" with Taiwan. National Security Council officials also argued against issuing a visa to Lee. However, after the Senate voted 97 to 1 and the House of Representatives voted 360 to 0 in support of a visa in May, the president gave in to congressional pressure and decided that Lee should receive a visa.[9]

Leaders in Beijing considered the U.S. decision a serious challenge to China's opposition to Taiwan's independence movement. A Chinese Foreign Ministry statement charged that this was Lee's latest step in his efforts to create "one China and one Taiwan."[10] When he returned from Cornell, a Xinhua News Agency commentary observed that Lee and pro-independence supporters "are now very swollen with arrogance." A joint *Xinhua–People's Daily* commentary argued that Lee had used his visit to gain U.S. support for independence. Moreover, Taiwan appeared to dare Beijing to try to stop its drive for independence. Just before his departure for Cornell, Lee personally observed military exercises in which Taiwan forces practiced defense against a People's Liberation Army (PLA) attempt to land on Taiwan. Then, Taiwan announced that it was prepared to spend $1 billion to secure admission to the United Nations.[11]

China believed that U.S. policy drift had encouraged Lee Teng-hui to seek sovereignty for Taiwan. Moreover, the visa decision followed a succession of similarly important decisions since the end of the Cold War. In 1992 George Bush approved the sale of 150 F-16 military planes to Taiwan. The sale not only violated the August 17, 1982, U.S.-China communiqué on U.S. arms sales to Taiwan but also suggested increased U.S. support for Taiwan in its conflict with China.[12] Then in 1994 the Clinton administration revised its policy on U.S. government contacts with Taiwan, raising the protocol level for U.S. treatment of Taiwan officials. Thus, as a leading Chinese authority observed, Washington's decision to issue the visa was not an isolated incident. Rather, it was the latest step in a dangerous post–Cold War trend that could lead to a Taiwan declaration of independence.[13] The *People's Daily* observed that if the trend continued, "Lee Teng-hui will have less to fear in colluding with 'Taiwan independence forces.'"[14]

Moreover, Lee's visit also had implications for other countries' Taiwan policies, including Japanese and West European policies. Lee had already carried out "golf diplomacy" in Southeast Asia and soon he might be traveling around the globe, gaining greater legitimacy for himself and for Taiwan independence. As a *Xinhua* commentary explained, Lee was the "chief behind-the-scenes backer" of Taiwan's independence movement. He aimed to use his visit to the United States to "boost Taiwan's status with the help of foreigners and to achieve a 'domino effect' leading to the international community's recognition of Taiwan's 'political status.'"[15]

Beijing understood that the catalyst for Washington's changing policy was political pressure on the White House. But it did not care, for regardless of the cause of U.S. policy change, "China cannot help but show great concern and vigilance" for the trend in U.S. policy.[16] As a Chinese Foreign Ministry statement explained, there are "stubborn anti-China elements in the U.S. Congress," but the U.S. government must "exercise its power and influence to . . . honor the international commitments it has made." The statement went on to observe that if policymakers "only attach importance to pressure from certain pro-Taiwan forces, Sino-U.S. relations will . . . even regress."[17]

Moreover, despite Christopher's April statement to Qian that a visit by Lee Teng-hui would be "inconsistent with an unofficial relationship," after the fact the administration argued that the visa decision was in fact consistent with U.S.-China understandings. On June 8, 1995, President Clinton explained to Chinese ambassador Li Daoyu that there had been no major change in U.S. policy. The State Department held that the decision was "completely consistent with the . . . three communiqués that form the basis" of U.S.-China relations. Assistant Secretary of State Winston Lord seemed to dismiss the significance of the decision when he characterized it as a mere "tactical change." In early July Christopher said that the visit was not "violative" of the U.S.-China "basic relationship" but was "quite compatible" with unofficial U.S.-Taiwan relations. Although it was clear that the administration would oppose additional visits by Lee to the United States, U.S. declaratory policy allowed room for ongoing policy change.[18]

Beijing, however, sought more than mere U.S. reaffirmation of the three U.S.-China joint communiqués. It was determined to compel the Clinton administration to formally commit the United States to a one-

China policy and to the status quo in its relationship with Taiwan. In a July meeting with former secretary of state Henry Kissinger, Foreign Minister Qian insisted that "what is imperative is that the United States make concrete moves to eliminate the disastrous effects of its permitting Lee's visit." Prime Minister Li Peng demanded that Washington "take practical measures" to correct its mistaken decision.[19]

Beijing retaliated to the visa decision by canceling the imminent visits to Washington by Defense Minister Chi Haotian and State Counselor Li Guixian and by cutting short a visit to the United States by the Chinese air force chief of staff. It also suspended bilateral discussions over arms proliferation and human rights. Following Lee's visit, Beijing called home its ambassador for "consultations" and rejected U.S. suggestions that the two sides hold high-level talks to restore previsit cooperation.[20]

China's diplomacy included a show of force. Chinese leaders were united in using force to signal that the Taiwan issue was a "question of war and peace" and that the United States "could be dragged into military conflict" over Taiwan.[21] On July 18 China announced that from July 21 to July 28 it would conduct missile tests and naval and air exercises in the waters near Taiwan. It launched six surface-to-surface missiles approximately one hundred miles from Taiwan.[22] The Chinese Foreign Ministry spokesman explained that "[w]hat we are going to do is make the U.S. realize the importance of U.S.-China relations to prompt it to take the right track."[23] The tests and exercises concluded three days before Qian Qichen and Warren Christopher would meet in Brunei for the first high-level U.S.-China meeting since Lee Teng-hui received his visa. The meeting would be Washington's first opportunity to inform Beijing whether it would "take practical measures" to end its support for Taiwan independence.

China's use of force had a second target: Lee Teng-hui and public support in Taiwan for Lee's pro-independence activities.[24] By using force Chinese leaders wanted to signal to Taiwan that a declaration of independence risked war with the mainland. They believed that their relatively conciliatory overtures, including Jiang Zemin's January 1995 eight-point proposal for mainland-Taiwan cooperation, and their tolerance of Lee's pragmatic diplomacy had eroded the credibility of

Chinese deterrence.[25] From China's perspective, the missile tests and naval exercises were thus necessary to signal its determination to curtail Taiwan's march toward independence and to make clear that a formal declaration of independence would result in war.[26]

U.S. Resistance to Chinese Demands

The agenda for the August 1 Christopher-Qian meeting in Brunei was clear. The two sides would attempt to reach sufficient agreement on U.S. policy toward Taiwan so that they could focus on other issues, including arms proliferation, trade, and human rights. Before the meeting Qian told the press that China appreciated U.S. statements that Washington would continue to abide by the one-China policy, but he recalled the Chinese expression that "words must count and deeds must yield results."[27] Qian wanted Washington to adopt new commitments that would limit U.S. policy and constrain Taiwan.

Christopher presented Qian with a confidential letter from President Clinton to President Jiang Zemin in which Clinton stated that U.S. policy opposed Taiwan independence, did not support Taiwan membership in the United Nations, and did not support a two-China policy or a policy of one China and one Taiwan. Although Washington expected that such assurances would mollify China, these were basically the same confidential commitments U.S. presidents had been making to Chinese leaders since Nixon visited China in 1972.[28] Christopher also tried to assure Qian that the U.S. decision to issue Lee a visa did not indicate that future visits would be routine. He did not rule them out, but he said that Lee's visit was a "special" situation and that future visits would be personal, unofficial, rare, and decided on a case-by-case basis.[29] While Christopher tried to reassure China with well-established U.S. commitments, he adopted a low-key posture toward Chinese military activities. He merely reiterated the mild State Department position that such activities do not contribute to "peace and stability in the area."[30]

Beijing was not satisfied with confidential and vague U.S. assurances, however. Following the Brunei meeting, Qian said that Christopher's statements were helpful but that the "true value of a promise is shown in real action." Prime Minister Li Peng explained that although Christopher and Qian held a positive meeting in Brunei, "it is not enough to make oral statements and what is important is to translate the statements into actions." China's Foreign Ministry insisted that the "top priority" was for the United States to "translate" its assurances into "concrete actions."[31]

Moreover, Chinese diplomacy had failed to curtail Lee Teng-hui's "adventuresome" foreign policy, including his call for Taiwan to be admitted to the United Nations. In late July, just a few days after China began its July military maneuvers, Taiwan launched its own missile and naval exercises. It also announced that it would conduct live artillery tests in August. Rather than succumb to Chinese pressure, Lee was "still stubbornly challenging the 'one-China' principle." Liu Huaqing, vice chairman of the Chinese Central Military Commission, observed that because Taiwan's leaders had purchased foreign weaponry, they could be "cocky" and resist reunification.[32]

China's next opportunity to press the United States was during Under Secretary of State Peter Tarnoff's visit to Beijing in late August. On August 15, before Tarnoff's arrival, China began a second round of missile tests and naval exercises near Taiwan. Both exercises were scheduled to last until August 25, the day of Tarnoff's arrival in China. The Chinese media explained that the July military operations had been effective in undermining support for Lee and his efforts to gain UN membership for Taiwan. Nonetheless, Lee remained stubborn and the United States had yet to make new commitments in opposition to Taiwan independence. Thus, to underscore its determination, China now carried out live artillery exercises and missile tests. Moreover, the Chinese-influenced Hong Kong media reported that the August exercises simulated a naval blockade of Taiwan and a response to U.S. military intervention.[33]

Before Tarnoff's arrival, Chinese leaders also defined their new demands on the United States. They would welcome a U.S.-China summit, but they also wanted public affirmation of the commitments that Clinton had made in his letter to Jiang Zemin. They suggested that the summit issue a fourth U.S.-China communiqué, which would address the subject of future visits to the United States by Taiwan's leaders and embody the "three nos" in Clinton's letter—no to Taiwan independence, no to a two-China policy, and no to Taiwan membership in the United Nations.

Once again, however, the United States adopted a low-key posture toward Chinese use of force and its demands for U.S. policy change. A State Department spokesperson simply repeated the now well-known phrase that the United States believed that China's missile tests "do not contribute to peace and stability in the region." In his meetings with Vice Foreign Minister Li Zhaoxing, Tarnoff privately conveyed previous U.S. assurances regarding Taiwan independence and Taiwan membership in the United Nations and reiterated that future visits to the United States by Taiwan's leaders would be rare. The Chinese Foreign Ministry responded that the talks were useful but maintained that "whether Sino-U.S. relations can be restored to normal depends on whether the U.S. side will take actions to honor its commitments."[34] Jiang Zemin then told former president George Bush that "oral undertakings are not enough; we demand . . . practical and effective measures" to remove the consequences of Lee's visit and to "avert the recurrence of big ups and downs" in U.S.-China relations. Prime Minister Li told Bush that China wanted "concrete actions."[35]

The dispute over Taiwan had become enmeshed in negotiations over a U.S.-China summit. At issue was the summit agenda. President Jiang would be in New York in late October 1995 to attend the celebration of the fiftieth anniversary of the UN General Assembly and could travel to Washington for a summit. But whereas China wanted the summit to focus on negotiations over the Taiwan issue, the State Department believed that it had made sufficient concessions to satisfy Chinese concerns. Nor would it agree to a summit in which the focus was on the Taiwan issue. It believed that such a summit would be tension-ridden, would only serve Chinese interests in one-upping Taiwan, and would not address the issues the United States cared about—arms proliferation, trade, and human rights.[36]

Washington brusquely dismissed China's demand. Before Vice Foreign Minister Li Zhaoxing resumed his discussions with Under Secretary of State Tarnoff in Washington, the State Department declared that the United States would not agree to any communiqué regarding visits to the United States by Taiwan leaders or "that deals in any way, shape or form with the subject of Taiwan because our position on Taiwan is clear." It explained that after repeated discussions and exchange of letters, the U.S. position is "abundantly clear" and it "is not going to change." Thus, "the stage is over in the relationship" in which the United States would try to mollify Beijing's concerns over the Taiwan issue.[37] Moreover, on September 13 President Clinton met with the Dalai Lama at the White House, revealing his ongoing willingness to consider domestic politics when making China policy.

The United States remained interested in a U.S.-China summit but insisted that "whether or not it takes place will depend on how much progress we make in U.S.-China relations." Progress for the United States meant Chinese willingness to reach agreement on human rights, arms proliferation, and trade.[38] After Li's talks with Tarnoff and a brief meeting with Christopher on September 22, the State Department explained that a summit meeting required a "stable" relationship in which the two sides "get beyond" the Taiwan issue. Li described his talks with Tarnoff as "very frank and useful."[39]

China faced a de facto U.S. ultimatum: either drop the Taiwan issue or forgo a summit. On September 27 Christopher and Qian met in New York to discuss the terms for a summit. Four days earlier the United States had delivered to Taiwan two E-2T early airborne warning-and-command aircraft. The timing of the delivery of the advanced aircraft to Taiwan may have been coincidental, but it underscored U.S. determination to resist Chinese pressure.[40]

Faced with the U.S. ultimatum, China on October 2 accepted the U.S. terms for a summit. The focus of the summit would be not Taiwan but nonproliferation. Without receiving any U.S. concessions on Taiwan, Qian told Christopher that China would suspend its assistance to Iran's nuclear energy program. He explained to the press that China appreciated U.S. commitments regarding Taiwan and that it was ready to work for greater U.S.-China cooperation. Notably absent from Qian's remarks were any complaints regarding U.S. Taiwan policy and demands for "practical measures." China had apparently followed U.S. advice to get beyond the Taiwan issue. Christopher thus instructed Tarnoff to continue his discussions with Li regarding a summit. Finally, after three more rounds of Tarnoff-Li meetings, on October 2 the two sides announced that Presidents Jiang and Clinton would meet on October 24 at the Lincoln Center in New York. Beijing then announced that its ambassador would soon return to Washington, D.C. Following the summit, China agreed to resume the U.S.-China military dialogue and to hold discussions on trade and other bilateral issues.[41]

THE CONFRONTATION OVER TAIWAN

The Clinton administration had withstood Chinese pressure to make significant concessions regarding Taiwan and secured an important Chinese concession regarding nuclear energy cooperation with Iran. Regarding visits by Taiwan's leaders to the United States, Clinton reaffirmed to Jiang that such visits would be "unofficial, private, and rare" and decided on a case-by-case basis. And as in the past, Clinton offered confidential assurances that Washington would oppose Taiwan independence and membership in the United Nations. He also repeated the administration's ambiguous assurances regarding future visits by Taiwan leaders to the United States. Otherwise, the summit agenda paid scant attention to the Taiwan issue. Instead it focused on such issues as trade disputes, arms proliferation, human rights, international crime, and environmental protection, all of which reflected the administration's interest in Chinese cooperation with U.S. objectives.[42]

Moreover, the Clinton administration had achieved its goals while retaining its negotiating leverage in summit diplomacy. Beijing had wanted a "state visit" in Washington, replete with a state banquet and military honors, but the White House had agreed to hold only an unofficial meeting in Washington. Thus, Washington could use Beijing's continued interest in an official Washington summit to extract additional concessions. The State Department explained that an unofficial summit "most appropriately reflects the current standing of U.S.-China relations."[43]

Administration officials were pleased with the summit and the direction of U.S.-China relations. Assistant Secretary of State Lord reported that Chinese leaders agreed with the U.S. position that the two sides can discuss issues sensitive to China (i.e., Taiwan), but that "we have to get on with the broad agenda." After the disruptions caused by Lee's visit to Cornell, China and the United States were now "resuming momentum" toward resolving other problems. Robert Suettinger, director of Asian Affairs for the National Security Council, similarly believed that the summit enabled the two sides to make "significant progress."[44] When Secretary of State Christopher met with Foreign Minister Qian in mid-November in Osaka, he reported that China was now prepared for a constructive discussion of the Taiwan issue. Lord said that he was confident that Chinese leaders "understand" that administration officials had "reaffirmed as much as we're capable of doing" on U.S.-Taiwan policy.[45]

But Chinese leaders were not satisfied, for there had been no fundamental change in U.S. policy since Lee's visit. They believed that the United States had not made commitments regarding the Taiwan issue. China agreed to the summit and had made the concessions necessary to make the summit successful, but it had not accepted Washington's Taiwan policy, nor had it demoted the priority of the Taiwan issue on the U.S.-China agenda.[46] Rather, it had decided to shelve the issue until its leverage improved. Even after Qian Qichen announced that China had agreed to the New York summit, he said that "we do not think that this is enough because a complete agreement . . . has not been reached." Immediately following the summit, Qian said that Clinton and Jiang had held a "positive and useful meeting," but "this does not mean that the Taiwan issue will not again be the main issue affecting U.S.-China relations." And whereas in Osaka Christopher was upbeat about U.S.-China relations, Qian said that the "differences and contradictions" between Washington and Beijing "need to be addressed and tackled."[47]

China agreed to the New York summit because it had turned its focus to the December election for members of the Taiwan legislature and it needed stable U.S.-China relations to enhance its effort to coerce Lee Teng-hui to stop his pro-independence activities. Despite China's repeated military exercises and missile tests, Lee defied Chinese warnings. In September Taiwan carried out its own missile tests, and in early October it held ground, air, and naval exercises simulating a response to an enemy attempt to land on Taiwan. It also insisted that Tokyo invite Lee to attend the Asia Pacific Economic

Cooperation (APEC) summit in Japan.[48] After visiting the United States, Lee was now aiming for Japan. Moreover, Taiwan leaders had been closely watching U.S.-China diplomacy. They stressed the U.S. refusal to consider a fourth communiqué and emphasized U.S. criticism of China's military activities, but they minimized the importance of the U.S.-China summit. China observed this pattern and suggested that Lee was creating a domestic environment supportive of his independence efforts.[49]

China responded to the failure of its U.S. policy by escalating its use of force. In October, following the announcement of the New York summit, Jiang Zemin, accompanied by China's senior military leadership, observed PLA air force and navy exercises and boarded a command ship to observe a "high-tech war game" of submarines, destroyers, and missile launchings. Also on display were China's bombers and nuclear and conventional submarines. The focus of the event was Chinese military modernization, but the Foreign Ministry stressed that the maneuvers also demonstrated China's resolve to safeguard sovereignty and territorial integrity.[50] Equally important, Jiang had directly associated himself with China's determination to resist militarily Taiwan independence, underscoring the unity of the Chinese leadership on this issue.

The October maneuvers were a prelude to more serious coercive diplomacy aimed at Taiwan's December 2 election for members of the Legislative Assembly. The mere holding of an election on Taiwan might enhance the international legitimacy of Taiwan's independence movement. The election was also an important opportunity for the people of Taiwan to pass judgment on Lee Teng-hui's mainland policy. Given Lee's recent successes and the impression of U.S. support for Taiwan, China was concerned that public optimism might result in a victory for the Democratic Progressive Party (DPP), Taiwan's pro-independence party. Finally, Lee might use the election and the pressures of campaign politics as an excuse to take another step toward establishing formal sovereignty for Taiwan.

On November 15, just as the two-week campaign period before the Taiwan election began and when Assistant Secretary of Defense Joseph Nye was in Beijing to resume the U.S.-China military dialogue, China began another round of military activities. Unlike with the previous exercises, Beijing openly declared that these exercises were aimed at Taiwan and designed to maintain the "unity" of China and to resist the "splittist" activities of Taiwan's pro-independence forces. It also declared that the "Nanjing military theater," rather than the Nanjing military region, was responsible for the exercises, suggesting that China had gone on war footing. The exercise included a simulation of an amphibious PLA landing on a Taiwan-held island and attacks on a mock-up of Taiwan's largest airport. The exercise included Chinese land, naval, and air forces. It demonstrated the "military's resolve and capability to defend national sovereignty and . . . safeguard the motherland's unity."[51] It was a "most serious warning" of China's "determination to firmly oppose and contain Taiwan independence" through "so-called 'democratic procedures' with the support of foreign sources."[52]

Beijing could draw considerable satisfaction from its coercive diplomacy. Lee Teng-hui's Nationalist Party, which had been expected to win an easy victory, held on to its majority by only two seats. The most surprising outcome was the success of the New Party, composed of candidates highly critical of Lee's provocative mainland policy. Although the New Party had been formed only two years earlier, all of its candidates were elected and it increased its total seats in the legislature. The outcome had "vindicated" Chinese forceful opposition to Taiwan independence.[53]

Although China's latest round of exercises was by far the largest and most threatening, the United States responded with conspicuous silence. No officials at the White House, the State Department, or the Defense Department discussed the maneuvers with the media or in public speeches. In his mid-November visit to Beijing, despite the recent exercises and strong Chinese warnings to him against U.S. "interference" in the Taiwan issue, Assistant Secretary of Defense Nye only privately reiterated U.S. advice that China's exercises were counterproductive. The focus of his visit remained his briefing for Chinese leaders on the U.S.-Japan alliance, which stressed that the strengthened alliance was not aimed at China, and U.S. interest in renewing the U.S.-China military dialogue. When a Chinese foreign policy analyst asked how the United States would respond to a mainland attack on Taiwan, Nye responded that it would depend on the immediate circumstances. He observed that in 1950 the United States had said that it would not become involved in Korea but that it quickly reversed itself. Other than this cautious response to a question from a think-tank analyst, Nye did not press China on its military activities.[54]

On December 19 the U.S. aircraft carrier *Nimitz* passed through the Taiwan Strait, the first such transit by a U.S. aircraft carrier since the normalization of U.S.-China relations in 1979. Neither a political gesture nor a quiet warning to Chinese leaders, the transit was an unpublicized detour to avoid delays caused by bad weather. Because the carrier avoided advertising its presence to China, U.S. officials believed that Chinese leaders were unaware of its presence.[55]

The administration's response to China's military exercises was intentionally low key. Since the first round of the exercises in the summer, U.S. officials had understood that the White House had contributed to U.S.-China conflict by failing to keep its pledges regarding Taiwan and they did not want to further aggravate the situation by overreacting to China's exercises. They also believed that as the "offended party" Beijing needed to express its anger. Moreover, as one NSC official later explained, the United States wanted Taiwan to understand that its "actions have consequences," that provoking China was not cost free. Thus, as long as China did not threaten Taiwan with war, the United States was not eager to rise to its defense.[56]

But China did not simply want to blow off steam and coerce Taiwan to end its independence diplomacy. Its exercises were also targeted at U.S. policy. They were a key part of China's effort to coerce the United States into changing its Taiwan policy. In this respect, U.S. silence suggested disinterest for Chinese capabilities and threats and its intention to continue to resist Chinese demands. To Chinese leaders, the White House had yet to get the message that the United States was challenging a vital Chinese interest and that it had to adjust its policy. China's leaders thus concluded that the next round of PLA activities should be even more provocative to show the United States its determination to use force against Taiwan independence.[57]

Chinese planning had considerable urgency because Taiwan was preparing for direct elections for president on March 23, 1996. This would be the first democratic election of a Taiwan leader and would add domestic and international legitimacy to sovereignty for Taiwan. Furthermore, campaign politics might encourage Lee to use the independence issue to raise support for his candidacy. Finally, China had to worry about the possibility of a victory for Peng Ming-min, the outspoken pro-independence DPP candidate for president.

In the lead-up to the March 1996 elections, Taiwan's candidates insisted that Taiwan could challenge mainland threats. Lee Teng-hui declared that of all the presidential candidates, only he had the "capability, wisdom, and guts to handle cross-strait relations." Two weeks later he said that the effect of the PLA exercises was "diminishing" and that the mainland was "not pleased with our foreign trips, but we must also say that we are not pleased with their military exercises. Shall we say that we have broken even?"[58] DPP candidate Peng Ming-min promised a friendly policy toward the mainland, but only if it "recognizes Taiwan as a sovereign and independent state." If the PLA carried out aggression against Taiwan, Taiwan's military capability would inflict a "heavy price" on the mainland.[59]

Simultaneously, Taiwan stressed U.S. support for Taiwan. In late January it revealed to the media that the *Nimitz* had passed through the Taiwan Strait in December, declared its appreciation to the U.S. Congress for appealing to the White House to expedite delivery of the Patriot missiles to Taiwan, and announced forthcoming antisubmarine exercises. In early February it announced that it had taken delivery of a missile frigate, which would contribute to Taiwan's antisubmarine and air defense, and that it would substantially increase its defense budget to deal with the greater military threat from the mainland. Taiwan seemed intent on using the United States to resist mainland pressure.[60]

Moreover, Washington seemed to support Taiwan's independence drive. On January 6, despite China's "solemn representations," the Clinton administration approved a visa for Taiwan vice president Li Yuan-zu to transit Los Angeles on his way to Guatemala, insisting that the decision was not inconsistent with unofficial relations with Taiwan. China expressed its "strong displeasure" at the decision.[61] Then on January 31 the White House again ignored Chinese warnings and approved two additional transit visas for Li to travel round-trip between Taiwan and Haiti. En route to Haiti he planned to spend two nights in the United States, visiting San Francisco and Miami. On his return to Taiwan he planned to stay one night in Los Angeles. Although the administration needed more than a week to make the decision, it insisted that the visa was a "routine matter" that should not affect U.S.-China relations.[62]

China attacked Washington's encouragement of Taiwan independence and warned Taiwan to go no further toward independence. In late December 1995 the director of the Institute of Taiwan Studies wrote that Taiwan's "separatists" were on the verge of danger and that the Taiwan people should "warn these separatists in all seriousness to rein themselves in at the brink of the precipice."[63] In January Prime Minister Li Peng said that China's commitment to use force was "directed . . . against the schemes of foreign forces . . . to bring about 'Taiwan independence.'" Since Lee's visit to Cornell, China had demonstrated its "determination and ability to safeguard . . . sovereignty and territorial integrity." In early March Jiang Zemin told China's National People's Congress (NPC) that if Taiwan did not abandon its independence activities, "the struggle between China and Taiwan will not stop." Qian Qichen told NPC delegates that the main danger is Taiwan independence with international support. "If this situation occurs, it will be disastrous."[64]

China backed up its verbal threats with coercive diplomacy. From late January through February the PLA massed more than one hundred thousand troops in Fujian Province.[65] The size of China's deployments caught Washington's attention. Administration officials stressed that they did not believe that the exercises were a prelude to an attack and that there was no military threat to Taiwan, but they warned Beijing not to adopt provocative actions. When Vice Foreign Minister Li Zhaoxing visited Washington in early February, U.S. officials told him that China should not intimidate Taiwan and should work to reduce tension in the strait. The administration also used military signals to weigh in against Chinese policy. On February 6 Secretary of Defense William Perry said that he did not yet consider China's use of its military a threat to Taiwan, but he admitted that he was concerned. The same day the Pentagon reported that a U.S. naval vessel was transiting the Taiwan Strait. The next day, Assistant Secretary of State Lord told the Senate Foreign Relations Committee that the administration had stressed to Beijing its "deep concern" over PLA activities. He warned that the administration was closely watching developments and that if hostilities occurred, the "impact . . . would be extremely serious." The State Department announced that since January 26 the administration's senior national security advisers had held a series of meetings to assess Beijing's activities and that these meetings would continue.[66]

Nonetheless, China pushed ahead with its plans for military maneuvers. It believed that it had to raise the stakes to make the United States understand the risks of its Taiwan policy.[67] U.S. silence during the December maneuvers suggested that Washington had become accustomed to Chinese military exercises, so that to get U.S. attention China had to carry out more provocative exercises.[68] Moreover, Taiwan seemed unfazed by PRC threats. During the first months of 1996 it conducted military maneuvers suggesting its resistance to the mainland's "anti-splittist, anti-Taiwan struggle."[69]

On March 4 China announced that the PLA would conduct surface-to-surface missile tests from March 8 to March 18. The target areas were waters just off the coast of Taiwan's two largest port cities, one of which was barely twenty miles from the northern port of Keelung. After careful study, Chinese leaders had concluded that if the target zones were not close to Taiwan, the tests would be ineffective in opposing Taiwan "splittism" and U.S. policy toward Taiwan.[70] When asked whether the likelihood of a mainland attack on Taiwan had increased, a Foreign Ministry spokesperson responded that "if Taiwan declares 'independence' or if foreign forces meddle, the Chinese Government will not sit by idly."[71]

On March 7, despite vigorous and repeated discussions between U.S. and Chinese diplomats and U.S. advice that China not proceed with its missile tests, the PLA fired three M-9 missiles into the target zones.[72] That day Defense Minister Chi Haotian explained to the Fujian delegates to the NPC that "we have more troops stationed in Fujian because we are facing a grim situation, in which Lee Teng-hui and his gang are vainly attempting to split China. . . . We must heighten our vigilance." A

March 8 joint editorial of *People's Daily* and the PLA's *Liberation Army Daily* warned of the danger of allowing Lee Teng-hui to continue to advocate Taiwan independence. It explained that China retained the right to use force to oppose "interference by foreign forces . . . and their attempt to promote 'Taiwan independence.' [We will] exert all our efforts to defend our country's reunification. We mean what we say."[73]

The Clinton administration understood that the PLA was not preparing to attack Taiwan but instead was trying to affect the election and Taiwan's independence movement. As Secretary of Defense Perry explained, attacking Taiwan would be "a dumb thing" for China to do, observing that it was not capable of invading Taiwan. Although Perry believed that China had the ability to harass Taiwan, he observed that "it does not make any sense. . . . I do not expect China to be attacking Taiwan." The State Department explained that the missile tests were an exercise in the political use of force and did not "presage any broader military effort." Moreover, following the March 7 missile launches, through various diplomatic channels, including Vice Foreign Minister Liu Huaqiu's discussions in Washington, China had assured the United States that it did not intend to attack Taiwan.[74]

Nonetheless, Washington had to react. China had ignored U.S. warnings, and its missile tests challenged U.S. credibility. Administration officials believed that if the United States did not forcefully respond, China would doubt Washington's commitment to a peaceful resolution of the Taiwan conflict. China would be encouraged to escalate its threat in the coming years, increasing the likelihood of hostilities and a far more serious U.S.-China crisis. The Defense Department explained that Washington needed to communicate its determination that China resolve its differences with Taiwan peacefully. It could not allow Chinese leaders to conclude that "the U.S. had lost interest in that area of the world." As Perry later recalled, the United States had to demonstrate its "military resolve" regarding its Taiwan policy.[75]

Equally significant, U.S. leaders believed that failure to respond to China's actions would have called into doubt U.S. commitments to remaining an active East Asian power in the post–Cold War era and to fulfilling its bilateral security commitments to regional allies. The United States' reputation as a "loyal" ally was at stake. Christopher explained that "because Asian and Pacific nations looked to the United States to preserve stability in the region, we had to take action to calm the situation."[76]

On March 7 Vice Foreign Minister Liu Huaqiu visited Washington to hold prearranged discussions with national security adviser Anthony Lake. Earlier that day, China had tested its M-9 missiles. Liu's visit offered the administration an opportunity to express its determination to respond to China's exercises and to forcefully advise China to end its missile tests. To strengthen the administration's message, Secretary of State Christopher and Secretary of Defense Perry joined Lake for his evening meal with Liu. As secretary of defense, Perry delivered the tough words. He told Liu that the Chinese missile tests "bracketing Taiwan" were "reckless" and "aggressive" and could be seen as a threat to U.S. interests. He warned Liu that the United States "had more than enough military capability to protect its vital national security interests in the region and is prepared to demonstrate that." He then said that China would make a mistake if it continued the missile tests. Lake told Liu that the Chinese exercises threatened vital U.S. security interests in the western Pacific and that China should stop its provocations and resume its cooperative policies toward Taiwan.[77]

China ignored Washington's warnings. On March 9 it announced that from March 12 to March 20 it would conduct air and naval exercises with live ammunition in the waters near Taiwan.[78] China and the United States were involved in a test of wills. But their respective objectives were very different. Beijing aimed to coerce Taiwan leaders into abandoning their independence activities, to coerce the Taiwan voters into voting against independence, and to coerce the United States into adopting more public and determined opposition to Taiwan independence. Washington, on the other hand, however much it may have opposed Taiwan's movement toward independence, aimed to uphold the credibility of its commitment to a peaceful resolution of the Taiwan conflict and to remain a reliable security partner to its regional allies. Despite their different objectives, China and the United States both had important interests at stake.

Following dinner with Liu Huaqiu on March 8, Perry decided that China's missile tests required the United States to conduct a show of force. He suggested that a carrier battle group sail through Taiwan Strait. But after consultations with NSC advisers, who advocated a less provocative display of force, and with General John Shali-kashvili, who preferred to keep the carrier farther from China's coastal weaponry, Perry agreed to a more cautious plan.[79] Perry then announced that the United States would deploy two aircraft carrier battle groups to observe China's behavior. He ordered the *Independence* battle group from Okinawa to the waters east of Taiwan and the *Nimitz* carrier group from the Persian Gulf to the Philippine Sea, which would allow it to join the *Independence* on short notice. Perry explained that China's insistence that its missile tests were routine was "baloney" and that they were meant to intimidate Taiwan. He said that the message of the U.S. carriers was that "the United States has a national interest in the security and the stability in the western Pacific region. We have a powerful military force there to help us carry out our national interests." The State Department concurred, explaining that the carriers indicated U.S. interest in a peaceful outcome to mainland-Taiwan differences.[80]

The United States was determined to protect the credibility of its commitment to defend its interests, but China was equally determined to protect its territorial integrity. Indeed, Beijing feared that the U.S. carrier deployments and the U.S. commitment to defend Taiwan might encourage Lee to take another step toward independence. The Chinese Foreign Ministry warned the United States that it was unwise to deploy the carriers: "If this . . . is regarded by the Taiwan authorities as . . . supporting and conniving" with Taiwan's "splitting the motherland, that would be very dangerous." Foreign Minister Qian said that it was not China but the United States that was "reckless."[81]

China launched its second set of March exercises as scheduled on March 12 and its fourth M-9 missile test on March 13. Then on March 15 it announced that from March 18 to March 25 the PLA would conduct joint air, ground, and naval exercises near Pingtan Island, ten nautical miles from Taiwan-controlled islands. The March 15 joint editorial of *People's Daily* and *Liberation Army Daily* warned that if Lee Teng-hui "insists on going his way and clings obstinately to promoting 'Taiwan independence' . . . or if foreign forces interfere in

China's unification," then China would "make every effort to safe-guard the motherland's reunification."[82]

Despite China's succession of exercises and missile tests, the Clinton administration remained confident that the PLA would not attack Taiwan. Throughout the confrontation there was no sense of tension in U.S. decision making. Having deployed the two carriers, the administration believed that its credibility was secure. Thus, with the exception of some verbal boasting of its naval prowess, Washington did not engage in further escalation of military signaling.[83] The United States observed the remainder of the Chinese exercises, Taiwan conducted its first presidential election, and there was neither war nor a Taiwan declaration of independence.

THE AFTERMATH: ASSESSING COERCIVE DIPLOMACY VERSUS DETERRENCE

The United States and China held two very different objectives in the 1995–96 confrontation over Taiwan. China used force to achieve tangible policy gains; the United States used force to achieve reputational gains. Because they sought different types of objectives, both were able to achieve their respective objective. But both also paid a price for their success.

The Costs and Benefits of Chinese Use of Force

Following the confrontation, Washington exercised caution in U.S.-Taiwan relations. Although it would not automatically deny visas to Taiwan officials, it issued only transit visas and limited the time and activities of Taiwan leaders in the United States. When Washington issued a transit visa for Vice President Lien Chan in January 1997, it insisted that he agree not to conduct any public activities. When his spokesman held a meeting with reporters at the Los Angeles airport, the White House required him to cut short his visit. When Lee Teng-hui requested a transit visa in September 1997, he was permitted to transit through Hawaii, but he was unable to schedule appointments with Hawaiian state officials. China appreciated Washington's effort to control Taiwan's independence activities.[84] Its silence on subsequent visas for Taiwan officials suggested that it was satisfied with U.S. sensitivity to Chinese interests.

Washington signaled its caution in other ways. When Taiwan's leaders traveled to Washington in late March 1996 to purchase U.S. arms, the Clinton administration did not agree to new sales. Then in mid-1997, in his Senate confirmation hearings, Stanley Roth, the Clinton administration's nominee for assistant secretary of state for East Asian and Pacific affairs, acknowledged that the 1995 decision to grant Lee Teng-hui a visa had been a "serious mistake."[85]

Most important, China made gains in influencing U.S. policy toward Taiwan's status in world affairs and in bilateral U.S.-China relations.[86] Before March 1996 the Clinton administration had followed the practice of presidents since Richard Nixon by making only confidential assurances regarding its opposition to Taiwan independence. It refused to change its declaratory policy on Taiwan's role in international politics, and it insisted that the negotiations over the Taiwan issue be removed from the agenda of U.S.-China summits. It was also reluctant to hold an "official" summit with Jiang Zemin.

Following the March exercises, there was widespread recognition in the administration that the U.S.-China relationship was "broke" and that it had to be "fixed." Thus, Secretary of State Christopher's May 1996 speech on U.S.-China relations reflected the administration's first effort to place the U.S.-China relationship, and the Taiwan issue, within a larger, comprehensive strategic perspective. The State Department also believed that U.S.-China summits could help to put the relationship on the right track. In July 1996, during his visit to Beijing, National Security Adviser Lake suggested that the two countries exchange summits. Then in November 1996 Clinton and Jiang met in Manila and agreed to exchange state visits in 1997 and 1998.[87]

China was pleased with U.S. initiatives, but it remained focused on the Taiwan issue. From November until the Washington summit in October 1997, China publicly pressed the United States to strengthen its opposition to Taiwan independence. In his June 1997 meeting with Secretary of State Madeleine Albright to plan for the summit, Foreign Minister Qian insisted that Taiwan was the most important and sensitive issue in the relationship. In August he repeated this to National

Security Adviser Samuel Berger and warned that the Taiwan issue had the potential to set back U.S.-China relations.[88]

In contrast to the 1995 diplomacy over the Clinton-Jiang meeting in New York, in 1997 not only did the Clinton administration not insist that China drop its demands on U.S.-Taiwan policy as a precondition to a summit meeting, but it also made a concession. During the October summit, Clinton assured Jiang that the United States did not support a two-China policy, did not support Taiwan independence, and did not support Taiwan membership in the United Nations or in other international organizations requiring sovereignty for membership. White House and State Department officials publicly reported the president's assurances. Although China had wanted Clinton's assurances included in the official summit statement, this was nonetheless the first time that the U.S. government had publicly and explicitly stated that it did not support Taiwan independence. Thereafter, other U.S. officials, including Secretary of State Albright, made similar statements. The administration made important gains on arms proliferation, human rights, and other issues, but in a clear break with the past it had negotiated and compromised on the Taiwan issue.[89]

Taiwan remained on the negotiating agenda during the preparations for President Clinton's 1998 visit to Beijing. This time China wanted Clinton to make a public announcement in China of U.S. policy toward Taiwan independence. In light of China's concessions, including providing the president with an opportunity to deliver on Chinese television an unedited speech and an agreement to a nuclear nontargeting pact, the president expressed personally U.S. policy on Taiwan in an open forum in Shanghai.[90] Although China had not secured a written U.S. statement or a fourth communiqué and the president's statement of the "three nos" contained nothing new regarding actual U.S. policy toward Taiwan and did not require change in U.S. behavior, this was the first time that a U.S. president had ever publicly stated that the United States did not support Taiwan independence. Since 1971 China had sought such a statement, and the United States had adamantly refused to make it. Before March 1996 Washington had refused even to consider changes in its Taiwan policy, regardless of Chinese quid pro quos, but in the aftermath of

China's coercive diplomacy the Taiwan issue had become an undisputed part of U.S.-China summit negotiations.

China was only partly successful regarding Taiwan. On the one hand, the DPP fared poorly in the March elections and subsequently adopted a cautious mainland policy to increase its appeal to the voters.[91] In addition, immediately after the elections Taiwan postponed plans for live-fire military exercises based on Mazu, the offshore island close to the mainland, and Lee Teng-hui indicated that he would limit his travel abroad. He explained that having just been elected president, he would have a "full agenda" and "no time for overseas visits for quite a while, and now I certainly have no plans to visit the United States." His foreign minister explained that Lee would only make trips that would not create trouble and that he did not want "to bring damage" to Taiwan.[92]

Nonetheless, Lee Teng-hui won a significant victory in the three-way presidential race, capturing 52 percent of the vote.[93] Moreover, it was clear that Lee's postelection caution was only a tactical response to the U.S.-China confrontation and Chinese pressure. He soon resumed Taiwan's effort to join the United Nations, and his subordinates resumed transit diplomacy. The next year he sought a transit visa from the United States. Then in July 1999, just before an important meeting in the cross-strait dialogue, he provocatively described the mainland-Taiwan relationship as a "special state-to-state relationship." His aides explained that the state-to-state formulation had been under discussion for more than a year, that Taiwan could no longer adhere to the one-China formula, and that the new formulation was Taiwan's new definition for mainland-Taiwan ties. Lee seemed bent on seeking Taiwan independence and Chinese leaders were outraged. Beijing canceled the forthcoming meeting between senior leaders Wang Daohan and Koo Chen-fu, conducted extensive military exercises in Fujian, and repeatedly sent its military aircraft over the midline of the Taiwan Strait.[94]

Nonetheless, China's new relationship with the United States paid off. Because Washington was concerned that Lee's statement could lead to renewed tension, it pressured him to modify his policy. The State Department indicated that it held Lee responsible for the suspended mainland-Taiwan dialogue and that it expected Taiwan to make the necessary clarification to allow the dialogue to resume. President Clinton quickly called Jiang Zemin to reassure him that the United States remained committed to a one-China policy, effectively aligning the United States with China in opposition to Taiwan's policy. The president also announced that he had postponed an arms sales mission to Taiwan by Defense Department officials to avoid exacerbating the situation. When Clinton met with Jiang in New Zealand in September, he cautioned China against using military force against Taiwan, but he also raised the Taiwan issue to reassert U.S. support for a one-China policy and to explain that he believed that Lee's statement "had made things more difficult for both China and the United States."[95]

China's successful coercive diplomacy came at a price. Its missile tests aggravated concern for Chinese power in Southeast Asia. After the March confrontation, the region intensified its focus on "the rise of China" and its implications for regional stability. Surprisingly, however, this was a short-lived phenomenon. First, some of the countries in Southeast Asia held Taiwan's diplomacy responsible for China's missile tests and for the ensuing regional tension. In addition, Beijing's currency policy following the onset of the Asian financial crisis in late 1997 earned widespread praise for China's responsible use of its financial power. Since then, although the region remains concerned about Chinese power in the evolving regional order, China's reputation has been no worse than it was before the 1996 confrontation.[96]

China incurred a greater cost in its relationship with the United States. The March confrontation exacerbated controversy in the United States over U.S. policy toward China and Taiwan and gave Taiwan's supporters a greater voice in U.S. policy debates. Thus, although members of Congress have been more reluctant to force the president's hand on potentially provocative issues, having learned a lesson from China's reaction to Lee's visit to Cornell, they have been increasingly eager to use China policy to score political points with the electorate and weaken the White House. This has made it more difficult for the president to develop cooperative policies toward China and to manage the U.S. arms sales relationship with Taiwan.

The 1996 confrontation focused the Pentagon's attention on the U.S.-China conflict over Taiwan as the most likely source of U.S. involvement in a major war. Since then, planning for war with China has become a Pentagon priority, with implications for budgets and weapons acquisition. Pentagon and congressional interest in theater missile defense, including cooperation with Taiwan on this system, has been to a significant degree a reaction to China's March 1996 missile tests. In addition, during the confrontation the Pentagon was alarmed at how little communication there was between Taiwan and U.S. defense officials. Since then, it has sought greater coordination between the two militaries in preparation for U.S.-Taiwan cooperation in a war with China, with implications for U.S.-Taiwan military relations and for China's effort to isolate Taiwan.[97]

Chinese leaders acknowledge the costs of their coercive diplomacy, but they believe that had they adopted less provocative policies and failed to get Washington's attention, independence sentiments in Taiwan would have remained high and U.S. policy would have continued to encourage Taiwan independence. Shortly after the confrontation, Prime Minister Li Peng gloated that Americans in and out of government "have come to realize the importance of China." He observed that this is "progress because before they miscalculated the situation. They thought that . . . China was no longer important. . . . But facts have negated these ideas." Chinese leaders accept the costs of coercive diplomacy as the necessary trade-off for the gains they made in U.S. policy toward Taiwan and the resulting caution among the Taiwan electorate.[98]

Chinese threats made the people of Taiwan less likely than ever to consider unification. The New Party has become irrelevant in Taiwan politics, while the victory of Chen Shui-bian, the DPP candidate in the 2000 presidential election, suggests Taiwan's growing resentment at mainland threats. Greater threat perception has also further encouraged Taiwan to develop political and military relationships with the United States. Thus, China's ability to expand mainland-Taiwan economic relations and to develop the cross-strait dialogue on the basis of the "one-China principle" has been more difficult since March 1996. Nevertheless, China's policy had never been predicated on the assumption that diplomacy could win the affection of the people on Taiwan or persuade Taiwan to loosen its ties with the United States. Rather, economic cooperation aims to make Taiwan increasingly dependent on the Chinese economy, diplomacy aims to manage the relationship to maintain stability for the long term, during which Taiwan will be absorbed into the mainland, and deterrence aims to prevent independence in the short term. Hence, from China's perspective, coercive diplomacy did not hurt the prospects of unification, but it did reduce the momentum toward independence.

The Costs and Benefits of U.S. Use of Force

The United States benefited from deterrence diplomacy. It maintained its reputation for resisting Chinese use of force against Taiwan and maintained the confidence of its allies that it was prepared to use force to maintain regional stability. Many Chinese leaders were surprised by the U.S. deployment of the two carriers, underscoring that they had miscalculated U.S. resolve to resist Chinese use of force. Their miscalculation affected not only U.S.-China relations but also the outcome of the Taiwan election. The U.S. response offset any impact China's use of force might have otherwise had on Beijing's effort to curb Taiwan's independence movement. Following the confrontation, uncertainty in China over U.S. intentions significantly diminished. Chinese policymakers must now assume that regardless of the source of a future crisis, including a formal Taiwan declaration of sovereign independence, the United States will almost certainly intervene militarily against Chinese use of force.[99]

Greater Chinese certainty regarding U.S. intervention has injected an element of uncertainty into China's Taiwan policy. Now that the cost for China of military retaliation against Taiwan independence is better understood—military conflict with the United States and thus derailment of China's economic modernization program and greater inability to manage its complex and troubling societal issues—Beijing has given greater attention to retaliatory measures that reduce the likelihood of U.S. intervention. A few well-informed Chinese even question China's commitment to retaliate militarily against Taiwan independence and suggest less costly options, including political use of force.[100] Although all Chinese recognize that the alternatives to military retaliation are fraught with problems, including implications for Chinese strategic credibility in Asia and the government's domestic legitimacy, that even a quiet and limited discussion exists underscores the success of U.S. use of force for its deterrence posture.

Washington's deployment of the two carriers also bolstered its strategic position in Asia. In the aftermath of the Cold War there had been considerable regional uncertainty over the U.S. role in Asia and heightened concern over the "rise of China." The combination of these two trends had challenged Washington's reputation to defend its regional strategic partners. Following the 1996 U.S. show of force, there has been greater confidence throughout Asia that the United States is committed to remaining an Asian power. This heightened confidence reflects many factors, including the strengthening of the U.S.-Japan security treaty. Nonetheless, the U.S. response to Chinese use of force made an important contribution to sustaining regional confidence in U.S. resolve.[101]

The costs for the United States of deterrence diplomacy mirrored Chinese costs for its coercive diplomacy. Although Washington achieved its immediate policy objectives, U.S. policy affected perceptions of the United States in China's political arena and within the PLA. U.S. ability to threaten China without risk angered, frustrated, and embarrassed many Chinese. U.S. gunboat diplomacy reminded Chinese of their humiliation by the imperialists' gunboat diplomacy directed at China during the nineteenth century. Some Chinese policymakers were especially angry insofar as the United States had been assured that China would not attack Taiwan; they believed the deployment of the aircraft carriers was unnecessary and aimed only to humiliate China. The net effect of U.S. policy was to establish a consensus in China among both urban citizens and elites that the United States is China's "semi-enemy."[102] Just as the U.S. reaction to China's "missile diplomacy" strengthened opposition in the United States to U.S.-China cooperation, U.S. "gunboat diplomacy" hardened Chinese attitudes toward the United States, making it more difficult for Chinese policymakers to cooperate with U.S. foreign policy interests, even as they understand the imperative to avoid U.S.-China conflict.

U.S. policy also influenced the PLA. Chinese leaders believe that the deployment of the two carriers increased the U.S. commitment to defend Taiwan, tying U.S. credibility to Taiwan's security. They are now convinced that the mainland-Taiwan conflict will compel the United States to intervene.[103] Thus the PLA is planning for war against the United States, with implications both for the domestic politics of China's U.S. policy and for PLA hardware acquisitions. China's increased deployment of M-9 missiles in Fujian Province and its cruise missile program reflect its understanding that missiles may be the only weapon that China can use to deter Taiwan independence because it is the only Chinese conventional weapon that the United States cannot defeat.[104] China began negotiations to purchase Russian Sovremennyi destroyers in 1996 after the U.S.-China confrontation. One important mission for the destroyers and their Sunburn missiles is to give pause to the United States before it decides to intervene in the next confrontation in the Taiwan Strait. Although China's military modernization program might have led to such deployments on its own, the pace, quantity, and quality of China's deployments have been affected by the assumption that war with Taiwan means war with the United States.[105] U.S. policy contributed to the development of a more capable and determined Chinese adversary.

Finally, similar to the outcome of China's coercive diplomacy, U.S. policy influenced Washington's relationship with Taiwan. Since 1979 U.S. policy toward mainland-Taiwan relations had been characterized by considerable ambiguity. Washington had opposed mainland use of force, but it had also implicitly opposed provocative Taiwan diplomacy that promoted Taiwan sovereign independence. These two policies created ambiguity over how the United States would respond to mainland use of force against a Taiwan declaration of independence, which promoted caution in both Beijing and Taipei. But just as U.S. deterrence diplomacy reduced uncertainty in Beijing over U.S. policy, it increased confidence in Taiwan that regardless of the source of conflict, the United States will intervene to protect Taiwan. Although Washington retains considerable leverage over Taiwan, it is now more difficult for the United States to persuade Taiwan to forgo destabilizing diplomacy.

The benefits of U.S. policy outweighed the costs. On the one hand, the United States gained Chinese caution and regional confidence in its presence in Asia. On the other hand, the costs of inaction could have been very high—greater Chinese militancy against Taiwan and less cooperation from its Asian security partners. At stake was the post–Cold War regional security order. Administration officials also believed that the deployment of two carriers was the minimum display of force that would succeed. Just as China had to use missile tests to get the attention of U.S. leaders, Washington's response had to get the attention of Chinese leaders and leaders throughout Asia. U.S. deterrence diplomacy was necessary and justified the costs.

CONCLUSION: THE LESSONS OF 1996

U.S. policy drift and the March 1996 confrontation reflected White House susceptibility to congressional pressure, which in turn reflected Taiwan lobbying on behalf of its independence diplomacy. Administration policymakers understood that U.S. interests lay in rejecting a visa for Lee Teng-hui and they resisted further change in U.S. policy toward Taiwan, but they were unable to sway the president's thinking. Following the confrontation, the White House readily returned U.S. policy to the status quo of 1994, suggesting that the intervening U.S.-China confrontation, including the U.S. show of force, was unnecessary and avoidable. The missed opportunity and the resultant costs are thus all the more deplorable.

The source of instability in U.S.-China-Taiwan relations was Taiwan's revisionism and its effect on U.S. policy. After coming to power, Lee Teng-hui sought a new international role for Taiwan that was destined to provoke the mainland and cause U.S.-China friction. He was also determined to use Taiwan's relationship with the United States to further his goals. In responding to Lee's efforts, the Clinton administration not only deviated from its understanding with Beijing regarding U.S.-Taiwan relations but also implicitly abetted Taiwan's attempt to move the United States toward abandoning its one-China policy and to establish for Taiwan an independent status in international politics.

Beijing used coercive diplomacy to attempt to compel Taiwan to curtail its independence activities and to accommodate itself to a declaratory policy that Taiwan is part of Chinese sovereignty. Beijing also adopted coercive diplomacy to end the developing trend in President Clinton's Taiwan policy and compel him to return to the policy of his predecessors. Beijing understood that domestic politics was the source of U.S. policy change, including the 1992 F-16 sale, the 1994 Taiwan policy review, and the 1995 decision to issue a visa to Lee Teng-hui. But it was the policy, rather than its sources, that mattered to China. It used force to persuade the administration that appeasement of the "Taiwan lobby" was not risk free and to compel Clinton to incur the domestic costs necessary to change U.S. policy toward Taiwan. The 1997 and 1998 U.S.-China summits and the administration's statements on Taiwan—the "three nos"—reflected the changes in U.S. policy.

The 1996 Taiwan Strait confrontation further reveals how easy it can be for the United States and China to stumble into a collision. The United States is committed to the defense of Taiwan, but it found itself in a confrontation with China that originated over a conflict of interest peripheral to U.S. security—the international legal status of Taiwan. Moreover, Taiwan continues to challenge the diplomatic status quo. In 2002 Taiwan's leader, Chen Shui-bian, reported that Taiwan's diplomacy was based on there being a "country" on each side of the Taiwan Strait, eliciting concern in both China and the United States that Taiwan's quest for independence would once again destabilize cross-strait relations.

Washington cannot permit U.S. ideological support for Taiwan's democracy or Taiwan's democratic politics to determine the politics of war and peace between the United States and China.[106] The United States must make policy in the U.S. interest, not in Taiwan's interest. Although both the Clinton and the George W. Bush administrations have cautioned Taiwan that the United States does not support Taiwan independence,[107] Washington has yet to tell Taiwan that it would not participate in a war to defend a Taiwan declaration of independence. Reduced Taiwan confidence in U.S. support would help to constrain Taiwan's independence diplomacy, contributing to cross-strait stability.

But while constraining Taiwan, the United States must also maintain its deterrence of PRC use of force. It can enhance its superiority in long-range precision-guided weaponry and in command-and-control facilities. And it can continue to develop and forward-deploy not only aircraft carriers but also Trident nuclear-powered guided missile submarines, platforms that enable the United States to deliver precision-guided weaponry with minimal risk of casualties, thus reducing PRC expectations that asymmetric capabilities or a fait accompli strategy could deter U.S. defense of Taiwan.[108]

While deterrence constrains the likelihood of war, the United States can support peaceful resolution of the Taiwan conflict. As China's modernization continues and economic and social integration between the mainland and Taiwan continues to deepen, both sides may exercise greater caution and the impediments to a compromise solution will likely decrease. By the end of 2001 more than three hundred thousand Taiwanese were living in Shanghai and more than thirty thousand Taiwan companies had manufacturing facilities there. In 2002 a Taiwan bank opened its first representative office in China, Chinese and Taiwanese state-owned energy corporations developed a joint venture for oil exploration, and Chinese firms began recruiting Taiwan financial and technology experts. There has also been progress toward establishing direct trade across the strait.[109] Taiwan and Chinese membership in the World Trade Organization will accelerate these developments.

U.S. policy in the 1996 Taiwan Strait confrontation bolstered U.S. credibility in East Asia and contributed to deterrence of PRC use of force. But deterrence is no guarantee of long-term stability. Rather, it creates a window of opportunity for diplomacy to minimize the likelihood of future conflict. Over the next decade the cross-strait relationship will likely become more amenable to diplomatic solution. Rather than simply relying on deterrence, the United States should welcome the trend in mainland-Taiwan economic and societal relations as an opportunity to mitigate the cross-strait conflict and as a potential source of conflict resolution, thus contributing to U.S. interest as well as stability in East Asia.

NOTES

Unless otherwise noted, interviews cited below were conducted by the author during 2000.

The author is grateful to United States Institute of Peace for its support of research travel to China and to Robert Art, Patrick Cronin, Joseph Fewsmith, Steven Goldstein, Ronald Montaperto, Barry Posen, Alan Romberg, Robert Suettinger, and Allen Whiting for their helpful comments.

1. See, for example, John W. Garver, *Face Off: China, the United States, and Taiwan's Democratization* (Seattle: University of Washington Press, 1997); and Arthur Waldron, "How Not to Deal with China," *Commentary* 103, no. 3 (March 1997): 44–49.

2. The distinction between coercive diplomacy and compellence is not obvious. Thomas C. Schelling's description of compellence is nearly identical to Alexander L. George's later definition of coercive diplomacy: action that aims to "persuade an opponent to stop or reverse an action." See Thomas C. Schelling, *Arms and Influence* (Westport, Conn.: Greenwood Press, 1976), 69–72; and Alexander George, "Coercive Diplomacy: Definition and Characteristics," in *The Limits of Coercive Diplomacy*, ed. Alexander L. George and William E. Simons (Boulder, Colo.: Westview Press, 1994), 7. Either term can capture Chinese behavior. This chapter uses the term "coercive diplomacy" rather than "compellence" to describe Chinese policy, if only because "coercive diplomacy" has become the more familiar term. (Cf. Robert Art's distinction between compellence and coercive diplomacy in chapter 1 of this volume, p. 9.)

Moreover, the distinction between coercion and deterrence is often not clear. As Schelling observes, when a state seeks to end the continuance of another state's policy, there are elements of both deterrence and compellence (coercion). Schelling, *Arms and Influence*, 77. It can be argued that there are elements of both deterrence and coercion in Chinese behavior. But compellence/coercive diplomacy better captures Chinese behavior, because China took the initiative and maintained its policy of threatening the use of force until it received a response from Taiwan and the United States in terms of concrete policy change. Paul Gordon Lauren calls this pattern "defensive coercion." See Paul Gordon Lauren, "Theories of Bargaining with Threats of Force: Deterrence and Coercive Diplomacy," in *Diplomacy: New Approaches in History, Theory, and Policy*, ed. Paul Gordon Lauren (New York: Free Press, 1979), 192–193. See also Thomas C. Schelling, *The Strategy of Conflict* (New York: Oxford University Press, 1960), 195–196; and Lawrence Freedman, "Strategic Coercion," in *Strategic Coercion: Concepts and Cases*, ed. Lawrence Freedman (New York: Oxford University Press, 1998), 15–20.

3. The relationship among reputation, credibility, commitment, and deterrence follows Schelling, *Arms and Conflict*, 42–43. For an extensive discussion of the relationship between reputation and deterrence, see Jonathan Mercer, *Reputation and International Politics* (Ithaca, N.Y.: Cornell University Press, 1996), chap 1.

4. Much of the following analysis of Chinese policy is based on extensive interviews the author conducted during visits to Beijing between 1996 and 2000 with senior civilian and military specialists on U.S.-China relations and Taiwan in government think tanks and universities. These policy analysts are advisers to such government agencies as the State Council, the Ministry of Foreign Affairs, the Ministry of Security, and the People's Liberation Army. They frequently participate in government meetings regarding policy toward the United States and Taiwan. For obvious reasons, I have not disclosed their identities.

5. On the role of use of force in coercive diplomacy see Alexander L. George and William Simons, "Findings and Conclusions," in *The Limits of Coercive Diplomacy*, 273–279; and Freedman, "Strategic Coercion," 20–23.

6. This use of "deterrence" follows the definition of deterrence in Glenn H. Snyder, *Deterrence and Defense: Toward a Theory of National Security* (Princeton, N.J.: Princeton University Press, 1961), 3. Washington believed that its commitments were "interdependent," so that its follow-through in March 1996 on its commitment to Taiwan would affect the credibility of its future commitment to both Taiwan and other regional actors. On the interdependence of commitments, see Schelling, *Arms and Influence*, 55–59; and Mercer, *Reputation and International Politics*, 36–37. On the difficulty of managing allies' perceptions to maintain a reputation for loyalty, see Glenn H. Snyder, *Alliance Politics* (Ithaca, N.Y.: Cornell University Press, 1997). On the role of force in signaling reputation to both adversaries and allies, see Robert Jervis, *The Logic of Images in International Relations* (Princeton, N.J.: Princeton University Press, 1970). For a more general discussion of the political use of force, see Barry M. Blechman and Stephen S. Kaplan, *Force without War: U.S. Armed Forces as a Political Instrument* (Washington, D.C.: Brookings Institution, 1978). On the role of the U.S. Navy in signaling intentions, see James Cable, *Gunboat Diplomacy, 1919–1979* (New York: St. Martin's Press, 1981), 81–83.

7. As Mercer *(Reputation and International Politics)* points out, sometimes leaders believe commitments are interdependent when, in fact, they are not. This case, however, is one in which U.S. behavior in March 1996 clearly affected China's assessment of U.S. future resolve on the Taiwan issue and likely affected the assessment of other countries toward their own security, so that U.S. policy was appropriate and successful.

8. The three communiqués are the 1979 normalization of relations communiqué, the 1982 communiqué on U.S. arms sales to China, and the 1992 Shanghai communiqué. The text of the communiqués can be found in Robert S. Ross, *Negotiating Cooperation: U.S.-China Relations, 1969–1989* (Stanford, Calif.: Stanford University Press, 1995).

9. Warren Christopher, *In the Stream of History: Shaping Foreign Policy for a New Era* (Stanford, Calif.: Stanford University Press, 1998), 286–287; and Robert Suettinger, director of Asian Affairs, National Security Council, interview with author. On the role of Congress and domestic politics in U.S. policy toward Taiwan, see Robert G. Sutter, "Domestic Politics and U.S.-China-Taiwan Triangle: The 1995–1996 Taiwan Strait Conflict and Its Aftermath," in *After the Cold War: Domestic Factors and U.S.-China Relations*, ed. Robert S. Ross (Armonk, N.Y.: M. E. Sharpe, 1998).

10. "PRC Foreign Ministry Statement (May 23, 1995)," *Xinhua*, May 22, 1995, in Foreign Broadcast Information Service-China (hereafter FBIS-China), May 23, 1995, 2–3.

11. Commentary, "Where Does the United States Really Want to Lead Sino-U.S. Relations?" *Xinhua*, June 17, 1995, in FBIS-China, June 19, 1995, 10–12; and Commentary, "A Self-Vindication of Advocacy for Splitting the Motherland," *Xinhua* and *People's Daily*, July 23, 1995, FBIS-China, July 24, 1995, 91–93. See also, for example, Ren Fan, "The U.S. Government Should Change Its Course Immediately," *People's Daily*, June 13, 1995, in FBIS-China, June 16, 1995, 7. Taiwan's military exercises are reported in *Lien Ho Pao* (Taipei), May 26, 1995, in FBIS-China, June 5, 1995, 89–90; and Agence France-Presse, May 30, 1995, in FBIS-China, May 30, 1995, 85. For China's reaction to the exercises, see *Xinhua*, June 27, 1995, in FBIS-China, June 27, 1995, 90. Taiwan's effort to enter the United Nations is discussed in Di Xiangqian, "Money Diplomacy Goes against the Popular Will in Taiwan," *People's Daily*, July 12, 1995, FBIS-China, July 18, 1995, 77–78; and in Central News Agency (Taipei), June 28, 1995.

12. For a discussion of the arms sales communiqué, see John. H. Holdridge, *Crossing the Divide: An Insider's Account of Normalization of U.S.-China Relations* (New York: Rowman and Littlefield, 1997), chaps. 13, 14; and Ross, *Negotiating Cooperation*, chap. 6. See also James Mann, *About Face: A History of America's Curious Relationship with China, from Nixon to Clinton* (New York: Alfred A. Knopf, 1999).

13. See the remarks by Wang Jisi in *Wen Wei Po*, August 29, 1995, in FBIS-China, September 13, 1995, 6–7. See also the discussion of U.S. policy in 1994 in Wang Li, *Bolan Qifu: Zhong Mei Guanxi Yanbian de Quzhe Licheng* (Roaring waves: The tortuous process of the evolution of U.S.-China relations) (Beijing: Shijie Zhishi Chuban She, 1998), 297–298. On the new U.S. policy toward Taiwan officials, see also Steven Greenhouse, "U.S., Despite Critics, Is to Expand Taiwan Ties," *New York Times*, September 7, 1994, A5.

14. Chinese policy analysts, interviews with author; Ren Fan, "The U.S. Government Should Change Its Course Immediately," 7; and *Zhongguo Tongxun She*, May 29, 1995, in FBIS-China, June 2, 1995, 5.

15. Chinese policy analysts, interviews with author; Commentary, "The Protective Umbrella and Chief Behind-the-Scenes Backer for 'Taiwan Independence,'" *Xinhua*, August 2, 1995, in FBIS-China, August 3, 1995, 43–44.

16. For a sophisticated analysis of the domestic politics of U.S. China policy, see Niu Jun, "Perspective of U.S. Policy toward China," *Guangming Ribao*, September 14, 1995, in FBIS-China, September 26, 1995, 4–6.

17. "PRC Foreign Ministry Statement (May 23, 1995)," 3. See also Commentary, "Where Does the United States Really Want to Lead Sino-U.S. Relations?" 11.

18. Suettinger, interview with author; Department of State daily press briefing, May 24, 1995; and on-the-record briefing by Assistant Secretary of State Winston Lord, May 30, 1995. Warren Christopher made his remarks on *News Hour*, July 11, 1995. See the Chinese analysis of U.S. "ambiguity" in He Chong, "Will the Talks between the Chinese Foreign Minister and the U.S. Secretary of State Improve Sino-U.S. Ties?" *Zhongguo Tongxun She*, August 1, 1995, in FBIS-China, August 1, 1995, 6. Chinese policy analysts, interviews with author.

19. Qian Qichen's and Li Peng's remarks are in *Xinhua*, July 4, 1995, in FBIS-China, July 5, 1995, 8–9. See also the July 8, 1995, statement by the Chinese Foreign Ministry spokesman in *Zhongguo Xinwen She*, July 13, 1995, in FBIS-China, July 14, 1995, 1; and Chen Dawei, "To Make Amends for the Damage Done to U.S. Relations with China, the United States Must Give Up Its Cold War Mode of Thinking," *Zhongguo Tongxun She*, June 23, 1995, in FBIS-China, June 29, 1995, 3–4.

20. On the cancellations, see U.S. Department of State, daily press briefings, May 24 and 26, 1995, and Assistant Secretary of State Winston Lord, press briefing, May 30, 1995; and *Xinhua*, May 26, 1995, in FBIS-China, May 26, 1995, 3. For subsequent Chinese moves, see *Xinhua*, June 16, 1995, in FBIS-China, June 19, 1995, 1; and Agence France-Presse, June 22, 1995, in FBIS-China, June 22, 1995, 1.

21. Chinese policy analysts, interviews with author. For a discussion of the politics of China's hard-line policy preferences, see Michael D. Swaine,

"Chinese Decision-Making toward Taiwan, 1978–1997," in *The Making of Chinese Foreign and Security Policy in the Era of Reform: 1978–2000*, ed. David M. Lampton (Stanford, Calif.: Stanford University Press, 2001); and You Ji, "Changing Leadership Consensus: The Domestic Context of the War Games," in *Across the Taiwan Strait: Mainland China, Taiwan, and the 1995–1996 Crisis*, ed. Suisheng Zhao (New York: Routledge, 1999).

22. *Xinhua*, July 18, 1995, in FBIS-China, July 19, 1995, 13; and Agence France-Presse, August 11, 1995, in FBIS-China, August 11, 1995, 13.

23. Chinese Foreign Ministry spokesman, quoted in *South China Morning Post*, August 1, 1995, in FBIS-China, August 1, 1995, 5.

24. For a discussion of the domestic politics of Taiwan's mainland policy, see Steven M. Goldstein, "The Cross-Strait Talks of 1993–the Rest of the Story: Domestic Politics and Taiwan's Mainland Policy," in *Across the Taiwan Strait*.

25. See Suisheng Zhao, "Changing Leadership Perceptions: The Adoption of a Coercive Strategy," in *Across the Taiwan Strait*; and Swaine, "Chinese Decision-Making toward Taiwan, 1978–1997."

26. Chinese policy analysts, interviews with author.

27. See the U.S. Department of State, text of the August 1, 1995, press availability of Warren Christopher and Qian Qichen, released in Bandar Seri Begawan, Brunei, August 1, 1995.

28. Mann, *About Face*, 330. On the commitments of previous administrations, see also Ross, *Negotiating Cooperation*. See also the Chinese account of the meeting in *Xinhua*, August 1, 1995, FBIS-China, August 2, 1995, 4.

29. Christopher, *In the Stream of History*, 289. See also Warren Christopher, speech to the National Press Club, Washington, D.C., July 28, 1995; and Michael Dobbs, "U.S., China Agree to Talks on Relations," *Washington Post*, August 2, 1995, A27.

30. U.S. Department of State, daily press briefings, July 14, 1995, and August 11, 1995; and Suettinger, interview with author.

31. *Xinhua*, August 1, 1995, in FBIS-China, August 2, 1995, 4; August 17, 1995, in FBIS-China, August 17, 1995, 5; and August 24, 1995, in FBIS-China, August 24, 1995, 1–2.

32. Commentator, "Lee Teng-hui Stubbornly Challenges the 'One-China' Principle," *Xinhua*, August 23, 1995, in FBIS-China, August 23, 1995, 50. On Taiwan's maneuvers, see Agence France-Presse, July 25, 1995, in FBIS-China, July 25, 1995, 41; and Voice of Free China, August 1, 1995,

in FBIS-China, August 2, 1995, 78. Liu's comments are in *Ta Kung Pao*, September 4, 1995, in FBIS-China, September 7, 1995, 32.

33. Agence France-Presse, August 26, 1995, in FBIS-China, August 28, 1995, 81–82; *Zhongguo Tongxun She*, August 15, 1995, in FBIS-China, August 17, 1995, 57; and *Ming Pao*, August 16, 1995, in FBIS-China, August 18, 1995, 27–28.

34. Gong Li, *Zhong Mei Guanxi Redian Toushi* (Perspective on hotspots in China-U.S. relations) (Harbin: Heilongjiang Chuban She, 1996), 159; U.S. Department of State, daily press briefings, August 11, 1995, and August 28, 1995; and *Xinhua*, August 27, 1995, in FBIS-China, August 28, 1995, 3, and August 29, 1995, in FBIS-China, August 30, 1995, 1.

35. *Xinhua*, September 8, and 11, 1995, both in FBIS-China, September 11, 1995, 13–15.

36. Suettinger and other administration officials, interviews with author.

37. U.S. Department of State, daily press briefings, September 18 and 21, 1995.

38. Ibid., September 18, 1995.

39. U.S. Department of State, daily press briefing, September 22, 1995; and *Xinhua*, September 23, 1995, in FBIS-China, September 25, 1995, 7.

40. Central News Agency, September 25, 1995, in FBIS-China, September 25, 1995, 73.

41. On the Chinese suspension of the nuclear energy agreement and the decision to move ahead with summit discussions between Tarnoff and Li, see U.S. Department of State, daily press briefing, September 29, 1995. Qian's remarks are in *Xinhua*, September 27, 1995, in FBIS-China, September 28, 1995, 11–12, and October 1, 1995, in FBIS-China, October 2, 1995, 11. The return of the ambassador is reported in *Kyodo*, October 17, 1995, in FBIS-China, October 17, 1995, 1. On military exchanges, see *Zhongguo Tongxun She*, October 31, 1995, in FBIS-China, November 1, 1995, 1.

42. See the postsummit briefing by officials from the U.S. State Department and National Security Council, Warwick Hotel, New York, October 24, 1995; Zhu Chenghu, ed., *Zhong Mei Guanxi de Fazhan Bianhua ji qi Qushi* (Developing change in China-U.S. relations and its trend) (Nanjing: Jiangsu Renmin Chuban She, 1998), 190–191; *Xinhua*, October 25, 1995, in FBIS-China, October 25, 1995, 18; and Clinton administration official, interview with author.

43. U.S. Department of State, daily press briefing, October 2, 1995; and Policy Planning Staff deputy director, interview with author.

44. U.S. Department of State and National Security Council officials, postsummit briefing, October 24, 1995.

45. November 16, 1995, press availability of Warren Christopher and Qian Qichen, New Otani Hotel, Tokyo; and briefing by Assistant Secretary of State Winston Lord at the Royal Hotel, Osaka, Japan, November 16, 1995.

46. Gong, *Zhong Mei Guanxi Redian Toushi*, 160; and Chinese policy analysts, interviews with author.

47. *Xinhua*, October 1, 1995, in FBIS-China, October 2, 1995, 11, and October 26, 1995, in FBIS-China, October 27, 1995, 2–3; and press availability of Christopher and Qian, New Otani Hotel, Tokyo.

48. *Chung-Yang Jih-Pao*, September 15, 1995, in FBIS-China, September 18, 1995, 53; and Central News Agency, October 4, 1995, in FBIS-China, October 4, 1995, 91. For a Chinese analysis of the exercises, see Tang Zhengshui, *Zhong Mei Qiju zhong de Taiwan Wenti: 1969.1–1999.12* (The Taiwan issue in U.S.-China chess: 1969.1–1999.12) (Shanghai: Shanghai Renmin Chuban She, 2000), 413–414. On the APEC meeting, see Central News Agency, October 18, 1995, in FBIS-China, October 18, 1995, 89.

49. Central News Agency, August 17, 1995, in FBIS-China, August 17, 1995, 58; *Chung Yang Jih Pao*, December 1, 1995, in FBIS-China, December 6, 1995, 101; and Central People's Radio, November 4, 1995, in FBIS-China, November 6, 1995, 60.

50. *Xinhua*, October 18, 1995, in FBIS-China, October 18, 1995, 25–26; and *Zhongguo Xinwen She*, October 19, 1995, in FBIS-China, October 20, 1995, 2.

51. Tang, *Zhong Mei Qiju zhong de Taiwan Wenti*, 414; *Xinhua*, November 25, 1995, in FBIS-China, document FBIS-CHI-95-227; *Ping Kuo Jih Pao*, November 27, 1995, in FBIS-China, November 27, 1995, 24–25; and Suettinger, interview with author. On the Nye visit, see *Zhongguo Xinwen She*, November 15, 1995, in FBIS-China, November 16, 1995, 4–5.

52. See the comments of Xin Qi in *Wen Wei Pao*, November 27, 1995, in FBIS-China, November 28, 1995, 72.

53. Chinese policy analysts, interviews with author; and *Hong Kong Standard*, December 4, 1995, in FBIS-China, December 4, 1995, 15. For a full discussion of the elections, see Shelley Rigger, *Politics in Taiwan: Voting for Democracy* (New York: Routledge, 1999), 172–174.

54. Joseph Nye, assistant secretary of defense for international security affairs, interview with author; Patrick E. Tyler, "China-U.S. Ties Warm a Bit as China-Taiwan Relations Chill," *New York Times*, November 18, 1995, A3;

"Perry Voices Concern for Taiwan," *New York Times*, February 7, 1996, A3; and Garver, *Face Off*, 85–86.

55. Central News Agency, January 27, 1996, in FBIS-China, January 29, 1996, 83; and U.S. Department of State, daily press briefing, January 26, 1996. The State Department and the NSC were persuaded by the Pentagon that its interest in sending the *Nimitz* through the strait was to avoid bad weather, rather than to send China a quiet yet persuasive signal and, thus, did not object. Nye, Suettinger, and other administration officials, interviews with author. Garver, *Face Off*, 87–89; and Li Yihu, ed., *Zhengzhi Dubo zhong de Taiwan* (Taiwan in a political gamble) (Beijing: Youyi Chuban She, 1999), 224.

56. Suettinger and Nye, interviews with author.

57. Chinese policy analysts, interviews with author.

58. For Lee's remarks, see the English translation of his speech distributed by Nationalist Party campaign headquarters, in FBIS-China, February 12, 1996, 83–84; and live telecast of Lee Teng-hui news conference, China Broadcasting Corporation (Taipei), February 23, 1996, in FBIS-China, February 26, 1996, 55.

59. "Taiwan Election Candidate Gives China Ultimatum," Reuters, February 23, 1996.

60. On Taiwan's publicizing the passage of the *Nimitz*, see Christopher, *In the Stream of History*, 426; Central News Agency, January 27, 1996, in FBIS-China, January 29, 1996, 83; and Central News Agency, January 27, 1996, in FBIS-China, document FBIS-CHI-96-019. See the extensive PRC discussion of this period in Taiwan's U.S. policy, in particular Taiwan's manipulation of the passage of the *Nimitz*, in Tang, *Zhong Mei Qiju zhong de Taiwan Wenti*, 417–421.

61. "U.S. Visa to Taiwan Aide," *New York Times*, January 7, 1996, A9; U.S. Department of State, daily press briefing, January 5, 1996; and *Xinhua*, January 9, 1996, in FBIS-China, January 11, 1996, 2.

62. U.S. Department of State, daily press briefings, January 23 and 31, 1996; and China Radio International, February 2, 1996, in FBIS-China, February 2, 1996, 1.

63. Jiang Dianming, "Safeguarding State Sovereignty Is the Greatest Public Opinion," *Wen Wei Pao*, December 24, 1995, in FBIS-China, February 5, 1996, 68–69.

64. *Xinhua*, January 30, 1996, in FBIS-China, January 31, 1996, 75–77; and *Zhongguo Xinwen She*, March 8, 1996, in FBIS-China, March 11, 1996, 10. See also Yan Xuetong, "U.S. Policy toward Taiwan and Tension in the Taiwan Strait," *Liaowang*, March 4, 1996, in FBIS-China, March 15, 1996, 5–6.

65. Associated Press, February 6, 1996; U.S. Department of State, daily press briefing, February 14, 1996; R. Jeffrey Smith, "China Plans Maneuvers Off Taiwan," *Washington Post*, February 5, 1996, A1; and Steven Mufson, "China Masses Troops on Coast Near Taiwan," *Washington Post*, February 14, 1996, A16.

66. Associated Press, February 6, 1996; U.S. Senate Committee on Foreign Relations, testimony by Assistant Secretary of State Winston Lord before the Subcommittee on East Asia and the Pacific, February 7, 1996; and U.S. Department of State, daily press briefings, February 13 and 14, 1996.

67. Chinese policy analysts, interviews with author.

68. Ibid.

69. See the discussion in Tang, *Zhong Mei Qiju zhong de Taiwan Wenti*, 421–422.

70. *Xinhua*, March 4, 1995, FBIS-China, March 5, 1996, 68; and Central News Agency, March 7, 1995, in FBIS-China, March 7, 1996, 81. Chinese policy analysts, interviews with author.

71. China Radio International, March 5, 1996, in FBIS-China, March 6, 1996, 1.

72. Agence France-Presse, March 8, 1996, in FBIS-China, March 8, 1996, 37; U.S. Department of State, daily press briefings, March 7 and 8, 1996; and White House, press briefing, March 7, 1996. Note that throughout the period, Chinese missile tests did not interfere with shipping in or out of Taiwan. See Central News Agency, March 8, 1996, in FBIS-China, document FBIS-CHI-96-047, and March 13, 1996, in FBIS-China, document FBIS-CHI-96-50.

73. *Wen Wei Po*, March 9, 1996, in FBIS-China, March 11, 1996, 15; and "Lee Teng-hui Practicing Taiwan Independence Is the Biggest Danger for Taiwan," *People's Daily* and *Liberation Army Daily*, March 8, 1996, in FBIS-China, March 11, 1996, 83–84.

74. Secretary of Defense William Perry, comments at the National Press Club, Washington, D.C., February 28, 1996; U.S. Department of State, daily press briefing, March 5, 1996; and U.S. Department of Defense, news briefing, March 14, 1996. See also Christopher, *In the Stream of History*, 427; Patrick E. Tyler, "China Signaling U.S. That It Will Not Invade Taiwan," *New York Times*, March 13, 1996, A3; and Chinese policy analysts, interviews with author.

75. U.S. Department of Defense, news briefing, March 14, 1996; Ashton B. Carter and William J. Perry, *Preventive Defense: A New Security Strategy for America* (Washington, D.C.: Brookings Institution, 1999), 92–93.

76. Christopher, *In the Stream of History*, 427. See also U.S. Department of Defense, news briefing, March 14, 1996.

77. See Perry's comments at the U.S. Department of Defense news briefing, December 8, 1996; and Carter and Perry, *Preventive Defense*, 96.

78. *Xinhua*, March 9, 1996, in FBIS-China, March 9, 1996, 54.

79. Suettinger, interview with author. See also Mann, *About Face*, 336–337; Carter and Perry, *Preventive Defense*, 96–99; and Patrick Tyler, *A Great Wall: Six Presidents and China* (New York: Public Affairs, 1999), 33.

80. American Forces Press Service, March 11, 1996; U.S. Department of Defense, news briefings, March 11, 12, 14, and 16, 1996; and Suettinger and other administration officials, interviews with author. Note that although the *Nimitz* was ordered to proceed to waters near Taiwan, it was also ordered to sail at a deliberate pace and it never reached Taiwan's vicinity. U.S. official, interview with author. Note also that Chinese leaders were aware of the deliberate pace of the *Nimitz*. Chinese policy analysts, interviews with author.

81. Central People's Radio, March 12, 1996, in FBIS-China, document FBIS-CHI-96-50; and *Xinhua*, March 8, 1996, in FBIS-China, document FBIS-CHI-96-47. See also He Chong, "Amassing U.S. Warships Is an Act of Playing with Fire," *Zhongguo Tongxun She*, March 13, 1996, in FBIS-China, March 14, 1996, 3.

82. Agence France-Presse, March 12, 1996, in FBIS-China, document FBIS-CHI-96-50; Central News Agency, March 13, 1996, in FBIS-China, document FBIS-CHI-96-50; China Broadcasting Corporation (Taipei), March 15, 1996, in FBIS-China, March 15, 1996, 92; Central News Agency, March 20, 1996, in FBIS-China, document FBIS-CHI-96-55; and *People's Daily* and *Liberation Army Daily*, "Safeguarding the Motherland's Unity Is the People's Army Bound Duty," March 15, 1996, in FBIS-China, March 18, 1996, 78–79. Note that China canceled two of its planned missile tests. It did not target the closure zone of the east side of Taiwan. These tests would have been the most provocative, because firing missiles into this zone would have required China to send the missiles directly over Taiwan. Suettinger, interview with author. See also Tyler, *A Great Wall*, 31, which notes that China readied "more than a dozen missiles" for firing. Chinese leaders did not carry out these tests, probably because they had determined that the prior tests had accomplished China's political objectives and because the U.S. show of force had made them more cautious.

83. White House, press briefing, March 12, 1996; and Suettinger, interview with author. Note that despite the lack of tension, the NSC worked with the Defense Department to prepare a number of scenarios in which U.S. forces would engage the PLA. Regarding the bravado, Secretary of Defense

Perry used China's ongoing exercises to remind Beijing that the United States had the "best damn navy in the world." See Rupert Cornwell, "Taiwan Fans Flames in the War of Words," *Independent* (London), March 20, 1996, 9; and U.S. Department of State, press briefing, March 19, 1996. See also Mann, *About Face*, 337–338. China carried out its own bravado after the dispatch of the carriers. See the interviews with PLA generals in *Ta Kung Pao*, March 13, 1996, in FBIS-China, document FBIS-CHI-96-50. Also note that on March 22 the Defense Department and China reported that each had taken the initiative to delay a visit to the United States by Minister of Defense Chi Haotian. U.S. Department of Defense, news release, ref. no. 149-96; and *Xinhua*, March 22, 1996, in FBIS-China, March 25, 1996, 3. See also Carter and Perry, *Preventive Defense*, 99.

84. Richard Bush, director, American Institute in Taiwan, interview with author; Central News Agency, January 15, 1996, in FBIS-China, document FBIS-CHI-97-011, January 8, 1996, in FBIS-China, document FBIS-CHI-97-06, and July 24, 1997; and Keith B. Richburg, "Taiwan Again an Issue in U.S.-China Relations," *Washington Post*, July 27, 1997, A24. China's appreciation of U.S. management of Taiwan's transit visas is reflected in He Jixiong, "Lee Teng-hui's 'Transit Diplomacy' Can Hardly Succeed," *Zhongguo Tongxun She*, September 4, 1997, in FBIS-China, document FBIS-CHI-97-248. China's protest of the Lien transit visa is reported in Agence France-Presse, January 7, 1997, in FBIS-China, document FBIS-CHI-97-04.

85. *Lien Ho Pao*, March 27, 1996, in FBIS-China, April 11, 1996, 88–89. On Stanley Roth's statement, see his nomination hearing before the U.S. Senate Committee on Foreign Relations, July 27, 1997.

86. This is the consensus among Chinese policy analysts. See also, for example, Zhu, *Zhong Mei Guanxi de Fazhan ji qi Qushi*, 195–196; and Tang, *Zhong Mei Qiju zhong de Taiwan Wenti*, 447–448.

87. Suettinger and other administration officials, interviews with author. See Warren Christopher, "American Interests and the U.S.-China Relationship" (speech to the Asia Society, the Council on Foreign Relations, and the National Committee on U.S.-China Relations, May 17, 1996); *Zhongguo Tongxun She*, July 8, 1996, in FBIS-China, document FBIS-CHI-96-133; and Central People's Radio, June 8, 1996, in FBIS-China, July 9, 1996, 6. On the Clinton-Jiang meeting in Manila, see *Xinhua*, November 24, 1996, in FBIS-China, document FBIS-CHI-96-228.

88. *Xinhua*, June 30, 1997, in FBIS-China, document FBIS-CHI-97-181, and August 12, 1997, in FBIS-China, document FBIS-CHI-97-224.

89. White House, background press briefing by senior administration officials, October 29, 1997; U.S. Department of State, daily press briefing,

October 31, 1997; administration official, interview with author; and Madeleine Albright, press conference at the Beijing International Club Hotel, April 30, 1998. Note that the president's August 1995 letter to Jiang Zemin stated that Washington "opposed" independence for Taiwan. By the 1997 summit the administration had shifted to "does not support" independence for Taiwan. See Mann, *About Face*, 330, 355–358.

90. See the president's June 30, 1998, remarks at the Shanghai Library, released by the White House, Office of the Press Secretary; and Suettinger, interview with author.

91. For a discussion of the outcome of the 1996 presidential elections, see Rigger, *Politics in Taiwan*, 175–177.

92. "Taiwan Postpones War Games off China," *New York Times*, April 3, 1996, A9; Central News Agency, April 3, 1996, in FBIS-China, April 3, 1996, 85, and March 28, 1996, in FBIS-China, March 28, 1996, 92–93; and Agence France-Presse, March 19, 1996, in FBIS-China, March 19, 1996, 96. See also the text of Lee's interview with *Newsweek*, in Central News Agency, May 13, 1996, in FBIS-China, May 14, 1996, 70–71.

93. Rigger, *Politics in Taiwan*, 175–177. Note that the outcome of the elections was likely influenced by the deployment of the two carriers, an implicit signal of U.S. support for Lee Teng-hui. This is a widespread view in China. See Wang Jisi, "Dui Hua Zhengce" (Policy toward China), in *Gaochu Busheng Han: Lengzhang hou Meiguo Quanqiu Zhanlue he Shijie Diwei* (Intolerable cold at the height: Post–Cold War U.S. global strategy and world position), ed. Wang Jisi (Beijing: Shijie Zhishi Chuban She, 1999), 263.

94. "Taiwan Foreign Minister Vows No Halt to UN Push," Reuters, June 10, 1999; Central News Agency, July 14, 1999, and *Chung Yang Jih Pao*, July 14, 1999, in FBIS-China, document FBIS-CHI-1999-0714; and *Lien-Ho Pao*, July 13, 1999, in FBIS-China, document FBIS-CHI-1999-0715. On the exercises, see Agence France-Presse, August 5, 1999, in FBIS-China, document FBIS-CHI-1999-0805; *Ta Kung Pao*, September 10, 1999, in FBIS-China, document FBIS-CHI-1999-0910; and *Wen Wei Po*, September 11, 1999, in FBIS-China, document FBIS-CHI-1999-0912. See also U.S. Department of State, daily press briefing, August 3, 1999.

95. U.S. Department of State, daily press briefings, July 13 and 14, 1999; House Committee on International Relations, testimony of Deputy Secretary of State Susan Shirk before the Asia and Pacific Subcommittee, September 15, 1999; Philip Shenon, "U.S. Cancels Military Aides' Visit to Taiwan," *New York Times*, July 22, 1999, A8; and David E. Sanger, "Clinton and Jiang Heal Rift and Set New Trade Course," *New York Times*, September 12, 1999, A1.

96. See Yuen Foong Khong, "Singapore: A Time for Economic and Political Engagement," and Amitav Acharya, "Containment, Engagement, or Counter-Dominance," in *Engaging China: The Management of an Emerging Power*, ed. Alastair Iain Johnston and Robert S. Ross (New York: Routledge, 1999), 124–125, 138, 145; and Jusuf Wanandi, "ASEAN's China Strategy: Towards Deeper Engagement," *Survival* 38, no. 2 (autumn 1996): 124–127.

97. For a discussion of U.S. missile defense cooperation with Taiwan, see Thomas J. Christensen, "Theater Missile Defense and Taiwan's Security," *Orbis* 44, no. 1 (winter 2000): 79–90; and Michael O'Hanlon, "Star Wars Strikes Back," *Foreign Affairs* 78, no. 6 (November-December 1999): 77. See also U.S. Department of Defense, "Report to Congress on Theater Missile Defense Architecture Options for the Asia-Pacific Region," May 4, 1999. For a discussion of the implications of the March confrontation for U.S.-Taiwan relations, see Steven M. Goldstein and Randall Schriver, "An Uncertain Relationship: The United States, Taiwan, and the Taiwan Relations Act," *China Quarterly*, no. 165 (March 2001): 147–172.

98. Chinese policy analysts, interviews with author. Li Peng's comments are in *Financial Times*, June 11, 1996, in FBIS-China, June 11, 1996, 1–2.

99. Shi Yinhong, "Kunnan yu Xuance: Dui Taiwan Wenti de Sikao" (Difficulty and choice: Thoughts on the Taiwan issue), *Zhanlue yu Guanli* (Strategy and management), no. 5 (1999): 3–4; and Chinese policy analysts, interviews with author. Regarding the outcome of the election, this is the suggestion of Wang, "Dui Hua Zhengce," 263. This analysis is challenged by reports that Chinese deployment of its strategic and attack submarines on March 13 compelled the United States to redeploy the carrier *Independence* an additional one hundred miles from the Chinese coast. See Su Ge, *Meiguo dui Hua Zhengce yu Taiwan Wenti* (Beijing: Shijie Zhishi Chuban She, 1998), 750. Yet this report is, at best, unreliable, as it based on an uninformed U.S. Chinese-language newspaper account. See "Zhonggong Shisi suo He Qianting Chu Hai" (Fourteen Chinese communist nuclear submarines go to sea), *Shijie Ribao* (World daily) (New York), March 19, 1996, 1; and Su, *Meiguo dui Hua Zhengce yu Taiwan Wenti* 750, n. 4. U.S. officials uniformly disagree with this and similar reports.

100. This is the argument of Shi, "Kunnan yu Xuance," 4; and Chinese policy analysts, interviews with author.

101. Countries throughout the region adopted a cautious attitude toward the U.S. response, lest they alienate China on a sensitive issue in Chinese foreign policy. Their reaction reflected the common concern of allies of entrapment versus abandonment, and they chose to split the difference. They were concerned that enhanced U.S. commitment to the defense of

Taiwan might enhance their security vis-à-vis China but might also drag them into a conflict over Taiwan. See the discussion of entrapment and abandonment in Glenn H. Snyder, "The Security Dilemma in Alliance Politics," *World Politics* 36, no. 4 (July 1984): 461–495. Beneath the caution, there was evidence of general support for the U.S. response. See, for example, the transcript of the March 12, 1996, Japanese foreign ministry press conference in Foreign Broadcast Information Service–East Asia, March 13, 1996, 7–12; Nigel Holloway, "Strait Talking," *Far Eastern Economic Review* (March 21, 1996): 16; "Asians Laud Us Privately," *Far Eastern Economic Review* (April 4, 1996): 17; and *Strategic Survey, 1995/96* (London: Institute for International Strategic Studies, 1996), 178–179.

102. Chinese policy analysts, interviews with author.

103. Shi, "'Kunnan yu Xuance: Dui Taiwan Wenti de Sikao," 4; and Chinese policy analysts, interviews with author.

104. Ibid. For discussions of post–March 1996 Chinese strategy and military acquisitions relevant to the Taiwan theater, see You Ji, *The Armed Forces of China* (New York: I. B. Tauris, 1999), 99–100; Tai Ming Cheung, "Chinese Military Preparations against Taiwan over the Next Ten Years," and Bates Gill, "Chinese Military Hardware and Technology Acquisition of Concern to Taiwan," in *Crisis in the Taiwan Strait*, ed. James R. Lilley and Chuck Downs (Washington, D.C.: National Defense University Press, 1997).

105. On the Sovremennyi destroyers, see *Interfax*, April 18, 1997, in FBIS-Central Eurasia, document 97-108; and He Chong, "China's Purchase of Russian-Made Sovremenny-Class Destroyer Attracts Attention," *Zhongguo Tongxun She*, February 12, 2000, in FBIS-China, document FBIS-CHI-2000-212. For a discussion of China's military modernization program and its implications for the Taiwan Strait, see Bates Gill and Michael O'Hanlon, "China's Hollow Military," *National Interest*, no. 56 (summer 1999); and Larry M. Wortzel, *The Chinese Armed Forces in the Twenty-First Century* (Carlisle, Penn.: Strategic Studies Institute, U.S. Army War College, 1999).

106. Proving a negative is difficult, yet it is clear that the origins of the 1996 confrontation lay in Taiwan's lobbying of Congress and congressional pressure on the president. It is also important to stress that Taiwan's lobbying did not reflect the pressure of Taiwan's democracy, which is a constant in U.S.-Taiwan relations. Taiwan's electorate has been cautious regarding independence diplomacy and the risk of war with the mainland. Lee Teng-hui was not responding to public opinion, but leading public opinion, and Chen Shui-bian had to abandon his support for independence in order to win the presidency in 2000, suggesting that a confrontation over Taiwan was not inevitable. This further suggests that Taiwan public opinion can be influenced by cautious U.S. policy toward Taiwan. On the politics of the 2000 campaign, including public attitudes toward Taiwan independence, see Shelly Rigger, "Taiwan Rides the Democratic Dragon," *Washington Quarterly* 23, no. 2 (spring 2000).

107. On the Bush administration, see, for example, Deputy Secretary of State Richard Armitage's press conference, Beijing, August 26, 2002.

108. On the Trident submarine and the trend in forward deployments, see Owen R. Cote, Jr., *The Future of the Trident Force: Enabling Access in Access Constrained Environments* (Cambridge, Mass.: Security Studies Program, Massachusetts Institute of Technology, 2002); U.S. Department of Defense, *Quadrennial Defense Report* (Washington, D.C.: U.S. Department of Defense, 2001); and James Dao, "Army to Move Some Weapons Out of Europe," *New York Times*, August 31, 2001, 16. For a discussion of U.S. deterrence of mainland use of force, see Robert S. Ross, "Deterrence Works: Escalation Dominance, Chinese Use of Force, and U.S. Policy," *International Security* 27, no. 2 (fall 2002).

109. Mark Landler, "Money Might Not Be Able to Buy Political Ties, Either," *New York Times*, December 9, 2001, 4; "Taiwan and China Ink Landmark Oil Exploration Pact," Reuters, May 16, 2002; "Mainland to Hire Hi-Tech, Financial Experts from Taiwan," Agence France-Presse, May 24, 2002; "Taiwan Leader Urged to Honour 'Direct Links' Pledge," *China Daily*, May 22, 2002; and "Taiwan Govt to Submit Bill on Direct China Links," Associated Press, June 4, 2002.

7

Coercive Diplomacy against Iraq, 1990–98

JON B. ALTERMAN

IRAQ HAS BEEN A RATHER PECULIAR FOE of the United States. Badly mismatched in terms of population, wealth, military strength, or almost any other conceivable measure, Iraq seems poorly positioned to win any confrontation. Equally unclear is why Iraq would want to provoke a confrontation with the United States. There is no ideological imperative to do so, and the countries arguably share an interest in a constant and stable flow of oil out of Iraq and its oil-rich neighbors.

How much more puzzling, then, that Iraq has emerged as one of the longer-running security challenges for the United States and battlefield opponent for U.S. military forces. For the past twelve years, U.S. officials have tried, with varying degrees of international cooperation and with varying degrees of success, to use the theories of coercive diplomacy to counter Iraqi threats. The success of such a strategy is unclear, because it is impossible to know what Iraq might have done had the United States pursued another strategy. But two things are relatively clear. The first is that the outcome of the past twelve years—no serious attack by Iraq on its neighbors and no substantial gains in its nuclear, biological, and chemical weapons programs—would have been one of the more optimistic predictions of Iraqi behavior in the early 1990s. The efforts of the past twelve years have not all been in vain. Equally important, though, another twelve years of the same policies could scarcely be expected to produce similar results. By the first years of the twenty-first century, sanctions were visibly fraying, as international resolve diminished and Iraqi officials became increasingly adept at circumventing restrictions on their country's income and spending. A new strategy would need to be found.

This chapter concentrates on episodes in the 1990s in which the U.S. government attempted to use coercive diplomacy against Iraq. Such a policy took place in the context of a broader policy of containment and deterrence—a policy that enjoyed far wider international support than U.S. efforts to coercively induce specific Iraqi actions. This chapter seeks to understand how coercive diplomacy might have been applied better in the years following the Iraqi invasion of Kuwait. It also seeks to explain how the United States should approach its future policy toward dilemmas like those posed by Iraqi behavior in the period under study.

The chapter concludes that several aspects of the Iraqi case made it a poor candidate for coercive diplomacy after the early 1990s and that the appropriateness of such a policy only declined over time. These aspects include but are not limited to the drawn-out nature of the conflict, the relatively large number of confrontations, the nature of the target regime, limited will in the United States for coercive measures, and the difficulties of coalition maintenance.

Few of those factors, however, were predictable from the outset. In addition, U.S. policy toward Iraq was particularly burdened by an expanding set of increasingly ill-defined goals. It is far easier to use coercive diplomacy to achieve a limited, positive outcome in the short term than to manage a number of competing goals over more than a decade. The passage of time undermines both coalition maintenance and resolve at home, which in turn make application of a coercive diplomacy strategy extraordinarily difficult.

The coercive diplomacy discussion in this chapter deals primarily with the period from August 1990 to December 1998. Before August 1990 U.S. policy was to engage Iraq, not coerce it. Iraq had seemed to emerge contrite from a long and bloody war with Iran, and "the widely shared view in the international community was that Saddam Hussein was following a more moderate path."[1] After December 1998

U.S. policy was not to coerce the regime in Baghdad but rather to remove it. That month, high-ranking U.S. officials announced that a primary goal of U.S. policy was to achieve "regime change" in Iraq. Given the repressiveness of the regime at home and its isolation abroad, regime change would seem to represent a death sentence for Baghdad's brutal leaders. Although Alexander George notes that regime change is a potential goal of coercive diplomacy, it is hard to imagine that he is referring to cases in which regime change would almost certainly be suicidal for the current leadership. In such conditions, it seems impossible to construct a set of consequences more dire than removing the leadership from power.[2]

The round of coercive diplomacy that ended with a U.S.-led military attack in March 2003 confirms the difficulty of coercing regime change in cases like Iraq. The Bush administration, however, avoided many of the pitfalls outlined in this chapter by keeping diplomatic confrontations focused and limited in time.

IRAQ AND COERCIVE DIPLOMACY

George envisions three possible goals for coercive diplomacy: to use the threat of force or limited force to persuade an adversary to "stop short of the goal" of an action currently under way; to persuade the adversary to undo an action already carried out; and to achieve "a cessation of the opponent's hostile behavior through a demand for change in the composition of the adversary's government or in the nature of the regime."[3] From 1990 to 1998 the United States sought explicitly to use the threat of force or limited force to achieve the first two goals. While changing the regime in Baghdad was a desire of the U.S government throughout that period, its efforts were generally directed not so much at persuading the Iraqi government to be more inclusive or to change its nature as at removing the government itself.

The episodes of coercive diplomacy did not occur in isolation but rather were one tool among many that the United States employed. In that regard, U.S. ambassador April Glaspie's widely criticized demarche to Saddam Hussein a week before Iraq's invasion of Kuwait was diplomacy, but it does not appear to have been coercive. According to Iraqi transcripts of the discussion, which the State Department reportedly has not contested, Glaspie expressed her concern over the situation on Iraq's southern border but never threatened any sort of military, economic, or political response if Iraq were to cross into Kuwait.[4]

By contrast, Operation Desert Storm was coercive, but it was not diplomacy. While a great deal of diplomacy went into assembling a coalition of a score of countries to confront Iraq, on the Iraqi end the war was a pure exercise of overwhelming military force. The allied forces did not fight a "limited war" with the goal of liberating Kuwait; rather, allied forces continued to fight the Iraqi army in retreat, although they did stop short of destroying the Republican Guard or marching on Baghdad. In this, pressure from Arab (and especially Saudi and Egyptian) coalition allies strongly influenced U.S. government decision making. The peace that emerged was not so much negotiated as accepted by the Iraqis, and it amounted to acceptance of relevant UN Security Council resolutions.

Desert Shield and Its Aftermath

From August 2, 1990—the day the Iraqi army invaded Kuwait—until the bombs began falling on January 16, 1991, it was not clear that force would be required to coerce Iraqi troops into withdrawing.[5] Indeed, at the time of the Iraqi invasion U.S. policy had been leaning the other way, favoring engagement with Iraq rather than sanctions against it. National Security Directive 26, signed by President Bush on October 2, 1989, called for expanded "economic and political incentives for Iraq" and concluded that "normal relations between the United States and Iraq would serve our longer-term interests and promote stability in both the Gulf and the Middle East."[6] Although the actual aid extended to Iraq was relatively meager—mostly in the form of Commodity Credit Corporation guarantees and Export-Import Bank development loan credits—the gestures were enough to set off alarm bells in Congress. In the first half of 1990, the administration curtailed its courtship of Iraq, partly in response to congressional pressure and partly in response to Iraq's weapons development efforts and its open threats directed at neighboring states.

The Iraqi invasion of Kuwait on August 2 forced a complete rethinking of U.S. policy toward Iraq. George Bush was a former permanent representative to the United Nations and a dedicated internationalist, and his first instinct was to build an international coalition. He called his ambassador to the United Nations, Thomas Pickering, immediately upon learning of the invasion and urged him to try to convene an emergency meeting of the Security Council to condemn the Iraqi move. Bush's early tilt toward the United Nations paid off with the rapid adoption of sweeping UN sanctions against Iraq just four days after the invasion. In addition, Bush rapidly built up allied (and especially American) forces in the Arabian Peninsula in the weeks and months following. Under Operation Desert Shield, more than forty thousand U.S. troops were in place in the region within a month of the Iraqi invasion, and four hundred thousand were in place by November 1990.

George Bush's actions in the weeks immediately before the invasion do not appear to represent an application of coercive diplomacy. As Iraqi troops and materiel gathered on the Kuwaiti border in July 1990 the U.S. government heeded the advice of its allies to tread softly and not aggravate the situation.[7] Whether or not a demonstration of force could have deterred Saddam Hussein from invading Kuwait is unclear, but the United States clearly chose not to try. Of course, Saddam's invasion was not completely predictable, and U.S. action must be seen within the framework of the prevailing uncertainty of the time.

Following the invasion, the coercive elements of U.S. policy took some time to fall into place. National Security Adviser Brent Scowcroft asked his senior Middle East aide on the National Security Council (NSC) to draft an "overview memo" in the immediate aftermath of the invasion. That memo advised, "We don't need to decide where to draw any lines just yet, but we do need to take steps—moving forces, pressing allies and reluctant Arabs, etc. that would at least give us a real choice if current efforts fall short."[8] The clear implication is that the United States began to deploy troops more to preserve U.S. options than to provoke a precise Iraqi response, which an orthodox application of coercive diplomacy would require. In this way, U.S. actions were along the lines of one of George's alternative nonmilitary strategies, namely, "buying time to explore a negotiated settlement."[9]

One might make the case that the UN sanctions played a role in convincing Saddam to stop short of moving from Kuwait into Saudi Arabia.

As such, the UN sanctions (which the United States took the lead on imposing) would represent a successful use of coercive diplomacy because the target state stopped short of its goal. Such a case is tenuous, however. Although U.S. officials clearly feared an Iraqi invasion of Saudi Arabia, there is no evidence in the public domain to suggest that such an invasion was in the offing.[10]

Interestingly, Secretary of State James A. Baker III explicitly states in his memoirs that the U.S. government's actions in August 1990 were intended "to deter an Iraqi move into Saudi Arabia . . . [and undo] Iraq's invasion of Kuwait by the pursuit of a policy of *coercive diplomacy* against Saddam Hussein" (emphasis added). As envisioned by Baker, carrying out such a plan meant "we would begin with diplomatic pressure, then add economic pressure . . . and finally move toward military pressure by gradually increasing American troop strength in the Gulf."[11]

Although it may be only a question of nuance, Baker's conceptualization of coercive diplomacy differs from Alexander George's in this instance. Baker emphasizes a "ratcheting up" process, a sort of "try-and-see" approach to tactics other than war, while retaining war as an ultimate possibility. Although Baker clearly targets Iraqi behavior, he does not actively seek to understand the motivations behind that behavior. George's concept of strategic diplomacy, however, is carefully constructed around the idea of understanding one's adversary. George suggests that policymakers attempting to apply coercive diplomacy need to accomplish four tasks: assign values to the variables in the coercive diplomacy model, settle on what variant of coercive diplomacy to pursue, replace the assumption of a "rational" opponent with an empirically derived model, and take contextual variables into account.

The key in all of this is to understand how the adversary perceives his interests. The task is hard enough with most adversaries, but when one comes from a cultural, familial, and political background as foreign to most U.S. analysts as Saddam Hussein's, the task is even harder. One cannot know at this point what U.S. government assessments of Iraqi intentions, likely reactions, and pressure points had been, or how the Bush administration used such assessments. Yet the memoirs of U.S. officials suggest they gave greater emphasis to building an anti-Saddam coalition and to following a try-and-see approach than to calculating how key pressure points might persuade Saddam to disgorge Kuwait.

Diplomatic efforts to resolve the conflict took center stage in November, when the Soviet Union emerged as a key intermediary between the United States and Iraq. Efforts to bring Iraqi foreign minister Tariq Aziz to Washington and send Baker to Baghdad foundered on disagreements over agendas, dates, and participants. As late as January 9 Baker met with Aziz in Geneva and attempted to deliver a letter of warning from George Bush to Saddam Hussein.[12] Aziz read the letter and refused to convey it on the grounds that its tone was "contrary to the traditions of correspondence between heads of state."[13]

While U.S. and allied threats to Saddam Hussein before the outbreak of war were not specific, their tone was clear. Bush's letter of January 9 stated baldly, "What is at issue here is not the future of Kuwait—it will be free, its government will be restored—but rather the future of Iraq. . . . Iraq cannot and will not be able to hold on to Kuwait or exact a price for leaving."[14] It is possible that Iraqi officials judged that the threats of the United States and the international community were not credible. It is also possible that they believed that the costs of complying with those threats—in terms of both international prestige and domestic politics—outweighed the costs of noncompliance. In any event, the United States and its allies appear to have delivered the threat of the use of force clearly.

As U.S. military capabilities in the region expanded into the winter, U.S. policy began to look more and more like an application of coercive diplomacy. The demands were clear, and the threat was direct, credible, and potent. The decision facing Iraqi officials—withdrawal or war—grew more stark, and while they chose the latter, it was not because of a lack of evident allied resolve.

When the threats were not heeded, allied forces began a month-long air campaign with approximately one hundred thousand sorties, followed by a 100-hour ground war. There are varying estimates of Iraqi casualties, ranging from twenty-five thousand to as many as one hundred fifty thousand. Iraq also lost a sizable portion of its weaponry, and when the dust settled, only 15 percent of its electrical grid was still operational.[15]

This last episode, Operation Desert Storm, represents not coercive diplomacy but pure coercion. Unable to win Iraqi withdrawal through diplomatic activity, sanctions, or threats, the United States and its allies took to the battlefield and won decisively. Rather than serve as a successful model of coercive diplomacy, Operation Desert Storm was intended in part to build credibility so that the next adversary might prove more susceptible to similar ultimata in the future.[16] What was not anticipated was that the target of such ultimata would again be Saddam Hussein and that the confrontation would follow right after the end of the war.

One can speculate endlessly about why coercive diplomacy failed to win Saddam's withdrawal from Kuwait. Absent much better information than exists about Iraqi internal decision making, hard and fast conclusions are difficult. One possible conclusion is that coercive diplomacy failed because Saddam Hussein simply miscalculated the likelihood of massive military action or the outcome of such action. Given what we know about his impatience with conflicting views, it is certainly possible that he blundered into war. If that is the case, it is unclear what the United States or its allies could have done to improve Iraqi analysis. Iraqi decision making is a notoriously closed process, and individuals' efforts to influence it are carried out at their peril.

Another possibility is that Saddam Hussein concluded that he would pay the greatest price if he succumbed to U.S. and allied threats. Because Saddam had been so bold in his proclamation that Kuwait was part of Iraq, he may have judged that his internal position would be untenable if he were to collapse in the face of foreign pressure. If that were the case, Saddam would have been susceptible to U.S. carrots that would have supported his internal position in exchange for retreating from Kuwait. Were one to adjudge that Saddam's overriding interest was to stay in power, a U.S. policy that preserved his ability to stay in power if he withdrew immediately from Kuwait and threatened his power were he to remain there might have dislodged Iraqi troops without firing a shot. Such a policy, though, may have been anathema to the Bush administration. As the crisis continued there were signs that a key Bush administration goal was, in fact, to end the regime, making such offers out of the question. The administration's "nightmare scenario" appears to have been partial Iraqi compliance with coalition demands, which would have undermined coalition resolve to go to war.[17]

Safe Havens (1991)

In the days following the official end of hostilities in the Gulf War, uprisings began in the Kurdish north and the Shiite south of Iraq. Inspired in part by George Bush's admonition to "take matters into their own hands," local militias began to take on government forces.

The uprisings posed a quandary for U.S. policymakers. In one respect, anything that created problems for Saddam was good. But the separatist movements were also deeply problematic for the United States and its allies in the region. Turkish officials were reportedly concerned that Kurdish separatism in Iraq would spill over into the Kurdish regions of Turkey; U.S. officials and some regional allies were also concerned by the possibility that Iranian-backed Shiites in the south could form a breakaway alliance with Iran. Uprisings in both regions raised the possibility that the United States would be drawn into an open-ended war with Iraq immediately after war had just ended. Such a war would have had a difficult time finding public support in the United States. Finally, U.S. decision makers wanted Iraq weakened but not destroyed so that it could remain a check against Iranian power in the region.

In the event, the Bush administration admonished the Iraqis that it would attack any Iraqi units using chemical weapons but went no further. Such a warning was consonant with earlier U.S. warnings that the administration would not tolerate the use of chemical or biological weapons against allied troops in the war. When Saddam began to use helicopters to battle the uprisings, the U.S. government complained that he had violated the terms of the cease-fire but took no immediate action against him.

Partly at the urging of Turkey, allied forces dispatched more than twenty thousand soldiers to the north of Iraq in April 1991 to create a safe haven for Kurdish populations. Under Operation Provide Comfort, the tide of more than two million Kurdish refugees streaming into Turkey and Iran was stemmed, and Kurds even began to return to northern Iraq. Iraq massed troops on the border of the northern enclave in the autumn of 1991, but after several initial confrontations the Iraqis backed off (until moving on the enclave in August 1996, described later). The northern zone, which existed into 2003, has been a strange hybrid. It has had no legal standing as a separate entity, but it is not controlled by the government of Iraq. Since May 1991 the United Nations has controlled the disbursement of relief supplies.

This incident is a more limited example of coercive diplomacy, since the United States and its allies made few demands on Iraq. Rather, the United States, France, and Britain moved troops into the north and established refugee camps, while the Iraqis agreed not to challenge the northern zone.

Saddam made no such efforts to cease his attacks in the south, where foreign inaction was driven by discomfort with a possible Iranian hand in the uprisings. Consequently, the government of Iraq was able to brutally suppress the Shiites and even drain the marshes where many revolting Shiite communities were based. In August 1992, the United States and the United Kingdom created a no-fly zone in southern Iraq, but that move may have been intended more to restrain future Iraqi threats against its neighbors than to protect the Shiite population.

Confrontations over No-Fly Zones and Inspections (1991–93)

The government of Iraq agreed to thorough arms control inspections as a condition of the 1991 cease-fire but did so under duress. Even early on in the inspection process it became clear that while Iraq was forthcoming about some elements of its arsenal, it continued to hold a good deal back. In July 1991 Iraqi troops fired warning shots at inspectors seeking to intercept trucks carrying calutrons, which are used in nuclear programs. Two months later weapons inspectors located a cache of documents indicating that the Iraqis were developing a clandestine nuclear program. In a bizarre standoff, the inspectors refused to surrender the documents back to the Iraqis, and for four days the Iraqis denied them permission to leave the parking lot of the building they had just inspected. The Iraqis relented after the Security Council threatened to use force, and the United States announced the dispatch of ninety-six Patriot missiles and additional troops to Saudi Arabia.

On other occasions in the subsequent months, Iraqi troops obstructed inspectors and even blocked them from destroying equipment as specified in the 1991 cease-fire. Iraqi actions drew a condemnation from the Security Council in February 1992, which declared Iraq in "material breach" of the UN resolutions and promised serious consequences if Iraq did not desist. In this matter, the Iraqis backed down three days after being officially informed of the Security Council's decision. There was also a seventeen-day standoff outside the Ministry of Agriculture in July 1992, which United Nations Commission on Iraq (UNSCOM) inspectors were seeking to enter for evidence of Iraq's ballistic missile development program. In this case the inspectors withdrew.

Tensions peaked in the final days of the Bush administration. In January 1993 Iraq moved surface-to-air missiles into the southern no-fly zone and argued that UNSCOM inspectors could travel only on Iraqi government planes to enter Iraq and conduct their inspections. At the same time there were reports of skirmishes between Kuwaiti and Iraqi troops on the border, and Iraqi troops moved into the DMZ to retrieve Silkworm missiles they had left behind in the war.

In response, more than one hundred French, British, and U.S. planes bombed targets on January 13. On January 17 forty U.S.-launched Tomahawk missiles attacked the Djilah Industrial Park in Zafaraniyya, which was thought to be connected to the Iraqi nuclear program; the next day seventy-five British, French, and U.S. aircraft bombed sites in the southern no-fly zone. On January 19 Saddam Hussein announced a unilateral cease-fire to mark the end of the Bush administration.

The United States does appear to have been engaged in an exercise of coercive diplomacy on these occasions, with mixed results. Clear demands with broad international support were often effective in reversing Iraqi actions. Yet while the United States and its allies were able to reverse these individual Iraqi actions, they were unable to reverse Iraqi behavior. Indeed, rather than moving toward cooperation with the international community, Iraqi behavior during this period appears to have been a carefully calibrated mechanism to test Western responses and wear down Western resolve.

Operation Vigilant Warrior (1994)

On October 5, 1994, U.S. intelligence analysts noted the massing of two Iraqi Republican Guard armored divisions near the Kuwaiti border, numbering some fifty thousand soldiers. The massing of troops was accompanied by Iraqi threats to expel UNSCOM weapons inspectors from Iraq. The move became public on October 7. In response to the Iraqi troop movement, the United States swiftly deployed thousands of troops to the area and began moving tens of thousands more. The United Kingdom and France also sent token naval assets to the Gulf. The administration made its move public by leaking it to CNN correspondent Wolf Blitzer on the morning of October 9. The next day Iraq announced that the troops were being withdrawn from the border area, but the United States expressed skepticism, continued its deployment, and announced that it would send hundreds of additional aircraft to the Gulf. Whether the Iraqi deployment represented a testing of the waters or was merely a feint to show bravado is unclear. What was clearer was that the United States took the threat seriously and acted to move forces with extreme speed. Because of the forward deployment of so much materiel in the region, a U.S. threat to meet an Iraqi invasion forcefully was credible.

Perhaps more than any other episode in the U.S. confrontation with Iraq, Operation Vigilant Warrior appears to have been a successful application of coercive diplomacy, even though it lies between coercive diplomacy and deterrence (since it was chiefly intended to preempt a future Iraqi action, rather than curtail or roll back an action that had already taken place). The U.S. action took place in a relatively confined time frame, the demands were specific, and the threat of force was real. While we cannot understand Saddam's motivations for massing troops, he clearly calculated that he was better off retreating than pushing the exercise to its conclusion.

Iraqi Thrust into the North (1996)

In August 1996 fighting escalated between two rival Kurdish factions, the Patriotic Union of Kurdistan (PUK) and the Kurdistan Democratic Party (KDP). The PUK, which was receiving some support from Iran, was making strides. In response to a request for assistance against the PUK from KDP leader Massoud Barzani, Iraqi troops entered the "safe haven" area of the north on August 29 and occupied the local capital of Irbīl two days later. The Iraqi army swept in with thirty thousand to forty thousand troops and extensive police and intelligence personnel. They killed more than one hundred lightly armed Kurdish troops and arrested nineteen members of the opposition group, the Iraqi National Congress (INC), who were never seen again. According to at least one account, CIA officers who were working with INC members in Salahuddin fled just ahead of the Iraqi tanks, leaving their clients to the Iraqis.[18]

In response to the Iraqi offensive, the United States launched forty-four cruise missiles against targets four hundred miles south of the zone of fighting on September 3 and expanded the southern no-fly zone by seventy miles, from the 32d parallel to the 33d. The United States did not provide air cover for the PUK fighters and ensured that its military intervention remained well outside the zone of conflict. Iraqi troops withdrew from Irbīl within days of the initial invasion, thus sparing any long-term U.S. response.

Despite the apparent clarity of winning an Iraqi withdrawal from the north after the U.S. missile strike, this episode does not appear to have been a successful application of coercive diplomacy for two reasons. First, the Iraqis were arguably able to achieve their goals in the brief time they were in Irbīl, rounding up oppositionists and neutralizing any insurgency. Viewed in this light, the Iraqi retreat was not a response to U.S. threats or U.S. force but a sign that its goals had already been accomplished. Any presumptive U.S. victory was illusory, since the outcome of Saddam's short stay in Irbīl was the destruction of the CIA's significant operations there. Second, there is no evidence that cruise missile attacks on targets in the south were either sufficiently punishing in and of themselves or indicative of enough future punishment to sway Iraqi behavior. More than the previous con-frontations, Saddam's incursion into Irbīl suggests that he had begun to understand U.S. diplomacy and the use of force and had begun to take actions that served his interests while limiting the U.S. response.

Defiance of UNSCOM (1997–98)

As UNSCOM inspections of Iraq progressed, inspectors came to believe that Iraq was implementing a concerted program of obstruc-tion, deception, and outright lies. In response, UNSCOM began to concentrate on understanding the deception mechanism, in addi-tion to conducting its overall inspection work. This operation, called "Shake the Tree," was directed by Scott Ritter, a hard-charging for-mer U.S. marine. Relying heavily on satellite imagery, signals intel-ligence, and other assistance from cooperating governments, Shake the Tree laid bare the pattern of Iraqi deception, led by intelligence services close to the Iraqi leadership. The actions also antagonized the government of Iraq, which increasingly obstructed the inspectors and denied them access to sites all over the country.[19]

In the face of such confrontations, the Security Council expressed grave and increasing concern about Iraq's "clear and flagrant viola-tions" of its obligations.[20] Despite the Security Council's protests, Iraq moved to bar U.S. inspectors from participating in UNSCOM activities on October 29, 1997, leading to a withdrawal of all UNSCOM inspec-tors from Iraq. Iraq readmitted inspectors the following month after solemnly promising "full compliance," but in December 1997 Iraq constructed a category of sites called "Presidential and Sovereign," which inspectors would not be allowed to visit.

Amid growing war clouds in February 1998, UN secretary-general Kofi Annan traveled to Baghdad to defuse the crisis. He emerged on February 23 with a memorandum of understanding in which Iraq reconfirmed its acceptance of the relevant Security Council resolutions and promised to grant the inspectors full access to suspect sites in the country.

U.S. officials were reportedly enraged by Annan's efforts, believing he had won only a Pyrrhic victory. They remained deeply skeptical that Annan had won Saddam's cooperation on inspections; instead, they believed that Annan's actions represented a high watermark for international obstruction of U.S. efforts to force Iraqi compliance. Indeed, Annan's energetic and high-profile diplomacy (which Americans whispered was part of an effort to secure the Nobel Peace Prize for himself) forcefully reminded Americans that the confrontation with Saddam Hussein's Iraq was not a bilateral one with the United States but a multilateral one predicated on Security Council resolutions and international law.

At the same time, evidence has emerged to suggest that the U.S. government was having second thoughts about coercive arms control in this period. Scott Ritter has charged that between November 1997 and August 1998 the U.S. government had called off UNSCOM inspectors at least seven times when they were on the verge of uncovering evidence of Iraqi noncompliance with relevant Security Council resolutions, for fear that discovery of noncompliance would precipitate a crisis that the United States hoped to avoid. The effect of the charge was to further weaken the U.S. exercise of coercive diplomacy, because it suggested a lack of U.S. resolve to back up its threats with force.

Operation Desert Fox (1998)

Kofi Annan's February victory was short-lived, as Iraq suspended its cooperation with UNSCOM in August 1998 and then announced unilaterally in October that all UNSCOM work in Iraq should cease. The inspectors left Iraq on November 9–12. After U.S. warplanes were in the air to bomb Iraq on November 14, Iraq announced that inspectors could return and that the Iraqis would cooperate fully. Inspections resumed on November 18, with a warning that the United States and its allies would strike if, in fact, full Iraqi cooperation was not forthcoming. In his report to the Security Council on December 15, UNSCOM chairman Richard Butler noted several instances (out of several hundred inspections) in which the Iraqis did not fully comply with UNSCOM demands. U.S.-British air strikes began shortly after midnight on December 17 and lasted four days, ending just before the Muslim holy month of Ramadan. In all, something like six hundred sorties and four hundred missile strikes were carried out against one hundred or so targets in Iraq.

The events leading up to Operation Desert Fox may have marked the death rattle of coercive diplomacy against Iraq. While Saddam had complied with UNSCOM's demands in limited cases under specific military threat, the United States and its allies were unable to change the overall pattern of Iraqi behavior. Iraq single-mindedly worked to undermine both the inspections and the international support for sanctions and achieved significant success in doing so. Operation Desert Fox further undermined international support for containment of Iraq and resulted in the termination of weapons inspections. Viewed in this light, Saddam Hussein may have made the quite rational calculation that his defiance of U.S. demands was in his interest since he could withstand whatever the United States was willing to deliver and use such strikes to build international support and lock in gains he sought.

Pursuing "Containment Plus"

The United States appears to have adopted a new policy toward Iraq in the aftermath of Operation Desert Fox. On the one hand, Anglo-American air strikes against Iraqi targets were increased. While the lethality of these strikes was relatively low, the cost to Iraq in terms of prestige and of replacing destroyed facilities was high. Repeated air strikes made clear that Iraq was defenseless against Anglo-American assaults and were no doubt intended to take a toll on the Iraqi army.

On the other hand, the Clinton administration made "regime change" the centerpiece of its policy toward Iraq.[21] In so doing, the administration made any Iraqi cooperation with U.S. demands unlikely. If coercion is to work, the coerced must believe that the use of force will stop if the offending action stops. As long as the stated goal of U.S. policy was to overthrow the regime, it legitimated any and all Iraqi efforts to defy U.S. policy since its ultimate goal was not disarmament, containment, or deterrence, but regime change. One can argue about whether there were any circumstances under which Iraq would cooperate with U.S. disarmament commands, and, given the Iraqis' past behavior, it seems unlikely that they would have fully complied in any event. But an avowed policy of regime change took all "carrots" out of the equation and made clear that the current regime was locked in a life-or-death struggle with the United States. The dynamic made Iraqi intransigence more likely, especially given the U.S. inability to establish a bill of particulars against Iraqi actions that could galvanize the international community. By pointedly dismissing the possibility of offering any "carrots" to the Iraqi regime, the U.S. government had given up on using coercive diplomacy to influence the regime of Saddam Hussein.

An Elective War?

When the Bush administration came into office in January 2001, it resolved to revise U.S. policy toward Iraq. In the latter years of the Clinton administration, the Bush administration believed, Iraq policy had badly unraveled. Inspections had ended, international support for sanctions was eroding, and the regime was able to combine black-market kickbacks, smuggling, sanctions busting, and a variety of other tactics to gain access to billions of dollars annually. The clear trajectory was for the dismantlement of the coercive disarmament regime that had been imposed a decade earlier, probably in a matter of a few years.

From the beginning, the Bush administration encompassed two schools of thought when it came to Iraq policy. One school favored "smart sanctions," which is to say a sanctions regime that enjoyed more international support, worked more efficiently, and took less of a toll on Iraqi civilians. The other favored a more robust policy of regime change and contained many advocates of using the fissiparous Iraqi expatriate opposition as a key element of that change.

The early round of the debate went to the "smart sanctions" faction, which won international approval for a new sanctions regime in May 2001. But after al Qaeda's catastrophic terrorist attack of September 11, 2001, the balance tilted toward the regime-change faction. The argument this faction made—that Saddam's unpredictability made him undeterrable and that his pursuit of weapons of mass destruction would give him the capability of a catastrophic attack even worse than that of September 11—gained increasing traction in a year when so much of U.S. foreign policy swung behind the ideas of combating terrorism and preempting national security threats.

The U.S. policy debate over Iraq reached something of a crescendo in August 2002, but in a strange way: it wasn't much of a debate. Rather, it was a series of leaks and counterleaks that seemed to indicate the creation of war plans and the movement of troops, without a debate on the advisability of starting a war against Iraq. Most administration officials portrayed the conflict in solely U.S.-Iraqi terms, leaving many erstwhile Arab and European partners feeling neglected and hurt.

On September 12, 2002, in a speech before the UN General Assembly, President Bush laid out the case for action against Iraq and invited international cooperation. After months of concern from the international community that the U.S. government was more interested in acting vigorously against Iraq than in having international sanction to do so, Bush said, "My nation will work with the U.N. Security Council to meet our common challenge. . . . We will work with the U.N. Security Council for the necessary resolutions." Bush did not completely forswear the unilateral card, however. He added, "The Security Council resolutions will be enforced—the just demands of peace and security will be met—or action will be unavoidable."²² By demonstrating his willingness to act unilaterally, Bush was able to win passage of a new resolution, 1441, which codified past Iraqi noncompliance and promised "serious consequences" if full compliance were not forthcoming.

In a way, by the fall of 2002 the United States had adopted a strategy of coercive diplomacy against its allies, arguing that it would strike Iraq unilaterally if they did not support robust and effective action against the Iraqi regime. The incentives for the allies to cooperate were several, but two are clear. First, if action were inevitable, futile gestures to halt such action would only incur U.S. wrath while providing no benefit. Second, such gestures would highlight the impotence, if not irrelevance, of the protesting party or parties. Although allies would not be the target of a U.S. strike, the potential blow to their influence and prestige was hoped to be sufficient to cause them to mute their criticism and drop obstacles to U.S. action against Iraq.

In the event, international criticism persisted, as did U.S. perceptions of noncompliance, and the United States went to war again in March 2003. Although some claimed that the Bush administration had already decided to go to war, and thus entered negotiations in bad faith, U.S. adherence to the principles of coercive diplomacy was clear: the desired actions were clearly specified, the threat of force was credible, and the time allowed for compliance was clearly bounded.

ANALYSIS

There are five particular aspects of the Iraqi case that demonstrate the difficulties of the United States' employing a strategy of coercive diplomacy against a determined adversary.

1. Unilateralism, Multilateralism, and Their Contradictions

Coercion (and the threat of coercion) is most precisely applied by unitary actors, but the legitimacy of coercion must come from multilateral actors. The confrontation between Iraq and the international community was neither a bilateral conflict nor a multilateral one, but rather a conflict that had bilateral and multilateral components and that required their coordination or, even better, their integration.

After Iraq's invasion of Kuwait, the United States assumed the lead role in confronting and sometimes battling the Iraqi regime. This role arose from U.S. global leadership, as well as the U.S. strategic interest in protecting friendly regimes in the Persian Gulf and ensuring the unencumbered flow of oil from the Gulf to U.S. allies (and, to a much lesser extent, to the United States itself). Yet the coalition confronting Iraq waxed and waned over time. The Desert Storm military coalition gathered twenty-nine countries. While U.S. troops formed the bulk of the fighting force, the coalition also included major Arab powers such as Egypt and Saudi Arabia, thereby undermining any Iraqi claim that the force represented outside powers invading the Arab world. Thereafter, the conflict veered between being an essentially bilateral (U.S./Iraqi, or sometimes U.S.-British/Iraqi) conflict and being a multilateral (coalition/Iraqi or UN/Iraqi) conflict.

In the aftermath of the Iraqi invasion of Kuwait, the United States worked assiduously to build international support for rolling back the invasion. Part of that support came in the form of the UN sanctions mentioned earlier. But in June 1993 the United States acted unilaterally when it bombed Iraqi intelligence headquarters in Baghdad in retribution for evidence linking Iraq to a plot to assassinate former president George Bush. The United States also acted unilaterally in October 1994 when it deployed an additional fifty-four thousand troops to Kuwait in response to Iraqi troops massing near the Kuwaiti border. In February

1998, after Iraqi obstruction of weapons inspectors, the United States and Britain pulled back from the brink of war after UN secretary-general Kofi Annan negotiated a memorandum of understanding with Baghdad that secured Iraqi promises to cooperate more fully with weapons inspections. The U.S.-British air attacks of December 1998, which followed within days of a negative report from UNSCOM's chairman regarding Iraqi cooperation, appear to have been carried out through coordination with the chairman but without the approval of the Security Council or the secretary-general.

One important question to be resolved is whether multilateralism has its moment in an international conflict. As the memory of Iraqi actions receded and nations felt no immediate threat from Iraq, it proved increasingly difficult to maintain a coalition to support the practice of coercive diplomacy against the Iraqis. Indeed, even the consensus for containment receded. One option for the United States, adopted in 2003, was to abandon the desire for Security Council consensus and instead to form a narrower coalition with clearer goals and a clearer will to pursue them. Such a choice sacrifices international legitimacy, but it may be worthwhile if the outcome would be significantly improved.

2. Coercive Diplomacy within Containment and Deterrence

The coercive diplomacy aspect of policy toward Iraq was embedded in a larger policy based on containment and deterrence. While the containment of Iraq had clear UN sanction, the deterrent aspects of U.S. policy toward Iraq had somewhat less clear UN sanction and were carried out primarily by U.S., and to some degree British, forces. They included the forward basing of troops and equipment in the Gulf region and aggressive patrolling of no-fly zones in northern and southern Iraq. The deterrent elements were ongoing and intended to send a clear message that Iraqi aggression against neighboring states would meet with a swift and punishing response. The coercive diplomacy aspects of U.S. policy were distinguished from the containment and deterrence components in that they were bounded in time and the individual actions had observable outcomes.

It is more difficult to judge the long-term efficacy of coercive actions. Although individual coercive actions may be successful in the short term, they may actually be a failure in the longer term because of negative effects on coalition cohesion, target motivation, or even coercer motivation. Coercive diplomacy was only one component of U.S. policy toward Iraq, and in some cases it undermined, or at least weakened, other elements of that policy. This was particularly true in the way perceived U.S. unilateralism vis-à-vis Iraq undermined international support for containment.

3. Highly Iterative Confrontations

The third particular aspect of the Iraqi case was its unusually iterative nature. Conflicts rose to a crescendo again and again and often resulted in the limited use of armed force. The conflict was striking, then, not only for its duration but also for the repeated cycles of violence short of all-out war.

Over time Iraq learned how to deal successfully with the international community. It adopted policies of "cheat and retreat," testing limits and then quickly stepping back from the brink when punishment seemed imminent. In its invasion of the Kurdish areas in the north, the Iraqi army made a quick thrust and then retreated before a concerted allied response could be assembled. Iraq also showed great skill in dividing the international coalition, publicly offering images of mass Iraqi suffering and privately offering remuneration to lending nations such as France and Russia. Time after time Saddam Hussein admitted weapons inspectors unconditionally and then swiftly moved to constrain their activities. While Saddam did not call the tune, he became familiar with the one that was being played, and he learned to live with it, if not how to make his country thrive despite it.

Viewed in this light, Saddam Hussein apparently used his series of confrontations with Western coercive diplomacy as an educational opportunity. He was more difficult to coerce in 1998 than he was in 1991 because he understood well the limits of Western resolve and the ways to undermine that resolve (through coalition splintering and other tactics). While Daniel Byman and Matthew Waxman urge that coercion be seen as a dynamic process, such admonitions may be insufficient.[23] Over time, repeated efforts to employ coercive diplomacy may tilt the balance in favor of the target country because of the relative robustness of possible counter-coercion strategies combined with a fine-tuned understanding of likely responses to defiance by the target country.

4. A Highly Motivated but Difficult-to-Understand Adversary

Alexander George's model of coercive diplomacy admittedly relies on the "assumption of a 'rational' opponent; that is, it assumes that the adversary will be receptive to and will correctly evaluate information that is critical to the question of whether the costs and risks of not complying will outweigh the gains to be expected from pursuing the course of action."[24] What George really means by rational, however, is that theorists or policymakers can anticipate the calculations of the target country. The two are not necessarily the same.

A leader such as Saddam Hussein is a particularly difficult target for coercive diplomacy. This stems in part from his violent background and in part from the way his interest in his own survival has trumped the well-being of his country to an overwhelming extent. U.S. models are predicated on political leaders who seek to preserve their armies, their assets, and their infrastructure. In the Iraqi case, the United States may have faced an adversary who made calculations based only on his individual interests and who controlled a political system alien to anything U.S. analysts themselves had known. With Saddam Hussein's status so tied up in his aura of power and invincibility, he may have calculated that the cost of compliance outweighed the cost of defiance since signs of weakness in the international arena could threaten his grip on power at home. In the words of one scholar of Iraq, since Saddam Hussein came to power, "whenever Iraq's foreign interests clashed with perceived domestic security interests, the latter has always prevailed."[25]

In such circumstances not only was the Iraqi leadership unswayed by long-running sanctions; it may even have concluded that maintaining the sanctions; was in its interest. Counterintuitive though such a prospect may be, it has a certain amount of rationality. The shortages caused by sanctions allowed the regime to reward and punish individuals and groups and created black markets from which the regime could profit. In this way, sanctions helped entrench the regime. The mechanism for selling oil also allowed the regime to enrich itself by pocketing smuggling proceeds, as well to make profits by manipulating the prices of oil futures. Finally, the appalling humanitarian situation in Iraq undermined international support for the continued containment of Iraq, thereby splitting the anti-Iraq coalition and making future military action less likely.[26]

If such calculations were in play, U.S. threats to launch cruise missile attacks or even air strikes at Iraqi targets were unlikely to yield Iraqi compliance since the Iraqi leadership calculated on a completely different—yet still rational—basis than countries are expected to use.

5. Changing Goals and Unchanging Authority

A final characteristic of the U.S.-Iraqi confrontation is that U.S. goals changed but the stated authority for those goals did not. This characteristic is peculiar to the Iraqi case, but it may be replicated in similar confrontations in the future. In particular, the United Nations levied sanctions against Iraq on August 6, 1990 (and revised them on September 25, 1990) in response to the Iraqi invasion of Kuwait. Those same sanctions were institutionalized with the passage of a resolution on April 2, 1991, following the cease-fire and fixed to remain until Iraq cooperated fully and completely with the UN-dictated arms control provisions. They were being used a decade later to ensure the continued containment of Iraq. Similarly, authority for Anglo-American no-fly zones in the north and south of Iraq was originally granted to protect populations under attack, but those zones were clearly used later to maintain pressure on the Iraqi regime.

The complication for U.S. policy was that the U.S. government had a clear preference for coercion backed by multilateral support,[27] yet that support was increasingly undermined by a reliance on outdated mandates. Such an environment induced U.S. partners to announce their distance from U.S. policy (as indeed the French, the Russians, and many Arab governments did) and actually eroded the ability of the United States to marshal international support for its actions.

ASSESSMENT AND POLICY RECOMMENDATIONS

The balance sheet for coercive diplomacy against Iraq is mixed. The strategies that the United States and the international community applied to Iraq cannot be evaluated normatively but rather only in comparison with the likely outcomes of alternative policies. In addition, the United States did not need to pursue the most effective policy. As David Baldwin suggests, a less effective policy may be preferable to a more effective one if the differential in costs is sufficient.[28] Finally, it is unclear if the various branches of the U.S. government shared a single measure for success. The military was avowedly hostile to being held accountable for political outcomes and insisted on being judged solely on the basis of mission completion. The State Department had its own measures for success (presumably relying on its success at winning international support for coercive moves), and the White House yet others. Under such conditions, any such assessment is tenuous.

Taken on the whole and viewed retrospectively, U.S. policy seems to have been a qualified success. The threat of force and occasional limited use of force contributed to "keeping Saddam in his box" from 1991 to 2002. Saddam sometimes threatened his neighbors, but those threats were limited and always effectively countered. Inspections revealed a great deal about Iraqi weapons development programs and certainly slowed (if not completely halted) Iraqi efforts in that direction.

The cost of the U.S. policy, however, was extremely high in terms of dollars, troop morale, and Iraqi lives. In order to enable the United States to pursue the occasional coercion of Iraq, the United States prepositioned billions of dollars of equipment in the Gulf, increased its standing force there, and periodically deployed even more troops to the region during crises. Policing the no-fly zones in the north and south of Iraq imposed a significant burden on U.S. pilots and support crew, who had to be away from home for months at a time and live through hot Arabian summers. Unused, coercive power morphs into deterrent power, and the costs of maintaining a significant deterrent to Iraqi behavior were high.

In addition, one account estimated that sanctions imposed on Iraq because of the government's efforts to develop weapons of mass destruction themselves caused more deaths than all weapons of mass destruction throughout history.[29] While U.S. policy was not wholly responsible for increased child mortality in Iraq, that policy certainly contributed to it. According to a UNICEF survey published in August 1999, both infant mortality and under-age-five mortality more than doubled in the decade of sanctions in those parts of Iraq under Saddam Hussein's control.[30]

Another cost was the way the past decade's events undermined the credibility of the United Nations, which insisted on Iraqi compliance but was unwilling to enforce it. In addition, the events induced the United States to have basically one-dimensional and occasionally strained relationships with the nations of the Persian Gulf, which concentrated on military threats at the expense of domestic development.

Finally, U.S. policy contributed to strengthening Saddam Hussein's hold on his people and on the presidency of his country. While U.S. policies appear to have denied the regime resources that it could have used to threaten its neighbors militarily, those policies also helped provide it with the resources to consolidate control over its own people.

CONCLUSION

Iraq proved to be a difficult target to coerce, in part because the government put such high value on engaging in the proscribed behavior. With such a highly motivated adversary acting over such an extended period of time, U.S. officials faced a difficult task in their efforts to shape Iraqi actions. The passage of time eroded international consensus on actions against Iraq, isolating U.S. policy from the original Gulf War coalition and from the UN authority that gave rise to it.

In this regard, Byman and Waxman's admonition to view coercion as a dynamic rather than a static process seems especially apt.[31] Iraq responded clearly to U.S. strategy by splitting the United States off from its allies. It did so by partial compliance with U.S. demands, by appeals for solidarity, and by highlighting the suffering of the Iraqi population. Just as the United States ramped up its forces and hit Iraqi targets time after time, so, too, did Iraq pick off members of the allied coalition. The vote to establish UNMOVIC as a successor to UNSCOM in December 1999 was certainly a great Iraqi victory: the new organization's mandate was significantly weakened to take account of French, Russian, and Chinese concerns, yet in the end those countries declined to vote in favor of the new organization anyway.

As the United States continued its efforts to isolate Iraq, Iraq succeeded in its efforts to isolate the United States. The question is not what U.S. coercive power can achieve, since it is clear that the United States enjoys overwhelming military superiority over Iraq. The question is rather where the limits of coercive diplomacy lie, since for most of this period the United States was far less motivated to engage in an escalation than the Iraqis were.

For coercive diplomacy, there are several lessons. The most important is that coercive diplomacy works best in the short term, for several reasons:

- the will of the coercer is the highest at that point;

- the coercer's reprisals for noncompliance are least predictable;

- the coerced has had the least opportunity to devise counterstrategies to coercion; and

- the authority for action is most closely tailored to the prevailing conditions.

The Iraq experience also revealed multilateralism to be a double-edged sword, conferring legitimacy but hamstringing implementation. Finally, the UN framework for confronting Iraqi behavior became threadbare over time. It was never devised to do what it subsequently did, nor to do it for so long.

It is hard to imagine an end to the U.S. confrontation with Iraq other than a change of regime in Baghdad—a change that the Bush administration chose to precipitate rather than wait for. The benefits and costs of this choice will take some time to become apparent.

NOTES

The author wishes to thank the editors, Daniel Byman, and Andrew Parasiliti for their helpful comments on earlier versions of this paper. There remains much with which they disagree here.

1. Kenneth I. Juster, "The United States and Iraq: Perils of Engagement," in *Honey and Vinegar: Incentives, Sanctions, and Foreign Policy*, ed. Richard N. Haass and Meghan L. O'Sullivan (Washington, D.C.: Brookings Institution Press, 2000), 55. For a sympathetic assessment of this policy, see Laurie Mylroie, "The Baghdad Alternative," *Orbis* (summer 1988).

2. One could argue that the U.S. shift toward a policy of overthrow represented a continuation of coercive diplomacy, with the aim of coercing the Iraqi people to overthrow their extant government. My own view is that coercive diplomacy properly remains at the state level, and that directly coercing populations veers toward engaging noncombatants in an inappropriate way.

3. Alexander L. George, "Coercive Diplomacy," in *The Limits of Coercive Diplomacy*, 2d ed., ed. Alexander L. George and William Simons (Boulder, Colo.: Westview Press, 1994), 8–9.

4. "The Glaspie Transcript: Saddam Meets the Ambassador (July 25, 1990)," in *The Gulf War Reader*, ed. Micah L. Sifry and Christopher Cerf (New York: Times Books, 1991), 122–136.

5. See, for example, Admiral William Crowe's testimony to the Senate Armed Services Committee on November 28, 1990, reprinted in Sifry and Cerf, *The Gulf War Reader*, 234–237.

6. George Bush, quoted in Juster, "The United States and Iraq," 55–56.

7. See George Bush and Brent Scowcroft, *A World Transformed* (New York: Alfred A. Knopf, 1998), 309–312; and James A. Baker, *The Politics of Diplomacy* (New York: G. P. Putnam's Sons, 1995), 271–272.

8. Bush and Scowcroft, *A World Transformed*, 322.

9. George, "Coercive Diplomacy," 8.

10. One interesting possibility is that in this case, Iraq was trying to employ coercive diplomacy against Saudi Arabia, possibly seeking accommodation on debt repayment, oil production, or U.S. presence. Andrew Parasiliti, personal correspondence with author, September 24, 2000.

11. Baker, *The Politics of Diplomacy*, 277.

12. The text of the letter, which suggested an allied attack would destroy the Iraqi military establishment, is reprinted in Sifry and Cerf, *The Gulf War Reader*, 178–179.

13. Transcript of press conference with James Baker and Tariq Aziz, reprinted in Sifry and Cerf, *The Gulf War Reader*, 173.

14. Sifry and Cerf, *The Gulf War Reader*, 179.

15. U.S. News and World Report, *Triumph without Victory: The Unreported History of the Persian Gulf War* (New York: Times Books, 1992), 410.

16. Americans and Russians shared dismay at Saddam Hussein's behavior. In August 1990 President George Bush said, "We do have a chance at a new world order. And I'd like to think that out of this dreary performance by Saddam Hussein there could be now an opportunity for peace throughout all the Middle East." Meanwhile, Russian foreign minister Eduard Shevardnadze echoed that language, terming Saddam Hussein's action "an act of terrorism against the emerging new world order." "Confrontation in the Gulf" (press conference excerpts), *New York Times*, August 31, 1992, A11; and Paul Lewis, "Confrontation in the Gulf," *New York Times*, September 26, 1992, A1.

17. Alexander George, "The Role of Force in Diplomacy," in *The Use of Force after the Cold War*, ed. H. W. Brands (College Station: Texas A&M University Press, 2000).

18. Andrew Cockburn and Patrick Cockburn, *Out of the Ashes: The Resurrection of Saddam Hussein* (New York: HarperCollins, 1999), 241–242.

19. See Peter J. Boyer, "Scott Ritter's Private War," *New Yorker*, November 9, 1998.

20. United Nations Security Council Resolution 1115 (unanimously adopted on June 21, 1997).

21. The shift in strategy was partly driven by congressional demands. President Clinton signed the Iraq Liberation Act into law on October 31, 1998, but it was not until early December 1998 that the administration's formula of "containment plus" for Iraq became "containment plus regime change."

22. See www.whitehouse.gov/news/releases/2002/09/print/20020912-1.html.

23. Daniel L. Byman and Matthew C. Waxman, *Confronting Iraq: U.S. Policy and the Use of Force since the Gulf War* (Santa Monica, Calif.: RAND, 2000), 8–10.

24. George, "Coercive Diplomacy," 13.

25. Amatzia Baram, *Building toward Crisis: Saddam Husayn's Strategy* *for Survival* (Washington, D.C.: Washington Institute for Near East Policy, 1998), 2.

26. I am indebted to Ambassador Richard Murphy for his thoughtful comments along these lines.

27. See Daniel Byman and Matthew Waxman, "Defeating U.S. Coercion," *Survival* 41, no. 2 (summer 1999): 108.

28. David A. Baldwin, "The Sanctions Debate and the Logic of Choice," *International Security* 24, no. 3 (winter 1999-2000): 86.

29. John and Karl Mueller, "The Real Weapons of Mass Destruction," *Foreign Affairs* 78, no. 3 (May-June 1999): 51.

30. Three northern provinces are beyond the control of Saddam Hussein. Mortality rates in those areas, while higher than before sanctions were imposed, are significantly lower than in the rest of Iraq. See UNICEF, *Child and Maternal Mortality Survey: Preliminary Report (Iraq)*, July 1999, 9, available at www.unicef.org/reseval/iraq.htm.

31. Byman and Waxman, "Defeating U.S. Coercion," 86–88.

8

Coercive Diplomacy and the Response to Terrorism

MARTHA CRENSHAW

ERRORISM HAS PROVED TO BE A DIFFICULT TEST for coercive diplomacy. U.S. counterterrorism policy cannot routinely meet the basic requirements of the strategy. When coercive diplomacy is applied, the conditions that would make it successful are rarely met. While the United States has sometimes been effective in changing the policies of states that instigate or assist terrorism, it has not found an appropriate mix of threat and reward that could constrain the behavior of nonstate adversaries.

This chapter focuses on the U.S. response to terrorism from 1993 to the "war on terrorism" launched in 2001. It first outlines the general contours of the threat as it developed after the Cold War. This overview is followed by analysis of the general concept of coercive diplomacy in relation to terrorist strategies. The propositions thus generated are then tested against the instances of post–Cold War counterterrorism policy that most closely fit the definition of the concept of coercive diplomacy. These cases, when military force was used or threatened, provide the best basis for evaluating the success or failure of the strategy. They include the retaliatory strike against Iraq in 1993, threats against Iran following the bombing of U.S. military facilities in Saudi Arabia in 1996, cruise missile attacks against Sudan and Afghanistan in 1998, and efforts to compel the Taliban to yield Osama

Bin Laden after September 11, 2001. The chapter concludes by assessing the strengths and weaknesses of coercive diplomacy as a response to terrorism.

THE CONTEXT

When the Clinton administration took office in 1993, the threat of terrorism appeared to be receding. The incidence of international terrorism was diminishing. Iraq had been defeated in the Gulf War. The last remaining hostages in Lebanon had been released. The ideological hostility of the Cold War had evaporated. The Israeli-Palestinian conflict was on the brink of transformation. A multilateral consensus against terrorism seemed feasible, with the United Nations assuming a more active role. Under UN auspices, for example, sanctions were implemented against Libya in order to bring to trial the Libyan agents accused of the bombing of Pan Am 103 in 1988.

The Clinton administration inherited a policy that had been applied reasonably consistently since 1972. It had four key principles: (1) no concessions to terrorist demands, (2) the imposition of diplomatic and economic sanctions against states that sponsored terrorism, (3) enforcement of the rule of law by bringing terrorists to trial, and (4) multilateral cooperation. It was accepted that the United States would take the lead in all these areas, yet frustration over lack of international cooperation often led to unilateral U.S. action. The Department of State officially designated six countries as sponsors of terrorism, which invoked automatic unilateral sanctions: Cuba, Iran, Iraq, Libya, North Korea, and Syria.

In addition, the 1986 attack on Libya had established a precedent for the use of retaliatory air power, although its effectiveness was questioned.[1] Earlier that year a task force led by Vice President George Bush had concluded that the "judicious employment of military force" might be necessary to a deterrent strategy. The report noted that a military show of force would be less risky than the use of force and might successfully intimidate terrorists and their sponsors. However, the task force also warned that a show of force could be considered gunboat diplomacy, that it might be perceived as a challenge rather than a credible threat, and, most important, that failure could require escalation to an active military response.[2]

The Clinton administration initially assumed a moderate stance toward terrorism. In contrast to the strong rhetoric of the Reagan years, the president's public speeches treated terrorism not as a major national security issue but as one of a series of modern transnational, or "border-crossing," threats, along with drug trafficking, global organized crime, epidemics of disease, and environmental disasters.

Immediately, however, three developments made terrorism a priority: highly destructive attacks on U.S. territory from both domestic and foreign sources, the terrorist use of chemical weapons, and the emergence of new terrorist actors hostile to U.S. interests. The close sequencing of terrorist attacks in different locations, the diversity of terrorist sources, and the geographical scope of terrorism heightened the salience of the threat.

The first shock came in February 1993, with the first bombing of the World Trade Center. Subsequent judicial investigations revealed that the perpetrators were transnational actors, independent of state sponsorship, not a familiar organization from the past. As information was gathered over the next two years, the United States identified an amorphous group composed of Egyptian religious dissidents, veterans of the war against the Soviet Union in Afghanistan, and freelancers. Arrests in 1995 revealed that the conspirators, led by Ramzi Youcef, had plans to bomb the Lincoln and Holland Tunnels and other buildings in New York as well as U.S. airliners over the Pacific. They seemed to represent a "new" global terrorism, with nonnegotiable demands, decentralized structures, and worldwide connections.

At the same time, the "old" state-sponsored terrorism continued to challenge U.S. interests. In April 1993 Kuwaiti authorities uncovered a plot to assassinate former president Bush during a visit to Kuwait. In June the United States retaliated against Baghdad for its complicity in the thwarted attack.

Less than two years later, in March 1995, the Aum Shinrikyo religious cult disseminated sarin gas in the Tokyo subways, killing eleven people and injuring as many as five thousand. U.S. policymakers feared that this first terrorist use of chemical weapons would establish a dangerous precedent for a "catastrophic" terrorism that the United States was ill equipped to combat.

Within the month a truck-bomb exploded in front of the federal building in Oklahoma City, leaving 168 people dead. The bombing exposed the country's domestic vulnerability to mass-casualty terrorism and reinforced the apprehensions inspired by the World Trade Center bombing two years earlier. Combined with the Tokyo subway attack, these incidents raised the specter of an even more deadly terrorist attack against the U.S. homeland in the future.

Although concern, especially in Congress, mounted over inadequate "domestic preparedness," U.S. interests abroad continued to be at risk, particularly military forces stationed in Saudi Arabia. Two bombings in 1995 and 1996 were the most serious attacks on U.S. targets outside the country since the 1983 bombing of the U.S. Marine barracks in Lebanon and the 1988 midair bombing of Pan Am 103. In November 1995 an attack on a Saudi National Guard office in Riyadh used by U.S. military trainers killed five U.S. citizens.[3] In June 1996 a truck-bomb at the Khobar Towers military housing complex in Dhahran killed nineteen U.S. airmen and wounded more than two hundred U.S. citizens. The Saudi government charged that Iran was responsible, and the United States considered but rejected military retaliation.

In July 1996 attention was again drawn to internal dangers. A small bomb at the Olympic Games in Atlanta led the secretary of defense to cut short a trip to Australia out of fear that it was part of a large-scale conspiracy, possibly connected to the Khobar Towers attack.[4] Fortunately, the initial reports turned out to be exaggerated.

Nevertheless, domestic worries about terrorism increased, focused especially on the prospective use of weapons of mass destruction, or WMD. In May 1998 the president signed two presidential decision directives designed to upgrade the country's counterterrorism capability. These measures dealt primarily with the organization of the government to combat terrorism and with domestic defenses against threats to the nation's infrastructure, such as attacks on telecommunications or banking systems. The president appointed a national coordinator for security, infrastructure protection, and counterterrorism on the staff of the National Security Council (NSC).

In August 1998 the nation was shocked again when bombs exploded simultaneously at U.S. embassies in Kenya and Tanzania, resulting in 301 deaths and more than 5,000 wounded. The bombings were charged to Osama Bin Laden, whom U.S. authorities had recognized as a threat since at least 1996. The United States struck back with cruise missile attacks against Bin Laden's training camps in Afghanistan and against a pharmaceuticals plant in Sudan, which was purportedly developing chemical weapons for Bin Laden. Sudan's general support for Islamic extremist terrorism had long been an irritant to the United States, and the country had been added to the State Department's list of state sponsors of terrorism in 1993.

In early December 1999 the United States received intelligence information that Bin Laden planned a series of attacks on U.S. citizens around the world to coincide with the New Year. Jordanian authorities had disrupted a plot to attack tourist sites in Jordan and Israel. A few days later, U.S. customs agents arrested an Algerian crossing the Canadian border into Seattle. Bomb-making materials were found in his car, and he had been trained in camps operated by Bin Laden in Afghanistan. His target was Los Angeles International Airport.

In October 2000 the U.S. military suffered another serious blow when the destroyer USS *Cole* was bombed in Yemen during a refueling stop. U.S. and Yemeni authorities suspected that Bin Laden was responsible for the attack, which killed seventeen U.S. sailors and crippled the ship, although definitive proof was lacking.

Terrorism was not an issue in the 2000 presidential campaign. On assuming office, the Bush administration did not consider it a top priority of the administration. The president's attention focused on domestic policy.

Over the spring and summer of 2001, U.S. intelligence agencies noticed an increased volume of communications among affiliates of the Bin Laden network and warned the government that a major attack was imminent. They could not predict, however, where or when or how an attack might occur. On the morning of September 11, the United States was the victim of a terrorist attack of unprecedented destructiveness. The inventiveness of the plot and the complexity of the planning also pointed to a new level of terrorism. The loss of the

World Trade Center and a wing of the Pentagon, as well as recognition that the White House or the Capitol might also have been destroyed, thrust terrorism to the top of the national security agenda. Eliminating the threat from al Qaeda suddenly became the nation's top priority.

TERRORISM AND COERCIVE DIPLOMACY

For terrorism, as for other cases, coercive diplomacy is designed to persuade an opponent to stop an action already undertaken or actively threatened. It is not uncommon for coercive diplomacy to confront an adversary who is also engaged in a form of compellence, as in the case of international terrorist adversaries seeking the government's withdrawal from a political commitment.[5] Each party, the government and the terrorist, wants to erode the other's motivation to continue and tries to understand what the other values most. Each wants to create the expectation of costs of sufficient magnitude that the other will back down. Each attempts to calibrate the amount of force necessary to overcome the other's disinclination to comply with its demands. Subjective perceptions or estimates of the credibility and strength of threats are critical to each party's decision making. Positive inducements are difficult for both sides since the conflict typically has a zero-sum quality. Certain asymmetries are also inherent in this relationship of reciprocal compellence. Each side threatens to punish the other for noncompliance, but the coercing state's power to escalate beyond the exemplary use of force far exceeds the terrorist's capabilities. On the other hand, the terrorist is likely to be more risk acceptant.

Terrorism, however, imposes unusual constraints on coercive diplomacy that are absent in the other cases examined in this volume.[6] Consider first the identities of the targets of coercive diplomacy. They are nonstate groups or states that are already isolated. Thus, governments are typically dealing with opponents lacking reliable internal control or valuable assets. Furthermore, the defending state is often trying to change the behavior of a loose alliance of states, nonstates, and autonomous individuals with ambiguous and complex interrelationships. Any strategy of coercive diplomacy must thus be directed toward multiple targets simultaneously, and each target's susceptibility to pressure and willingness to transgress vary. What is wanted of them will also vary. Thus, the defender has a complicated task involving critical trade-offs among different interests.

In addition, assessing the nature and intensity of the adversary's motivation is problematic. It is difficult for decision makers to put themselves in the frame of reference of the adversary. Because the essence of terrorism is concealment and deception, information about terrorist intentions is inherently difficult to obtain. When information is lacking, decision makers are tempted to rely on prior assumptions about motivation rather than on analysis of specific circumstances. Furthermore, a tendency to assume intention from behavior as well as poor understanding can lead states to focus on opportunities and vulnerabilities rather than on motivation. The propensity of policymakers to develop stereotypes and preconceptions that stress the fanaticism and irrationality of the adversary is reinforced when acts of terrorism are notably destructive and provocative. For example, policymakers may be tempted to ascribe terrorism to blind rage rather than instrumental reasoning, to personalize the adversary, and to see the enemy as monolithic. Terrorists' aspirations may be seen as unlimited and their demands nonnegotiable from the outset. Lack of knowledge makes it hard to assess the accuracy of these assumptions.

However, asymmetrical motivation is probably always in favor of the nonstate terrorist, and in favor of some state actors as well. Neither survival nor material power is at stake for the United States, however painful terrorist attacks are. In contrast, for the terrorist, everything may be at stake. Terrorism is the only reason for the existence of some nonstate actors.[7] Moreover, precisely because of their superior motivation, and because terrorism is so unacceptable a method, the defending state is likely to want to destroy the terrorist organization, not just change its behavior. Reassurances that one's aims are limited may not be credible even at the early stages of a coercive strategy. Under these circumstances the nonstate will have little incentive to abandon terrorism. States sponsoring terrorism have more to lose by resisting demands for compliance, but their isolation may also limit their interests beyond terrorism. If the coercer explicitly or implicitly seeks the displacement of the offending government, then compliance is unlikely unless some faction of the regime defects.

While identifying the terrorist opponent and understanding his motivations are difficult, gaining sufficiently precise and timely warning of his intention to attack in order to communicate a counterthreat and a sense of urgency is almost impossible. Terrorism depends on surprise. Furthermore, if a government learns of and exposes a terrorist plot, it may simply deflect the terrorists onto alternative targets or alter the timing of their attack. Identifying concrete assets to threaten or damage is also difficult. First, terrorism requires few material resources. Second, the assets a nonstate actor possesses, such as physical bases or financial resources, are necessarily within the domain of a state, so that considerations of sovereignty and other foreign policy interests are involved. A government cannot track, locate, or punish nonstates without the cooperation of states. Terrorism may be considered private rather than public violence, but there is no private space within which terrorists can operate.

Another difficulty is that coercing states cannot judge the effect of a threat or an initial use of demonstrative force since typically there can only be evidence of noncompliance.[8] Even if an adversary should renounce terrorism and disarm, it requires significant trust to accept such promises since terrorism is an economical and thus easily resumed strategy. Verification is tricky. The coercer must usually infer compliance from the absence of overt noncompliance, which is inconclusive and even dangerous. This constraint also makes it difficult to use an ultimatum to create a sense of urgency.

Another problem with the use of threats or demonstrative force is that terrorist adversaries may not perceive the use of force as punishment. In fact, the purpose of terrorism may be to provoke overreaction. A limited punitive response may reward them by providing recognition and even legitimacy among their constituents. The resort to military force may erode the coercer's status as the victim, causing a loss of moral high ground. It can alienate allies who prefer persuasion to coercion. And it can lead to an endless cycle of revenge and retaliation.

A strategy of coercive diplomacy is further complicated because the coercing state seeks not only to curb present terrorism but also to dissuade future terrorists. The goal is to compel existing terrorist actors to stop and to deter successors from starting. Using more destructive force than coercive diplomacy strictly requires may be essential to the long-term purpose of deterrence, but extreme punitiveness may exacerbate the existing conflict. Escalation can jeopardize the postcrisis relationship that the coercing government seeks, which may be based on interaction with a different set of actors than those currently posing a threat.

The government's secrecy requirements also weaken coercive diplomacy. Any meaningful threat to the terrorist in advance of an anticipated attack publicizes what the government knows and permits the terrorist to design around the government's threats. Concealing plans to threaten or use force may be an operational necessity. However, maintaining strict secrecy is an impediment to building the necessary domestic or international political consensus to ensure policy legitimacy. Lack of consultation before the response almost guarantees public criticism afterward. In the aftermath, security considerations also restrict the government's ability to justify its actions, since persuasive explanations would reveal sensitive intelligence information. Furthermore, covert preemption of an attack cannot usually be revealed to the public. Thus, failures are visible, while successes mostly are not.

Liberal democracies are restricted to a proportional and discriminating use of force. They are reluctant to incur casualties among their own forces or among noncombatants on the opponent's side. They are sensitive to reputation and to international norms governing the use of force. For these reasons, threatening escalation should an initial exemplary use of force fail can be difficult. On the other hand, public demand for action after a terrorist outrage may lead the government to respond rashly. It is the public, after all, that is targeted in the most spectacular acts of terrorism. The government's response to terrorism may come to depend more on public expectations—or decision makers' perceptions of those expectations—than on calculations of the adversary's reaction. Moreover, the defending state that offers positive inducements for stopping terrorism is vulnerable to charges of being "soft on terrorism."

Because terrorism is a form of surprise attack outside the context of war, it usually takes time to identify and locate the perpetrators. By the time the government acquires convincing evidence of responsibility, the public's outrage may have dissipated and justifying a punitive response will be difficult. However, responding quickly without conclusive information will likely appear clumsy and vindictive.

In sum, the specific properties of terrorism complicate the case for coercive diplomacy. The strategic interaction between government and terrorist is a form of reciprocal compellence. The targets of coercive diplomacy are multiple, shifting, and diffuse. Their material assets are few and meager by conventional measures of state power. Not only are nonstate actors hard to identify and understand, but they deliberately conceal their intentions. Their tactics depend on surprise and deception. Governments lack tactical warning of attacks. The terrorist can also be expected to be more highly motivated and more risk acceptant than the coercing government. Moreover, the government must look to the future and practice deterrence, preemption, prevention, and coercive diplomacy simultaneously. The government must also be concerned with policy legitimacy, since both domestic support and international cooperation are essential to an effective counterterrorist strategy.

THE U.S. RESPONSE TO TERRORISM BEFORE SEPTEMBER 11

The instances that are analyzed in depth are the best illustrations of the applicability and effectiveness of coercive diplomacy in U.S. counterterrorist policy after the end of the Cold War and before the attacks of September 11, 2001. The analysis focuses on situations involving the use or threat of military force, which is an essential component of a strategy of coercive diplomacy. Selecting these cases as focal points for a detailed examination of U.S. decision making provides empirical evidence for the theoretical propositions sketched earlier, permits comparisons to be made among cases, and establishes a foundation for drawing conclusions about the effectiveness of coercive diplomacy against terrorism. This approach also distinguishes U.S. policy before the September attacks from policy after the attacks.

Retaliation against Iraq, 1993

The case of retaliation against Iraq is the most straightforward case of the application of coercive diplomacy.[9] The provocation was a plot to kill former president Bush in a car-bomb attack during his visit to Kuwait in April. FBI and CIA investigations produced convincing evidence that the Iraqi Intelligence Service was behind the attempt. The information included confessions by two of the sixteen suspects arrested by Kuwaiti authorities, physical evidence from the bomb, and threats by Saddam Hussein to seek revenge against Bush for his leadership of the anti-Iraq coalition during the 1991 Gulf War. President Clinton referred to incontrovertible evidence of Iraq's guilt as well as to Saddam Hussein's past behavior: "We should not be surprised by such deeds, coming, as they do, from a regime like Saddam Hussein's, which has ruled by atrocity, slaughtered its own people, invaded two neighbors, attacked others and engaged in chemical and environmental warfare. Saddam has repeatedly violated the will and conscience of the international community, but this attempt at revenge by a tyrant against the leader of the world coalition that defeated him in war is particularly loathsome and cowardly."[10]

The decision to use force against Iraq was carefully considered, and the process was strictly secret. It was reached after two months of intensive investigation, the conclusion of final reports from the CIA and the FBI, and long meetings between Clinton and top aides in the final week.[11] Apparently, no more than five presidential aides knew of the discussions. The Pentagon had been drawing up a list of possible military responses for several weeks before the decision, including targeting Saddam Hussein's personal command post and military headquarters. The option that was chosen was, as the president explained, "firm and commensurate." The target was directly related to the offending behavior, and the method comported no risks for U.S. forces. Two U.S. Navy ships in the Persian Gulf and the Red Sea fired twenty-three Tomahawk cruise missiles directly at the headquarters of the Iraqi Intelligence Service in central Baghdad. The purpose, according to the president and to top military officials, was to send a message to the people responsible for planning the operation, not to

target Saddam Hussein himself. They acknowledged that it was a
show of force rather than an attempt to destroy the regime. As General Colin Powell put it, the intention was to "smack him whenever
it's necessary." The president explained the attack's purpose as deterring further violence or "outlawed behavior." The United States chose
to attack in the early hours of the morning in Baghdad, to avoid civilian casualties, and the attack was delayed a day in order to avoid the
Muslim sabbath.

The United States also explicitly retained the option to escalate if
necessary. Military officials stated publicly on several occasions that they
did not rule out future military action. Clinton explained in his public
address: "If Saddam and his regime contemplate further illegal
provocative actions, they can be certain of our response."

Although the attack was unilateral, the United States had apparently consulted Britain far in advance and informed some of its allies
just before the attack. The United States also called for an emergency
Security Council meeting and justified the attack in terms of Article
51 of the UN Charter. The operation was kept carefully separate from
the UN-authorized military actions against Iraq in the no-fly zone.

The administration quickly declared the attack a success, although
only sixteen of the twenty-three cruise missiles hit their intended targets. Three hit a residential housing area outside the intelligence
headquarters complex, killing eight civilians, according to official
Iraqi accounts that the United States did not dispute. U.S. officials
claimed that major damage was done to the Iraqi facility, although
they declined to be specific about the potential political impact of the
raid on Iraq's future behavior. At home, Congress was generally favorable to the decision, and the president received high approval ratings
in public opinion polls.[12] However, conservative columnist William
Safire criticized Clinton for choosing the weakest military option, a
"pitiful wristslap," in response to a provocation that was actually an
act of war.[13] Among U.S. allies, the British government supported
a limited, proportional response, although opposition parties denounced the raid as a calculated reprisal.[14] Critics also warned that
the strike would only strengthen Islamic extremists. In the Middle
East only the Kuwaiti government enthusiastically supported the U.S.

attack. Other Arab states criticized the action on the grounds that an anti-U.S. backlash would strengthen Saddam Hussein.[15] They noted that the United States had not acted decisively to stop ethnic cleansing in Bosnia, indicating a lack of balance and objectivity in U.S. foreign policy.

As for the effect of the raid on Iraq's subsequent behavior, no concrete evidence linked Iraqi agents to further acts of anti-U.S. terrorism in the 1990s. It is possible, then, to infer compliance from the lack of evidence of noncompliance. However, Paul Pillar, former deputy chief of the Counterterrorist Center of the CIA, argued that the U.S. effort had only a minimal effect and was unlikely to have deterred Saddam Hussein from further action.[16] Although temporarily weakened by the need to rebuild its intelligence networks, Iraq retained its capability for action. Iraq's primary focus became the anti-regime opposition in Iraq and abroad. The government also sheltered various rejectionist Palestinian terrorist groups such as the Abu Nidal organization and provided financial support for the families of "suicide" bombers in Palestine.

After September 11 the Bush administration charged repeatedly that Iraq was linked to al Qaeda. Iraqi support for terrorism was cited as one reason for the shift in U.S. strategy to a preemptive posture.

The Reaction to the Khobar Towers Bombing, June 1996

The truck-bomb attack was directed against a U.S. military complex that housed almost three thousand personnel participating in Joint Task Force/Southwest Asia, charged with enforcing the no-fly zone in Iraq. The explosion killed 19 U.S. airmen, wounded 372 other U.S. citizens, and injured more than 200 non-Americans. At least four classified CIA reports had warned of a terrorist threat to the housing complex since the November 1995 bombing that the Saudi government had traced to domestic Sunni opposition groups.[17] The perpetrators of that bombing had been executed just three weeks earlier, and retaliation was expected. The Department of Defense concluded that although tactical intelligence was lacking, there was "considerable" information that terrorists had both the capability and the intention of attacking.[18]

The first routine step was to send an FBI team to assist in the investigations, but the United States had "woefully inadequate intelligence" about the opposition within Saudi Arabia.[19] This assessment was subsequently confirmed by the Defense Department's report on the bombing, issued in September. The reasons for this blind spot were both general and specific. Intelligence gathering in friendly countries cannot exceed the bounds of the host government's tolerance, and the Saudi government was unusually sensitive to U.S. intrusion. Apparently, the United States relied primarily on the royal family for information, and only after the bombing was a special CIA task force organized to analyze security in Saudi Arabia. There were also reports of uneven cooperation between the FBI and the Saudi Ministry of the Interior in the investigation into the bombings. Saudi authorities were said to be deeply concerned about secrecy and the possibility of leaks on the U.S. side.

Nevertheless, in mid-October the Clinton administration was said to be actively considering a more aggressive response, including preemptive strikes and covert operations.[20] An internal policy debate was sparked not only by the bombing but also by Republican criticism during the presidential election campaign, especially charges of being "soft on terrorism" from Republican candidate Robert Dole and House Speaker Newt Gingrich. In September CIA director John Deutch had reluctantly gone public to defend the CIA against criticism, announcing in a speech that the CIA was drawing up a list of military options as well as improving its intelligence capabilities.[21]

Decision makers disagreed, however, over whether to target states or nonstates, a recurrent theme in counterterrorism policy debates. They also argued over the potential effectiveness of military action and the risks it comported. They had to acknowledge, however, that the primary alternative to force—economic and diplomatic sanctions against Iran, including a comprehensive trade embargo imposed by Congress in 1995—had not curbed Iranian support for terrorism. Shortly before the Khobar Towers bombing, Secretary of State Warren Christopher had publicly condemned Iran for its leadership in encouraging and financing terrorism designed to disrupt the Middle East peace process, specifically suicide bombings by Palestinian

Islamic Jihad and Hamas in Israel.[22] He made no mention of a possible direct Iranian threat to the United States and recommended only increased economic pressure in order to deny Iran the resources to finance its support for terrorism. The question of responsibility was also disputed. Among the NSC staff, Richard Clarke apparently argued that Iran was guilty, but Anthony Lake believed that the case was circumstantial.[23] Similarly, Syria was known to allow Iranian agents to use Syrian territory to recruit Islamic militants for training in Iran. However, the U.S. need for Syrian support in the Middle East peace process limited its options.

By November Saudi authorities had arrested forty suspects in the bombing. Press reports claimed that the Saudi government was convinced that Iran had sponsored the attack.[24] The perpetrators were said to be members of a wing of Hizbullah, a Lebanese Islamic organization trained and equipped by Iran and known for the 1983 U.S. Marines barracks bombing. Other evidence was said to indicate a direct Iranian connection, possibly with Syrian assistance. However, U.S. officials appeared unconvinced; in public they were cautious and noncommittal. When Secretary of Defense William Perry suggested openly that Iran might be behind the bombing, other officials immediately replied that he lacked evidence. Some officials suggested privately that Saudi Arabia might find it convenient to blame foreign or Shiite sources rather than domestic Sunni extremists. Saudi Arabia still appeared reluctant to provide conclusive evidence to the United States, perhaps out of fear that the United States would respond precipitately. A show of force or limited punitive strike against Iran would put Saudi Arabia at risk, not the United States. FBI officials were said to be frustrated and dissatisfied over the progress of the "joint" investigation; they had not been allowed to see the specific evidence linking Iran to the attack. Even so, to allay Saudi fears of leaks, information about the investigation was tightly restricted within the U.S. official community.

After the elections in the United States, Saudi authorities gave FBI director Louis Freeh more detailed information linking Iran to the bombing.[25] The Saudi government remained divided, however, over what response to recommend. Some officials favored a strong policy that might include punitive military strikes or an international trade embargo, such as the one approved by the Security Council against Libya in order to compel the surrender of the agents accused of the Pan Am 103 bombing. Others urged restraint and moderation.

Although the timing was not opportune—some U.S. officials remained skeptical about Saudi claims, the administration was in a postelection transition period, and the FBI had not had time to evaluate the Saudi evidence—the discussion of policy options resumed in December.[26] Because the Saudi information was highly sensitive, only top officials were briefed fully, including National Security Adviser Anthony Lake, CIA director John Deutch, and Secretary of Defense William Perry. Alternatives included selective military strikes to shut down Iran's oil export terminal at Kharg Island or to destroy Iran's navy. The United States could also blockade Iranian ports or impose a selective embargo on shipping. Attacks on Hizbullah training camps in Lebanon would be a less confrontational and more proportional military option, but they would not directly damage Iran's interests. The fact that these discussions were leaked to the press could be interpreted as a veiled threat, and Iran apparently expected a strike at this time since its forces were placed on alert. It is not clear, however, whether the threats were meaningful to Iran.

By January 1998 the administration still hesitated, feeling that the evidence linking Iran to the bombing was not definitive enough to justify admittedly risky military action or even to expose Iran in order to mobilize support for sanctions.[27] Saudi Arabia still would not allow FBI access to the imprisoned suspects (all Saudi citizens) or provide comprehensive evidence. The previous December FBI director Freeh had told the families of victims that no indictments or charges were imminent. Nevertheless, by late 1998 or early 1999 U.S. officials had apparently acquired convincing evidence that Iran was behind the attack, even if it was insufficient for prosecution.[28]

Instead of publicizing the information, the administration decided to use it secretly in order to try to induce Iran to abandon terrorism. In May 1997 Mohammed Khatemi's election as president of Iran had led to rapprochement with Saudi Arabia, concluding in an agreement not to support further acts of terrorism. As its critics had urged, the administration decided to pursue an accommodationist strategy in the interest of shifting the regime toward a more moderate stance. In fact, administration officials appeared uncomfortable when reminded of the earlier threats of retaliation. Rather than threatening confrontation, in August 1999 Clinton sent a secret letter to Khatemi.[29] The letter, which had been drafted months earlier but not sent, apparently asked for Iranian cooperation in solving the problem of the bombing, which was cited as the most important barrier to a policy of engagement. Congressional opposition, including charges that the administration was deliberately ignoring Iran's role in Khobar Towers, prevented the administration from changing policy without progress on the issue. But the administration had already begun to reduce unilateral sanctions against Iran and to issue public statements that communicated understanding of Iran's resentment of the United States. Iran, however, remained obstinate. At this point the United States again began to refer publicly to possible Iranian involvement, suggesting that Iranian officials were implicated but that it was unclear whether the government itself had directed the attack. Moderates dominated Iranian parliamentary elections in February 2000, further complicating the problem of combining coercion and diplomacy.

There were no further direct Iranian attacks on U.S. interests, but Iran remained on the State Department's list of state sponsors of terrorism.[30] In January 2002 President Bush singled out Iran as part of the "axis of evil." The government was also suspected of aiding Palestinian groups conducting bombings in Israel and of assisting al Qaeda militants fleeing Afghanistan.

Military Strikes against Sudan and Afghanistan, 1998

Cruise missile attacks on targets in Sudan and Afghanistan in response to the bombings of the U.S. embassies in Kenya and Tanzania were the most obvious use of military force against terrorism before September 11. However, the 1998 bombings must be interpreted in the context of increasing reliance on covert operations to apprehend or kill Bin Laden and disrupt al Qaeda operations, beginning before 1998 and extending to September 2001.

Bin Laden was first identified as a serious threat during investigations into the 1993 World Trade Center bombing.[31] In 1991, after

Saudi Arabia expelled him, he moved to Sudan. In 1994, at U.S. insti-
gation, Saudi authorities stripped him of his citizenship and much of
his property and assets. By May 1996 the United States and Saudi
Arabia had convinced Sudan to expel him. Apparently, the United
States urged Saudi Arabia and Egypt to accept him but they refused,
and the president did not want to spend his political capital on the
issue. Sudan was reportedly willing to turn him over to the United
States, but the Justice Department lacked the evidence to mount a
trial. In order to build regional support for efforts to induce Sudan to
expel him, the United States circulated a dossier accusing Bin Laden
of training the Somalis who attacked U.S. forces in 1993, a role he was
pleased to acknowledge.[32]

Thus Bin Laden took refuge in Afghanistan on the eve of the Taliban's takeover. As the State Department's 1997 report on terrorism
noted, from August 1996 on, Bin Laden became "very vocal in
expressing his approval of and intent to use terrorism."[33] In March
1997, in an interview with CNN, for example, he declared a jihad
against the United States, ostensibly as a response to U.S. support for
Israel, its military presence in Saudi Arabia, and its "aggressive intervention against Muslims in the whole world."[34] This campaign culminated in 1998 with the establishment of an "International Front for
Islamic Holy War against the Jews and Crusaders," which effectively
merged the Egyptian Islamic Jihad and al Qaeda.[35] The front issued
an appeal for attacks on U.S. civil and military targets around the
world in order to force a U.S. withdrawal from Saudi Arabia and an
end to the Israeli occupation of Jerusalem. Although Bin Laden had
no clerical authority, the appeal was presented as a *fatwa*, or religious
edict, which all Muslims were called on to obey.[36]

In 1996 the United States had already launched a grand jury investigation into Bin Laden's activities, and the CIA had begun to "disrupt"
his network, often with the assistance of foreign governments. By June
1997 the National Security Agency was monitoring telephone conversations in Nairobi. A sealed indictment in June 1998 provided a basis
for the arrests of twenty-one al Qaeda militants during the summer. It
charged Bin Laden and his associates with attacks on U.S. and UN
troops in Somalia and accused him of leading a terrorist conspiracy in

concert with Sudan, Iraq, and Iran. Press reports later indicated the United States was simultaneously plotting a raid into Afghanistan to arrest Bin Laden, as a result of a 1998 finding by President Clinton authorizing specific covert operations that included blocking Bin Laden's financial assets and exercising close surveillance. A worldwide alert issued by the Department of State in March 1998 drew attention to threats against U.S. military and civilians following the February 23 *fatwa*.

Although Sudan had expelled Bin Laden, it continued to support terrorism, in the U.S. view. In 1993 the country had been added to the State Department's list of state sponsors because it provided a base of operations for several terrorist groups, including Hizbullah. In 1995 U.S. intelligence agencies found that Bin Laden and Sudan were cooperating to produce chemical weapons to use against the United States in Saudi Arabia.[37] However, owing to the risk of terrorism (reportedly including an assassination attempt against Anthony Lake), the CIA's Khartoum station was shut down in 1995, and the embassy staff was removed for security reasons in 1996. The UN Security Council imposed sanctions when Sudan refused to turn over three Egyptian dissidents linked to an assassination attempt against Egyptian president Hosni Mubarak. In the summer of 1997 U.S. suspicions that Sudan might be developing chemical weapons deepened. In November the United States imposed a wide range of economic sanctions.[38] The 1997 State Department annual report accused Sudan of harboring terrorist organizations and assisting Iran in its support of radical Islamic groups. At approximately the same time, the United States began investigating the Al Shifa pharmaceuticals plant, and in July and August 1998 the CIA issued intelligence reports detailing links between the plant and Bin Laden. In fact, an August 4 report referred to new intelligence indicating that Bin Laden had already acquired chemical weapons and might be ready to attack.

There were, however, divisions of opinion within the administration, as there would be throughout Clinton's term. Supporters of a less confrontational approach pointed to positive aspects of Sudan's behavior: assistance in apprehending the world-famous terrorist "Carlos" in 1994; reinstitution of visa requirements for Muslim visitors in 1995;

expulsion of Bin Laden in 1996; and offers in February 1997 and June 1998 to assist in combating terrorism. Unimpressed, Assistant Secretary of State for African Affairs Susan Rice dismissed these offers as a "charm offensive."[39]

Before the embassy bombings, Afghanistan was not a primary area of U.S. interest. The United States did not recognize the Taliban government. Afghanistan had ceased to be of strategic importance after the Soviet withdrawal in 1989, and the country was isolated during the period of anarchy that followed the collapse of the government in 1992. When the Taliban seized power in 1996, the United States was not alarmed.[40] Its extremist creed was perceived as "antimodern" rather than "anti-Western," and its opposition to Iran was welcome. Pakistan and Saudi Arabia, both U.S. allies, were the regime's main outside contacts.

The August bombings of the embassies in Kenya and Tanzania surprised U.S. authorities. Added to the difficulties of obtaining credible and specific intelligence warnings, bureaucratic coordination was a problem, both between agencies and between Washington and the field. According to the reports of the Accountability Review Boards, in Dar es Salaam, a "low-threat" post, no information or intelligence warned of a possible attack. In Kenya, a "medium-threat" post, no intelligence reports were received immediately before the bombing, but earlier reports referred explicitly to threats of vehicle-bombs and assassinations. These reports, however, were discounted because the sources were discredited or the information was imprecise. It was also believed that actions taken by the CIA and the FBI to confront Bin Laden in Nairobi, including telephone intercepts, raids, and arrests, had effectively eliminated the threat by the latter part of 1997, although in May 1998 surveillance resumed. However, the FBI and the CIA may not have shared what they knew with the State Department.[41] For its part, the State Department found the threat of crime more immediate and specific, a critical "daily reality." The ambassador to Kenya was more sensitive to the threat of terrorism, but her requests for the construction of a less vulnerable building were not met.

On August 20, thirteen days after the embassy bombings, the United States launched six or seven Tomahawk cruise missiles against the Al

Shifa pharmaceuticals plant in Khartoum. Probably sixty to seventy missiles, launched from navy ships in the Red Sea and the Persian Gulf, struck a complex of base, support, and training camps used by Bin Laden in Afghanistan, near the Pakistani border. The Defense Department released few details, but later accounts disclosed that Pakistan was not informed of the operation in advance and that two of the targeted camps were run by Pakistani intelligence services.[42]

Secrecy, controversy, and a growing sense of urgency had characterized the decision-making process.[43] President Clinton, Secretary of Defense William Cohen, Secretary of State Madeleine Albright, Under Secretary of State Thomas Pickering, CIA director George Tenet, National Security Adviser Samuel Berger, and Chairman of the Joint Chiefs of Staff General Henry Hugh Shelton were the key participants. On the NSC staff, Richard Clarke, now the national coordinator for counterterrorism, played a "pivotal role in planning the operation on behalf of the President," according to press reports.[44] An NSC staff member was quoted as saying, "For the first time, the White House is treating terrorism as a national-security problem, and not as a law-enforcement problem. America has joined the battle."[45]

On August 8, the day after the embassy bombings, presidential advisers asked the Pentagon Joint Staff and the CIA, including the Counterterrorist Center, to draw up a list of possible targets. Approximately twenty sites were selected in Sudan, Afghanistan, and an unidentified third nation. Four days later, the list was narrowed according to the evidence linking each target to terrorism and the risks involved, including the danger of hitting civilians. On August 13, however, the CIA received information that Bin Laden and his key associates planned to meet in Afghanistan on August 20, and this date was selected for the attack.[46] The intelligence report also indicated that he might be planning further attacks, possibly using chemical weapons. This development imparted a new sense of urgency to the deliberations.

On August 19, with one day left to select the targets, a meeting was held at the White House to decide on final recommendations for the president. The code name of the operation, Infinite Reach, was not coincidental; the administration was apparently determined to demonstrate that it could strike two targets simultaneously, to match the adversary. The choices were the camps in Afghanistan and two targets in Sudan: the Al Shifa pharmaceuticals plant and a tannery linked to Bin Laden. The attacks were to take place at night, in order to avoid civilian casualties.

The decision to target training camps in Afghanistan was not questioned, but the choice of the Al Shifa plant was contentious. The secrecy surrounding the decision and the haste with which it was made may have precluded a broader examination of the evidence linking Al Shifa to chemical weapons production, and some analysts in the CIA and the State Department remained unconvinced. The FBI and the Defense Intelligence Agency were apparently excluded from the decision, although the FBI was responsible for constructing the legal case to prosecute Bin Laden. Tenet apparently warned that the link between Bin Laden and the factory was indirect and inferential. Berger, however, later countered that the choice of target was not questioned and that the only objections concerned the wisdom of striking Sudan after Bin Laden had left. He concluded the meeting by warning of the consequences if the United States failed to act and Bin Laden then launched a chemical attack.[47]

Apparently, General Shelton also criticized the targeting plan. He felt that the tannery should be taken off the list because it was not involved in chemical weapons production and the attack might cause civilian casualties. He then explained the plans for a military strike to other officers among the Joint Chiefs, who shared his doubts. Later that day Berger informed the president of their objections, and the tannery was dropped from the list.

On the afternoon of August 19 Richard Clarke summoned other administration officials responsible for counterterrorism to his office at the NSC and told them to remain through the evening in order to prepare a public response to follow the bombing. These advisers had not been consulted about the targets and reacted with skepticism when told of the decision, according to reports that Clarke later denied. Similarly, as word of the prospective military strike leaked out, CIA and State Department analysts expressed doubts about the choice of targets. Pickering and Albright were shown a report by the

State Department's Bureau of Intelligence and Research questioning the Al Shifa evidence, but they held firm.

The strike against Sudan provoked extensive debate and criticism, primarily in the domestic press and among the U.S. political elite. Top U.S. officials, especially Secretary Albright, vigorously defended the action in terms of a mix of objectives—self-defense, preemption, disruption, and deterrence. Albright appeared on all four major television networks to make the case. The U.S. refusal to provide the intelligence information on which the choice of targets was based, on grounds of the need for secrecy, exacerbated the controversy. Almost immediately critics charged that the U.S. government was wrong on several counts in its public explanations that the Al Shifa plant was set up to manufacture chemical weapons.[48] The Clinton administration then revealed some of its information, insisting that soil samples the CIA had taken from the plant grounds had traces of Empta, a precursor chemical for the production of VX nerve gas.[49]

After the August strikes, the United States kept up the pressure on Bin Laden and al Qaeda. A "Small Group" of the Cabinet met almost weekly, and a Counterterrorism Security Group led by Richard Clarke met two or three times a week. In early September 1998, for example, six bombers were sent to Guam on a training mission characterized as a show of force aimed at Bin Laden, and the secretary of defense was quoted more than once as not ruling out the possibility of further military strikes.[50] Apparently, the major constraint was time. Using air bases in the Middle East was considered too politically sensitive, but U.S. decision makers insisted on precise weapons. These restrictions meant that cruise missiles had to be launched from ships and required a minimum of six hours' notice. Moreover, U.S. policy was apparently not to strike just any al Qaeda asset but to pinpoint Bin Laden and top al Qaeda leaders, who were moving targets.[51] Clinton had reportedly authorized the CIA or its local recruits to use lethal military force against Bin Laden and his top associates, to the extent of shooting down civilian aircraft should he attempt to leave Afghanistan. In December 1998 CIA director Tenet had issued a written "declaration of war" against Bin Laden, but this move did not lead to budget shifts or reassignment of personnel, nor was his intent known widely through the intelligence community.[52]

The Joint Chiefs opposed using Special Forces in a limited military operation, rejecting such proposals from Clinton's advisers as too risky and "naive." Moreover, a raid by Delta Force, for example, would have taken twelve to fourteen hours' advance notice. On the other hand, the White House did not sense that there was sufficient popular support for a major combat commitment, which is what the military recommended. Clinton was also said to fear an embarrassing mistake.[53]

U.S. policy also stressed law enforcement and sanctions. On August 20 President Clinton had added al Qaeda to the government's official list of terrorist organizations, which blocked their U.S. assets and prohibited all financial transactions. A $5 million reward was offered for Bin Laden's arrest. With the cooperation of the Kenyan and Tanzanian governments, as well as other allies, the U.S. criminal investigation produced a series of indictments. Within a week after the military strikes, the FBI had brought two suspects back to the United States for trial, and arrests continued at a regular pace. In November and December additional indictments were returned, including charges against Bin Laden.

Another critical part of U.S. policy was pressing Afghanistan to extradite Bin Laden. In October 1999, at U.S. urging, the UN Security Council imposed a deadline of thirty days for the turnover of Bin Laden to a country where he would be tried. The council threatened sanctions to freeze the country's economic assets abroad and curtail international flights by the national airline (the United States had already imposed a unilateral embargo). The Taliban's desire to assume the UN seat still held by representatives of the former regime suggested that a bargain might be possible. However, Taliban leaders replied that they had already restricted Bin Laden's movements and communications but that they could not turn him over. Accordingly, in November sanctions were imposed despite the Taliban's request for a delay. The Taliban's foreign minister, Wakil Ahmad Muttawakil, responded, "We will never hand over Osama bin Laden, and we will not force him out. He will remain free in defiance of America. . . . We will not hand him to an infidel nation."[54]

Still U.S. officials continued to meet with representatives of the Taliban, reiterating the message that the United States was always prepared to talk but that Bin Laden had to be surrendered.[55] The administration declined the Taliban's offer to convene a panel of Islamic scholars to decide the issue. According to later press reports, U.S. threats then were as "stark" as those issued after September 11 by the Bush administration.[56] If so, they were not implemented.

The United States also worked to persuade Saudi Arabia, Pakistan, and the United Arab Emirates, the only governments with diplomatic relations with Afghanistan, to secure compliance. The State Department coordinator for counterterrorism, Michael Sheehan, was said to have written a secret memorandum calling for more vigorous efforts to cut off financing, sanctuary, and other support from friendly states, Pakistan in particular.[57] Sheehan's memo was said to urge the administration to make terrorism the central issue in U.S. policy toward Pakistan, but it had only slight effect.

Pakistan had been an important conduit for aid to the rebels during the war against the Soviet Union, and a number of Islamic groups operating in Pakistan had well-known ties to the Taliban. The Pakistani Interservices Intelligence Division (ISI) was connected not only to the Taliban, and thus indirectly to al Qaeda, but to the Harakat ul-Mujadeen, a Kashmiri organization added to the State Department's list of foreign terrorist groups in 1997. The 1998 cruise missile attack on the ISI-run training camps for Kashmiri militants had been a warning signal. Adding to these complications, General Pervez Musharraf seized power in a military coup in October 1999. The United States was thus restrained by Pakistan's status as an ally and by the worry that isolating the regime would interfere with other U.S. policy goals such as restoring democracy and controlling nuclear proliferation.[58] And Pakistan had been helpful in past instances, such as by arresting Ramzi Youcef in 1995.

Sudan also continued to be an irritant. The 1998 military strike had gained the regime some sympathy in the Arab world. Moreover, U.S. allies, such as Canada, began to show increased interest in investing in the country's oil industry, and Great Britain returned its ambassador. Within the Clinton administration an intense dispute over policy toward

Sudan broke into the headlines in late November 1999. Hard-liners argued for a tougher policy of isolation and pressure. Officials in the Africa bureaus of the State Department and the NSC backed legislation to permit the United States to give food assistance directly to Christian rebels in southern Sudan, who had been fighting the northern-dominated Islamic government since the early 1980s. (Previous legislation had prohibited such assistance.) Other officials, including the State Department's Bureau of Refugee Affairs and two former ambassadors, opposed intervention in the civil war as well as the use of food as a weapon of war. The U.S. embassy remained closed; Under Secretary of State Pickering sought to reopen it, but the Africa bureau countered his efforts. The State Department did appoint a special envoy to Sudan, but the United States still seemed determined to isolate the regime even though the FBI reported that any former terrorist camps in Sudan had been vacated.[59]

In early December 1999 the United States received intelligence information that Bin Laden planned a series of attacks on U.S. citizens around the world to coincide with the New Year.[60] Jordanian authorities had broken up a plot to attack tourist sites in Jordan and Israel. At the White House, George Tenet and Richard Clarke worked for a month to produce a "Millennium Threats Plan" to disrupt terrorist planning through arrests of members of Bin Laden's network by allies around the world. After considerable argument, the White House also decided to issue a public alert on December 11.

Three days later, customs agents arrested an Algerian, Ahmed Rassam, crossing the Canadian border into Seattle. Some 130 pounds of explosives as well as detonators were in his car, and he was found to have trained in camps operated by Bin Laden in Afghanistan.[61] This surprise prompted the United States to issue a direct threat. Michael Sheehan telephoned the Taliban's foreign minister to warn him that the United States would not tolerate a refusal to turn over Bin Laden while disavowing responsibility for his actions. Apparently, Sheehan hinted that the United States would use military force against Afghanistan should terrorist attacks occur. This message was reinforced in the State Department's 1999 annual report on terrorism, which declared that "[t]he United States repeatedly made clear to the Taliban that they will be held responsible for any terrorist acts undertaken by Bin Laden while he is in their territory."[62] Yet there were no specific public threats or an ultimatum.

In anticipation of the year's end, efforts to help European allies arrest suspected terrorists abroad were stepped up. After a further warning on December 21, which increased airport security and placed U.S. military bases on high alert, the president reassured the public that the holiday season would not be disturbed. On December 30 the FBI began questioning Arab Americans who appeared suspicious, and operational response teams were placed on the ready in Europe and the United States. Clarke's Counterterrorism Subgroup kept watch in a top-secret communications vault through New Year's Eve and concluded with relief that on this occasion the battle had been won. It seemed that the huge increase in the counterterrorism budget—over 90 percent since 1995—had been worth it. However, Clarke was quoted as saying, "It's not enough to be in a cat-and-mouse game, warning about his plots. . . . We need to seriously think about doing more. Our goal should be to so erode his network of organizations that they no longer pose a serious threat."[63]

In fact, by March 2000 U.S. officials were optimistic.[64] International cooperation had produced arrests in Britain, Germany, Canada, the United States, Jordan, and Pakistan. Experts agreed that Bin Laden had been significantly weakened, although his reputation among Islamic militants remained high. The United States also continued covert operations in Afghanistan. The Predator drone had recently been deployed, and the administration was pursuing the idea of equipping it with a Hellfire missile.

However, efforts to persuade Pakistan to change its policies proved unproductive. In a brief visit in March, Clinton asked Musharraf to halt incursions across the Line of Control in Kashmir and to crack down on militant groups operating in Pakistan, as well as to help pressure the Taliban to turn over Bin Laden. Musharraf was apparently reassuring on the last point but made no concrete promises. He denied that Pakistan was supporting violence against India in Kashmir. The United States had to be content with having made its position clear.[65]

As general policy, the State Department stressed "political and diplomatic efforts that reduce the space in which terrorists operate," criminal punishment for the perpetrators of terrorist acts, "depoliticizing the message of terrorism," and international cooperation. The instruments of counterterrorism policy were listed as U.S. leadership, zero tolerance for terrorism, and "draining the swamp" to deny terrorists safe refuge.[66] The 1999 annual report, an unusually detailed statement of policy, called for efforts to drain the "swamps" where governments were too sympathetic or weak to control terrorists. The aim of U.S. policy was to "compel" these states to end their support for terrorism through the use of political and economic pressures and "other means as necessary."[67] The report explained that the United States sought to remove states from the terrorism business entirely by persuading them to rejoin the community of nations committed to ending the threat. A "zero-tolerance" policy would delineate the steps state sponsors must take to be removed from the official list. Other policy differences would not be allowed to stand in the way. The report mentioned positive signs shown in North Korea and Syria, although no similarly veiled overtures were extended to Iran, Sudan, or Afghanistan. In fact, both Afghanistan and Pakistan were criticized, as well as Iran, although neither state was added to the list of state sponsors.[68] The report did recognize that Afghanistan was not otherwise hostile to U.S. interests, which could be interpreted as a positive signal.[69]

The policy of offering cautious inducements to state sponsors was further accentuated in June, when Secretary of State Albright explained that the Clinton administration had officially replaced the label "rogue states" with the more innocuous term "states of concern."[70] The change reflected a belief that more "gentle" terms and a more "nuanced" American vocabulary would advance internal reforms more effectively. Specific mention was made of North Korea, Iran, and Libya. In October the secretary of state paid an official visit to North Korea.

The United States also opened a counterterrorist "dialogue" with Sudan, although unilateral sanctions remained in force. By the summer of 2000 Sudan was eager to see UN sanctions lifted (even though they had not been strictly enforced) and, more ambitiously, lobbied for a regional seat on the Security Council.[71] The Sudanese argued that their behavior had changed and reminded Washington that the previous December Sudan's president had dismissed his radical Islamic mentor. Sudan had also improved its relationships with Ethiopia and Egypt.

U.S. policy toward nonstates also appeared to shift slightly by the spring of 2000. The 1999 State Department report announced that the goal of U.S. policy was to "eliminate the use of terrorism as a policy instrument," not destroy the organization in question. Should nonstates cease using terrorism, they would be removed from the State Department's list of terrorist organizations. Otherwise, they were reminded of the severe sanctions mandated by legislation enacted in 1996: members and representatives of "FTOs" (foreign terrorist organizations) are ineligible for U.S. visas and subject to exclusion from the country, their funds are blocked, and no U.S. citizen or person within U.S. jurisdiction can provide any material support or resources. This message was probably intended for organizations other than al Qaeda, however.

The National Commission on Terrorism took a more hard-line approach, reflecting differences of opinion between Congress and the administration.[72] Its June 2000 report recommended that Afghanistan be added to the list of state sponsors and that Pakistan be considered for classification as a state "not cooperating fully," which requires the imposition of limited sanctions. It also recommended strengthening sanctions and legal penalties across the board as well as expanded FBI and CIA efforts to disrupt and prosecute nonstate actors.

In September the State Department added the Islamic Movement of Uzbekistan (IMU) to the list of foreign terrorist organizations. Administration officials explained that the IMU and other Islamic militants in the former Soviet republics in Central Asia were receiving financial support and training from Bin Laden's network.[73]

On October 12, 2000, in Yemen, a small boat armed with explosives rammed the naval destroyer *Cole* in the Aden harbor. Circumstantial evidence pointed to Bin Laden's involvement, although U.S. officials could not make a definitive case that would justify military retaliation. Yemeni authorities were reluctant to cooperate beyond a modest extent, which slowed and frustrated FBI investigations. In turn, the U.S. ambassador to Yemen, Barbara Bodine, was irritated by the FBI. Yemeni security police did discover, however, that an attack on another U.S. ship had failed the previous January and that planning for the bombing may have started as early as 1997.

In spite of official U.S. caution, a retaliatory missile attack was widely expected. Within the ranks of the NSC, Richard Clarke was said to have favored bombing al Qaeda training camps in Afghanistan.[74] In December Yemeni president Ali Abdullah Saleh warned against a repetition of the 1998 attack against Afghanistan. It would be a mistake, he said, for a great power to use disproportionate force against a weaker enemy. Instead, if the case against Bin Laden could be proved, the United States should apprehend and prosecute him.[75]

In fact, in public the secretary of state and the president stressed accountability and did not threaten force. The president, at the end of his term, was absorbed with negotiating a peaceful settlement to the Israeli-Palestinian conflict. A retaliatory strike would have undermined that process. Thus, in addition to ongoing covert operations, the United States urged stiffer sanctions against Afghanistan, including an arms embargo, to force the Taliban to hand over Bin Laden and close all training camps for Islamic militants.[76] Russia supported the U.S. resolution submitted to the UN Security Council, but Pakistan rejected new sanctions, substantially reducing their potential effectiveness.

Terrorism was not an issue in the 2000 presidential campaign. The Bush administration entered office without a great sense of urgency.[77] In January Richard Clarke briefed Condoleezza Rice on the terrorist threat.[78] He apparently described a strategy paper that the Clinton NSC had declined to take up in December. In it he had recommended a number of actions to break up or "roll back" al Qaeda, including the introduction of Special Forces into Afghanistan, air strikes on the training camps, and increased support for the Northern Alliance. However, the proposals were not considered until April, and the policy review process did not conclude until September 4.

Beginning in late March, and continuing into the summer, intelligence agencies noted an unprecedented increase in threat reporting.

However, tactical warning, or "actionable detail," was lacking.[79] The Fourth of July, for example, was considered a likely target date, and the State Department issued a worldwide caution on June 22. On June 26 the State Department presented a demarche to Taliban representatives in Pakistan. The Defense Department issued four threat warnings in June and July. There were indications of a planned attack on the president at the Genoa summit meeting in mid-July. The CIA briefed the president on August 6, apparently at his request.

COERCIVE DIPLOMACY AND THE WAR ON TERRORISM

After the September 11 attacks, coercive diplomacy was no longer an option for responding directly to the threat from al Qaeda, if it had ever been. The "war on terrorism" assumed a strategy of destruction leading to defeat. However, the Bush administration did attempt, unsuccessfully, to coerce the Taliban into giving up Bin Laden. Pakistan was also forced to reverse its policy of support for the Taliban, although it is hard to know what mixture of threat and reward the United States employed in this case.

The Bush administration decided immediately that both the Taliban and Pakistan, as well as the rest of the world, should be told "you're for us or against us."[80] In the days following the attacks, the president and the secretary of state both telephoned General Musharraf to demand Pakistani assistance. In his conversation on September 13, Powell was said to have been set to throw a "brushback pitch." The ambassador to Pakistan then visited Musharraf to specify the details. On September 19 Musharraf delivered a televised speech to the nation in which he dramatically announced his support for the United States. He contended that Pakistan's survival was at stake and alluded to the danger that India, having quickly proposed allowing the United States to use its air and naval bases, would exploit Pakistan's isolation and even have it declared a state sponsor of terrorism.[81] He was rewarded with the lifting of sanctions, massive debt relief, and substantial economic assistance. Pakistan became the third-largest beneficiary of U.S. aid, after Israel and Egypt. The alternative was bleak. Pakistan would become a pariah state relegated to crushing poverty and internal instability. It would be vulnerable to Indian pressure. The U.S. war on terrorism could extend to military strikes against local militant groups operating in Afghanistan and Kashmir from Pakistani territory or to the seizure of Pakistan's nuclear facilities should they appear likely to fall into the hands of Islamic extremists.

Thus the U.S. government first communicated its demand to the Taliban to turn Bin Laden over for trial via a Pakistani military delegation led by General Mahmood Ahmed, the head of the ISI, within days after September 11.[82] The demand was accompanied by threats of military action, and heavy bombers and other military forces were moved to bases within striking range of Afghanistan.

The Taliban's response was equivocal. It rejected the demand, but Mullah Omar asked the United States for patience and for more information linking Bin Laden to the attacks. Apparently, Mullah Omar suggested that were he to surrender Bin Laden, he would need the endorsement of the Organization of the Islamic Conference, an organization of fifty Muslim nations dominated by Saudi Arabia.[83]

More contradictory signals followed. On September 20 a clerical grand council, or *shura*, issued a *fatwa* declaring that Bin Laden should be persuaded to leave the country immediately. The *shura* asked Mullah Omar to implement the decision. The United States, however, rejected the move as inadequate. Statements from officials at the Afghan embassy in Islamabad were contradictory; some said that there would be no surrender, while others said that Bin Laden might surrender voluntarily.

During this time Bush decided to issue a public ultimatum, to be communicated in his speech to Congress on the evening of September 20. The idea apparently came from Prime Minister Tony Blair. The speech demanded that the Taliban deliver to the United States all al Qaeda leaders, release all foreign nationals, close all terrorist training camps, and hand over all terrorists to "appropriate authorities." The president concluded: "These demands are not open to negotiation or discussion. The Taliban must act, and act immediately. They will hand over the terrorists, or they will share in their fate."[84] No deadline was imposed nor was a reward offered, at least not in public. Within hours, a Taliban emissary announced defiantly that its "final decision" was to reject the ultimatum: "So the only master of the world wants to threaten us. But make no mistake: Afghanistan . . . is a swamp. People enter here laughing, are exiting injured."[85] The Taliban official implied that Mullah Omar had overruled the *shura's* decree that Bin Laden be asked to leave Afghanistan. It was not certain, however, that Taliban officials had the power to hand over Bin Laden should they wish to.

As the United States kept up a steady pace of military preparations, Mullah Omar issued his own demand and counterthreat that the United States withdraw its military forces from the Persian Gulf and end its "partisanship" in Palestine or risk involvement in a "vain and bloody war."[86] Yet Taliban officials at the embassy in Pakistan read a statement from the Foreign Affairs Ministry asking "the American people to urge their authorities to save the people of Afghanistan and America from the impacts and consequences and untoward problems of a war." The Taliban faced a growing refugee crisis—more than a million people were said to have fled the cities in anticipation of war—as well as diplomatic isolation. The United Arab Emirates and Saudi Arabia severed diplomatic ties and Pakistan withdrew its diplomats.

Possibly hoping to exploit divisions within the Taliban ranks, the United States asked the Pakistani ISI officials who had remained in Afghanistan after their first unsuccessful mission to go back to the Taliban and repeat the U.S. demand. This request apparently preceded a public Pakistani warning that it did not want to see a new government in Afghanistan, particularly one constructed as a result of U.S. support for the Northern Alliance.[87] The Pakistani overture appeared to bear fruit when the Taliban issued another statement announcing that Bin Laden had been asked to leave. Interpreting this development as a hopeful sign, or at least as a reprieve, and desperate to avoid war, Musharraf again sent General Mahmood Ahmed, the head of the ISI. This time he was accompanied by a group of militant Islamic clerics who had taught many of the Taliban, including Mullah Omar, at madrassahs in Pakistan. The mission went to Kandahar to meet with Mullah Omar himself.[88] Pakistani authorities hoped that the group of clerics could serve as a substitute for the Islamic Conference that Mullah Omar had initially called for and that they could persuade him that resistance only harmed the cause of Islam. Information about political conditions in Afghanistan had become scarce since Western reporters had been expelled, but there were indications that the Taliban's authority was eroding.

However, within almost a day the Pakistani mission was rebuffed.[89] One of the Pakistani clerics reported that Mullah Omar was not afraid of war. Some of the military officers in the delegation suggested that the Taliban's leaders had no grasp of U.S. military power or of the outrage that the September 11 attacks had provoked. One Pakistani official reportedly said, "You tell them they may die, and the Taliban with them, and they are unmoved." Furthermore, while the Pakistani clerics had the advantage of being credible intermediaries, they were also fundamentally unsympathetic to the U.S. demands.

This failure as well as contradictory statements from the Afghani ambassador to Pakistan may have convinced the U.S. government to apply more coercion. Bush secretly approved aid for the Northern Alliance as well as psychological operations (e.g., radio broadcasts and air drops of leaflets) as a "nonmilitary" way of pressuring the Taliban. The presence of Special Forces in Afghanistan was reported in the press. Defense Secretary Donald Rumsfeld set out on a tour of the region to build a supporting coalition, including Uzbekistan. It also became evident to the Taliban that the ISI and the CIA were trying to persuade Pashtun warlords in the border areas to defect.[90]

The Taliban's response was to hedge and try to buy time. The ambassador to Pakistan said that although the request to leave had been delivered to Bin Laden, he had not answered. Both Rumsfeld and Musharraf expressed public doubt that the Taliban would give him up.[91] Nevertheless, Pakistan resolved to send a third delegation to Kandahar, this time of clerics only, on October 2. Simultaneously, a blunt public threat came from Tony Blair on October 2. In a speech to the Labour Party annual conference he asserted: "I say to the Taliban: surrender the terrorists, or surrender power."[92] Within the day the Taliban's ambassador to Pakistan appealed to the United States not to initiate military action, saying that while Taliban leaders still required proof of Bin Laden's complicity, they were ready to negotiate with Washington.[93] He suggested that Bin Laden might be turned over to some third country, but he also replied to Tony Blair's threat earlier that day: only Allah, he said, could overthrow the Taliban. At the same time Mullah Omar continued to issue belligerent statements, in particular condemning U.S. moves to build a coalition to support the return of the former king, Zahir Shah. In tacit recognition of Pakistani complaints that they, too, lacked evidence, the U.S. ambassador to Pakistan visited Musharraf to brief him on Bin Laden's role.

In Washington, on October 6 Bush again publicly threatened Taliban leaders that they had been warned and that time was running out.[94] Winter would be closing in by mid-November, which also marked the start of Ramadan. Military mobilization was proceeding rapidly, with a thousand troops from the Tenth Mountain Division deployed in Uzbekistan and allied assistance lined up. It was clear that the United States intended to use force to disable the Taliban's air defenses in order to facilitate ground operations.

The Taliban responded by (1) preparing for military action, especialy by trying to ensure the loyalty of regional commanders, (2) issuing rhetorical threats of a "holy war," and (3) offering to release eight imprisoned Christian aid workers *if* the United States stopped its threats, in effect making them hostages.[95] A spokesman reiterated the well-established Taliban position that it lacked evidence of Bin Laden's guilt, and he denied that there were terrorist training camps in Afghanistan in which the September 11 hijackers could have trained. Press reports now referred to splits within the Taliban ranks, with a more "realist" faction favoring compromise.

On October 7 the U.S. and British military campaign opened with cruise missile and long-range bomber attacks. Bush announced that the actions were designed not only to disrupt terrorism but also to damage the Taliban's military capabilities. Taliban leaders had been warned, he said, and now they would pay a price for resisting U.S. demands.[96] Secretary of Defense Rumsfeld added that the goal was to punish the Taliban and weaken it so severely that it would not be able to withstand an assault from the Northern Alliance or other opposition groups. The targets were military airfields, air defense sites, and command centers, including Mullah Omar's residence in Kandahar.[97] On the second day of bombing, the United States attacked Afghan ground forces north of Kabul who were fighting Northern Alliance units. Rumsfeld announced that a U.S. goal was to help Afghan forces interested in overthrowing and expelling the Taliban. After three days, the United States effectively controlled Afghan air space and began bombing troop facilities and other ground force targets using cluster bombs and other "area munitions." The next stage would involve helicopter gunships and special operations forces.

On October 11, in a White House news conference, Bush offered to reconsider the military offensive if the Taliban surrendered Bin Laden.[98] You have a second chance, he said, to cough up him and his people. Then the United States would reconsider its actions in Afghanistan. He also spoke for the first time of the prospect of nation building in Afghanistan, looking forward to a post-Taliban era.

The Taliban quickly rejected the invitation but said that it would begin discussions *if* the bombing stopped. A top Taliban leader, the second in command to Mullah Omar, responded: "We would be ready to hand him over to a third country. It can be negotiated provided the U.S gives us evidence and the Taliban are assured that the country is neutral and will not be influenced by the United States."[99]

Bush countered by telling reporters emphatically and repeatedly: "When I said no negotiations, I meant no negotiations," "this is non-negotiable," "there's nothing to negotiate about," and "there is no negotiation, period."[100] He refused to discuss the question of providing evidence since "we know he's guilty." He reiterated the demands set out in his September 20 speech to Congress: the Taliban must turn over Bin Laden and the al Qaeda organization; destroy the terrorist camps and give the United States access to them; protect all foreign journalists, diplomats, and aid workers; and release all foreign nationals in custody.

In the meantime Powell left Washington for a visit to Pakistan, India, and China. He arrived in Islamabad on the evening of October 15. There he learned that meetings between the Taliban's foreign minister and Pakistani officials, including the head of the military intelligence directorate, had resulted in a request for a bombing pause while Taliban moderates tried to persuade Mullah Omar to agree to hand over Bin Laden.[101] At least two or three days would be required for officials in Kabul to travel to Kandahar, since the bombing campaign had cut off all communications and made travel by road or helicopter too dangerous. Most observers interpreted the move as a sign of a split in Taliban ranks. Otherwise, the intentions behind the request were not clear: was it a sign of a genuine difference of opinion or an attempt to confuse and buy time? If the plea was sincere, was it likely that Mullah Omar could be convinced to change his mind, or that he could be displaced? Observers commented that the Taliban foreign minister was not a close associate of Mullah Omar. And, as was the case with earlier offers, it was not certain that the Taliban could implement a promise to turn over Bin Laden, given the strength of al Qaeda forces as well as the disruption caused by the bombing campaign.

Probably as both an attempt to encourage defections within Taliban ranks by offering a reward for compromise and a concession to Pakistan's interests, Powell agreed with Musharraf that moderate elements of the Taliban could participate in a new Afghani government.[102] Powell's message was ambiguous, however. He referred to "listening to" the Taliban movement and "taking them into account," since the Taliban could not be "exported," but he also insisted that this "particular regime" had to go. It was also unclear whether Bin Laden had to be surrendered as a condition for "moderate" participation. In the previous twenty-four hours, bombing of Taliban positions near Kabul had escalated, although the United States generally refrained from attacking the Taliban front lines that prevented the Northern Alliance from moving against Kabul or Mazar-i-Sharif. The prospects for bargaining were further diminished when a spokesman for the Northern Alliance refused adamantly to accept any Taliban members in a future coalition government.

The day after the Powell-Musharraf news conference in Islamabad, Mullah Omar sent a radio message encouraging Taliban troops to continue to fight the infidel. He promised that they would triumph as they had over the Soviet Union in the 1980s. He added, "We will succeed whether we live or die. Death will definitely come one day. We are not worried about death. We should die as Muslims. It does not matter whether we die today or tomorrow. The goal is martyrdom."[103] The regime's last remaining ambassador, Mullah Abdul Salam Zaeef, just having returned to Pakistan from a week in Afghanistan, echoed his resolve. He denied that there was a "moderate" Taliban: "All the Taliban are the same, and they follow the views of the leadership. . . . On the issue of Osama, there is no change in that. Osama is a faith issue, and we are not going to change our faith for anyone."[104]

On October 19 the United States launched a helicopter commando raid against Mullah Omar's compound, the first large-scale commando attack since the intervention in Somalia in 1993. Two days later, bombing of Taliban front-line defenses around Kabul began, and Powell indicated that the Northern Alliance would be encouraged to move on Kabul. The United States had lost patience. The military campaign could no longer wait for Taliban compliance or a defection by "moderates."[105] The aim was now decisive military victory and the replacement of the regime.

CONCLUSION

The Record

The record of coercive diplomacy is not encouraging. The outcomes of even the simplest cases of state-sponsored terrorism are not clear-cut.[106] The response to Iraq in 1993 can be considered an example of appropriately implemented coercive diplomacy, but its success or failure is hard to judge. That assessment depends on whether the United States was attempting to halt direct attacks on U.S. targets or force Iraq out of the business of supporting terrorism altogether. If the judgment is based on the first assumption, then compliance can only be inferred from lack of evidence of noncompliance. This is a weak standard, since Iraq never admitted to having organized the plot against President Bush, much less to having complied with U.S. demands not to continue. If the judgment is based on the second assumption, then coercive diplomacy failed.

The case of Iran in 1996 is even more problematic. A conclusion about whether or not coercive diplomacy was employed depends on estimating the seriousness of U.S. threats of military retaliation for the

1996 Khobar Towers bombing. Although the United States decided not to use force, Iran, like Iraq, did not directly attack U.S. targets again. However, like Iraq, Iran also stayed in the terrorism business and refused to cooperate in resolving the dispute over responsibility for the Khobar Towers bombing. The United States was initially constrained from using force by lack of information that linked Iran conclusively to the bombing. When the evidence was finally acquired, internal changes in Iran had made the use of force too costly in terms of its effect on other policy interests, especially reforming Iran. Saudi Arabia's reluctance to share data, in part a consequence of the fear of unilateral U.S. retaliation, contributed to the U.S. dilemma. Thus, paradoxically, a willingness to use force made it less feasible. Furthermore, unlike with the case of Iraq, the administration was divided over how to respond to Iran.

Dealing with the more lethal and ambiguous threat of al Qaeda was even more complicated. This conflict was a zero-sum game. One cannot conclude either that the United States employed coercive diplomacy or that coercive diplomacy would have been an appropriate response to such an adversary, however expertly applied. From the beginning, the U.S. strategy was not to induce Bin Laden and al Qaeda to stop terrorism but to disrupt and destroy so as to make continued terrorism impossible. It was not the group's collective intentions but its capabilities that mattered.[107] The cruise missile attacks in 1998 were not so much exemplary uses of coercive force as symbolic statements of political commitment to combating terrorism. They inflicted little pain on al Qaeda. Covert operations in Afghanistan were meant to arrest or kill Bin Laden.[108] After 1998 Bin Laden's indictment by a U.S. court could not be ignored in the interest of striking a bargain. Coercive diplomacy and a strategy of law enforcement, or "bringing to justice," may not be complementary.

Furthermore, even if coercive diplomacy had been the intent, and al Qaeda not been impervious to coercion, its use would not necessarily have prevented specific attacks, notably those of September 11. Although the United States received streams of warnings, none were specific or timely enough to issue a threat or use demonstrative force to compel al Qaeda to desist. This limitation on coercive diplomacy was exacerbated by the organizational structure of al

Qaeda. Cells such as the one organized by Mohammed Atta operated with considerable autonomy. Changing the calculations of the top leadership at the last minute would probably not have defeated a plot already in the last planning stages.

Coercive diplomacy was more relevant when it came to altering the behavior of the states that directly or indirectly assisted al Qaeda, but significant constraints existed. First, consider Sudan. The 1998 attack on the Al Shifa pharmaceuticals plant might be interpreted as a demonstration of force, but it was modest. Perhaps the strike communicated to Sudan that any further assistance to Bin Laden would be similarly punished, but the likelihood of escalation was low. Sudan's behavior improved, but probably not as the result of threats of military force. The United States also resisted opportunities to offer rewards. Perhaps Sudan's behavior was not threatening enough. Sudan, after all, had expelled Bin Laden. It took measures to reduce its ties to radical Islamic groups and offered other positive signals. The links to terrorism that remained were hard to prove. As a consequence of these ambiguities, U.S. officials disagreed on the subject of how to treat Sudan. None of these factors are favorable for successful coercive diplomacy.

Pakistan was also a difficult case. Pakistan's support for the Taliban was not disguised, and the United States tried unsuccessfully to exploit Pakistan's leverage over the Taliban to cut its ties with al Qaeda. However, before September 11 the United States hesitated to put pressure on Pakistan, placing other foreign policy interests ahead of preventing terrorism. The United States objected to Pakistan's support for militant groups operating in Kashmir and distrusted Pakistan because of the ISI's connections with the Taliban, but the Clinton administration took almost no visible action beyond the cruise missile attack on the ISI-run training camps in Afghanistan in 1998.

Policy shifted after September 11. The Bush administration both promised rewards and threatened punishment, but it is hard to know whether these threats included military force. The threats, which were kept private, probably centered on economic and political costs. However, Pakistan's conflict with India and the risk of domestic unrest created at least an implicit sense of threat. This case shows that it is difficult to coerce allies whose assistance is needed even when they are uncooperative.

The least ambiguous case is the unsuccessful use of coercive diplomacy to induce the Taliban to turn over Bin Laden. Under both administrations, the objective of coercive diplomacy was precise. It was communicated clearly. After 1998 the Clinton administration combined threats and rewards, although in principle officials rejected the idea of "rewarding terrorism." The 1998 cruise missile attacks were balanced against normalization of relations, which presumably meant the removal of sanctions and official recognition of the regime. The public record does not show any specific threats or the insistence on an ultimatum. Various options for coercion were apparently considered—aid to the Northern Alliance, for example—but rejected. Rhetorical threats were not implemented, even after the discovery of al Qaeda plots in December 1999 and the USS *Cole* bombing in October 2000.

After September 11 the Bush administration continued coercive diplomacy. Bush gave the Taliban several "second chances" after issuing a public ultimatum for compliance and even after launching military operations. However, the Taliban leadership may not have believed U.S. promises. In October the offer to "moderates" of a place in a future government was a threat to the leaders who were clearly not moderates. As coercive military pressure mounted, the Taliban's ability to comply decreased correspondingly. This relationship suggests another potential paradox: as the defending state escalates the use of force, the ability of the adversary to comply decreases. The adversary may become more willing but less able. At this point, the United States had superior motivation, but Taliban leaders may not have recognized it, despite Pakistan's efforts to convince them. The Taliban may have mistaken not just the new U.S. willingness to conduct a ground war but the prospect that a war could be fought at so little cost. Pakistani intermediaries reported that the Taliban had no conception of U.S. capabilities or motivation after September 11. One could argue that the Bush administration should have been more patient in waiting for a response to its demands, and the public use of an ultimatum by both Bush and Blair may have set back efforts to reach a compromise. However, the United States had made the same demand consistently since 1998. The Taliban had taken three years to consider its options. Situational factors (the advent of winter and of Ramadan) also constrained the Bush administration's choices.

Implications

It is important for a government to know which adversaries can be coerced and which cannot. This determination is harder to make in the case of states than of nonstates, probably because policymakers assume that states possess tangible assets that their leaders and citizens value enough not to want to risk losing them. A regime may be willing to sacrifice its hold on power rather than comply with the coercer's demands. Furthermore, the government may be mistaken in believing that the regime that is assisting terrorism can comply with its demands. Possibly the Taliban leaders believed that turning over Bin Laden would cost them their tenure anyway, because the surrender would remove what legitimacy they had. As they said, it was an issue of faith. Possibly the Taliban was also so dependent on or intermingled with al Qaeda forces that it had no control over Bin Laden from the outset.

Before September 11 the United States found it difficult to threaten escalation or to communicate a sense of urgency. Terrorism was not the top national security priority. One could blame lack of domestic public support, owing to failure to recognize the threat or aversion to U.S. military casualties.[109] However, the Clinton administration did not advocate or try to justify a stronger coercive policy against the Taliban or against Pakistan. The anticipation of international disapproval of the use of force might also have restricted policy choices. Furthermore, the hiatus between the last months of the Clinton administration and the Bush administration's conclusion of the policy review process the next fall created a policy vacuum.

Many questions remain. One is whether the Taliban's compliance with the demand to turn over Bin Laden and his associates and to shut down al Qaeda's training camps would actually have halted terrorism or prevented the September 11 attacks. The hijacking plot, like most other spectacular terrorist attacks, was initiated years in advance. Al Qaeda might have survived without sanctuary in

Afghanistan. The leadership of Bin Laden may not be critical to the organization's existence.

Another question concerns the alternatives to coercive diplomacy. Was there a strategy with a better conceptual fit, leaving aside the issue of whether it would be politically acceptable? Even the "war on terrorism" has not guaranteed long-term success. Terrorism is extraordinarily hard to control, much less defeat, especially in the short term. The outcomes of policies are highly uncertain and contingent. Neither scholars nor practitioners know precisely how and why campaigns of terrorism end.[110] Expectations of what coercive diplomacy can achieve may be too high.

Policymakers need a mix of strategies. They also need to be consistent and clear about the strategies they are using, to ensure that they are compatible with each other, and to tailor them to a range of different actors, not all of whom are adversaries. Policymakers must resign themselves to dealing with high levels of ambiguity, complexity, and uncertainty. Success and failure will be hard to judge.

NOTES

1. See Tim Zimmermann, "Coercive Diplomacy and Libya," in *The Limits of Coercive Diplomacy*, 2d ed., ed. Alexander L. George and William E. Simons (Boulder, Colo.: Westview Press, 1994), 201–228. The United States had also used limited military force in efforts to apprehend individual terrorist suspects.

2. *Public Report of the Vice President's Task Force on Combating Terrorism* (Washington, D.C.: U.S. Government Printing Office, February 1986), esp. 9, 13.

3. In April 1996 Saudi authorities televised the confessions of four religious militants who claimed to be motivated by dissatisfaction with the regime. Three had fought in the wars in Afghanistan, Bosnia, and Chechnya. In May they were executed.

4. See "A False Alarm (This Time): Preventive Defense against Catastrophic Terrorism," in Ashton B. Carter and William J. Perry, *Preventive Defense: A New Security Strategy for America*, ed. Ashton B. Carter and William J. Perry (Washington, D.C.: Brookings Institution, 1999), 143–174.

5. See Martha Crenshaw, "The Logic of Terrorism: Terrorism as the

Product of Strategic Choice," in *Origins of Terrorism: Psychologies, Ideologies, Theologies, States of Mind*, ed. Walter Reich (Cambridge: Woodrow Wilson International Center for Scholars and Cambridge University Press, 1990).

6. On the question of how to coerce terrorists, see Joseph Lepgold, "Hypotheses on Vulnerability: Are Terrorists and Drug Traffickers Coerceable?" in *Strategic Coercion: Concepts and Cases*, ed. Lawrence Freedman (New York and Oxford: Oxford University Press, 1998); and Ian O. Lesser, "Countering the New Terrorism: Implications for Strategy," in *Countering the New Terrorism*, ed. Ian O. Lesser et al. (Santa Monica, Calif.: RAND, 1999). See also Daniel Byman and Matthew Waxman, *The Dynamics of Coercion: American Foreign Policy and the Limits of Military Might* (Cambridge: Cambridge University Press and RAND, 2002).

7. Some nonstates have alternatives to terrorism, while others do not. This is an important consideration in choosing a defensive or coercive strategy.

8. Zimmermann, "Coercive Diplomacy and Libya," 204.

9. This account is based on David Von Drehle and R. Jeffrey Smith, "U.S. Strikes Iraq for Plot to Kill Bush," *Washington Post*, June 27, 1993; and Eric Schmitt, "Raid on Baghdad," *New York Times*, June 28, 1993.

10. The text of the president's statement on June 26 can be found in *Washington Post*, June 27, 1993, A20.

11. The Kuwaiti trial of the accused plotters had not been completed, however.

12. Richard L. Berke, "Raid on Baghdad: Poll Shows Raid on Iraq Buoyed Clinton's Popularity," *New York Times*, June 29, 1993.

13. William Safire, "Slapping Saddam's Wrist," *New York Times*, June 28, 1993.

14. Martin Walker and Michael White, "Clinton Sparks Anger Abroad," *Guardian*, June 29, 1993.

15. Stephen Hubbell, "Arab States Condemn US Strike on Baghdad," *Christian Science Monitor*, June 29, 1993.

16. Paul Pillar, *Terrorism and U.S. Foreign Policy* (Washington, D.C.: Brookings Institution Press, 2001), 103–104.

17. R. Jeffrey Smith, "Critics 'Wrong,' CIA Chief Says," *Washington Post*, September 6, 1996.

18. See U.S. Department of Defense, *Report to the President and Congress on the Protection of U.S. Forces Deployed Abroad* (with the Downing

Investigation Report, August 30, 1996) (Washington, D.C.: September 15, 1996). In June 2001 indictments returned before the U.S. District Court in Alexandria, Virginia, revealed that plans for the attack started in 1993 and that the Saudis had arrested some members of the group before the bombing.

19. Jeff Gerth and Elaine Sciolino, "U.S. Takes Hard Look at Saudis with Bombing and Shah in Mind," *New York Times*, December 1, 1996.

20. David B. Ottaway, "U.S. Considers Slugging It Out with International Terrorism," *Washington Post*, October 17, 1996.

21. See Smith, "Critics 'Wrong,' CIA Chief Says." Smith also notes that Deutch's speech was remarkably lacking in detail, apparently because its contents had been strongly debated within the agency. The opponents of disclosure seemed to prevail. The CIA was apparently uncomfortable about defending the agency against partisan attacks, but National Security Adviser Anthony Lake was angry. Deutch also announced that the CIA was establishing a new "terrorist warning group."

22. Warren Christopher, "Fighting Terrorism: Challenges for Peacemakers" (address to the Washington Institute for Near East Policy, May 21, 1996), in *U.S. Department of State Dispatch*, June 3, 1996, 277–279.

23. Michael Dobbs, "An Obscure Chief in U.S. War on Terror," *Washington Post*, April 2, 2000. In 1994 Lake had described a moderate and non-threatening policy toward Iran, suggesting that normal relations would be "conceivable" if Iran ceased its support for terrorism and its challenge to non-proliferation principles. He described U.S. policy as isolation and containment. See "Confronting Backlash States," *Foreign Affairs* (March-April 1994).

24. R. Jeffrey Smith, "Saudis Hold 40 Suspects in GI Quarters Bombing," *Washington Post*, November 1, 1996. The details of the Saudi findings and U.S. response come primarily from this reporting.

25. R. Jeffrey Smith, "Saudis Offer Data to U.S. Linking Extremists, Bomb," *Washington Post*, December 11, 1996.

26. Thomas W. Lippman and Bradley Graham, "U.S. Mulls Possible Response to Iran in Saudi Bombing," *Washington Post*, December 22, 1996. See also Robin Wright, "Iran Braces to Get Blamed for Bombing," *Los Angeles Times*, December 25, 1996.

27. R. Jeffrey Smith, "New Questions about Old Issues," *Washington Post*, January 8, 1998. Alternatively, a conclusive demonstration of Iranian complicity might persuade U.S. allies to support economic sanctions. The following April, when a German court concluded that Iran's "Committee for Special Operations" had ordered the assassinations of Kurdish dissidents, the State Department seized the opportunity to criticize the Europeans for maintaining a "critical dialogue" with Iran. The European Union was asked again to join in U.S. sanctions in order to contain Iran. See Alan Cowell, "Berlin Court Says Top Iran Leaders Ordered Killings," *New York Times*, April 11, 1997. The government was also coming under criticism at home for its policy of "dual containment" of Iraq and Iran. An impressive trio of former officials warned that although direct attacks on Americans called for retaliation, containment was not a solution to the general problem of terrorism. They urged that Iran's support for terrorism be addressed by "specific policy instruments," not the current crude and counterproductive attempt to isolate the entire country. They also advocated incentives for cooperation. See Zbigniew Brzezinski, Brent Scowcroft, and Richard Murphy, "Differentiated Containment," *Foreign Affairs* 76, no. 3 (May-June 1997): 20–41.

28. Jane Perlez and James Risen, "Clinton Seeks an Opening to Iran," *New York Times*, December 3, 1999. The indictments handed down in June 2001 did not name or charge any Iranians, although the involvement of Iranian military officials was described.

29. Ibid.

30. See U.S. Department of State, Office of the Secretary of State and Office of the Coordinator for Counterterrorism, *Patterns of Global Terrorism*, for the years 1996, 1997, 1998, and 1999.

31. On U.S. awareness of the threat before the August bombings, see Vernon Loeb, "Where the CIA Wages Its New World War," *Washington Post*, September 9, 1998; Benjamin Weiser, "Saudi Is Indicted in Bomb Attacks on U.S. Embassies," and "Senior Aide Implicating Bin Laden in Terrorism," *New York Times*, November 5, 1998, and December 3, 1998, respectively; and James Risen and Benjamin Weiser, "Before Bombings, Omens and Fears," *New York Times*, January 9, 1999. Further information was revealed during the trial in New York of some of those responsible, from January to July 2001. Extensive coverage can be found in the *New York Times*, and much of the trial testimony has been made public.

32. See "Planning for Terror but Failing to Act," *New York Times*, December 30, 2001. This lengthy overview has helped inform the following discussion.

33. U.S. Department of State, *Patterns of Global Terrorism: 1997.*

34. Osama bin Laden, interview with Peter Arnett, accessed at CNN's homepage, "CNN/Time Impact: Holy Terror?"

35. See Rohan Gunaratna, *Inside al Qaeda: Global Network of Terror* (New York: Columbia University Press, 2002).

36. The text is available at www.fas.org/irp/world/para/docs/980223-

fatwa.htm. Bin Laden also gave an interview to ABC News in May. See "Talking with Terror's Banker" on www.abcnews.com. See also the analysis of the declaration by Bernard Lewis, "License to Kill," *Foreign Affairs* 77, no. 6 (November-December 1998): 14–19.

37. Details of U.S. information about Sudan and chemical weapons production are taken from James Risen, "To Bomb Sudan Plant, or Not: A Year Later, Debates Rankle," *New York Times*, October 27, 1999.

38. Thomas W. Lippman, "Clinton Imposes Sanctions on Sudan, Freezes Assets," *Washington Post*, November 5, 1997.

39. Tim Weiner and James Risen, "Decision to Strike Factory in Sudan Based on Surmise," *New York Times*, September 21, 1998.

40. Michael Dobbs, "Analysts Feel Militia Could End Anarchy," *Washington Post*, September 28, 1996.

41. See *Report of the Accountability Review Boards: Bombings of the US Embassies in Nairobi, Kenya and Dar es Salaam, Tanzania on August 7, 1998.* January 11, 1999. Available at www/zgram.net/embassybombing.htm. See further details from the classified report in Risen and Weiser, "Before Bombings, Omens and Fears." According to this account, the Kenyan authorities arrested a group of suspects, but the CIA station chief declined to interview them. Also see Benjamin Weiser, "U.S. to Offer Detailed Trail of bin Laden in Bomb Trial," *New York Times*, January 13, 2001.

42. Seymour Hersh, "The Missiles of August," *New Yorker*, October 12, 1998, 34–41. See also James Risen and Judith Miller, "Pakistani Intelligence Had Ties to al Qaeda," *New York Times*, October 29, 2001.

43. See Hersh, "The Missiles of August," and Risen, "To Bomb Sudan Plant, or Not." The following description of the decision-making process is based largely on these accounts, and also on background interviews with some officials. See also Tim Weiner and Steven Lee Myers, "Flaws in U.S. Account Raise Questions on Strike in Sudan," *New York Times*, August 29, 1998; and Weiner and Risen, "Decision to Strike Factory in Sudan Based on Surmise."

44. Risen, "To Bomb Sudan Plant, or Not."

45. Hersh, "The Missiles of August."

46. It appears that the aim was not so much to kill Bin Laden (although this would have been a welcome side effect) but to demonstrate U.S. knowledge of his location.

47. Former NSC staff members Daniel Benjamin and Steven Simon report that the decision was unanimous and argue that the press underestimated the importance of Al Shifa. Daniel Benjamin and Steven Simon, "A Failure of Intelligence?" in *Striking Terror: America's New War*, ed.

Robert B. Silvers and Barbara Epstein (New York: New York Review of Books, 2002). Benjamin and Simon are also the authors of *The Age of Sacred Terror* (New York: Random House, 2002).

48. See Michael Barletta, "Chemical Weapons in the Sudan: Allegations and Evidence," *Nonproliferation Review* 6, no. 1 (fall 1998): 1–37. As a counter to this view, consult Benjamin and Simon, "A Failure of Intelligence?"

49. Risen, "To Bomb Sudan Plant, or Not"; and Tim Weiner and Steven Lee Myers, "U.S. Notes Gaps in Data about Drug Plant but Defends Attack," *New York Times*, September 3, 1998. See also James Risen and David Johnston, "Experts Find No Arms Chemicals at Bombed Sudan Plant," *New York Times*, February 9, 1999, and the discussion in Paul Pillar, *Terrorism and U.S. Foreign Policy* (Washington, D.C.: Brookings Institution Press, 2001), 107–109.

50. "Bombers Sent to Train on Guam," *New York Times*, September 3, 1998.

51. See Barton Gellman, "Clinton's Covert War" and "Terrorism Wasn't a Top Priority," *Washington Post*, National Weekly Edition, January 7–13 and 14–20, 2002, respectively. Both provide details on the 1998–2000 period.

52. *Joint Inquiry Staff Statement, Part I*, September 18, 2002, available on the House and Senate Intelligence Committee websites (intelligence.house.gov and intelligence.senate.gov). See p. 10. In 1999 only three analysts were assigned full-time to tracking Bin Laden; there were five by 2000 (p. 18). The Counterterrorist Center staff doubled after September 11, from four hundred to eight hundred.

53. See Gellman, "Clinton's Covert War."

54. Wakil Ahmad Muttawakil, quoted in Pamela Constable, "U.N. Imposes Air, Economic Sanctions on Afghanistan," *Washington Post*, November 14, 1999.

55. Barbara Crossette, "U.S. Steps Up Pressure on Taliban to Deliver Osama bin Ladin," *New York Times*, October 19, 1999.

56. Gellman, "Clinton's Covert War."

57. See James Risen and Judith Miller, "Pakistani Intelligence Had Ties to Al Qaeda," *New York Times*, October 29, 2001.

58. See John Lancaster, "U.S. Pressures Pakistan to Cut Ties with Extremist Groups," *Washington Post*, January 26, 2000.

59. Among numerous press reports, see Jane Perlez, "U.S. Weighs Using Food as Support for Sudan Rebels" and "Friendly Fire: In a War, Even Food

Aid Can Kill," *New York Times*, November 29, 1999, and December 5, 1999, respectively. See also Mark Huband, "Debate Grows on How to Deal with Sudan," *Financial Times*, December 7, 1999. Susan Rice, the assistant secretary of state for African affairs, was said to view the Sudanese regime as "evil incarnate" and to be the main proponent of a hard-line policy.

60. Neil King, Jr., and David S. Cloud, "Casting a Global Net, U.S. Security Forces Survive Terrorist Test," *Wall Street Journal*, March 8, 2000. See also Dobbs, "An Obscure Chief in U.S. War on Terror."

61. He intended to bomb the Los Angeles International Airport, a target he chose himself, according to his testimony. See Laura Mansnerus and Judith Miller, "Terrorist Details His Training in Afghanistan," *New York Times*, July 4, 2001.

62. U.S. Department of State, *Patterns of Global Terrorism, 1999* (April 2000), 7.

63. Dobbs, "An Obscure Chief in U.S. War on Terror."

64. David A. Vise and Lorraine Adams, "Bin Ladin Weakened, Officials Say," *Washington Post*, March 11, 2000. However, shortly after this report Clinton canceled a visit to a village in Bangladesh during his South Asia visit, owing to threats from Bin Laden. See "Report on bin Laden Altered Clinton Plan," *New York Times*, March 21, 2000.

65. Jane Perlez, "Clinton Entreats Pakistan to Tread Lightly in Kashmir," *New York Times*, March 26, 2000. In fact, the Secret Service opposed the trip because of concerns about Clinton's safety. Extraordinary security precautions were taken, and the trip lasted only a few hours.

66. See Ambassador Michael Sheehan, "Post-Millennium Terrorism Review" (speech to the Brookings Institution, February 10, 2000), as well as his testimony before the House Committee on International Relations (July 12, 2000). See also "Fact Sheet: U.S. Counterterrorism Efforts since the 1998 U.S. Embassy Bombings in Africa," August 7, 2000. The texts are available on the Office of Counterterrorism's website, state.gov/s/ct.

67. In contrast, the 1998 report referred to "forcing" state sponsors to change their behavior. The reports usually appear in the spring of the following year. This view is also corroborated by later *Washington Post* interviews with Ambassador Michael Sheehan (see Gellman, "Clinton's Covert War").

68. In an interview with Judith Miller, Ambassador Sheehan explained that Afghanistan was not added to the list because the United States did not recognize the Taliban government, and that Pakistan was a "friendly state" trying to improve its record, which badly needed it. See "South Asia Called Major Terror Hub in a Survey by U.S.," *New York Times*, April 30, 2000.

69. However, in September Secretary of State Albright repeated the Clinton administration's demand that the regime agree to a broad-based democratic government. Barbara Crossette, "Taliban Open a Campaign to Gain Status at the U.N.," *New York Times*, September 21, 2000.

70. Christopher Marquis, "U.S. Declares 'Rogue Nations' Are Now 'States of Concern,'" *New York Times*, June 20, 2000.

71. Barbara Crossette, "Spurned Sudan, Looking for Foreign Support, Says It Has Changed," *New York Times*, June 21, 2000. See also Karl Vick, "Sudanese Leader Moves against Rival," *Washington Post*, December 15, 1999. The State Department's 2001 annual report explains the U.S. position. After the September 11 attacks, which Sudan condemned, Sudan pledged cooperation and was rewarded with the lifting of UN sanctions. However, U.S. unilateral sanctions remained in force.

72. National Commission on Terrorism, *Report to Congress: Countering the Changing Threat of International Terrorism* (Washington, D.C., June 5, 2000). The administration responded firmly that it was not considering sanctions against Pakistan.

73. Judith Miller, "U.S. Puts Uzbek Group on Its Terror List," *New York Times*, September 15, 2000. See also Ambassador Sheehan's testimony before the House Committee on International Relations, July 12, 2000. Afghanistan was said to be the "primary swamp of terrorism." On the other hand, Sheehan also argued that Bin Laden had no need for a state sponsor for material support. And he warned again that the Taliban would be held responsible should Bin Laden undertake any terrorist acts while based on its territory.

74. See "Planning for Terror but Failing to Act," *New York Times*, December 30, 2002.

75. John F. Burns, "Yemeni on Delicate Path in bin Laden Hunt," *New York Times*, December 15, 2000.

76. Barbara Crossette, "U.S. and Russia Ask Harsh Sanctions on Afghanistan," *New York Times*, December 8, 2000. An arms embargo might be considered an implied threat, since it would presumably handicap the Taliban in the internal struggle for power.

77. See David Johnston and James Risen, "Traces of Terrorism: The Intelligence Reports," and David E. Sanger and Elisabeth Bumiller, "Traces of Terrorism: The Overview," in *New York Times*, May 17, 2002; and Jane Perlez and David E. Sanger, "A Nation Challenged: State Department: Powell Says U.S. Had Signs, but Not Clear Ones, of a Plot," *New York Times*, October 3, 2001.

78. See the special report in *Time*, August 12, 2002.

79. In September 2002 a joint inquiry by the House and Senate Intelligence Committees produced an interim report. So far investigators had not found a "smoking gun" that would have alerted the government to a preventable attack. However, the government had received a stream of more general warnings, or "chatter." See *Joint Inquiry Staff Statement, Part I*, September 18, 2002, and "The Intelligence Community's Knowledge of the September 11 Hijackers prior to September 11, 2001," September 20, 2002. Both documents are available on the House and Senate Intelligence Committee websites. The report also noted that information on what the White House and the president knew remained classified. The report states that "high government officials" were briefed repeatedly.

80. See the series of reports by Dan Balz and Bob Woodward, "Ten Days in September," *Washington Post*, January 27–February 3, 2002.

81. Siddharth Varadarajan, "Musharraf Drops Taliban to Get Kashmir," *Times of India*, September 21, 2001. He refers to "relentless pressure" from the United States. See also Farhan Bokhari and Edward Luce, "Pakistan's Choice," *Financial Times*, September 18, 2001. J. N. Dixit, former Indian foreign minister, is quoted as saying that "America's war on terrorism is the best opportunity India has had to settle the Kashmir dispute in its favour once and for all."

82. John F. Burns, "Pakistani Defends Joining with U.S." and "Pakistanis Fail in Last-Ditch Bid to Persuade Taliban to Turn Over bin Laden," *New York Times*, September 20 and September 29, 2001, respectively. Delegations traveled both to Kandahar and to Kabul and met with the Taliban for two days.

83. See John F. Burns, "New Push to Get bin Laden to Agree to Quit Afghanistan," *New York Times*, September 28, 2001.

84. See the text of the president's speech at www.whitehouse.gov/news/releases/2001/09. The Taliban had imprisoned a group of Christian relief workers accused of proselytizing.

85. John F. Burns, "Clerics Answer 'No, No, No!' and Invoke Fates of Past Foes," *New York Times*, September 22, 2001.

86. John F. Burns, "U.S. Officers Are Meeting in Islamabad on War Plans," *New York Times*, September 25, 2001.

87. John F. Burns, "Pakistan Fights U.S. Move Linked to Anti-Taliban Drive," *New York Times*, September 26, 2001.

88. See Burns, "New Push to Get bin Laden to Agree to Quit Afghanistan." Burns refers to these talks as well as the earlier set as "negotiations."

89. The following account is based on Burns, "Pakistanis Fail in Last-Ditch Bid to Persuade Taliban to Turn Over bin Laden."

90. See Michael R. Gordon and Eric Schmitt, "Pentagon Tries to Avoid Using Pakistan Bases," and Douglas Frantz, "Taliban Say They Want to Negotiate with the U.S. Over bin Laden," *New York Times*, October 3, 2001.

91. John F. Burns, "Taliban Say They Hold bin Laden," *New York Times*, October 1, 2001.

92. See Sarah Lyall, "Tough Talk from Blair on Taliban," *New York Times*, October 3, 2001.

93. Frantz, "Taliban Say They Want to Negotiate with the U.S. over bin Laden." The ambassador appeared in Quetta, Pakistan, sixty miles from the Afghan border, where the local tribal chiefs had been meeting.

94. Elaine Sciolino and Steven Lee Myers, "Bush Says 'Time Is Running Out,'" *New York Times*, October 7, 2001.

95. John F. Burns, "Taliban Link Fate of Aid Workers to U.S. Action," *New York Times*, October 7, 2001.

96. Patrick E. Tyler, "U.S. and Britain Strike Afghanistan," and "Jets Pound Taliban Sites a 2nd Night," *New York Times*, October 8 and 9, 2001, respectively. The bombing involved fifteen land-based bombers and twenty-five strike aircraft from carriers. They used precision-guided bombs. U.S. warships and British submarines fired fifty Tomahawk cruise missiles.

97. Although this attack was reported at the time, only on October 15 did the secretary of defense admit openly that the air strikes had been targeting Mullah Omar since the first day of the air campaign. See Michael R. Gordon and Tim Weiner, "Taliban Leader a Target of U.S. Air Campaign," *New York Times*, October 16, 2001.

98. Patrick E. Tyler and Elisabeth Bumiller, "Bush Offers Taliban '2nd Chance' to Yield," *New York Times*, October 12, 2001.

99. Elisabeth Bumiller, "President Rejects Offer by Taliban for Negotiations," *New York Times*, October 15, 2001. Gunaratna argues that the Taliban might have turned Bin Laden over to Pakistan had the Bush administration given them more time (*Inside Al Qaeda*, 227).

100. Ibid.

101. John F. Burns, "Taliban Envoy Talks of a Deal over bin Laden," *New York Times*, October 16, 2001.

102. Patrick E. Tyler, "Powell Suggests Role for Taliban," *New York Times*, October 17, 2001.

103. John F. Burns, "Taliban Chief Urges Troops: Defy 'Infidel,'" *New York Times*, October 18, 2001.

104. Mullah Abdul Salam Zaeef, quoted in John F. Burns, "Don't Doubt Steadfastness of Taliban, Envoy Insists," *New York Times*, October 20, 2001. Maulvi Jalaluddin Haqqani, the commander of Taliban forces on the Pakistan border, also rejected the idea of Taliban participation in a postwar government, although Pakistan had encouraged him to consider the idea, and earlier Pakistani and U.S. intelligence agents had approached him about defecting. See John F. Burns, "Taliban Army Chief Scoffs at Report of Peace Talks," *New York Times*, October 21, 2001.

105. Michael R. Gordon, "U.S. Bombs Taliban's Forces on Front Lines," *New York Times*, October 22, 2001.

106. Access to classified information would undoubtedly yield a less tentative assessment.

107. Possibly these efforts might be interpreted as coercion at the individual rather than the group level, since militants might have been expected to lose enthusiasm for the cause once the costs of action mounted.

108. Even the 1998 cruise missile attack was meant to strike a group of senior leaders, including Bin Laden, so it might be interpreted as an assassination attempt as much as a demonstration of force.

109. Simon and Benjamin, for example, blame the press for labeling the attack on the Al Shifa pharmaceuticals a foreign policy blunder ("A Failure of Intelligence?" 292–299).

110. See Martha Crenshaw, "How Terrorism Declines," *Terrorism and Political Violence* 3, no. 1 (spring 1991): 69–87 (also in *Terrorism Research and Public Policy*, ed. Clark McCauley [London: Frank Cass, 1991]); and "Why Violence Is Rejected or Renounced: A Case Study of Oppositional Terrorism," in *The Natural History of Peace*, ed. Tom Gregor (Nashville, Tenn.: Vanderbilt University Press, 1996).

9

Coercive Diplomacy: What Do We Know?

ROBERT J. ART

HE PURPOSE OF THIS FINAL CHAPTER is to derive conclusions about the efficacy of coercive diplomacy and to offer guidelines for policymakers. The evidentiary basis for the analysis comes from the cases analyzed in chapters 2 through 8, supplemented by the earlier studies of Alexander George and his colleagues mentioned in chapter 1 and discussed more fully here.

To provide an overall assessment of coercive diplomacy, I address these five questions:

- Why is coercive diplomacy difficult?
- What are the prerequisites for the successful exercise of coercive diplomacy?
- What is the United States' experience with coercive diplomacy?
- When does coercive diplomacy work?
- What guidelines can be offered to U.S. policymakers who may contemplate resort to coercive diplomacy?

Before turning to these questions, however, a brief restatement of the concept of coercive diplomacy as laid out in the introduction is necessary.

Coercive diplomacy is a form of coercion or compellence, but it is to be distinguished from war. Coercive diplomacy has two hallmarks: it seeks to get a target to change its behavior, and it does so by threatening to use force, or by using force, but only in limited amounts. If we conceive of coercion to have three phases—threats to use force, demonstrative use of force, and full-scale use of force (or war)—coercive diplomacy encompasses only the first two phases. When we identify a coercive diplomatic gambit, threats to use force are easy to grasp and so, too, is war. Demonstrative use is more difficult to pin down. It encompasses both exemplary use and limited use. The former entails the use of force that is decidedly at the low end of force employment, just beyond the boundary of threat, and can involve a one-time demonstration or several demonstrations. Limited use means employing more amounts of force than for demonstrative use but not to the point that the boundary between limited use and full-scale war has been crossed. Admittedly, the line between limited use and war is not easy to draw, and it depends to a degree on the situation at hand. In general, however, the line should be drawn in terms of how much destruction is done to the target, not how much of its own military power the coercer draws upon. The central notion of coercive diplomacy is that it is "forceful persuasion," to borrow Alexander George's apt phrase, and the task is to "persuade an opponent to cease his aggression rather than bludgeon him into stopping."[1]

Coercion can succeed if coercive diplomacy fails. That is, the coercer may ultimately bend the target to its will but only after resorting to war. If war is necessary to change the target's behavior, however, then, by definition, coercive diplomacy has failed. Sometimes the coercer undertakes coercive diplomacy knowing full well that it will fail. These are instances of what can be termed "disingenuous" coercive diplomacy: this technique is viewed as a necessary political step to war, not a viable alternative to it. The coercer believes that threats or limited use of force will not work, but also that they must be tried and be seen to fail so that others—the coercer's domestic publics and political allies—can be shown that everything short of war has been tried, that it has not worked, and, consequently, that there is now no alternative to war. More often the coercer undertakes coercive diplomacy in the belief that it has a good chance of succeeding, thereby enabling war to be avoided. This can be termed "genuine" coercive diplomacy.

War, of course, does not have to follow a failed attempt at genuine coercive diplomacy; the coercer can simply give up its quest to change the target's behavior. This generally does not happen, however, for two reasons: a coercer does not resort to force or threats of force unless the interests at stake are of sufficient importance that it is willing to call out the ultimate weapon; and a coercer faces severe loss of credibility by backing down after threatening or using limited force. More likely, then, the coercer will persist in its actions, engaging in repeated acts of coercive diplomacy or resorting to war, and avoiding war only if some favorable compromise with the target is reached. Except for the 2001 Afghanistan and 1990–91 Iraqi cases, in which the calculations of the two Bush presidents were that sanctions and military threats would not work to coerce the Taliban and Saddam Hussein, our cases look to be ones of genuine coercive diplomacy—instances, that is, when the U.S. government hoped that coercive diplomacy would avert war and enable it to achieve its objectives.

WHY IS COERCIVE DIPLOMACY DIFFICULT?

Our case studies have shown that it is hard to make coercive diplomacy work, and the case studies by George and his colleagues (discussed below) reconfirm this conclusion. There are good theoretical reasons why coercive diplomacy is difficult. In particular, four factors, which stem from the inherent nature of coercive diplomacy and which therefore operate in every such attempt, explain why this technique is hard to pull off. In addition, depending on the specific situation, two other factors can manifest themselves, and when they are present, they make the successful exercise of coercive diplomacy even more difficult.

Compellence Is Difficult

First, coercive diplomacy is a form of compellence and, as Thomas Schelling observed, compellence is harder to pull off than deterrence. It is intrinsically more difficult to get a target to change its behavior than to keep its behavior as is.[2] Compellent actions require that the target alter its behavior in a manner quite visible to all in response to an equally visible initiative taken by the coercer. In contrast, deterrent threats are easier for the target to appear to have ignored or to acquiesce in without great loss of face. In deterrent situations the target can claim plausible deniability, maintaining that it had no intention of changing its behavior in the first place, or it can simply appear to ignore the deterrent threats while not changing its behavior. The target has no such plausible deniability in the case of compellence because its overt submission is required. Greater face is thus lost when a target, under pressure, reverses a course of action to which it has committed its prestige and devoted resources than when it simply persists in the same behavior.[3] Finally, compellence more directly engages the passions of the target state than does deterrence because of the pain and humiliation inflicted upon it, but passions, once engaged, are dangerous and produce boomerang effects: they cause the government to mobilize domestic opinion against the coercer, and they increase domestic support for the target government. Both effects perversely make the government more popular after it becomes subject to coercive action than it was before, with the ironic result that the target becomes less susceptible to coercive diplomacy. For these reasons, compellence is harder than deterrence.[4]

Denial, Punishment, and Risk Strategies Are Hard with Diplomatic and Demonstrative Uses of Force

Coercive diplomacy is a form of coercion, and coercion, as Robert Pape has argued, can be applied in a denial, punishment, or risk fashion.[5] Denial strategies seek to change an adversary's behavior by thwarting its military strategy. Denial takes aim at the target's military forces in order to undercut their effectiveness, seeking to stalemate these forces rather than bring outright military victory over them. A successful denial strategy is one that prevents the target from achieving its political objectives with its military strategy. Punishment strategies seek to change an adversary's behavior by raising the costs of its continued resistance. Punishment imposes pain, either directly to the target's population or to those assets that are important for the population's or the leadership's quality of life. A successful punishment strategy is one that causes the target to give way, not because its military strategy has been thwarted, but because the costs to its population have become too great. Risk strategies seek to change an adversary's behavior by raising the probability that it will suffer ever-greater punishment in the future if it fails to comply. Risk means escalation, and risk threatens more pain to the population or to its valuable assets. A successful risk strategy is one that causes the target to give way because it becomes convinced that the pain it will suffer from looming punishment is not worth the objectives it seeks.

To the extent that it is applied to produce risk, coercive diplomacy is inherently difficult to pull off because risk strategies, Pape tells us, are inherently difficult. They fail for several reasons.[6] For starters, risk strategies are successful to the extent that they create in the target's mind fear of future punishment sufficiently costly that the target changes its behavior. As Pape points out, however, the pain suffered from damage done in the present is greater than the pain imagined from damage done in the future. This happens because human beings discount the future, which means they value the present more. Risk should be conceived as future punishment, and imagined future pain hurts less than present pain. Moreover, because of political considerations, risk strategies are generally applied incrementally, with the coercer gradually ratcheting up the pain inflicted.[7] This produces more perverse effects: the target has time to adapt its tactics to reduce the damage done, time to get used to the pain being inflicted, and time to mobilize domestic opinion against the foreign intruder—all of which make the target better able to tolerate the pain being doled out by the coercer. Finally, when the pain is only threatened or is severely limited when inflicted, as is the case, by definition, with coercive diplomacy, then a coercive risk strategy becomes all the more difficult.

For similar reasons, punishment and denial strategies are difficult to execute with coercive diplomacy. After all, it is hard to inflict much punishment with coercive diplomacy: the limited use of force produces only limited punishment. Delivering limited punishment is not likely to cause a target that cares a great deal about its objectives to change course. Similarly, the threat to deny is not denial, and the limited use of force can produce only limited denial. Strictly speaking, coercive diplomacy cannot employ denial in the sense that it cannot use enough force to stalemate a target. Instead, to the extent that coercive diplomacy aims at denial, it employs "demonstrative denial." Through limited military action the coercer demonstrates to the target that the coercer can, if it so chooses, undercut the effectiveness of the target's military strategy but without actually undercutting it.

Whether the coercer intends to employ its military power to manipulate risk, inflict punishment, or execute denial, all three are hard to bring off when the employment of military power is severely constricted, as it is with coercive diplomacy. To the coercer, its threats and limited use are intended to signal its firm resolve to escalate the use of force—for risk, punishment, or denial purposes—unless the target knuckles under, but the target, especially a highly motivated one, can just as easily see threats and limited use as signaling weak resolve. After all, if the coercer cares that much about its objective, why pull its punches in the first place? What looks to the coercer as steely determination can appear to the target as an unwillingness or inability to employ large-scale use of force to attain its goal. Threats and limited use are not unequivocal in their meaning; they can be interpreted to signify both firmness and weakness in resolve, depending on the perspective of the viewer.

Some of these dynamics appear to have been at work in the Kosovo War. Before the war, the NATO allies thought that Slobodan Milosevic would cave in after a few days of bombing, because they concluded, incorrectly, that he had done so once before—in September 1995, after a period of short intensive bombing strikes against Serbian forces in Bosnia.[8] In 1999, however, Milosevic proved them wrong. Apparently, he believed that he could ride out a few days of bombing and calculated that the alliance could not hold together if it engaged in a sustained, heavy bombing campaign against him. Believing he could outlast the alliance, he forced NATO to resort to an extensive air campaign and ultimately to threaten a ground campaign in order to win the war.

In sum, neither significant punishment nor significant denial is possible with coercive diplomacy. Therefore, what coercive diplomacy can most easily communicate to the target is the increasing probability of more punishment to come if it fails to comply, which is risk, and also some indication of the denial powers of the coercer.

Estimating Resolve Is Difficult

The third reason that coercive diplomacy is hard to execute lies in the fact that estimating resolve both before and during a coercive diplomatic attempt is a tricky affair and therefore easy to get wrong. Resolve refers to the strength of a party's will to prevail, and the balance of resolve refers to whose will—the target's or the coercer's—is the stronger. Before the fact, the coercer can never know for certain whose resolve is the stronger—its own or the target's. Indeed, this is the function of the crisis produced by the resort to coercive diplomacy: to test the relative strength of the two parties' resolves. Coercive diplomatic attempts are games of chicken that reveal to the target and the coercer which one cares more about something and just how much more. After all, if the relative strength of the parties' resolves were known before coercive diplomacy began, then there would be no reason to begin it. If the target knew, for example, that it cared much less than the coercer and knew that the coercer was intent on getting its way no matter what, and if the coercer also knew that the target cared less than it did, then the target would most likely relent at the first signs of serious intent by the coercer. In serious disputes, however, this does not happen because each party cares intensely about its respective goals. Hence, the resulting crisis serves the function of demonstrating who cares more.

Even if the coercer accurately estimates the relative strength of the two parties' resolves before the crisis gets under way, this is no guarantee that their resolves will remain the same once the crisis begins. Indeed, once it begins, resolves can change and usually do, but generally in the direction of greater firmness by both parties. Each party digs in, in order to see how strongly the other cares. Moreover, when threats are made, and especially when some force is used, both sides are likely to harden their initial positions even more, because the use of force engages passions and almost always causes both the target and the coercer to stiffen their wills. As a consequence, both will bear more sacrifice in order to justify the pain already suffered.

Economists argue that sunk costs should be ignored when making current decisions. Their motto is, "Never throw good money after bad." Statesmen, however, cannot ignore sunk costs because of political considerations: the costs already incurred impel them to pour in even more resources. Their motto is, "Sacrifices already borne justify those currently being made." As a consequence, initial resolves are likely to harden, not weaken, under the impact of a coercive attempt; threats to use force are likely to lead to exemplary use; and exemplary use is likely to lead to full-scale use of force. Therefore, as Glenn Snyder and Paul Diesing have demonstrated, crises that look like games of chicken have an inherent dynamic toward escalation before they are resolved because neither party will give way at the outset.[9] None of this is to argue that coercive diplomacy is inevitably doomed to fail, only that the odds are not in its favor when the resulting crisis hardens the initial resolves of the parties.

Credibility and Power Are at Stake

Fourth, coercive diplomacy is difficult because the target has to worry about the effects of a confrontation not only on its credibility stakes but also on its power stakes.[10] Credibility stakes concern reputation; power stakes, capabilities. Both are involved in the target's calculations about whether to stand firm or give way to the coercer. Credibility considerations make compromise difficult enough for the target because they involve the following sorts of issues: if the target gives way on this matter, will this be the coercer's last demand, or is it only the first in a series of demands? Even if the coercer will not demand more, what will the effects of giving way to this coercer have on other would-be coercers? In this regard a target is in the same situation that British leaders were in when dealing with Hitler in the late 1930s: will appeasement satiate Hitler, or will it only whet his appetite and that of other potential coercers as well? Actions in the present always set precedents for the future, and the target can never ignore how its reactions to pressures from others will affect its reputation.

Power stakes are equally, if not more, important. Giving way to the coercer is usually not cost free for the target's power. For example, when the United Nations began to push for representative councils in Somalia in March 1993, Mohammed Farah Aideed, the most powerful of the Somali warlords, understood that he would lose a lot of territory and hence power if representative councils were to emerge in a reconstructed Somalia. He therefore resisted the establishment of these councils. Similarly, both Iraq and North Korea would have faced a significant weakening in their military power if they had acceded to U.S. demands to give up their programs to acquire weapons of mass destruction. North Korea demanded a great deal in return, and Iraq tried to do everything to thwart UN inspectors. Hence, when giving way means that the target's future capacity to resist is significantly diminished, its incentives to stand firm go up dramatically. In these situations a coercive diplomatic demand looks to the target like unilateral disarmament: actions that are being demanded of the target weaken its future power. Thus, giving way represents a double whammy for the target because both its reputation for resolve and its ability to stand firm are undercut.

The inherent difficulty of both compellent and risk strategies, the formidable task of estimating resolves before and during crises, and the target's concern for its power and credibility stakes—all make every attempt at coercive diplomacy hard, not easy, to bring off. Two other factors can complicate the task even further when they are present.

Multiple Coercers and Multiple Targets Complicate Coercive Diplomacy

Coercive diplomacy becomes even more demanding in situations in which more than a single coercer and a single target are present. If there is a coalition of coercers, it may be united in its overall goal, but more often than not, the coalition will be divided over the means to achieve the goal.[11] Sometimes the coalition will even be divided on the goal itself. If either is the case, then actions are required to keep the members united in their effort. The rub lies here: actions taken to hold the coalition together can degrade the military and diplomatic effectiveness of the coercive attempt.[12] If several targets are present, it becomes more difficult to design actions that coerce them all. Sometimes steps that coerce one of the parties can actually encourage the others to resist. Other times it may be necessary to favor one of the targets in order to induce the others to cooperate. The presence of two

or more targets thus requires that the coercer devise actions that ultimately induce all the targets to change their behavior. Neither holding together a coalition while maintaining its military effectiveness
nor devising actions to alter the behavior of all the targets is an easy
task to accomplish, and success in such situations requires finesse,
diplomacy, patience, compromise, and, oftentimes, duplicity. Thus,
two or more parties at either the target or the coercer end, or both,
complicate what is already an inherently difficult task.

Five of our cases—Bosnia, Kosovo, Iraq, Somalia, and even North
Korea—involved more than two parties, and complications ensued as
a consequence. Steven Burg and Paul Shoup report that NATO's
bombing in late August and early September 1995, which helped end
the Bosnian War, was a two-edged sword. It helped bring the Serbs to
the negotiating table, but it also encouraged the Muslims and Croats,
who were allied at that time, to continue to resist and achieve all their
goals through continued battle, using NATO as their air force. As a
consequence NATO had to walk a fine line between bombing the
Serbs enough to bring them to the negotiating table and bombing
them not so much that it pushed the Croatian-Muslim alliance away
from the negotiating table.[13] The Kosovo War witnessed serious conflicts among the NATO members over the selection of targets for the
bombing campaign. The United States wanted to escalate both the
scope and the intensity of the bombing more quickly than did many
of its European allies, and these conflicts threatened the cohesiveness
of the coalition and probably the efficiency of the bombing campaign,
even if they did not ultimately degrade the campaign's military effectiveness.[14] The coalition against Iraq, united during the war, began to
fall apart during the 1990s as members became more and more dis-
affected with the continuing costs of the sanctions. The intervention
in Somalia had to deal with dozens of factions vying for power, with
two of them, one led by Ali Mahdi Mohammed and the other by
Mohammed Farah Aideed, being the most important. Ali Mahdi
cooperated more with the United Nations than did Aideed, who
viewed the United Nations and the actions it took as hurting his interests and benefiting Ali Mahdi's. This set the stage for the armed confrontation that led to the collapse of the United Nations' mission in

Somalia.[15] Finally, even though the United States was the only coercer of North Korea, it could not ignore the views and interests of both South Korea and Japan, its close allies in the region. Their views made U.S. air strikes on North Korea's nuclear facilities difficult because of the fear they would release radioactive material that could disperse over both Japan and South Korea as well as re-ignite the Korean War.

Belief in "Counter-Coercion" Techniques Can Foil Coercive Diplomacy

Finally, if the target believes that it has the ability to counter the coercer's diplomatic and military pressures, then coercive diplomacy becomes so difficult that it will generally fail. The task for the coercer is to convince the target that sufficient pain and suffering will ensue if the target does not cease its actions. If the target believes that it can foil or significantly mitigate the coercer's measures or in turn impose risks on the coercer, through what are called "counter-coercion" techniques, which can be political, economic, or military in nature, then the target is much less likely to give way. Milosevic must have made such calculations when contemplating NATO's air war against him, because in the months before the war, Serbian military figures visited Iraq to see if they could learn how to thwart U.S. airpower. One device the Serbs hit upon was not to fire most of their surface-to-air missiles (SAMs) but instead to hold them back. This forced NATO pilots to fly at high altitudes over Kosovo and impeded their ability to knock out Serbian armor placed there. Thus, believing that he had the means to ride out an air war, Milosevic did not back down under NATO's threats.

Matters become especially vexing in those situations in which the target will not reveal its counter-coercion techniques for fear that doing so will negate their effectiveness. Not all counter-coercion techniques are undermined if the target makes them known beforehand to the coercer. Indeed, there are often strong incentives to make such measures known ahead of time if doing so will deter the coercer from undertaking his actions. For example, before the onset of the Persian Gulf War, Saddam Hussein argued that Americans could not suffer heavy casualties the way that Iraqis could, thereby attempting to make Iraqi willingness to suffer more than the Americans a counter-coercion tool for deterrence.[16] In the Kosovo conflict there is credible evidence that Milosevic believed his threat to expel large numbers of Albanians from Kosovo to surrounding states in order to destabilize them would deter the NATO alliance from launching the air war against him.[17] The counter-coercion measures that the target must conceal are those that the coercer can quickly design around once they become known, thereby enabling it to make the threat of significant punishment once again credible. In these cases the target has no incentive to forewarn the coercer of its counter-coercion techniques because such foreknowledge would degrade the target's defenses against the coercer's attack, not enhance deterrence of it.

The target's failure to reveal its counter-coercion techniques produces a perverse result: not only does it make the coercer's resort to coercive diplomacy more likely; it also raises the probability that the attempt will fail. Ignorant that its initial measures might be thwarted, the coercer will begin its coercive diplomatic maneuver. Confident that it can defend itself, the target then applies its counter-coercion methods to undermine the coercer's gambit once it begins. The coercer then works furiously to devise its own counters to the target's counters; the target responds in kind; both persist in their respective actions, pouring more into their respective efforts. In short, the dynamics of crisis behavior take over, and the confrontation escalates from threats and exemplary use to the third stage of coercion—war. Thus, when a target believes that it possesses effective counter-coercion techniques that cannot be revealed, it will not find the coercer's threats or exemplary use of force credible, and full-scale use of force will be required if the coercer wants to get its way.

In sum, these six factors explain why coercive diplomacy is difficult. The first four are "permanently operating factors" and explain why, even if executed well, coercive diplomacy often fails. The last two are occasional factors, present or absent depending on the exact nature of the coercive diplomatic attempt. The first five factors make coercive diplomacy inherently hard but not impossible. The last factor—the target's belief that it has effective counter-coercion techniques—makes it highly likely, if not guaranteed, that coercive diplomacy will fail.

WHAT ARE THE PREREQUISITES FOR SUCCESS?

Coercive diplomacy is hard to execute and therefore frequently fails, but it does not invariably fail. What, then, are the ingredients that enhance its chances for success?

Alexander George has distilled eight conditions that increase the likelihood, but do not guarantee, that coercive diplomacy will succeed.[18] They are (1) clarity about the objectives of coercive diplomacy, (2) strong motivation by the coercing state's leadership to accept the costs and risks of coercive diplomacy, (3) sufficient domestic and international support for the coercive action, (4) strong leadership by the coercer, (5) clarity regarding the precise terms of settlement of the crisis, (6) sense of urgency created by the coercer in the mind of the target state, (7) the target's fear of unacceptable escalation, and (8) asymmetry of motivation in favor of the coercer.

The importance of the first six ingredients is straightforward. If the coercer does not make clear what it wants from the target, the target will be hard-pressed to comply, although, as George points out, there may be some situations in which imprecision about objectives can be useful. If the coercer does not care a great deal about achieving its objectives, then it will not accept the costs and bear the risks necessary to attain them. If the coercer's leadership lacks adequate domestic support for its policies, then it will not be able to sustain them, and if it lacks adequate international support for them, its actions could be easily frustrated or undermined by other states. If the coercer's top-level decision makers do not provide consistently strong leadership, then the coercer's message can become disjointed, clarity in objectives can be lost, and sufficient domestic and international support will not be forthcoming. If the specific conditions that the target must meet to settle the crisis are not spelled out, the target may continue to resist. Clear objectives from the outset may negate the need for spelling out precise "surrender terms," but often in coercive diplomatic attempts the coercer's initial objectives may undergo some change because of the bargaining that takes place between it and the target. Other times the target may demand assurances from the coercer that it will meet its obligations under the bargained agreement. Under either scenario, specifying the terms of agreement amounts to writing a contract between the coercer and the target. Finally, if the target has no sense of urgency about complying with the coercer's demands, then the target can find all sorts of reasons not to comply.

These six ingredients facilitate the successful execution of coercive diplomacy, but they are not in themselves sufficient to produce target compliance. The last two ingredients are critical, and unless they are favorable for the coercer, the attempt will fail. First, the target must fear escalation by the coercer, whether for punishment or denial purposes, and the costs of such escalation must be unacceptable to it; otherwise, there will be no reason for the target to comply. Punishment and denial are delivered through the coercer's ability to increase the amount of force used against, and hence damage inflicted on, the target's populace, cities, or military forces. If the target does not fear the costs that will result from such escalation, then it will have no incentive to comply. This is the case, for example, when the target believes it has effective counter-coercion techniques to negate the coercer's escalatory threats (as discussed earlier). Second, if the coercer does not care more about achieving its objectives than the target cares about denying them, then coercive diplomacy will most likely fail because the target's resolve to resist and its willingness to bear pain will be greater than the coercer's will to prevail and its willingness to inflict pain. As George puts it, "the outcome of coercive diplomacy is extremely sensitive to the relative motivations of the two sides."[19]

Escalatory fears and motivational asymmetries are tightly interconnected. The target's willingness to bear future punishment of its population or degradation of its military forces, and hence its degree of fear about escalation, depend on the strength of its motivation to prevail. The stronger (the weaker) that motivation, the more (the less) pain and degradation the target will be willing to bear, and, consequently, the less (the more) fearful it will be about escalation. Similarly, the coercer's willingness to expend the resources necessary to prevail, and hence its willingness to take the attendant risks and costs involved in threatening escalation, depend on the strength of its motivation to prevail. The stronger (the weaker) that motivation, the more (the fewer) resources the coercer will commit and the greater (the smaller) risks it will take. In turn, the strength of both parties' motivations to prevail depends to a great degree on how much each values what it believes to be at stake in the dispute. Ultimately, the comparative worth of the respective interests that target and coercer are defending goes a long way toward determining the degree of escalatory fear of the target and the disparity in resolve between it and the coercer. Thus, the balance of interests plays a major role in the outcome of any coercive diplomatic gambit.

The worst situation for a coercer to be in, then, is one in which it cares a great deal less about achieving its objective than does the target. This is most likely to be the case when the coercer's primary goal is the humanitarian task of saving lives in a civil war. Here the asymmetry in motivation will be most unfavorable to the coercer, for reasons that Barry Posen perceptively lays out:

> It is quite likely that the will of the local party, the assailant, is stronger than that of the outside rescuers, because the stakes for the local party are so much greater. Indeed, outsiders are unlikely to have many classical "vital" interests at stake in these conflicts. Assailants often begin their depredations because of some deeply held beliefs about the necessity of their actions. These often reflect extreme interpretations of old disputes among communities. . . . It is extremely difficult for the rescuer to convince the assailant that it cares more, particularly when the source of the concern seems to be an erratic and capricious humanitarian impulse, which varies with the extent of international media coverage; the availability of other dramas in the global village; the skin color, culture or religion of the victims.[20]

In short, there is likely to be an inherently large asymmetry between the coercer's resolve and the target's in such situations, and when the target cares so much more about achieving its goals than does the coercer, coercive diplomacy is likely to fail.

Four of the cases presented in this book—Haiti, Bosnia, Somalia, and Kosovo—clearly demonstrate how hard it is to use coercive diplomacy to achieve humanitarian ends. Saving the lives of innocent noncombatants was not the only U.S. goal in these four cases. In the Haiti case the United States also worried about masses of refugees landing on its shores. In the Bosnian and Kosovo cases the viability of the NATO alliance also came to be an issue, and in the Somali case during the second phase, when the United Nations took over from the United States, the integrity of UN peacekeeping after the Cold War also became prime. Nevertheless, in all four cases the objective of saving innocent lives was a central concern, and in each case the United States attempted to rescue parties being attacked by their governments or by other third parties within a state—in Haiti, to protect the citizens from the army-dominated government; in Bosnia, to protect the Muslims from the Serbs and the Croats; in Somalia, to feed starving noncombatants whose hunger was being used as a weapon by the warring clans; and in Kosovo, to protect the Albanian Muslims from the Serbs. Kosovo and the second phase of the Somali operation were clear failures of coercive diplomacy (Somalia's first phase was a success); Bosnia and Haiti were borderline successes. Humanitarian interventions are demanding tasks for coercive diplomacy because the asymmetry in motivation is tilted against the coercer.

In sum, the successful exercise of coercive diplomacy is built upon eight ingredients. Six of these enhance the likelihood of success, but they alone cannot produce it. The last two—the target's fear of unacceptable escalation and the coercer's stronger will to prevail—are essential if the gambit is to have some chance of succeeding. If the last two ingredients are unfavorable to the coercer, the gambit will fail, no matter how favorable the other six are. If the last two are only marginally favorable to the coercer, the gambit's outcome is in doubt. Only when the last two decisively favor the coercer is there a fighting chance that coercive diplomacy will succeed.

What Is the U.S. Experience with Coercive Diplomacy?

Two general arguments have been developed thus far. First, a small number of powerful factors make coercive diplomacy intrinsically difficult to pull off; second, a large number of things must go right if it is to have a good chance of succeeding. Taken together, these two propositions should cause us to have modest expectations about coercive diplomacy. Does the evidence bear these expectations out? For the United States, at least, the answer is yes. Washington's coercive diplomatic gambits have failed more often than they have succeeded. Two sets of studies support this conclusion: the seven cases by George and his colleagues referred to earlier, all but one of which occurred during the Cold War; and the eight cases examined in this volume, all of which took place within the first dozen years after the Cold War's end.

The George Data

Of the seven cases in the first set of studies, only two—the 1961 Laotian crisis and the 1962 Cuban missile crisis—are clear successes.[21] In the Laotian case President Kennedy succeeded in preventing Pathet Lao forces from overrunning the key positions of the Royal Lao government. In the Cuban case he succeeded in getting Nikita Khrushchev to remove the missiles that he had put on the island. Laos was relatively easy to do because Kennedy sought limited objectives—a neutralized Laos rather than a stable noncommunist government for the country as a whole. Cuba was more difficult because it required the Soviet Union to reverse course by taking out the missiles that it had put in and thereby to suffer public humiliation at the hands of the United States.

Three cases—Japan before Pearl Harbor, Vietnam in 1965, and the 1990–91 Persian Gulf crisis—are clear failures. The United States failed to compel Japan to withdraw its forces from China in the late 1930s. It failed to get the North Vietnamese to stop their intervention in South Vietnam in the spring of 1965 by bombing North Vietnam. And it failed short of war in 1990–91 to force Saddam Hussein to leave Kuwait after he had invaded and occupied it. All three were hard cases for coercive diplomacy because the adversaries were highly motivated and because they would have had to reverse course and undo actions they had undertaken.

Two cases—Libya in 1985–86 and Nicaragua in the early 1980s—are ambiguous. (Ambiguous means that we cannot classify a case as a success or a failure because we cannot determine if U.S. actions helped produce the result.) The Reagan administration launched air strikes in April 1986 against Libya in order to compel Mu'ammar Gadhafi to end his support of terrorism. After those strikes, Gadhafi's support seems to have moderated somewhat, but as George points out, the case is ambiguous because other factors were at work that could help explain this moderation, such as more intensive counterterrorism efforts by the Europeans to thwart terrorist attacks and greater efforts by Gadhafi to hide his involvement in them. Moreover, although his support for terrorism may have moderated somewhat, it did not end. In the Nicaraguan case the Reagan administration sought to destabilize and then replace the Sandinista regime through economic sanctions and the creation of a Contra army to fight it. Ultimately, free elections were held in 1989 and a non-Sandinista candidate for the presidency won. George counts the case as ambiguous because although U.S. policy wore down Nicaragua's economy and weakened the Sandinista regime politically, the coercion worked in an unanticipated fashion—a way, ironically, that the United States resolutely opposed. The United States' coercive gambits galvanized Nicaragua's Central American neighbors to begin a seven-year-long effort to achieve a peaceful resolution of the situation in order to avoid direct U.S. military intervention. The irony is that these Central American efforts succeeded in spite of continual U.S. attempts to undermine them. Coercion ultimately worked, but in ways that the United States actively sought to thwart.

Thus, out of the seven cases that George and his colleagues examined, we have a clear success rate of 29 percent (two out of seven), a clear failure rate of 43 percent (three out of seven), and an ambiguous rate of 29 percent (two out of seven). If we give some credence to coercive diplomacy in the two ambiguous cases, we can raise the success rate somewhat, but it is hard to put a precise figure on how much. If the George data are an accurate guide to what we can expect from coercive diplomacy, then it has a little less than a one-in-three chance of outright success.

Our Data

The cases in this volume yield results that approximate those of George and his colleagues. Only two (Kosovo and North Korea) are crystal clear, and they are outright failures, although failure in the Korean case did not become apparent until eight years after a seemingly successful outcome. The other six are tougher calls. Bosnia and Haiti are borderline successes because they fall right on the line between coercive diplomacy and full-scale coercion. Somalia and Iraq are not single but complex cases of coercive diplomacy—Somalia consisting of two separate instances of coercive diplomacy, Iraq of six. Although there are both successes and failures within each case, overall both Somalia and Iraq have been judged failures. Similarly, the terrorism case consists of four separate incidents, only three of which can qualify as coercive diplomacy. Of those three, one is a success, but the other two are failures. The China case is the hardest to code for three reasons: the United States' actions were a response to China's own coercive diplomacy directed at Taiwan and the United States; the actions the United States took in response to China's were as much deterrent as coercive in nature; and the United States and Taiwan subsequently altered their behavior to a degree in response to Chinese pressure. For these reasons, the China case is coded as ambiguous.

Table 1 displays the success and failure rates of our eight cases of coercive diplomacy. If the coding of our eight cases in table 1 is correct, then we have a success rate of 25 percent (two out of eight), a failure rate of 63 percent (five out of eight), and an ambiguous rate of 13 percent (one out of eight). Thus, our cases yield a success rate of one out of four, compared with that of the George cases, of slightly more than one out of four.[22]

Borderline Successes. Bosnia and Haiti have been coded as successes, but both are clearly borderline cases and could arguably be classified as failures of coercive diplomacy if some criteria are emphasized over others. Consider first the Bosnian case.

Once it developed an interest in ending the Bosnian War, the United States, together with its NATO allies, succeeded in bringing it to an end but without having to wage full-scale war. The United States took two actions that clearly fall under the rubric of coercive diplomacy: NATO's air strikes and artillery barrages directed against Bosnian Serb positions from August 30 through mid-September 1995, and a concomitant U.S. threat to the Muslims to stop the bombing of Bosnian Serb positions if the Muslims did not agree to enter into negotiations.[23] Useful as they were, however, these coercive actions would not have brought the Bosnian War to an end without the Croatian-Muslim ground offensives in western Bosnia, especially the Croatian offensive that ejected the

Table 1. Success Rate of Case Studies

Case	Outcome
Somalia 1992–94	Failure
Haiti 1994	Success
North Korea 1994	Failure
Bosnia 1995	Success
China 1996	Ambiguous
Iraq 1990–98	Failure
Kosovo 1999	Failure
Terrorism, 1993, 1998, and 2001	Failure

Note: "Ambiguous" denotes an inability to classify the case as either a success or a failure because we cannot determine if U.S. actions helped produce the result.

Serbs from Krajina in early August. These offensives were crucial because they turned the tide of the ground war and made clear to the Bosnian Serbs that they were in danger of losing a great deal more if they did not settle soon.[24] Moreover, the United States had a heavy hand in training the Croats in the combined arms operations that proved so successful in Krajina.[25] Thus, in the late summer of 1995 NATO's use of force may have been limited, but limited force alone did not bring the Bosnian Serbs around: the Croatian-Muslim ground offensive significantly augmented Western coercive diplomacy. Nevertheless, even though this is a borderline case, on balance we have coded Bosnia a success because the U.S. and NATO use of force clearly fall within the coercive diplomacy rubric, even though another party allied with them was using all-out force.

Haiti is also a borderline case—somewhere between coercive diplomacy and full-scale coercion. The Haitian military refused to sign an agreement for a change of government that former president Jimmy Carter had worked out the day before U.S. troops began to land in Haiti. The military agreed to sign this agreement only the day after U.S. troops had landed. Nonetheless, the invasion that took place was a "forced but peaceful" one, without loss of life for either U.S. or Haitian forces, because the Haitian military, under actual invasion, approved the entry of U.S. forces. If the criterion for the successful exercise of coercive diplomacy is the absence of full-scale war, then Haiti is a success, but if the criterion for success is something short of outright invasion, then Haiti is a failure of coercive diplomacy. Because the forced invasion was peaceful, I have coded Haiti a success for coercive diplomacy, although such an invasion clearly skirts the boundary of war.

Multiple Cases and Failures. Kosovo is a clear failure because Milosevic refused in the end to bend to NATO's will. He refused to grant significant political autonomy to the Kosovar Albanians, and he resumed his counterinsurgency war against them in early 1999, partly, although not solely, because the Kosovo Liberation Army (KLA), which was not a party to the October 1998 cease-fire agreement between Richard Holbrooke and Milosevic, took advantage of the situation to regroup and renew its guerrilla tactics.[26] Milosevic subsequently resorted to his brutal repressive techniques, and in the spring of 1999 it took an air war, Russian abandonment of Milosevic, the threat to pound the Serb economy to pieces, and the threat of a NATO ground invasion to evict Serbian troops from Kosovo in order to achieve the West's goal of significant political autonomy for the Kosovars. Because the United States and its allies had to resort to war, however, coercive diplomacy failed.

North Korea, too, represents a clear failure of coercive diplomacy, although this did not become clear until the fall of 2002, when the North Koreans admitted that they had begun a second program to acquire nuclear weapons. From 1994 to 2002 the North Korean case looked to be a success, because in October 1994 the North Koreans signed the Agreed Framework with the United States, by which they consented to freeze their plutonium-reprocessing program. (If this was a success, though, it was a borderline one because it took Jimmy Carter's freelancing intervention in June 1994 to avert the path to war that the United States and North Korea appeared to be fixed on in the early summer.) The North Koreans continued to adhere to the plutonium-reprocessing provisions of the Agreed Framework, but in

1997 or 1998 they covertly began a second route to nuclear weapons acquisition—uranium enrichment—with the help of the Pakistanis.[27] This program violated two other terms of the Agreed Framework, specifically the North's commitment to implement the North-South Joint Declaration on the Denuclearization of the Korean Peninsula and its commitment to remain a party to the Treaty on the Nonproliferation of Nuclear Weapons.[28] Thus, even though North Korea had lived up to its pledge to freeze plutonium reprocessing, by beginning the uranium-enrichment program, it had violated other terms of the Agreed Framework and also, therefore, its spirit. For these reasons, coercive diplomacy ultimately failed in this case.

The terrorism cases are difficult calls. The first appears to be a success but could just as easily be classified as ambiguous; the second probably does not qualify as coercive diplomacy; and the third and fourth are clear failures. The first case consisted of U.S. retaliation to shore up deterrence. In 1993 the Iraqi Intelligence Service attempted to assassinate former president George Bush in a car-bomb attack while he was visiting Kuwait. The United States retaliated by bombing the headquarters of the Iraqi Intelligence Service in Baghdad. No Iraqi assassination attempts were made against Bush after that retaliation, so on the face of it, the bombing looks like a success. But the absence of any further assassination attempts may have been due as much to lack of opportunity as to a change in motive. Moreover, Iraq continued to engage in terrorism, directing its efforts against opponents of the regime, and it continued to provide support to other terrorist groups. Nevertheless, we have coded this instance as a success.

In the second case, after marshaling evidence that Iran was behind the 1996 bombing of the Khobar Towers barracks that housed U.S. troops in Saudi Arabia, the United States switched to a policy of strengthening the moderate elements in Iran and therefore tried only diplomacy, not coercion, to move Iran away from terrorism. Because no force was threatened or used, this is not a case of coercive diplomacy. In the third case the United States retaliated against Osama bin Laden after his attacks on the U.S. embassies in Kenya and Tanzania. It struck two states accused of aiding him—a presumed chemical weapons factory in Sudan and his training camps in Afghanistan. The second attack was probably designed to kill Bin Laden (killing is a form of coercion). These attacks clearly failed to coerce Bin Laden or his organization to stop the terrorist attacks because al Qaeda struck and crippled the U.S. destroyer *Cole* in 2000 and attacked the Pentagon and destroyed the New York City World Trade Towers in 2001. The fourth case—the attempt to coerce the Taliban government in the fall of 2001 to give up al Qaeda's leaders and close down its terrorist training camps—was a clear failure as war followed to achieve those ends. A generous interpretation of our three cases of coercive diplomacy against terrorists is that they are a mixed bag—one success and two failures. A tougher interpretation is that they represent an overall failure because the first case is ambiguous and because the last two cases, which were failures, are by far the more consequential of the three.

Between them, Somalia and Iraq contain eight separate incidents of coercive diplomacy. The Somali cases consist of a short-term success—the relief of widespread starvation with U.S. intervention in late 1992—but a longer-term failure: the inability in 1993 and 1994 to disarm the Somali clans, to put in place a program of civil reconstruction, to reconstruct a viable Somali government, and to strengthen the United Nations' capacity for peacekeeping and civilian reconstruction. As a consequence, for ten years Somalia was a country without an effective central government. Somalia is judged to be a failure because as important as stopping widespread starvation is, reconstructing the Somali state is even more important. A success on the lesser goal cannot fully compensate for failure on the weightier one.

Similarly, the Iraqi case from 1990 to 1998 consists of at least six discrete instances of U.S. coercive diplomatic gambits: the 1990–91 attempt, short of war, to get Iraq to leave Kuwait, which was a failure; the 1991 attempt to create safe havens for the Kurds in the north of Iraq and the Shiites in the south, which produced mixed results, succeeding in the north but failing in the south; the 1992–93 confrontations over no-fly zones and inspections, which again produced mixed results; the 1994 deployment of additional U.S. troops to Kuwait in response to an Iraqi buildup of forces on the Kuwaiti border, which was a success because Iraq withdrew its troops from the border; the 1996 cruise missile attacks on Iraq to punish it for sending troops into the Kurdish area in the north, which was probably a failure because Saddam Hussein's main goal was to neutralize any insurgency brewing in the area by killing the opposition and rooting out the CIA's operations there, not permanently reoccupying the area; and the British and U.S. bombing in December 1998 in response to Iraq's lack of full cooperation with UN inspectors, which failed to produce Iraqi cooperation.[29] The balance sheet here is unclear (three failures, one success, and two mixed cases), but overall I judge the Iraqi case to be a failure because in the two most important issues for coercive diplomacy during those eight years—reversing Iraq's invasion of Kuwait and getting Iraq to allow UN inspectors free access to its weapons of mass destruction program—the United States and its allies failed. It took a war to get Iraq out of Kuwait, and although the United Nations did destroy many of Iraq's weapons of mass destruction, it was unable to keep an active inspection program going much past 1997. Thus, while coercive diplomacy against Iraq took place within the larger context of containing Iraqi power, and while containment worked during this period, coercive diplomacy on balance did not.

The Ambiguous Case. The coercive diplomatic outcome in the Chinese case is ambiguous. The 1996 Taiwan Strait crisis is a good example of how deterrence and compellence become conflated in disputes when deterrence appears to be weakening. In March 1996 China engaged in coercive diplomacy vis-à-vis Taiwan and the United States when it test-fired missiles close to Taiwan. Its purpose was to compel the Taiwanese government to reverse what looked like creeping moves toward independence and to stop the United States from giving what looked like support for that goal. The United States responded by sending two aircraft carrier battle groups into the Taiwan Strait in order to strengthen its strategic commitment to Taiwan and to its other allies in East Asia. At one level this was shoring up deterrence, pure and simple: the United States is committed to the peaceful resolution of the Taiwan question and therefore opposes China's use of force to resolve it. The show of force in the strait was meant to signal—or signal once again—U.S. resolve to impose unacceptable costs on China should it resort to force to solve the Taiwan question. At another level U.S. actions can be viewed as compellent: to meet force with force—to match China's escalation in policy (its resort to force) with Washington's own escalation in order to compel China to de-escalate its policy and pursue the peaceful resolution of the Taiwan question. Whereas China's action was a clear coercive diplomatic maneuver, Washington's straddled the line between compellence and deterrence—engaging in coercive diplomacy to strengthen deterrence.

Because Washington's actions were a response to China's coercive diplomacy, and because they straddle deterrence and compellence, coding the case is difficult. After the U.S. show of force in the Taiwan Strait in 1996, China did not resort again to the use of force (as of this writing) against Taiwan to halt its movement toward political independence. This is probably due, however, as much to the fact that China's coercive actions against Taiwan produced a change in Taiwan's behavior and to the quiet but strong U.S. pressure on the Taiwanese to avoid steps toward independence that could provoke China's leaders once again to resort to their own coercive diplomacy as it was to Washington's forceful response.[30] For these reasons, I have coded the 1996 China case as ambiguous.

Requirements for Success

What light do the cases shed on George's eight ingredients for success laid out earlier? In general, our cases support his view that the more ingredients present, the greater the likelihood of success, and conversely, the fewer that are present, the greater the likelihood of failure. A larger number of ingredients were present in the successes than in the failures. Moreover, the cases also demonstrate the critical role of asymmetry in resolve and fear of escalation.

In the cases of failure (Somalia in its second phase, Iraq on the most important issues, Kosovo, North Korea, and the 2001 terrorism case), the asymmetry in motivation favored the target and, consequently, in each case the United States was not able to engender in the target sufficient fear of unacceptable escalation to bend it to Washington's will.

Several of the first six ingredients were also missing. In Somalia, once mass starvation had been dealt with, the United States' motivation to aid in the reconstruction of Somalia was not strong, which is why the asymmetry in motivation favored the Somali warlords. President Clinton also thought that there would not be sufficient domestic support for that policy once it cost some U.S. lives. In Kosovo, similarly, Clinton worried about domestic support if U.S. casualties ensued, and full international support was also not forthcoming because Milosevic felt he could count on Russia to bail him out. Declining international support for sanctions hampered Washington's coercive effort against Iraq after its eviction from Kuwait. In the North Korean case the United States must have engendered a sufficient sense of urgency in the North Koreans to induce them to sign the Agreed Framework in 1994, but it could not sustain that sense for long, because they covertly began another route to nuclear weapons acquisition three or so years later. In Afghanistan splits in the Taliban regime over compromising with the United States appeared, but ultimately al Qaeda was so central to the Taliban's control of the country that the regime would have engaged in "unilateral disarmament" had it turned over Bin Laden and his leadership cadre to the United States. In none of these cases does it appear that a sufficient sense of urgency was created in the target to produce a change in behavior.

For the successes, a larger number of ingredients appear to be present, and the United States was especially clear about the precise terms it was demanding for settlement of the crisis. In the first phase of the Somali operation, the U.S. mission was clearly defined, was limited in both scope and time, and had little effect on the power positions of the warring clans. In the Bosnian case nearly all the factors appeared to favor the United States and its allies but one: Milosevic could still look to Russia for some limited support because until the end Russia tried to fine-tune the agreement to suit Bosnian Serb interests. Milosevic and the Bosnian Serbs, however, ultimately settled because they feared the consequences of a continued Croatian-Muslim ground offensive and a further escalation in NATO's bombing. The Haitian case was almost a textbook example of all eight factors being favorable to the United States, save one: Clinton lacked domestic support for military action and in fact took action when the polls did not favor it. This probably contributed to the belief by the Haitian military that the United States would not invade the island to overthrow it, which is why the military resisted signing an agreement to change the government before the invasion occurred. The Haitian case illustrates that even when nearly all the ingredients for success are in place, success is not guaranteed.

Assessing the presence of the eight ingredients in the 1996 China and 1993 and 1998 terrorism cases is much more difficult. In all three the United States was not engaged in a classic coercive diplomatic gambit but instead was using force to shore up deterrence. These were, therefore, cases not of a direct crisis confrontation between the United States and a target, but rather of Washington's use of force after the target had taken its own actions—for demonstration of resolve in the Chinese case and for retaliation in the terrorism cases. The fact that none of the three followed the classic course of a coercive diplomatic encounter makes it difficult to gauge the role that the eight ingredients played. In all three cases the United States was strongly motivated, was clear in its objectives, and exercised strong leadership, but the degree of domestic and international support it had, the target's fear of unacceptable escalation and sense of urgency, and the strength of relative resolves remain difficult to pin down.

The Expanded Data Set

If we count the multiple coercive diplomacy incidents within the Somali, Iraqi, and terrorist cases as independent cases in their own right, we can expand the number of cases to sixteen and change the overall outcomes somewhat. Table 2 displays the coding of the expanded case set. The success rate is 31 percent (five out of sixteen); the failure rate is 50 percent (eight out of sixteen); the ambiguous rate drops to 6 percent (one out of sixteen); and the mixed rate (see table 2 for definition) becomes 13 percent (two of out sixteen). The assumption in this expanded data set, of course, is that all the multiple incidents in the Somali, Iraqi, and terrorist cases are of equal importance, an assumption that can be reasonably questioned.

Table 2. Success Rate of Case Studies

Case	Outcome
Somalia I 1992–93	Success
Somalia II 1993–94	Failure
Haiti 1994	Success
North Korea 1994	Failure
Bosnia 1995	Success
China 1996	Ambiguous
Iraq 1990–91	Failure
Iraq 1991	Mixed
Iraq 1992–93	Mixed
Iraq 1994	Success
Iraq 1996	Failure
Iraq 1998	Failure
Kosovo 1999	Failure
Terrorism I (Iraq, 1993)	Success
Terrorism II (Bin Laden, 1998)	Failure
Terrorism III (Afghanistan, 2001)	Failure

Note: "Ambiguous" denotes an inability to classify the case as either a success or a failure because we cannot determine if the United States' actions helped produce the result. "Mixed" implies that there were clearly identified elements of success and failure in the case such that it is neither an outright success nor a clear failure. Thus, "ambiguous" and "mixed" both denote an inability to classify the case as either a success or a failure, but for different reasons.

Whether considered as eight or sixteen cases, however, the results of our studies, at least when it comes to the successes, still accord reasonably well with those of George and his colleagues, as table 3 demonstrates. (The comparison is biased somewhat by the fact that there is

Table 3. Comparison of George Studies and Our Studies

Study	Success	Failure	Ambiguous	Mixed
George data: 7 cases	29%	43%	29%	
1990–2001 data: 8 cases	25%	63%	13%	
1990–2001 data: 16 cases	31%	50%	6%	12%
Combined cases: 22 cases	32%	45%	14%	9%

Note: The first, second, and third rows do not total 100 percent because the percentages have been rounded to the nearest whole number. The 1990–91 Iraqi case is included in both the George data and our data. The combined data set comprises twenty-two cases (George's seven cases and our sixteen cases, minus the double counting of the 1990–91 Iraqi case), of which seven are successes, ten failures, three ambiguous, and two mixed.

double counting of the 1990–91 Iraqi case.) Furthermore, if we combine George's and our expanded instances, we produce a set of twenty-two cases that constitutes the most important and best-studied U.S. attempts at coercive diplomacy since the late 1930s, even if these cases do not represent the universe of U.S. coercive diplomacy attempts. (The combined data set is twenty-two, not twenty-three cases; see the note to table 3.) The success and failure rates of this combined set are 32 and 45 percent, respectively. To the extent that these twenty-two cases are representative, the overall conclusion to be drawn is clear: coercive diplomacy is difficult to execute successfully, succeeding in only one-third of cases and failing in almost half.

WHEN DOES COERCIVE DIPLOMACY WORK?

Thus far, we have analyzed why coercive diplomacy is difficult; we have examined the prerequisites for (but not the guarantees of) success at coercive diplomacy; and we have reviewed and coded Washington's most salient attempts at coercive diplomacy since 1990. What we have not explained is why coercive diplomacy sometimes works and sometimes fails. To figure that out, we need to assess three additional factors to see if we can enhance our predictive capabilities. These factors are the role and timing of positive inducements, the nature of the demands that the coercer makes on the target, and the manner in which the coercer uses force against the target. Let us first see what theory says about the effects that these three factors should have; then we will look at what our cases reveal about the effects that they did have.

Theory

All other things being equal, the target should be more likely to comply with the coercer's demands if it is offered positive inducements in addition to coercion. If the target must bend to the coercer's will, carrots should help, especially if they enable the target to save face or provide it with resources that help it abandon its goal. Positive inducements can take the form of either new resources—for example, provision of reconstruction aid or other type of assistance—or the discontinuance of a punitive action previously undertaken—for example, the lifting of economic sanctions previously imposed. Positive inducements do not work in every coercive diplomatic situation, however. In those situations in which the target values its objective quite highly, positive inducements are less likely to reduce its resolve. In those situations in which the target can interpret positive inducements as signifying less than a steely resolve on the part of the coercer, their presence may actually backfire and strengthen the target's resolve. Positive inducements are likely to be most useful in those cases in which the target does not place the value of its goal above all its other interests.

In addition, positive inducements are likely to be most effective after coercion has already begun to change the target's calculus of cost and benefit. This means that positive inducements should not, in general, be offered before threats or limited use of force. In his strategy during the Cuban missile crisis, President Kennedy instinctively understood this. He knew that he would have to make concessions to Khrushchev to get the Soviet missiles out of Cuba, but his overriding priority at the outset was to make clear his determination to Khrushchev that the missiles had to come out. This became apparent when Adlai Stevenson, the U.S. ambassador to the United Nations, and others initially recommended concessions. President Kennedy had his brother Robert explain to Stevenson that inducements had to follow threat. As Robert Kennedy put it to Stevenson: "We will have to make a deal at the end, but we must stand absolutely firm now. Concessions must come at the end of negotiations, not at the beginning."[31]

The logic here is simple. If matters have reached the point of a crisis, then it is more likely that leading with inducements will signify to a target the coercer's weak, not its firm, resolve. Crises, remember, are games of chicken in which the relative strength of resolves is being tested, and the incentives of both parties in the initial stages of the confrontation are either to stand firm or to escalate. Offering inducements at the outset is likely to be viewed as a willingness to give way, and in the initial stages of a game of chicken, such willingness only emboldens the other party to stand firm or to demand even more. Therefore, the logic of a crisis provides clear incentives to the coercer to offer inducements to the target, if they are offered at all, only after the seriousness of the coercer's resolve has been communicated, in this case by threats or demonstrative use of force.[32] Thus, inducements can help the coercer to achieve its objectives, but only when offered at the appropriate time.[33]

Next, as George reminds us, "the strength of the opponent's motivation not to comply is highly dependent on what is demanded of him."[34] In this regard, George developed a trilogy of goals that the coercer can aim for: get the target to stop short of its goal (stop short), get the target to undo its action (undo action), or get the target to change its form of government or the regime in power (change government).[35] Although all three are difficult objectives, the first should be the easiest to bring about; the last, the most difficult; and the second, somewhere in between. The first should be the easiest because it is the one most akin to deterrence. To cause the target to stop short of a goal is equivalent to drawing a line in the sand and saying, "Stop here; go no further." The coercer does not demand that the target undo all it has done, only that it go no further. The target can accede to this demand more easily because it can claim that it never intended to go further, or it can simply stop its action without comment on why it did so. The last type of demand should be the most difficult because it requires a regime in power to commit suicide, and regimes do not willingly do that. The second type of demand should not be as hard as forcing a target's regime to commit suicide, but it clearly is more difficult than getting it to stop short of its goal. Undoing an action already taken requires that the target not only stop short but also reverse course, and that involves loss of face, admission of a weaker resolve, and the foregoing of the fruits of the action taken—none of which is easy.

To these three types of demand we must add a fourth, because several of our cases do not fall neatly into one of the three types. This type—do not repeat the action taken (do not repeat)—accounts for those cases when coercion is being applied for deterrent purposes. In these circumstances the coercer takes action or administers retaliation so as to shore up deterrence and get the adversary not to repeat its actions again. "Do not repeat" falls somewhere between stopping short and undoing an action in its inherent difficulty.

Finally, based upon the work of Robert Pape, we have some grounds to believe that coercive diplomacy should work better if it employs a denial rather than a risk or punishment strategy. Pape investigated the universe of cases in the twentieth century when airpower was used for coercive purposes. Granted, most of his cases involved outright war, not situations short of war like coercive diplomacy, and all of them involved disputes over territory, which is not the case for every one of our incidents. Nonetheless, Pape's conclusions are relevant for two reasons. First, the bulk of our cases involved the coercive use of airpower—either threat or limited use; second, Pape's cases are a particularly good test of the relative worth of denial and punishment (risk is a weak form of punishment), because force is used in much greater amounts in wartime than is the case for coercive diplomacy. Wartime uses sufficient force to give denial and punishment strategies a fair chance to work, unlike the case for coercive diplomacy in which, by definition, only limited punishment and demonstrative denial can occur.

Pape found that denial predicted thirty-seven out of forty cases correctly and, more important, when denial was medium or high, coercion worked 82 percent of the time. Neither risk nor punishment worked to anywhere near the same degree.[36] Risk strategies worked poorly for the reasons elaborated earlier. Punishment strategies worked poorly for many reasons. For our purposes, the most important is that light punishment of the target produced anger toward the coercer, whereas heavy punishment produced political apathy toward the target government.[37] Because coercive diplomacy cannot produce heavy punishment, the light punishment that it produces is likely to backfire against the coercer: it will merely rally the target population around its government. Denial worked well when it was medium to high because it prevented the target from achieving its political objectives through military means. Thwarted in its military strategy, the target was coerced into changing its behavior. Thus, if risk strategies are inherently difficult and if light punishment only angers a target population, then demonstrative denial should be the best hope for coercive diplomacy. Through demonstrative denial the coercer needs to convince the target that it can and that it will undercut the target's military strategy if it persists in its objectionable behavior.

In sum, theory tells us that success at coercive diplomacy should be enhanced (1) when positive inducements are offered, but only after force has been threatened or used, (2) when less, not more, is demanded of the target, and (3) when military force is threatened or used in a denial, not a risk or punishment, mode. What do our cases tell us?

Categorizing the Cases

To answer the question, we must first group our expanded set of sixteen cases by the type of demand the United States made upon the target. There is one case in which the United States wanted the target to stop short, three in which the United States wanted the target not to repeat its actions, ten in which the United States sought to undo the target's actions, and two in which the United States sought to change the target's government. Grouping the cases according to demand type yields the following:

1. *One "stop short" case:* in 1994, to induce North Korea to freeze in place its program to acquire nuclear weapons.

2. *Three "do not repeat" cases:* in 1993, to compel Saddam Hussein

not to try another assassination attempt against former president Bush; in 1996, to compel China not to use its own coercive diplomacy against Taiwan again; and in 1998, to deter Bin Laden from further attacks against U.S. targets.

3. *Ten "undo action" cases:* in 1990–91, to get Iraq out of Kuwait; in 1991, to end Iraqi actions against the Kurds and Shiites; in 1992–93, to establish no-fly zones in Iraq and to obtain access for UN inspectors; in 1992–93, to end the Somali warlords' use of starvation of civilians as a weapon of war; in 1994, to coerce Iraq into removing the troops that it had massed along the Iraqi-Kuwaiti border; in Bosnia in 1995, to roll back Serbian territorial conquests from 55 to 49 percent of the territory and to end the war; in 1996, to end Iraqi attacks against the Kurds; in 1998, to obtain access for UN inspectors in Iraq; in Kosovo in 1999, to end Serbian repression of the Albanian Kosovars; and in 2001, to get the Taliban to stop its support of al Qaeda, close its terrorist training camps, and turn over its leaders. (The North Korean case could also be classified in the "undo action" category, because the United States wanted the North Koreans to come clean on the plutonium that it believed they had reprocessed and to hand the material over to the International Atomic Energy Agency or subject it to the agency's safeguards. Thus, the United States wanted the North Koreans both to freeze their weapons program and to undo the progress that they had made on it, but the first goal was the more urgent, and the latter was deferred until the later steps embodied in the Agreed Framework.)

4. *Two "change government" cases:* in Somalia II in 1992–93, to create a central government by eroding the power of the Somali warlords; and in Haiti in 1994, to replace the military government with the democratically elected Aristide government.

Table 4 sorts the cases by demand type and then categorizes them according to whether positive inducements were offered, when they were offered, and how force was employed. The first column lists the case; the second, the demand type into which the goal falls; the third, the specific goal the United States sought; the fourth, the presence or absence of a positive inducement and the time of its offer; the fifth, whether force was used in a punishment or denial mode and how much punishment or denial took place; and the sixth, the success or failure of the attempt. Four conclusions emerge from table 4:

- success correlates well with positive inducements (three out of four instances in which inducements were offered resulted in success, and three out of five successes employed inducements);

- positive inducements appear to work best when offered after either threats or demonstrative use of force, or at the same time, but not before;

- success correlates well with high denial (four out of six instances in which high denial was present resulted in success, and high denial was present in four out of five successes); and

- little correlation appears to exist between demand type and success or failure.

The Power of Positive Inducements

Our expanded set of cases contains four instances in which positive inducements were offered—Haiti 1994, Bosnia 1995, Somalia 1992, and North Korea 1994—and all but the North Korean case resulted in success. In the Haitian case Raoul Cedras, the head of the military junta, and his ilk were offered a safe haven outside Haiti if they agreed to leave the country, but Cedras and the others made clear that they did not want to consider exile. Instead, what appeared to induce Cedras and the Haitian General Staff was the offer by General Colin Powell and Senator Sam Nunn of a U.S.-Haitian military agreement that would bring about a renewal and modernization of Haiti's armed forces. In the Bosnian case Milosevic wanted sanctions lifted, and amorphous promises to lift them were apparently made as early as September 1995, although they were not written down.[38] Some of the sanctions were subsequently lifted after the Dayton Peace Accords were signed, but the United States insisted on retaining others. In Somalia 1992–93, although no financial incentives were offered to the warring clans, a positive inducement of some sort was offered: the

Table 4. Case Studies by Demand Type, Positive Inducement, and Military Threat

Case	Demand Type	Specific U.S. Goal	Positive Inducement	Military Threat	Outcome
North Korea 1994	Stop short	Freeze nuclear weapons program	Yes; offered after threats	High denial	Failure
Terrorism I (Iraq 1993)	Do not repeat	Retaliate for assassination attempt	No	Low punishment	Success
Terrorism II (Bin Laden)	Do not repeat	Retaliate for embassy bombings	No	Low punishment or low denial	Failure
China 1996	Do not repeat	Show U.S. resolve and stop China from coercing Taiwan	No	Medium denial	Ambiguous
Somalia I 1992–93	Undo action	Stop starvation	Yes; not clear when offered	High denial	Success
Bosnia 1995	Undo action	Reduce Serbian conquest and end the war	Yes; offered after force used	High denial	Success
Kosovo 1999	Undo action	End Serbian repression of Kosovars	No	Low Denial	Failure
Iraq 1990–91	Undo action	Free Kuwait	No	High denial	Failure

Case	Type	Objective	Compliance	Denial/Punishment	Outcome
Iraq 1991	Undo action	Establish safe havens	No	High denial in north, low denial in south	Mixed
Iraq 1992–93	Undo action	Establish no-fly zones and access for UN Inspectors	No	Medium denial	Mixed
Iraq 1994	Undo action	Remove troops from border	No	High denial	Success
Iraq 1996	Undo action	End attack into Kurdish area	No	Low denial	Failure
Iraq 1998	Undo action	Access for UN inspectors	No	Low denial or low punishment	Failure
Terrorism III (Afghanistan, 2001)	Undo action	Turn over al Qaeda leaders and close terrorist training camps	No	High punishment	Failure
Somalia II 1993–94	Change government	Reconstruct government	No	Low denial	Failure
Haiti 1994	Change government	Install new government	Yes; offered after force threatened	High denial	Success

clans could keep their weapons as long as they did not interfere with the distribution of food to the starving civilians. In the North Korean case the United States put together a package that would provide North Korea with oil while new and more proliferation-resistant nuclear reactors were built for it. There was also the eventual prospect of normalized relations with the United States and the end of North Korea's diplomatic isolation, with all that that would mean for its failing economy.

Should we conclude from our data that positive inducements help produce favorable outcomes for the coercer? The answer appears to be yes, for three reasons. First, although two successes were produced without a positive inducement, they are in a special class by themselves. Both involved an Iraq that had been militarily defeated by the United States and that had not fully reconstituted its military power. Inducements did not need to be offered to a just-defeated state. In the 1994 case, moreover, overwhelming U.S. airpower in the theater, supplemented by reinforcements from the United States, could easily deter Iraq from attacking Kuwait once again and compel it to withdraw the two Republican Guard divisions that it had massed along the Kuwaiti border, and Iraq may have been only testing the waters anyway. U.S. actions in this case were on the border between deterrence and coercion, depending on how one reads Iraqi intentions at the time. Second, the one case in which inducements were offered and failure occurred—North Korea—is also special. Even though it falls into the "stop short" category, theoretically at the lower end of the spectrum of attainment difficulty, the substantive demand made of the North Koreans was a tough one to achieve. It involved "coercive disarmament"—requiring a small, insecure state to give up a powerful means of defense against an overwhelmingly powerful state. Third, George also found strong support in his cases for the utility of positive inducements. In his two outright successes—Laos in 1961 and Cuba in 1962, which also spanned two different demand types—substantial carrots were offered, whereas little or none were offered in the other five cases, all of which were either failures or ambiguous.[39]

The combined results from our cases and George's, however, by no means constitute overwhelming proof that positive inducements guarantee success. Too many qualifications surround their role to make such a claim. Recall that the offer to raise the sanctions on Serbia was made orally to Milosevic by Holbrooke, not written down, because the White House would not authorize a written offer.[40] Judging its effect on Milosevic is therefore difficult. Moreover, Milosevic had already decided to push the Bosnian Serbs to the table before the quasi-inducement was offered; it was the Bosnian Serbs who needed convincing, and the lifting of sanctions on Serbia would not affect them directly, if at all.[41] The inducements offered in the first Somalia operation were positive but in a special sense: nothing was offered to the warlords except a promise that their weapons would not be taken from them if they cooperated. The Haitian military reached agreement not to fight U.S. forces only as the invasion was under way, and because the military signed the change of government agreement only the day after the invasion began, the role played by the offer to reconstruct the military is difficult to assess. Finally, the inducements offered failed to prevent the North Koreans from undertaking a covert uranium-enrichment program to acquire nuclear weapons after they had frozen the plutonium route. Thus, because we have to qualify so heavily the role that inducements played in our three successful cases, and because they failed to bring lasting success in a fourth, we should treat the proposition that positive inducements help produce success as suggestive, not definitive.[42]

The Timing of Inducements

Our cases give credible support to the proposition that the timing of positive inducements matters. In two of the three cases in which positive inducements were offered and success was achieved, the inducements were offered only after the threat to use force was made or after force was used. In the Haitian case discussion of reconstructing the Haitian military took place after the threat of invasion was made. In the Bosnian case pointed hints by the U.S. negotiator Holbrooke about the lifting of sanctions on Serbia were made to Milosevic only after NATO had already started bombing Serb positions in Bosnia.

The timing of inducements in Somalia I is not wholly clear. From what we know, Ambassador Robert Oakley tried to precede the deployment of U.S. troops with his diplomatic mission, the purpose of which was to make crystal clear to the warlords how well armed U.S. troops were and how firm was their determination to use force if challenged. But at the same time, he also communicated to the warlords that the United States would not try to disarm them.[43] In Somalia I, then, either the threat preceded the inducement or threats and inducements were offered at roughly the same time. If the former is the case, then Somalia follows the same pattern as the first two successes; if the latter is the case, then it does not. In either event, however, the inducement did not precede the threat.

Even though the North Korean case was a failure, the timing of inducements followed the same pattern as for the successes, but a little more discussion is required because of the nature of the coercion employed. No official explicit public threats to use force were made, nor did an exemplary use of force take place, but two implicit military threats were employed—one public, the other private. At the end of March 1994, Secretary of Defense William Perry issued the implicit public threat, stating that the United States would stop North Korea from building a nuclear arsenal.[44] The second came in a private, face-to-face spoken communication in June 1994, at the height of the crisis. Ambassador Robert Gallucci, who led the U.S. negotiating team, told Kang Sok Ju, North Korea's vice foreign minister, that "President Clinton would not allow North Korea to become a nuclear weapons state and this negotiation has to succeed. You know what that means."[45] The implication was that if talks failed, then force would be used to prevent North Korea from proceeding with its nuclear weapons program. In addition to the military threat was an economic one: UN sanctions against North Korea.[46] Had sanctions been imposed, this could have led to war between the United States and North Korea, because Kang Sok Ju told Gallucci that North Korea did not recognize the United Nations as a neutral body (the United Nations waged war against North Korea in the Korean War), that a sanctions resolution would be taken as a violation of the Korean War armistice, and that such a violation would be considered an act of war.[47] Whatever the exact nature of the U.S. threats made in the summer of 1994, significant inducements, partly in the form of new reactors and heavy fuel oil, were offered to the North

Koreans in the fall, only after the coercive threats had been issued. Thus, even though coercive diplomacy ultimately failed, in the North Korean case inducements came after threats.[48]

In sum, our evidence about the timing of inducements by no means constitutes ironclad proof that positive inducements have their greatest effect only when offered after threats have been made or demonstrative use has been implemented. For that kind of proof, we need an additional set of cases, which we do not have, showing that when inducements were offered first, failure resulted.[49] Absent such a controlled comparison, again the evidence we have is suggestive, not definitive, about the proper timing of inducements, but it does accord with what theory tells us: offer inducements after threats or use of force, not before.

Degree of Denial and Outcome

Our cases also give qualified support to the proposition that high denial correlates well with success, but only if the meaning of high denial under conditions of coercive diplomacy is properly understood. As argued earlier, with coercive diplomacy an actor cannot militarily deny the target its ability to implement its military strategy. Instead, all the coercer can do is to demonstrate to the target by example what will happen to its military forces should it refuse to change its behavior. Demonstrative denial does not undercut the target's military strategy; rather, it shows that it can be undercut.

In four of our five successes, the United States appears to have posed a high denial capability to the target: Somalia 1992–93, Iraq 1994, Bosnia 1995, and Haiti 1994.[50] In Somalia in 1992 and 1993, the United States and its UN allies clearly had the capability to destroy any armed clan operatives that chose to interfere with the distribution of food in the areas where the United States and its allies operated, which was only in the southern part of the country.[51] In Iraq in 1994, when Saddam massed two Republican Guard armored divisions near the Kuwait border, the United States almost immediately deployed thousands of troops to the area, causing the Iraqis to withdraw. Similarly, in Bosnia in 1995, while U.S. and NATO airpower mostly disrupted Serbian communications and command and control, it could have devastated Serbian forces, especially where they would have had to mass against the Croatian-Muslim ground offensives.[52] In Haiti in 1994 there was no doubt that U.S. forces could easily have overwhelmed the Haitian armed forces had it come to a shooting war. In each of these four cases of success, the United States posed a high denial threat, although in none of them would execution of the threat have necessarily meant few or no U.S. casualties.

In two cases—Iraq 1990–91 and North Korea 1994—the United States had high denial capability, but coercive diplomacy failed. In the North Korean case the United States had the capability through air strikes to destroy North Korea's reprocessing facility at Yongbyon, as well as to destroy the 50-megawatt research reactor there, the ponds where the spent fuel rods were stored, the 200-megawatt reactor under construction, and the 600- to 800-megawatt reactor being built at Tae-chon.[53] This capability may have contributed to North Korea's willingness to agree to freeze its plutonium-reprocessing route to nuclear weapons and to continue to abide by its agreement, even after it covertly undertook the uranium-enrichment route. In the 1990–91 Iraqi case the United States also possessed a high denial capability, but Saddam Hussein seriously underestimated the potency of U.S. airpower and believed that the United States would not be willing to suffer the casualties necessary to dislodge him through a ground campaign.

One success (Iraq in 1993) was achieved without high denial capability. The United States fired twenty-three Tomahawk cruise missiles at the Iraqi Intelligence Service headquarters in central Baghdad because CIA and FBI investigations had produced conclusive evidence that the Intelligence Service was behind the attempted assassination of former president Bush. As noted earlier, the success of this case is not clear-cut because the absence of further attempts on Bush's life may have been due as much to lack of opportunity as to change in motive. Whichever is the case, the attack was punishment, not denial, because the United States could not deny Iraq's ability to undertake terrorism. In another case—Iraq in 1991—results were mixed. The United States had high denial capability in the north because it sent twenty thousand allied soldiers to establish a safe haven for the Kurds, but it chose not to create one for the Shiites in the south. It achieved success in the north but not in the south.

In sum, although high denial is not perfectly correlated with success, nor success with high denial, the relationship between high denial and success appears to be strong. High denial was present in four of the five cases of success; it may have partially succeeded in one case of failure; and it worked well in one of the mixed cases. In all the other cases, as the authors make clear in their respective chapters, the United States appears not to have posed a credible military capability to undercut the target's military strategy. In some cases punishment was the goal; in others, only low to medium denial could be demonstrated because of either political or military constraints on U.S. forces.

Demand Type and Outcome

Finally, there appears to be no firm relation between demand type and successful outcome, or if there is, our data cannot reveal it. There are successes in three of our four types of demand (one "do not repeat"; three "undo actions"; and one "change government"). Three of the five successes, however, had the helping hand of positive inducements; four of the five successes had the helping hand of high denial; and three of the five successes had both positive inducements and high denial. Consequently, from our data we can conclude either one of two things: (1) there is no firm relation between demand type and successful outcome or (2) the relative difficulty of demand is no barrier to a successful outcome when the coercer offers positive inducements, when the coercer has high denial capability, or when both are present. George reached a similar inconclusive result from his seven cases: "success or failure has little causal relation to the type of strategy [demand] attempted."[54]

On the basis of twenty-two cases, then, we have reasonable evidence that supports three major conclusions: (1) positive inducements help coercive diplomacy succeed but by no means guarantee success, (2) a high demonstrative denial capability helps but by no means guarantees success, and (3) no clear relation exists between the type of coercive objective sought and the likelihood of achieving success. None of these conclusions is as firm or fully satisfying as we would like, but all point to the wisdom of George's insight that coercive diplomacy is highly context dependent. That is, the particulars of the situation, especially factors such as the size of the gap between the resolve of the coercer and that of the target, the nature of the interests at stake for both parties, and the skill of the coercer, significantly influence the outcome.[55] These are qualitative factors even more difficult to gauge than the ones we have been dealing with thus far.

CONCLUSION: WHAT POLICY GUIDELINES CAN BE OFFERED?

Based on the logic and evidence presented, what guidelines can we give to policymakers who are contemplating resort to coercive diplomacy? Six seem in order.

- *First, coercive diplomacy is difficult and has a relatively low success rate.*

- *Second, it is difficult to estimate the likely outcome of any given coercive diplomatic gambit.*

- *Third, possession of military superiority over the target does not guarantee success at coercive diplomacy.*

- *Fourth, positive inducements seem to enhance the likelihood of success, but only if they are offered after the threatened or actual use of exemplary or limited force.*

- *Fifth, demonstrative denial works better than limited punishment for coercive diplomacy.*

- *Sixth, never resort to coercive diplomacy unless you are prepared to go to war should it fail, or unless you have devised a suitable political escape hatch if war is not acceptable.*

Because the fourth and fifth guidelines have already been discussed at length in the preceding section, I deal here with only the other four.

1. Coercive Diplomacy Is Difficult

As I argued earlier, coercive diplomacy is difficult because coercion in general is difficult and because coercive diplomacy is the most difficult form of coercion. The case studies presented in this volume, together with those George and his colleagues produced, show that coercive diplomacy has a success rate of 32 percent. Even that figure may be too high because two of our cases (Bosnia 1995 and Haiti 1994) were borderline successes and because one (Iraq 1993) may not be a success at all.[56] A tougher coding could easily rank all three as failures, driving the success rate down significantly.

Standing alone, this 32 percent figure lacks context, but fortunately we have some statistics on how other instruments and strategies compare—not as much as we would like but enough to provide some context within which to place the record of coercive diplomacy. The evidence concerning economic sanctions provides a useful starting point, because the imposition of sanctions is roughly analogous to what happens in coercive diplomacy: something is done to try to force a change in a target's behavior without going to war against it. Although the primary instrument of each differs (military versus economic), the objectives and general method of procedure of both are roughly the same. The evidence on sanctions is remarkably similar to our coercive diplomacy data. Gary Hufbauer, Jeffrey Schott, and Kimberly Elliot have produced the most comprehensive study to date of economic sanctions, having reviewed 120 cases in the twentieth century when sanctions were imposed. They concluded that sanctions worked 33 percent of the time to produce a modest change in the target's policies and 25 percent of the time to produce a major policy change.[57] These figures are not identical to the upper and lower bounds of the success rate for our coercive diplomacy cases, but they are close enough to support the proposition that coercion short of war through either economic or economic-military means is difficult and fails more than it succeeds.

Still, the data on sanctions do not provide sufficient context because it could be the case that most other types of diplomatic gambits also fail more than they succeed. Fortunately, we have one other evidentiary benchmark that shows this does not have to be the case and that helps put into comparative perspective the success rate of coercion short of war. It concerns extended deterrence—a diplomatic gambit wherein one state (the defender) tries to protect another (the protégé) from attack by a third party (the attacker). Paul Huth and Bruce Russett studied the universe of cases of extended deterrence—fifty-four such instances—from 1900 to 1980. They found that extended deterrence was successful in thirty-one of these cases, for a success rate of 57 percent.[58] The Huth-Russett study not only shows that some political-military uses of force can succeed more than they fail but also provides empirical support for the proposition that deterrence is easier than compellence.[59]

Table 5 displays the success rates for these three data sets. Taken together, the evidence about economic sanctions, coercive diplomacy, and extended deterrence gives us greater confidence that coercive diplomacy's success rate is not due simply to flawed execution and, therefore, that coercion short of war is indeed an inherently difficult enterprise.

Two final points need to be made about the inherent difficulty of coercive diplomacy. First, as stated earlier, it could be the case that no single strategy or political-military gambit works all that well; that the success rate of extended deterrence is an outlier; and, therefore, that the record for coercive diplomacy is nothing out of the ordinary. Short of a comprehensive study of how the various instruments of statecraft fare, all that we can conclude is that coercive diplomacy looks harder than extended deterrence and works a little more than one-third of the time.[60]

Second, it could be the case that our results are distorted by a selection effect bias.[61] Our cases and George's could represent only the most visible and difficult cases, and there could well be many less visible ones that are mostly successes. If that is so, then our results are clearly biased because we have selected only the difficult cases—precisely the ones in which failure is more likely than success. Short of a comprehensive study of U.S. attempts at coercive diplomacy from 1939 until the present, we cannot know how much, if at all, our conclusion suffers from a selection effect bias. Our judgment is that it does not, but if it does, the effect is likely small.

We have one benchmark study that provides partial support for this belief. In their comprehensive study of the employment of military power short of war, Barry Blechman and Stephen Kaplan analyzed

Table 5. Comparative Success Rates

Type of Strategy or Instrument	Success Rate
Coercive diplomacy	32%
Economic sanctions	25–33%
Extended deterrence	57%

thirty-three cases of Washington's use of force from 1946 to 1975. Each of these cases involved multiple objectives and multiple uses of force, and their data are not strictly comparable with ours. Nevertheless, Blechman and Kaplan concluded that deterrence was easier than compellence. Of the twenty-eight incidents they code as compellence, success was achieved in 68 percent of the cases after six months, but when the objectives were evaluated three years later, only 18 percent were successes. This compares with 85 percent and 67 percent, respectively, for the twenty cases they code as deterrence. We would probably call the bulk, but not all, of the incidents they code as compellence to be those of coercive diplomacy, and by inspection it appears that the cases at the extreme end of least ambitious, of which there appear to be about three, such as protection of U.S. military bases in Morocco in 1956, met with greater success than the cases with the more ambitious goals.[62] If a selection effect bias is present in our study, it is therefore probably small, but even if the bias is more pronounced than that, it still remains worthwhile for policymakers to know that the ballpark probability of success for the really tough cases of coercive diplomacy is around 32 percent.

2. Estimating Outcomes Is Difficult

We have seen that positive inducements and denial strategies enhance the likelihood of success at coercive diplomacy, but they alone cannot guarantee success because the size of the disparity in resolve between the coercer and the target plays a significant role in determining the outcome. Therefore, determining before the fact whether any given coercive diplomatic attempt will be successful is also hard, and again the problem derives from the inherent difficulty of estimating relative resolves.

First, before the coercive diplomatic crisis begins, the coercer cannot know the strength of the target's resolve compared with its own, nor can it fully know how strongly the target is attached to the interest it is trying to defend. Oftentimes in such situations, the coercer may not be fully certain about the strength of its own resolve and how firmly it is committed to the interests it is defending. The same may be true for the target. To complicate matters, the coercer will find it difficult to credibly communicate to the target just how strong its resolve is, because only resort to war will reveal the full lengths to which it is prepared to go to prevail. War, however, is generally not desired by the coercer since it has chosen coercive diplomacy in the hope of avoiding war. It is therefore inherently hard for the coercer to persuade the target that it is prepared to wage war if coercive diplomacy fails when the coercer has chosen a step short of war to signify the seriousness of its intent. Furthermore, for its part, the target will, more often than not, believe that it has effective counter-coercion instruments available to it, some of which it will want to hide and some or all of which will cause it to believe that it can persevere and ultimately prevail in the test of wills. If the coercer cannot fully reveal its resolve and if the target believes it can counter the coercer, then accurately predicting the outcome of the encounter is difficult. Finally, under the impact of events, wills can change, standing interests can take on different values, and new interests can be formed.

All these factors make *ex ante* estimation of outcomes extraordinarily difficult. As a consequence, the United States should be wary of putting high confidence in estimates about the likely outcome of any given coercive diplomatic attempt. This also means that it should put little confidence in the notion that the less demanding changes in a target's behavior are easier to bring about than the more demanding ones.

3. Military Superiority Is No Guarantee of Success

In every one of our cases, the United States possessed military capabilities far superior to the target's. If military superiority alone guaranteed success, then the United States should have had a 100 percent success rate. The fact that it had only a 32 percent success rate shows that the militarily stronger adversary does not necessarily prevail at coercive diplomacy.

The reason why is clear. Compare coercive diplomatic gambits to war. In war, if the wills (resolves) and skills of the opponents are equally matched, then the outcome is decided by relative military capabilities, and the party with superior military strength prevails. If the weaker party has the stronger will, it still cannot prevail against a stronger adversary unless that adversary cares so little about what is at stake that it will quit the fight, which is usually not the case once the war begins. After all, states do not wage war over things that one or both care little about; they wage war only over things that they both care a great deal about.

In coercive diplomacy, in contrast, will counts more heavily than capability. Clearly, capability counts to a degree. Both parties do make estimates of each other's power, calculating how much it can hurt the other, how well it can defend itself from the blows of the other, and to what extent it can foil the other's military strategy. These power estimates do affect resolve, especially when the target believes it possesses effective counter-coercion techniques that can thwart or mitigate the coercer's military power. However, military capability still takes second place to will in coercive diplomacy situations because estimates about the efficacy of military power are different from the actual use of military power. In a coercive diplomatic gambit the coercer employs only threats and limited force, not the full panoply of its military capabilities. Its purpose is to signal to the target just how far it is willing to go in its use of force without having to use much force. With military power partly sheathed, it is the value that each party puts on the objectives at stake that largely determines how many risks each will take and how many costs each will bear.[63] True, confidence about its military capability can strengthen a target's resolve, but the target must have a strong resolve to begin with because it can never be certain that its counter-coercion techniques will work as envisioned. It must therefore value the objective highly enough to take the risk that its counter-coercion techniques may well not work. At their core, then, coercive diplomatic crises are akin to games of chicken in which wills more than capabilities are being tested. In such situations the more the target values its objectives, the more pain it is willing to bear to achieve them, and hence the less likely the coercer is to succeed.

In all the cases we studied, the United States faced targets that, although militarily inferior, were initially more highly motivated than the United States. After all, in the bulk of our cases, the issues at stake between the United States and the target were vital for the target, but not for the United States, with the 1994 North Korean, 1990–91 Iraqi, and 2001 Afghanistan cases being the clear exceptions. How much military power the United States is prepared to commit, and therefore how far it is willing to go in signaling its intent to commit its vast resources, depends on how much the United States values the interests at stake. The United States can always militarily overwhelm such a target, but to win at coercive diplomacy, it must convince the target that the United States cares more about winning than does the target, and that the United States will use a sufficient portion of its superior strength to prevail. This is not easy to accomplish in situations in which the target views the issues at stake as vital. As a consequence, targets with strong wills but inferior military capabilities may well believe that their superior determination will offset their capabilities' deficit.

For all these reasons, the United States should never bank on the fact that being militarily stronger automatically brings victory in coercive diplomatic encounters the way it can in wars. Were that the case, the United States could dispense with war and do only coercive diplomacy.

4. Do Not Resort to Coercive Diplomacy Unless, Should It Fail, You Are Prepared to Go Down the Path of War or You Have Prepared a Suitable Political Escape Hatch

This advice does not imply that policymakers should eschew coercive diplomacy. Indeed, it is reasonable for U.S. national security decision makers to use it in order to achieve their objectives because coercion short of war, if it works, is cheaper than waging war. Because the odds are against success, however, the United States should not start down the road of coercive diplomacy unless it is willing to resort to war, or unless it has devised a political strategy that will enable it to back down without too much loss of face, should coercive diplomacy fail. To resort to coercive diplomacy and then to abandon pursuit of the objective when coercive diplomacy fails, if done too much, weakens the technique for future use and may well discredit it. Although it is true that the objectives at hand determine to a great degree how both the target and the coercer view the coercer's determination, repeated use of coercive diplomacy, followed by hasty retreats when strong resistance is encountered, cannot but have a negative effect on the coercer's reputation and, by extension, on its use of this technique. For this reason, if for no other, resort to coercive diplomacy should be undertaken only when the objectives sought are worth going to war for, or can somehow be easily discounted politically to the U.S. public and its external audiences, should coercive diplomacy fail. There is obviously a tension here, however, because if the objective is worth going to war for, it is more difficult to discount politically. Thus, although the temptation to try coercion on the cheap is great, the United States should not try it unless it is prepared to go the expensive route or can find a suitable escape hatch.

One final point needs to be made. Our two most serious cases of coercive diplomacy (Iraq and North Korea) involved coercion against states that were known to have, or were feared to have, nuclear, biological, and/or chemical (NBC) weapons. Iraq chose not to use its chemical and biological weapons against U.S. troops in the Gulf War because it feared that the United States would follow through on the threats it made to retaliate should Iraq use them. As far as we know, North Korea did not yet possess nuclear weapons in 1994, although it may have had enough fissile material to produce two atomic bombs. The future is not likely to be as easy. Someday the United States will confront another NBC-armed state that it wants to coerce, but unlike past cases, one whose reach easily extends beyond its region to U.S. shores. An NBC-armed state with a long reach will be much harder to push around than one that can target only U.S. forces or U.S. allies in its region. In such instances the risks to the United States will be much greater than they were for any of the cases surveyed in this volume, as they were during the Cold War confrontation between the United States and the Soviet Union. In that situation, neither power engaged in much direct coercion or coercive diplomacy against the other and the few instances in which either took place were extremely dangerous, as the Berlin crisis and the Cuban missile crisis demonstrated. Because the spread of NBC weapons can only increase the inherent difficulty of successfully implementing coercive diplomacy, the United States should work even harder than it has been doing to limit NBC weapons spread and to take even more seriously than it now does deterrence of hostile actions that threaten its interests in regions of importance to it. It is far better to prevent adverse situations from arising than to have to alter them once they do.

NOTES

This chapter has benefited greatly from the following: (1) the exchange of ideas at the two workshops on this project held at the United States Institute of Peace (I have borrowed liberally from the participants' interventions, especially those by the contributors to this volume); (2) presentations of this material in earlier drafts at Harvard University's Olin Institute for Strategic Studies, Harvard University's Belfer Center for Science and International Affairs, the University of Chicago's Program on International Security Policy, and Columbia University's Security Policy Speakers Series at the Institute of War and Peace Studies; and (3) the excellent comments by Nora Bensahel, Seyom Brown, Dan Byman, Steven Burg, Patrick Cronin, William Drennan, Dan Drezner, Robert Gallucci, Alexander George, Charles Glaser, John Mearsheimer, Nigel Quinney, Robert Pape, Barry Posen, Robert Ross, Kenneth Waltz, and Micah Zenko.

1. Alexander L. George, *Forceful Persuasion: Coercive Diplomacy as an Alternative to War* (Washington, D.C.: United States Institute of Peace Press, 1991), 5.

2. See Thomas C. Schelling, *Arms and Influence* (New Haven, Conn.: Yale University Press, 1966), 69–86; and Barry R. Posen, "Military Responses to Refugee Disasters," *International Security* 21, no. 1 (summer 1996): 79–81.

3. Schelling aptly summarized this difference: "There is another characteristic of compellent threats, arising in the need for affirmative action, that often distinguishes them from deterrent threats. It is that the very act of compliance—or doing what is demanded—is more conspicuously compliant,

more recognizable as submission under duress, than when an act is merely withheld in the face of a deterrent threat. Compliance is likely to be less casual, less capable of being rationalized as something that one was going to do anyhow." Schelling, *Arms and Influence*, 82.

4. In their comprehensive study of the employment of U.S. military power short of war from 1946 to 1975, Barry Blechman and Stephen Kaplan found empirical support for Schelling's insight. They concluded: "Favorable outcomes occurred far more frequently when the objective was to reinforce (assure or deter) behavior than when it was to modify (compel or induce) behavior, both in the short and the longer term." See Barry M. Blechman and Stephen S. Kaplan, *Force without War: U.S. Armed Forces as a Political Instrument* (Washington, D.C.: Brookings Institution, 1978), 107.

5. Robert A. Pape, *Bombing to Win: Air Power and Coercion* (Ithaca, N.Y.: Cornell University Press, 1996), 18–19.

6. Ibid., 28.

7. To the extent that coercive diplomacy manipulates risk, it becomes akin to what Schelling defined as a competition in risk taking: "a military-diplomatic maneuver with or without military engagement but with the outcome determined more by manipulation of risk than by actual contest of force." Schelling had in mind the Cuban missile crisis of 1962 when he spoke of a competition in risk taking; he implied that the United States and the Soviet Union were more or less equal in their ability to manipulate risk, even if their military forces were not equal. In the cases examined in this volume, the United States was clearly superior to its adversary in its ability to dominate militarily at any level and thereby to manipulate risk. In nearly all these cases, moreover, even though the United States was superior in both senses, it is still valid to view the cases partly as risk-taking competitions, because the use of force is never risk free for the coercing state and because the U.S. government was averse to suffering battlefield casualties in most, although not all, of these cases. Therefore, even though Washington's cities and civilians were not at risk, its soldiers were. Asymmetries in vulnerability were compensated for by Washington's (and its allies') sensitivity to loss of life, which was greater than that of the target states examined in this volume. Thus, in a risk-taking competition, parties see who is more willing to bear risk (to escalate) and hence who is more willing to suffer pain (casualties and destruction). Schelling, *Arms and Influence*, 166. See also Robert Jervis, *The Illogic of American Nuclear Strategy* (Ithaca, N.Y.: Cornell University Press, 1984), 129–148.

8. See Ivo H. Daalder and Michael E. O'Hanlon, *Winning Ugly: NATO's War to Save Kosovo* (Washington, D.C.: Brookings Institution, 2000), 91–96.

9. Glenn Snyder and Paul Diesing, *Conflict among Nations: Bargaining, Decision Making, and System Structure in International Crises* (Princeton, N.J.: Princeton University Press, 1977), 118–122. Games of chicken are resolved in one of three ways: one party gives way, both parties give way, or neither party gives way and war results.

10. I am indebted to Barry Posen for this distinction.

11. For a good analysis of the problems that coalitions present for coercion, see Daniel L. Byman and Matthew C. Waxman, *The Dynamics of Coercion: American Foreign Policy and the Limits of Military Might* (Cambridge: Cambridge University Press, 2002), chap. 6. For a structured and focused comparative study of coalitions and coercive diplomacy, see Andrew C. Winner, "You and What Army? Coalitions and Coercive Diplomacy" (Ph.D. diss., University of Maryland, 2002).

12. For a good analysis of reconciling coalition maintenance with military effectiveness, see Nora Bensahel, "The Coalition Paradox: The Politics of Military Cooperation" (Ph.D. diss., Department of Political Science, Stanford University, 1999).

13. Steven L. Burg and Paul S. Shoup, *The War in Bosnia-Herzegovina: Ethnic Conflict and International Intervention* (Armonk, N.Y.: M. E. Sharpe, 1999), 354–355.

14. See James P. Thomas, *The Military Challenges of Transatlantic Coalitions*, Adelphi Paper 333 (New York: Oxford University Press, 2000), 45–49; John E. Peters et al., *European Contributions to Operation Allied Force: Implications for Transatlantic Cooperation* (Santa Monica, Calif.: RAND, 2001); General Wesley K. Clark, *Waging Modern War* (New York: Public Affairs, 2001), chaps. 8, 9; and General Accounting Office, *Kosovo Air Operations: Need to Maintain Allied Cohesion Resulted in Doctrinal Departures*, GAO-01-784, July 2001, www.GAO.gov.

15. In Somalia there were also disagreements within the coalition of coercers. Italy disagreed with the UN approach of hunting down Aideed and did what it could, according to Nora Bensahel, to undermine this operation, including, according to anecdotal evidence, giving Aideed advance notice of UN activities. See Bensahel, "The Coalition Paradox," chap. 4.

16. When Saddam's declared willingness to suffer failed to deter the Americans from launching the war, and when the Americans refused to engage Iraqi forces in a ground war before allied airpower had done its job once the war began, Saddam tried to bring on the ground war and inflict heavy casualties on the Americans in order to provoke political opposition in the United States. As Michael Gordon and Bernard Trainor put it: "If the Americans would not march north to fight, the Iraqi army would go south and make them fight." This was the meaning of the battle of Khafji at the end of January 1991. In this case, however, with the war under way, surprise was necessary if the plan was to succeed. See Michael R. Gordon and General Bernard E. Trainor, *The Generals' War: The Inside Story of the Conflict in the Gulf* (Boston: Little, Brown, 1995), 269.

17. See Kelly M. Greenhill, "The Use of Refugees as Political and Military Weapons in the Kosovo Conflict," in *Yugoslavia Unraveled: Sovereignty, Self-Determination, Intervention,* ed. Raju G. C. Thomas (Lanham, Md.: Lexington Books, 2003).

18. This list is distilled from the following: George, *Forceful Persuasion,* 75–80; and Alexander L. George and William E. Simons, *The Limits of Coercive Diplomacy,* 2d ed. (Boulder, Colo.: Westview Press, 1994), 288.

19. George, *Forceful Persuasion,* 12.

20. Posen, "Military Responses to Refugee Disasters," 82.

21. See the chart in George, *The Limits of Coercive Diplomacy,* 270. For excellent summaries of all the cases, see George, *Forceful Persuasion.* This paragraph and the next are based on the analyses in these two books.

22. Both the George data set and ours include Washington's coercive diplomatic attempt in 1990–91 to force Saddam Hussein to withdraw from Kuwait. Because there is double counting of one case, this biases the comparison between the two data sets to a degree.

23. Burg and Shoup recount the threat: "On October 4 [1995] Holbrooke warned Izetbegovic that he was 'playing craps with the destiny of his country' by refusing to agree to a cease-fire, and added, 'If you want to let the fighting go on, that is your right, but do not expect the United States to be your air force.'" Burg and Shoup, *The War in Bosnia-Herzegovina,* 359. See also 354–359 for a fuller accounting of Holbrooke's pressure on the Croats and the Muslims.

24. Richard Holbrooke, *To End a War* (New York: Random House, 1998), 147–148.

25. Burg and Shoup, *The War in Bosnia-Herzegovina,* 339–340, 379.

26. An argument could be made that Kosovo consisted of two separate cases—the October 1998 case and the spring 1999 case—and that coercive diplomacy worked in the first instance but not in the second. In his chapter Steven Burg does not count the October 1998 cease-fire agreement as a successful exercise in coercive diplomacy because the demands made on Milosevic were limited and did not challenge the fundamental interests of the Serbs. The Serb summer-fall 1998 campaign against the KLA had significantly reduced it as a threat to Serbia's position in Kosovo, and as long as the October agreement did not produce big gains for the KLA, Milosevic could easily go along with it. The KLA was not party to the agreement, however, and the West had no leverage over it at this time. Finally, the October agreement did not reach a settlement acceptable to both the Serbs and the Kosovar Albanians. For all these reasons, we treat the October 1998 agreement more as a temporary cease-fire for Western pressure on Serbia than a discrete incident of coercive diplomacy.

27. David E. Sanger and James Dao, "U.S. Says Pakistan Gave Technology to North Korea," *New York Times*, October 18, 2002, A6.

28. The references to the Joint Declaration and the Nonproliferation Treaty are in sections III and IV of the Agreed Framework and can be found in Leon V. Sigal, *Disarming Strangers: Nuclear Diplomacy with North Korea* (Princeton, N.J.: Princeton University Press, 1998), 263–264. The Joint Declaration explicitly states: "South and North Korea shall not possess nuclear reprocessing and uranium enrichment facilities." The text of the Joint Declaration can be found at www.unikorea.go.kr/eng/policy/intral_view.php?db=Tab_3&boardno=295&content=D4129.htm&code=b21&flag=2.

29. Jon Alterman includes another case—Iraqi's defiance of UN inspectors in 1997–98—but there is no evidence of U.S. threats to use force, and therefore I omit it from this list. See Alterman's chapter in this volume.

30. For a good analysis of the pressure put by the U.S. government on Taipei, see Timothy W. Crawford, *Pivotal Deterrence and Peacemaking: Bargaining, Leverage, and Third-Party Statecraft* (Ithaca, N.Y.: Cornell University Press, 2003), chap. 8.

31. Robert Kennedy, quoted in Alexander L. George, *The Limits of Coercive Diplomacy*, 1st ed. (Boston: Little, Brown, 1971), 103. I am indebted to George for reminding me of this quotation.

32. For an interesting discussion of the role that threats and promises play in deterrence and compellence and that parallels some of the points made here about positive inducements, see James W. Davis, Jr., *Threats and Promises: The Pursuit of International Influence* (Baltimore: Johns Hopkins University Press, 2000).

33. In coercive diplomatic situations, some might want to argue that offering any inducements, whether before or after threats have been made and resolve communicated, weakens the coercer's resolve in the mind of the target and is therefore counterproductive. I do not find this line of argument persuasive because it ignores the role that inducements can play in affecting the target's calculus of costs and benefits. It is not contradictory to take the position that a threat increases the target's cost of resistance to the coercer's demands and an inducement increases the target's benefits in complying with the coercer's demands. Logic still favors offering inducements, if they are offered, after threats have been communicated but not before.

34. George, *Forceful Persuasion*, 12.

35. George, *The Limits of Coercive Diplomacy*, 2d ed., 8–9.

36. Pape, *Bombing to Win*, 51–53.

37. Ibid., 25.

38. Ivo Daalder (comments made at the United States Institute of Peace conference, Washington, D.C., October 27, 1999). Daalder worked at the National Security Council during the Clinton administration and handled the Balkans.

39. George says that in the Laos case the carrot offered was U.S. disengagement and the neutralization of Laos. In the Cuban missile crisis the carrot was the de facto agreement to remove U.S. missiles from Turkey in exchange for removal of Soviet missiles from Cuba. George, *Forceful Persuasion*, 27, 35.

40. Daalder (comments made at the United States Institute of Peace conference).

41. See Ivo H. Daalder, *Getting to Dayton: The Making of America's Bosnia Policy* (Washington, D.C.: Brookings Institution, 2000), 127–129.

42. Andrew Winner's data reinforce the tentative nature of the role that positive inducements play in producing success at coercive diplomacy. He examined ten cases in which a coalition of states engaged in coercive diplomacy. Three had to do with Congo from 1960 to 1963, seven with the Bosnian War from 1992 to 1995. Five attempts succeeded; five failed. All three Congo attempts were failures. Five of the seven Bosnian attempts succeeded. Winner lists five conditions that facilitate success in coercive diplomacy: (1) a threat of force that carries high costs to the target, (2) a threat that is credible, capable of being quickly used, and of low cost to the coercer, (3) a workable deadline for compliance, (4) clear and close-ended settlement terms, and (5) a positive inducement. Only five of his ten cases had the first four conditions present. Of these five, three offered positive inducements, one did not, and one was ambiguous about whether inducements were offered. Of the three that offered inducements, two succeeded and one failed; the ambiguous case succeeded. This evidence would appear to confirm the powerful role that inducements play if it were not for the fact that two of his five successes, which also did not have all of the first four conditions present, also offered no inducements. (The five cases where the first four conditions were present are not the same as the five successes.) See Winner, "You and What Army?" chap. 5, table 1, 516.

43. See Bensahel, "The Coalition Paradox," chap. 4. For a discussion of how Oakley proceeded, see also John L. Hirsch and Robert B. Oakley, *Somalia and Operation Restore Hope* (Washington, D.C.: United States Institute of Peace Press, 1995), chap. 5.

44. As William Drennan recounts in his chapter in this volume, Perry's words were: "We are going to stop them from doing that."

45. Robert Gallucci, telephone interview with author, December 6, 2001. A year earlier President Clinton had issued a military threat, not about North Korea's acquisition of nuclear weapons, but about their use if North Korea acquired them. On a visit to Seoul in July 1993 he stated that if North Korea ever used its nuclear weapons, "it would be the end of their country." See the *New York Times*, July 12, 1993.

46. By the middle of June 1994, all the permanent members of the Security Council except China had agreed to sanctions. At the time Gallucci calculated that after the Russians had agreed to sanctions, the Chinese may well have abstained on the vote, thereby permitting sanctions to be imposed. Don Oberdorfer reports that on June 10 the Chinese conveyed to the North Koreans that "although China continued to oppose sanctions, the strength of international opinion was such that China might not be able to veto them. Therefore, Beijing strongly urged Pyongyang to take action to accommodate international opinion on the nuclear issue in its own interest or face drastic consequences without Chinese protection." In his comprehensive study of the North Korean case, however, Leon Sigal argues that even had they abstained, the Chinese would never have enforced an oil embargo or other such stringent sanctions. Gallucci, interview with author; Don Oberdorfer, *The Two Koreas: A Contemporary History* (Reading, Mass.: Addison-Wesley, 1997), 320–321; and Sigal, *Disarming Strangers*, 58. For a general analysis of the efficacy of sanctions versus inducements in this case, see Daniel W. Drezner, *The Sanctions Paradox: Economic Statecraft and International Relations* (Cambridge: Cambridge University Press), 275–302.

47. Gallucci, telephone interview with author, May 29, 2002. In response to these warnings from North Korea, President Clinton had convened a National Security Council meeting on June 16. At the outset he gave final approval for "the drive for sanctions." Discussion at the meeting covered authorizing reinforcements to be sent to South Korea in anticipation of sanctions being imposed. Oberdorfer, *The Two Koreas*, 330; and Sigal, *Disarming Strangers*, 155. Oberdorfer reports that during his mission to Pyongyang in June, Carter "concluded that North Korea actually would have gone to war on a preemptive basis if sanctions had been imposed while the United States was engaging in a major military buildup in the area." Oberdorfer, *The Two Koreas*, 329.

48. One could make a strong case, and William Drennan does in his chapter, that the United States offered some inducements to the North Koreans in the summer of 1993 before threats were made. They included things such as the North Koreans inspecting U.S. bases in South Korea and the United States helping North Korea become part of the East Asian economic miracle. Gallucci terms these concessions window dressing, not offers of real substance. Sigal also agrees that the Clinton administration did not spell out inducements first. Gallucci, telephone interview with author, May 29, 2002; and Sigal, *Disarming Strangers*, 56. Drennan points out, however, that the Agreed Statement between the United States and North Korea of July 19, 1993, offered the prospect of a deal, with an inducement thrown in: if the North Koreans gave up their graphite-moderated reactors and associated nuclear facilities (such as reprocessing plants), they would get light-water reactors and the United States would explore ways to help North Korea obtain them. Gallucci maintains that the July 1993 Agreed Statement contains only the concept or suggestion of a deal, but that the United States made no commitments at that time. There was the prospect of help, but no clear offer of help was made until August 1994. In July 1993 the United States did not offer money to obtain the light-water reactors, and it had no idea at the time where the money would come from. Gallucci, interview with author, December 10, 2002. The text of the Agreed Statement of July 19, 1993, can be found in Sigal, *Disarming Strangers*, 260–261.

49. If Drennan's viewpoint is accepted—that the United States offered a positive inducement before a threat was made (see note 48)—then the North Korean case is one example where inducements were offered first and the coercive diplomatic attempt failed. Accepting Drennan's interpretation would strengthen the general argument that positive inducements should come after, not before, a threat is made.

50. Coding the degree of denial in each of our cases is not easy, because the degree of denial ultimately posed lies in the mind of the target, not that of the United States. It is the target's views about Washington's denial capability, not Washington's actions, that count. In most of our cases we have little direct evidence about how the target interpreted Washington's threats or limited use of force at the time that the threats were made or the force was used. Short of such direct evidence, I have had to use a surrogate for the target's views: I estimated the degree to which U.S. military threats, plans, and actions could have undercut the target's military strategy. Obviously, for a whole host of reasons, not the least of which is the substitution of my views for the target's, this is not a fully satisfactory way to proceed. Furthermore, there is always the criticism that all I did was to classify a case as high denial when it was a success. I have tried to avoid that trap by making independent estimates of the degree of denial that Washington's threats or demonstrative use of force appear to have posed to the target, but reasonable people can (and will) disagree on this coding.

51. For UNITAF deployments, see Hirsch and Oakley, *Somalia and Operation Restore Hope*, 66.

52. For the effects of NATO air strikes in late August and early September, see Burg and Shoup, *The War in Bosnia-Herzegovina*, 353–355.

53. Perry recounts in his memoirs that plans existed for "destroying key components at the reactor site with a military attack." In later public testimony he stated that the reprocessing facility was the main target. Gallucci remembers that the military strike being contemplated was much broader: antiaircraft and SAM (surface-to-missile) sites, the 5-megawatt reactor at Pyongyang, the spent fuel in the cooling ponds, the reprocessing plant, and the 50- and 200-megawatt reactors being built elsewhere. See Ashton B. Carter and William J. Perry, *Preventive Defense: A New Security for America* (Washington, D.C.: Brookings Institution, 1999), 128; Thomas W. Lippman, "U.S. Considered Attack on N. Korea, Perry Tells Panel," *Washington Post*, January 25, 1995; and Robert Gallucci, telephone interview with author, May 29, 2002.

54. George, *The Limits of Coercive Diplomacy*, 269, and table 2, 270.

55. Ibid., 291.

56. A good argument can be made that George's 1986 Libyan case should also be coded as a failure, not as ambiguous, because Libya's support for terrorism did not moderate but increased with the attack on Pam Am 103 and an Air France flight. I am indebted to Dan Byman for pointing this out to me.

57. Hufbauer and his associates divided their cases into five categories according to the policy goal sought: produce a modest policy change by the target, destabilize the target's government, disrupt minor military adventures by the target, impair the target's military potential, and produce major policy changes by the target. The success rates for these five categories are, respectively, 33 percent, 52 percent, 33 percent, 20 percent, and 25 percent. The first and last categories most closely approximate the nature of our cases— producing a change in the target's behavior. The destabilization cases achieved the highest success rate because they were accompanied by covert and quasi-military measures. When all the cases were averaged together, the overall success rate was 34 percent. See Gary Clyde Hufbauer, Jeffrey J. Schott, and Kimberly Ann Elliot, *Economic Sanctions Reconsidered: History* *and Current Policy,* 2d ed. (Washington, D.C.: Institute for International Economics, 1990), 93, 51. The data set has been updated through 1999 in preparation for a third edition and contains approximately 188 cases, but the overall success rate has changed only marginally. Kimberly Elliot, conversation with author. See also Kimberly Ann Elliot and Barbara L. Oegg, "Economic Sanctions Reconsidered—Again: Trends in Sanctions Policy in the 1990s" (paper prepared for the International Studies Association convention, March 23–26, 2002). Also consult the International Institute for Economics website for analysis of the 1900–1999 data set, www.iie.org.

58. Paul Huth and Bruce Russett, "What Makes Deterrence Work? Cases from 1900–1980," *World Politics* 36, no. 4 (July 1984): 505, table 1. Richard Lebow and Janice Stein challenged this result, but, for reasons that Huth and Russett lay out in their response to this critique, I find the Lebow-Stein critique unpersuasive. See Richard Ned Lebow and Janice Gross Stein, "Deterrence: The Elusive Dependent Variable," *World Politics* 42, no. 3 (April 1990): 336–369; and Paul Huth and Bruce Russett, "Testing Deterrence Theory: Rigor Makes a Difference," *World Politics* 42, no. 4 (July 1990): 466–501.

59. In reanalyzing the Huth-Russett data, James Fearon concluded that the success rate of deterrence was even higher in two categories. During the past one hundred years, when deterrence was applied by a major power against a minor one, it almost always worked. For the post-1945 cases, deterrence worked 80 percent of the time when the defender had nuclear weapons. See James D. Fearon, "Signaling versus the Balance of Power and Interests: An Empirical Test of a Crisis Bargaining Model," *Journal of Conflict Resolution* 38, no. 2 (June 1994): 253–255.

60. I have come across three studies that attempt to assess the relative utility of several instruments of statecraft. All three are valuable, but none fully provides the basis of comparison that we currently lack. See Russell J. Leng, *Interstate Crisis Behavior, 1816–1980* (Cambridge: Cambridge University Press, 1993); Martin Patchen, *Resolving Disputes between Nations: Coercion or Conciliation?* (Durham, N.C.: Duke University Press, 1988); and Brian M. Pollins, "Cannons and Capital: The Use of Coercive Diplomacy by Major Powers in the Twentieth Century," in *Reconstructing Realpolitik*, ed. Frank W. Wayman and Paul F. Diehl (Ann Arbor: University of Michigan Press, 1994), 29–54.

61. On selection effects, see James D. Fearon, "Selection Effects and Deterrence," *International Interactions* 28 (2002): 5–29.

62. See Blechman and Kaplan, *Force without War*, tables 3.1, 3.2, and 4.2.

63. Leng found this to be the case in a sample of forty crises drawn from the Correlates of War project: "The interests at stake . . . appeared to be a more powerful predictor than capabilities." The prediction concerned whether crises escalated to war. See Leng, *Interstate Crisis Behavior, 1816–1980*, 193.

Index

421

THE UNITED STATES AND COERCIVE DIPLOMACY

This book is set in Bodoni Light; the display type is Bodoni Medium. The Creative Shop designed the book's cover; Mike Chase designed and made up the pages. David Sweet copyedited the text, which was proofread by Karen Stough. The index was prepared by Sonsie Conroy. The book's editor was Nigel Quinney.